Photoshop® 7
Complete Course

tamm...

...n Kabili

Wiley Publishing, Inc.

Photoshop® 7 Complete Course

Published by:
Wiley Publishing, Inc.
909 Third Avenue
New York, NY 10022
www.wiley.com/compbooks

Published simultaneously in Canada

For general information on our other products and services or to obtain technical support, please contact our Customer Care Department within the U.S. at 800-762-2974, outside the U.S. at 317-572-3993, or fax 317-572-4002.

Library of Congress Control Number: 2002110249

ISBN: 0-7645-3684-2

Manufactured in the United States of America

10 9 8 7 6 5 4 3 2 1

» Credits

Publisher: Barry Pruett

Project Editor: Dana Rhodes Lesh

Acquisitions Editor: Michael Roney

Editorial Manager: Rev Mengle

Technical Editor: Lee Musick

Interior Designers: Edwin Kwo, Daniela Richardson

Cover Designer: Anthony Bunyan

Layout: Beth Brooks, Sean Decker, Melanie DesJardins, Kristine Leonardo, Kristin McMullan, Heather Pope, Erin Zeltner

Production: Kelly Emkow, Joyce Haughey, Gabriele McCann, Barry Offringa

Quality Control: Laura L. Bowman, Andy Hollandbeck, Susan Moritz, Charles Spencer

Contributing Artist: Sam Shipley

Special Help: Tim Borek, Cricket Franklin, Ted Padova, Wendy Peck, Daniela Richardson, Maureen Spears

» Dedication

To my beautiful, independent children, Ben, Coby, and Kate Kabili.

» Table of Contents

Introduction

Almost every Photoshop user that I know is self-taught. Some have managed to learn enough on their own to use the program for specific purposes. Others are still struggling to move beyond the basics. Anyone who has tried to learn this program on his or her own eventually realizes that there's more to knowing Photoshop than understanding how to work some of its tools. The real trick is in knowing how to use the program in context to create a professional-looking product — be it a page layout, a typographic logo, a Web design, a color-corrected photograph, or an art collage.

That's where this book comes in. It uses a project-based approach to teach you Photoshop in a way that takes into account context as well as technique. Here you'll learn not only how to use the many exciting tools that Photoshop offers, but also how to use those tools together to construct a design project from beginning to end. Each lesson builds on those that came before, giving you a chance to practice what you've learned and reinforcing those skills that you'll use over and over.

In short, this is more than just a book. It really is a complete, structured course that leads you through the intricacies of Photoshop while keeping an eye on the bigger creative picture. If you put your nose to the grindstone and work your way through the lessons in this book, I can assure you that you'll come away with a deeper understanding of Photoshop than you already have, whether you're a Photoshop beginner or a user with some experience. In the process, I hope you enjoy yourself and give yourself a pat on the back each time that you complete a piece of the final project, which you'll be working on throughout the book.

Is This Book for You?

The answer to this question is definitely yes if you are a serious student or teacher of Photoshop or if you are a designer, photographer, artist, architect, or other creative professional. The lessons offered in this course were designed with you in mind. And the project collages were created by seasoned Photoshop users who are artists and teachers themselves.

What's in this Book?

This course is divided into eight parts — a quick-start tutorial called the Confidence Builder and seven substantial parts. Here's an overview of what you'll find in each of these parts:

» **Confidence Builder:** You'll hit the ground running by working through this short tutorial. The Confidence Builder is a hands-on exercise that gives you a taste of basic Photoshop tools and techniques. It introduces you to how Photoshop works, while leading you through the creation of a simple collage.

» **Part I: Course Setup:** This is the only narrative section in the book. It contains introductory material about Photoshop and about this course:

» "Photoshop Basics" includes an overview of what you can do with Photoshop and a summary of the features that are new in Photoshop 7.

» "Project Overview" explains the project that you'll be creating as you work through this course and introduces the tutorial files that are provided for you on the CD-ROM at the back of the book. It also discusses how to install and use Photoshop 7 in various Macintosh and Windows operating systems.

» **Part II: Getting to Know Photoshop:** This is where you'll find the first of the tutorials that make up the format of the rest of the book. There are three sessions (chapters) in this part:

» Session 1, "Customizing Photoshop," uses tutorials to teach you how to access tools and commands, set preferences, and create custom-built workspaces and tool presets.

» Session 2, "Managing Documents," shows you how to create and save files, how to use the new File Browser to view and manage files, and various ways of fixing the mistakes that you're bound to make in Photoshop.

» Session 3, "Viewing Documents," covers image magnification, navigation in the document window, multiple document windows image information, screen display modes, image size, canvas size, and cropping.

» **Part III: Painting and Drawing:** This part covers how to paint and fill pixel-based images and how to draw vector-based objects:

» Session 4, "Choosing and Using Color," introduces Photoshop's color management system, foreground and background colors, the Color Picker, the Color palette, and color swatches.

» Session 5, "Painting and Filling with Pixels," covers various methods of filling pixel-based artwork with color, patterns, and gradients. It introduces the new Brushes palette and shows you how to define a custom brush. It also covers stroking and erasing.

» Session 6, "Drawing with Vectors," addresses a side of Photoshop that's less well-known — its vector-drawing capabilities. You'll explore the Pen tools, paths, and the easy-to-use Shape tool.

» **Part IV: Image Editing:** This part addresses the image-editing capabilities that are the heart of Photoshop:

» Session 7, "Selecting," covers the many methods of selecting part of an image so that you can edit its content, including selection tools and commands, the Quick Mask mode, feathering and anti-aliasing, storing selections in Alpha channels, and the Extract feature.

» Session 8, "Using Layers," explains everything you'll need to know about creating layers, layer visibility, layer locks, layer opacity, linking layers, layer sets, adjustment layers, and fill layers.

» Session 9, "Compositing Images," is all about making collages. In this session, you'll learn how to make images compatible and how to use layer masks, vector masks, blending sliders, rulers and guides, and blending modes.

» Session 10, "Filters, Layer Styles, and Special Effects," shows you how to add decorative effects to your images using different kinds of filters, customizable layer styles, the Liquify feature, and the History Brushes.

» **Part V: Text:** Here you'll learn all about using text in Photoshop:

» Session 11, "Creating and Formatting Text," covers the Type tools, point type, paragraph type, type formatting features, and the new spell check and find and replace features.

» Session 12, "Special Text Effects," is the place to practice some typographic effects, including warping text, using curves to make text visible on a photograph, rasterizing type, and displaying an image in text.

» **Part VI: Working with Photographs in the Digital Darkroom:** This part covers how to retouch and correct photographs in Photoshop:

» Session 13, "Using Darkroom Tools," looks at retouching with the Clone Stamp tool, the new Healing Brush tool, and the new Patch tool. It also addresses adjusting exposure, saturation, and focus in photographs.

» Session 14, "Controlling Tone," is about correcting tonal imbalance in photographs using auto-correction commands, levels, and curves.

» Session 15, "Adjusting Color," covers color correction with color balance, hue/saturation, curves, and variation adjustments.

» **Part VII: Preparing Art for Print and Web:** This part addresses output on the Web and in desktop and commercial printing:

» Session 16, "Creating Graphics, Pages, and Gallery Sites for the Web," is a comprehensive look at the many Web-related tasks that you can accomplish with Photoshop and its sister program, ImageReady.

» Session 17, "Printing," offers pointers for preparing images for desktop and commercial printing. This chapter is your payoff, because here you'll create proof prints of each of the project collages that you've created as you worked through the course.

Confidence Builder

This section gives you a chance to try out some of Photoshop's basic tools and commands as you build a simple collage. You'll get a quick look at features that are addressed in more detail in later sessions, including layers, selections, brushes, type, filters, layer styles, vector shapes, image adjustments, and combining images from multiple files. This hands-on overview of Photoshop basics will build your confidence as a Photoshop user and whet your appetite for future sessions.

Tutorial
» An Introduction to Photoshop

In this tutorial, you create a simple Photoshop collage from two images, using a variety of Photoshop features. You'll revisit each of the features that you use here in more detail in later sessions.

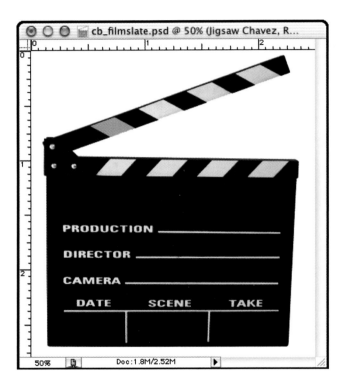

1. **Make sure that the Confidence Builder folder of tutorial files is on your hard drive.**
   The Confidence Builder files are included with the tutorial files on the CD-ROM at the back of the book. Before you get started, turn to Appendix A to find out how to put these files on your hard drive and how to prepare them for use with the tutorials.

If you're working on Windows 98 or Windows 2000, the tutorial files that you copy from the CD-ROM may start off as read-only files. You'll have to remove the read-only setting from the copies on your hard drive, or you won't be able to write over the copied files. See Appendix A for more instructions.

2. **Launch Photoshop.**

3. **Choose File→Open.**

4. **Navigate to** cb_filmslate.psd **in the Confidence Builder folder on your desktop and click Open.**

If you're a Windows user, you may not see the .psd file extension in the tutorial files. See Appendix A for instructions on how to reveal the hidden file extensions in Windows.

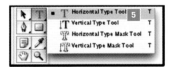

5. **Click the Horizontal Type tool in the toolbox.**
   The Type tool has several variations. If a variation other than the Horizontal Type tool is showing in the toolbox, click and hold that Type tool and choose the Horizontal Type tool from the fly-out menu.

<TIP>
If you're not sure what an icon means, move your cursor over the icon to reveal a ToolTip that identifies the icon and its keyboard shortcut.

6. **Click the Default Colors icon (the small black and white squares) in the toolbox. Then click the Switch Colors icon (the double-pointed arrow) in the toolbox.**

   This sets the Foreground Color box in the toolbox to white. The Type tool uses the Foreground color to create type. In Session 11, you'll find out how to change the color of type after it's been created.

7. **In the Options bar at the top of your screen, click the Font down arrow and choose Courier TT (or a font of your choice) from the drop-down list. Click the Font Size down arrow and choose 14 pt. Leave the other options at their defaults.**

   The Options bar is context sensitive, so it changes depending on the tool selected. It currently displays options for the Type tool.

8. **Click inside the document window and type** Jigsaw. **Press Return or Enter, and type** Chavez.

   Two lines of type appear where you inserted your cursor in the document. Notice that when you use the Type tool, Photoshop automatically creates a separate type layer in the Layers palette and names that layer based on the words that you typed.

9. **Click the Move tool in the toolbox.**

10. **Check that the Jigsaw Chavez type layer is highlighted in the Layers palette. In the document, click and drag to position the text near the lines in the film slate.**

    You're able to move the text separately from the rest of the image because the text is isolated on its own layer.

11. **Click the Type tool in the toolbox again. In the document, click and drag to highlight both lines of text.**

12. **In the Options bar, click the Palettes icon to open the Character palette.**

    The Character palette offers additional options for formatting what Photoshop calls point type (as distinguished from paragraph type, which is created inside of a bounding box). You'll find out more about both kinds of type in Session 11.

13. **In the Character palette, click the Leading down arrow and choose 18 pt from the drop-down list.**

    Increasing leading expands the amount of space between the two lines of type so that they more closely match the lines on the film slate.

14. **Click the Check Mark icon on the right of the Options bar.**

    Clicking the Check Mark icon commits the type edits that you just made and takes you out of type edit mode, enabling you to access the many menu commands that are unavailable when you're editing type.

15. **Check that the type layer is still selected in the Layers palette and click the New Layer icon at the bottom of the Layers palette. (If your Layers palette isn't open, first choose Window→Layers.)**

    This creates a new layer of transparent pixels above the layer that was selected in the Layers palette. Think of each layer as a piece of clear glass stacked one upon the other. You can add pixels of content to each layer, and wherever there is no content, you can see through to the layers below.

16. **In the Layers palette, double-click directly on the new layer's name, Layer 1. Rename the layer by typing** take **and press Return or Enter.**

    Photoshop 7 brings back this easy way of renaming layers. Be sure to double-click directly on the layer name, or you'll inadvertently cause the Layer Styles palette to open.

17. **Click the Brush tool in the toolbox.**

18. **Click the Brush Sample in the Options bar to open the Brush pop-up palette.**
You'll see a scrolling list of brush tips with previews of a stroke made with each brush. This is a new feature in Photoshop 7.

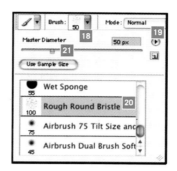

19. **Click the arrow on the right of the Brush pop-up palette and choose Large List from the drop-down list.**
This changes the view of the Brush pop-up palette to display each brush tip with its size and name.

20. **Scroll to the bottom of the Brush pop-up palette and choose the Rough Round Bristle brush.**

21. **Drag the Brush Size slider at the top of the Brush pop-up palette to 50 px.**

22. **Click and drag a line of white paint under the word TAKE on the film slate.**
Notice the painterly look this brush gives to your brushstroke. You'll find many more natural media brushes like this in Photoshop 7.

23. **Click the Brushes tab in the Palette well on the right of the Options bar to open the Brushes palette.**
Photoshop 7 brings back the Brushes palette that was missing from Photoshop 6. This Brushes palette offers many options for creating customized brush tips, which you'll have a chance to explore in Session 5.

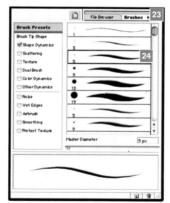

24. **Choose the Hard Round 5 pixel brush near the top of the Brush pop-up palette.**

25. **Click the New Layer icon in the Layers palette. Double-click the name of the new layer and rename it** date scene.

26. **Paint a date and scene number on the film slate in the document window.**

27. **Select the Move tool in the toolbox, and click and drag to position the date and scene on top of the film slate.**

28. **Click the Magic Wand tool in the toolbox.**

    You have to select pixels in an image before you can affect them with many of Photoshop's tools and commands. The Magic Wand tool is one of several ways of selecting pixels. You'll find out all about selecting in Session 7.

29. **Type** 18 **in the Tolerance box on the Options bar and make sure that there are check marks in the Anti-aliased and Contiguous fields.**

    Tolerance determines the color range of the pixels that the Magic Wand will select, based on color brightness. The lower the number, the narrower the range of colors that will be selected. Anti-aliased softens the edges of the selection. Contiguous limits the selection to pixels that are adjacent to one another.

30. **Make sure that the Background layer is selected in the Layers palette and click inside one of the white polygons on the film slate arm to select that polygon.**

    The animated dashes that appear around the polygon are called marching ants. They identify the selected area of an image. If your selected area is bigger than the area shown here, decrease Tolerance in the Options bar. If your selected area is smaller than the white polygon, increase Tolerance. Then click once in the image to deselect and click again in the white polygon to reselect it with the new tolerance setting.

31. **Double-click the Foreground Color box in the toolbox to open the Color Picker.**

    The Color Picker is one of several tools that you can use to select colors in Photoshop. You'll learn about others, such as the Swatches palette and the Color palette, in Session 4.

32. **Make sure that Only Web Colors is unchecked in the Color Picker. Move the Color slider to the blue area of the hue bar. Click a light gray-blue in the color field on the left side of the Color Picker and then click OK.**

    <TIP>

    If you want to use the exact same color that I did, type the following values in the R, G, and B fields at the bottom of the Color Picker, rather than follow step 32 — R:176, G:183, B:185. These are values for the red, green, and blue components of the color that you are choosing.

33. **Check that the background layer is still selected in the Layers palette. Press Option+Delete (Mac) or Alt+Delete (Windows) to fill the selected area on that layer with the gray-blue color in the Foreground Color box.**

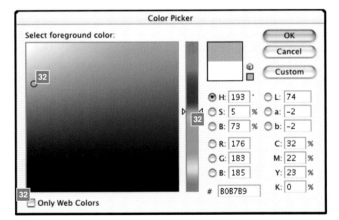

34. **Click anywhere in the image to deselect.**

35. **Repeat steps 28 through 34 to color two more of the white polygons on the film slate arm. Try using khaki (R:213, G:148, B:96) and light olive (R:195, G:199, B:143) or colors of your choice.**
    You may have to tweak the Tolerance setting in the Options bar to get an accurate selection of each polygon.

36. **Click and hold the Shape tool in the toolbox and choose Custom Shape Tool from the fly-out menu of hidden tools.**

37. **Click the Shape sample in the Options bar.**

38. **Click the arrow on the top right of the Shape pop-up palette and choose Objects from the drop-down list. In the dialog box that appears, click OK.**
    This replaces the default set of shapes with a different set of shapes.

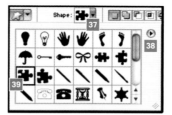

39. **Click one of the puzzle pieces in the Shape pop-up palette.**

40. **Click the Foreground Color box and choose a purple in the Color Picker (try R:124, G:90, B:123).**

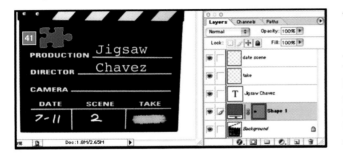

41. Click and drag in the document to draw a puzzle shape, adjusting its size and shape as you drag.

<NOTE>
The Shape tool automatically created a new shape layer in the Layers palette, labeled Shape 1. The shape layer has two thumbnails representing the two components of a shape — a pixel-based layer of color that fills the shape and a vector-based mask that outlines the shape. As you'll see in Session 6, a shape has crisp edges and can be scaled and adjusted without losing those sharp edges.

42. Click the Black Arrow tool (the Path Selection tool) in the toolbox.

43. Click and drag in the document window to position the puzzle piece on the left side of the film slate.

44. Double-click the name of the shape layer — Shape 1 — in the Layers palette. Type puzzle shape to rename the layer.

<TIP>
I recommend that you always give each of your layers a meaningful name to make the layers easy to identify.

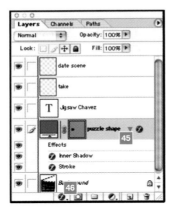

45. Make sure that the puzzle shape layer is selected in the Layers palette.

46. Click the Layer Style icon at the bottom of the Layers palette and choose Stroke from the drop-down list.
This causes the Layer Style dialog box to open, displaying options for the Stroke layer style.

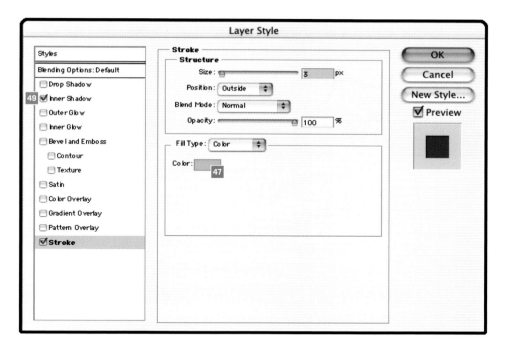

47. **Click the Stroke Color option on the right side of the Layer Style dialog box.**

This causes the Color Picker to open.

48. **Move your cursor out of the Color Picker, causing it to change to an eyedropper. Click in the document window on one of the polygons that you filled with color earlier in the tutorial. (I clicked on my light olive polygon.) Click OK in the Color Picker.**

This fills the Stroke Color option with a color sampled from the image and creates a stroke of that color around the puzzle shape.

49. **Click the Inner Shadow check box on the left side of the Layer Style dialog box.**

This adds an inner shadow to the layer style that you applied to the puzzle shape. In the Layers palette, the puzzle shape layer now displays sublayers of Stroke and Inner Shadow effects.

< T I P >

If you're having trouble seeing the stroke that you applied to the image, click a different layer in the Layers palette. This hides the vector outline around the puzzle shape, making it easier to see the stroke that you just added.

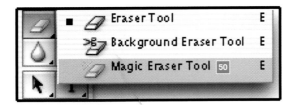

50. **Click and hold the Eraser tool in the toolbox and choose the Magic Eraser tool from the fly-out menu.**

51. **Select the background layer in the Layers palette and click the white area of the image in the document window.**
This causes the white pixels that were on the background layer to disappear, revealing a gray-and-white checkerboard pattern. The checkerboard is the symbol for transparent pixels.

52. **Double-click the layer named Layer 0 in the Layers palette and rename the layer by typing** slate.
You may be wondering where Layer 0 came from. Making the bottom layer transparent automatically converted that layer from a special background layer (which cannot include transparency) to a regular layer named Layer 0.

<NOTE>

The Magic Eraser tool selects pixels within a range of color (just like the Magic Wand tool) and deletes those pixels — all in one step. It's great for knocking out solid color backgrounds like this one. You'll learn more about the Magic Wand tool and its settings in Session 7.

53. **Make sure that the slate layer is selected in the Layers palette. Click inside the empty link field (the square just to the right of the eye icon) on each of the other layers.**
This links the other layers to the slate layer so that you can move all the layers together into a second file.

54. **Choose File→Open and navigate to** cb_walkofame.psd **in the Confidence Builder folder on your desktop. Click Open.**

<NOTE>

Windows users, don't be surprised if you don't see the .psd extension on the end of the cb_walkofame file. Open it anyway.

55. **Select the Move tool in the toolbox.**

56. **Click inside the film slate document window and drag into the walkofame document window.**

    The film slate appears in the walkofame image, and all the layers from the film slate image appear in the Layers palette of the walkofame image.

57. **Make sure that the slate layer is selected in the walkofame image. Choose Edit→Transform→Rotate.**

    A bounding box appears around the film slate in the walko-fame image.

58. **Move the cursor outside the bounding box so that it becomes a curved, double-pointed arrow. Click and drag to rotate the film slate and move it into a position like that shown here. Press Return or Enter to commit this transformation.**

    If you want to cancel the transformation while it's in progress, press Esc on your keyboard.

59. **Select the star walk layer in the walkofame image. Choose Image→Adjustments→Hue/Saturation.**

60. **Click the Colorize check box in the Hue/Saturation dialog box. Move the Hue slider to 25 and the Saturation slider to 40. Click OK.**

    This changes the star walk layer to sepia tones.

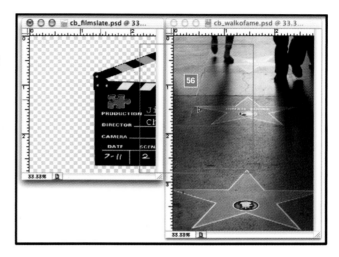

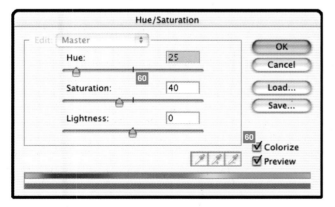

61. **Make sure that the star walk layer is still selected in the Layers palette. Choose Filter→Texture→Texturizer.**

62. **In the Texturizer dialog box, leave the settings at their defaults for now and click OK to apply the filter.**
    If you want to reduce the effect of this filter after applying it, choose Edit→Texturizer and move the Opacity slider to the left in the Fade dialog box.

63. **Choose File→Save to save your collage as** cb_walkofame.psd **in the Confidence Builder folder on your desktop.**
    This saves over the original file. You can always get a new copy of the original file from the CD-ROM if you need it.

<NOTE>
You've completed your first Photoshop collage using many of the program's fundamental features. Here's what the final result should look like. In the sessions that follow, you'll find out more about the tools and commands that you tried out here.

Part I
Course Setup

Photoshop Basics

An Overview of Photoshop 7

Photoshop is, hands down, the most comprehensive image-editing program available. It offers tools to satisfy the graphic needs of a wide range of professionals and hobbyists — from photographers and artists to print designers and Web developers.

The breadth and depth of Photoshop's features are unmatched. You can use it for lots of different tasks. Here's a list of the kinds of things that you can do with Photoshop. You'll get a chance to try these as you work through this book, but don't stop with these ideas. Your imagination and creativity are the only real limits on how you use this expansive program.

» Paint with pixel-based tools, including a variety of brushes, selections, fills, and layer masks.

» Draw with vector-based tools, including shape tools, pen tools, and vector masks.

» Retouch and manipulate photographs with toning, focus, and painting tools and with image adjustments.

» Collage images using layers, masks, and blending modes.

» Add special effects with filters and layer styles.

» Create editable, vector-based type.

» Make still, animated, and interactive graphics for the Web in Photoshop's companion program, ImageReady.

New Features in Photoshop 7

There's lots of anticipation among Photoshop users every time Adobe announces a new version of the program. Photoshop 7, like previous versions, didn't disappoint its fans. It has some major new features and lots of small changes that make it easier to use than ever. This section provides an overview of the most important new features in Photoshop 7.

New looks for OS X and Windows XP

One of the biggest changes in this version of Photoshop is that it is a native Macintosh OS X application. It also runs fine in Mac OS 9.1 and 9.2. (If you plan to install Photoshop 7 in both OS X and OS 9 on the same computer in order to use it with an older printer or program, be sure to read my advice on installing Photoshop 7 in Part I's "Project Overview.")

On the Windows side, Photoshop 7 is fully compatible with the new Windows XP operating system. It also runs in Windows 2000, 98, Me, and NT. The program works the same way across platforms and operating systems. I'll let you know about any small cross-platform differences you may encounter as you work through the tutorials.

From a stylistic viewpoint, Photoshop 7 is like a chameleon that wears different skins depending on the operating system in which it's running.

Photoshop 7 in Mac OS X.

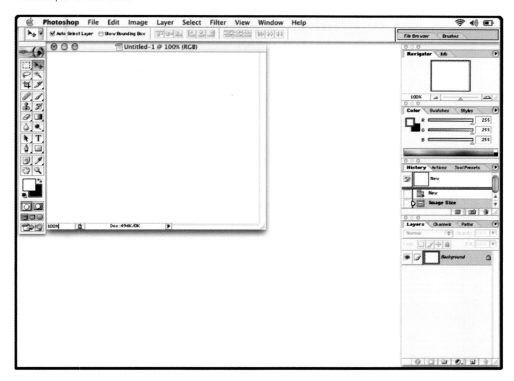

In Mac OS 9, Photoshop 7 looks like previous versions of the program. But in Mac OS X, Photoshop 7 reflects that operating system's aqua interface, three dimensional buttons, and drop shadows. It's a bright, clean look that I think creates an optimal environment for graphics work. There are a couple of interface differences between Photoshop in OS X and other operating systems. In OS X, you'll see a Photoshop menu at the top of the screen, to which the Preferences, Color Settings, and Quit commands have been moved. There's also a new menu command — Window➔Documents➔Minimize — from which you can minimize an open Photoshop document and send it to the OS X Dock.

Photoshop 7 in Windows XP.

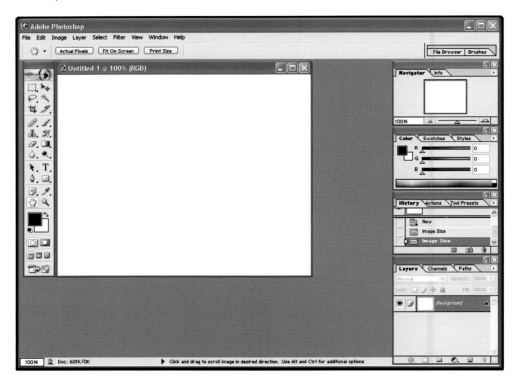

In Windows XP, the program takes on the crisp new look of that operating system, but the interface generally is the same as in other Windows environments.

Rollover tool icons

The tools in the Photoshop 7 toolbox now light up when you roll your cursor over them. This is true in both the Macintosh and Windows operating systems.

The File Browser

The File Browser is a major addition to Photoshop. It's an image viewer with extra features for managing and organizing files. In the File Browser, you can see thumbnails of all the images in a folder, view detailed information about each image, rename images, rank and sort them, rotate them, and organize them into folders. The File Browser is particularly useful for handling photos from digital cameras, which often come into your computer with meaningless names, without visual previews, and rotated the wrong way.

The Brushes palette

Photoshop 7 reintroduces the Brushes palette, which was missing from Photoshop 6. The Brushes palette has lots of new preset brushes to choose from, including some designed to give your digital painting a natural media look. It also has many options that you can use to create custom brushes and a dynamic size slider with which you can resize any brush on-the-fly.

The Healing Brush and Patch tools

The two new tools, Healing Brush and Patch, are similar to the Rubber Stamp tool, but they are specially designed for realistic retouching of hard-to-match areas of photographs, such as faces and hair. They copy content from one part of an image to another and blend the copied pixels with the texture and lighting of the retouched area. The Healing Brush stamps in content, and the Patch tool drags a selection of content to the target area.

Tool Presets

Each tool in Photoshop's toolbox has option settings. The new Tool Presets feature saves combinations of those settings, enabling you to design and reuse your own custom tools.

Custom workspaces

You have lots of freedom to rearrange Photoshop palettes on your desktop. Use the new custom workspace feature to save multiple palette configurations so that you can call up different arrangements to suit whatever task you're doing. If more than one person uses the same computer, each can store and use her own Photoshop workspace configuration.

Spell check

Photoshop 7 has a spell checker to help you keep your type error-free.

Miscellaneous features

Here are some of the numerous smaller changes to existing tools and palettes:

> » In the Layers palette, you now double-click on a layer to rename the layer. The Layers palette also offers some new Layer Blending methods (Hard Light, Vivid Light, Pin Light, Linear Burn, Linear Dodge, and Linear Light).

Also, the four kinds of layer locks are now managed by buttons rather than check boxes.

» All the brush tools have icons in the Options bar that open the Brushes palette for easy access.

» The Airbrush tool is no longer a standalone tool. It's now a setting in the Options bar for various brush tools.

» The Type tool has an additional anti-aliasing choice — the Sharp method.

» The Slice tool Options bar has a new Slice by Guides option. Slice line color and slice numbers options have moved to Preferences→Guides, Grid, & Slices.

» The Slice Select tool has a new Show/Hide Auto Slices option with which you can control the display of slices the program makes, so you can focus on those slices you make yourself.

» There's a new Auto-Color command in the Image menu, which does a pretty good job of removing color casts from photos.

» There's a new Pattern Maker command under the Filter menu. The Pattern Maker is particularly useful for making tiles to use as Web page backgrounds.

» The Document window status bar now shows Document Dimensions.

» The File→New dialog box offers preset document sizes.

» The Web Photo Gallery has been significantly upgraded with several new templates that you can use to automatically create a Web site right in Photoshop.

» In Photoshop's Save for Web window and in ImageReady 7's Optimize palette, you can make any color in a GIF transparent simply by clicking it. You can also use the new Transparency Dither feature to help create a GIF that you can place against a patterned background.

» ImageReady 7 has a redesigned Rollover palette that displays information about all the rollover slices in a document, as well as information about animation frames and image maps. There's also a new rollover state — the Selected state.

All of these changes make Photoshop 7 exciting for existing users without raising the learning curve for new users. You'll get a chance to work with these new features in the sessions that follow.

Project Overview

The Complete Course Project

This book is a tutorial-based course in Photoshop for students, educators, and design professionals. It will teach you not only how to use the features of Photoshop and ImageReady 7, but also how to apply those features in a practical context as you create a design project — a multipaged brochure for a film festival.

You'll create the collages for the brochure as you work through the tutorials in the book. Your reward for finishing all the tutorials will be completed collages for the pages of a brochure that you can print out on your inkjet or color laser printer or prepare for commercial printing. Use the printed product to remind yourself of the Photoshop techniques that you've learned, stimulate ideas for future projects, or show off your Photoshop skills to clients and friends.

Required Software

Adobe Photoshop 7

All the instructions and figures in this book are based on Adobe Photoshop 7. You can find a try-out version of Photoshop 7 on the book's CD-ROM. Check the Adobe Web site (www.adobe.com) for the latest update to the program.

What if you're stuck with using an older version of Photoshop? You can still work through this book, but you'll find that some features discussed here aren't available or are somewhat different in your version of the program. Photoshop 6 users will have an easier time with this book than users of even older releases because there aren't many drastic differences between Photoshop 6 and 7. I'll point out features that are new to Photoshop 7 as they come up.

Installing Photoshop 7

It's easy to install Photoshop 7 on any Windows operating system that supports the program — Windows 2000, 98, Me, NT, or the latest and greatest Windows XP. All you have to do is insert your application CD-ROM and follow the installation and setup instructions on your computer. *Note:* If you're a Windows user, you can skip the rest of this section on installing Photoshop 7.

Macintosh users have a little more thinking to do about how they want to use and install Photoshop 7. Figure out which of the following four scenarios describes your situation and follow the appropriate instructions.

Scenario 1 — Macintosh OS 9 only

You may be happy to know that you can install and use Photoshop 7 even if you don't have OS X. Just upgrade to OS 9.1 or 9.2, start up your computer in that operating system, and install Photoshop 7 as you would any application. You don't have to buy a special version of the program. The same installation disc works with Macintosh OS 9 or OS X.

Scenario 2 — Macintosh OS X only

The day may soon come when you'll have no need for OS 9 because you'll have upgraded all your programs and peripheral devices to OS X versions. If you're one of the rare people in that situation already, just start up your computer in OS X 10.1.3 or later and install Photoshop 7 directly into OS X.

Scenario 3 — Macintosh OS X and OS 9 Classic

You may be ready to run Photoshop 7 in OS X, but you still need OS 9 on your computer so that you can keep on using your non-OS X applications and peripherals.

You'd also like the option of sometimes running Photoshop in the same environment as your non–OS X applications so that you can move more easily between the programs.

The solution for you is to have both OS X (10.1.3 or later) and OS 9 (9.2 or later) installed on your computer, run the latter as OS 9 Classic (which is a simulation of OS 9 that runs from inside OS X), and make sure that your computer is booted in OS X when you install Photoshop 7. This causes all of Photoshop's support components to be installed in the proper places in both OS X and OS 9 Classic. Installing once from OS X is all you have to do.

This may sound more complicated than it really is. The following steps walk you through this Photoshop installation process and show you how to open Photoshop 7 in these different environments. These instructions assume that you've already installed both OS X and OS 9. If you've designated OS X as your startup operating system, just boot the computer as you normally would and skip to step 3 below. If OS 9 is your startup system, start with step 1.

1. **Click the Apple menu in Macintosh OS 9 and choose Control Panels→Startup Disk.**

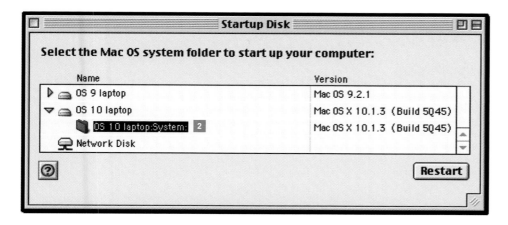

2. **Click the arrow next to the name of each drive or partition listed in the Startup Disk window to display the system folder on each hard drive. Click the system folder that contains your Macintosh OS X operating system. Click Restart.**
   This causes your computer to restart in OS X.

3. **Install Adobe Photoshop 7 from the application CD-ROM or install the try-out version from this book's accompanying CD-ROM.**
   That's all there is to installing Photoshop 7 in a dual operating system environment. In the next few steps, I'll show you how to set up your interface so that you can easily launch Photoshop 7 in either Macintosh OS X or Macintosh OS 9 Classic.

4. **Click the Finder icon on the far left of your OS X Dock to open the OS X Finder.**
   The OS X Dock is a convenient place from which to open frequently used items, such as the Finder, useful folders or files, and favorite applications.

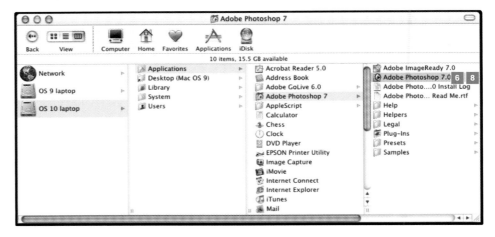

5. **Choose File→New Finder Window and navigate to your OS X drive→Applications→Adobe Photoshop 7 application folder.**

6. **Click once on the Adobe Photoshop 7.0 program icon in the Adobe Photoshop 7 application folder and drag a copy of that icon to the OS X Dock. Repeat this step with the Adobe ImageReady 7.0 program icon.**
   From now on, you'll be able to launch Photoshop or ImageReady in OS X by double-clicking its program icon in the Dock, which is visible from either OS X or from OS 9 Classic.

7. **Repeat steps 4 and 5.**

8. **Click once on the Adobe Photoshop 7.0 program icon in the Adobe Photoshop 7 application folder.**

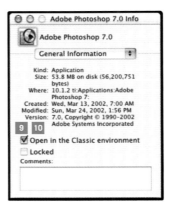

9. **Choose File→Show Info and in the Info window, place a check mark next to Open in the Classic Environment.**
   This causes Photoshop 7 to open in the OS 9 Classic environment, rather than in OS X, the next time you launch the program.

10. **Uncheck Open in the Classic Environment before closing the Info window because the next time you work with Photoshop 7 in this course, you'll want the program to open in OS X.**

Scenario 4 — Macintosh OS X, Macintosh OS 9 Classic, and Macintosh OS 9

Running Photoshop in OS X and OS 9 Classic may not meet all your needs. For example, you still may not be able to scan into or print from Photoshop 7 because your scanner and printer don't work from OS 9 Classic (which is all too typical) and the manufacturer hasn't yet released OS X drivers. You have another option. In addition to doing everything covered in the preceding steps, you can install a second copy of OS 9 in a separate partition or on a separate hard drive from the OS 9 operating system assigned to OS 9 Classic. Then install Photoshop 7 directly into the standalone copy of OS 9. If you need to use Photoshop 7 with your scanner, printer, or other device, install their drivers in the standalone OS 9 operating system, choose that system as the startup disk, and launch Photoshop 7 directly in OS 9. This is a more complex and time-consuming setup than those described in preceding paragraphs, so you may not want to attempt it right now. Just keep it in your back pocket as another option.

Setting Photoshop's Maximum Memory Allocation in Macintosh OS X

Windows users can skip this section too. Allocation of memory to Photoshop is a Macintosh-only issue because Windows automatically distributes memory among open applications. Macintosh users running Mac OS X are enjoying a similar kind of automatic memory allocation for the first time. Mac OS X takes care of RAM allocation on-the-fly, dynamically allocating memory among open programs according to what each program needs at any given time.

In previous Macintosh operating systems, you could set the exact amount of RAM that would be allocated to Photoshop whenever the program was open. In Macintosh OS X, there is no need for such a setting. The only control that you have over the dynamic allocation of memory to Photoshop is to limit the maximum percentage of total memory that Photoshop is allowed to claim. You'll learn how to do that here.

1. **Choose Photoshop→Preferences→Memory & Image Cache.**

<NOTE>
You won't find this preference if you're running Photoshop in OS 9 Classic or a standalone version of OS 9. It's only available in OS X.

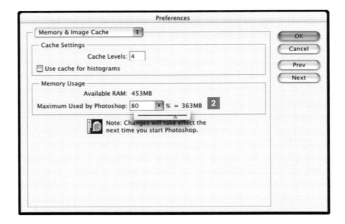

2. **Click the arrow on the field labeled Maximum Used by Photoshop, which you'll find in the Memory Usage area of the Preferences dialog box. Move the slider to 90% or lower. Click OK.**
This sets a cap on the maximum percentage of available RAM that OS X allocates to Photoshop. This stops Photoshop from hogging all the available RAM, which could negatively affect the performance of other open programs and of the operating system itself.

<NOTE>
It's a good idea to set Photoshop's maximum memory usage to something less than 100%, even if there are no other programs running, to avoid Photoshop interfering with the memory requirements of the operating system. However, there is no method other than experience for determining the exact size at which to set this preference. Simply try decreasing this setting if you plan to run other programs that will handle big files at the same time as Photoshop, and raising the setting if you'll be working only in Photoshop. If the performance of the operating system or of other programs seems to degrade, go back into the Preferences dialog box and lower this number.

Adobe ImageReady 7

Adobe ImageReady is a companion program to Photoshop that's designed for making images for the World Wide Web. ImageReady 7 ships free with Photoshop 7. You'll find ImageReady's launch file in the Adobe Photoshop application folder on your hard drive after you install Photoshop. In case you're wondering about the version numbering, you didn't miss anything; the last release of ImageReady, which came with Photoshop 6, was ImageReady 3. Adobe skipped a few version numbers for ImageReady so that its number would match that of the new Photoshop release.

Internet Explorer 4+ or Netscape Navigator 4+

You'll want a Web browser (Internet Explorer or Netscape Navigator version 4 or later) installed on your computer for use with the sessions on Web graphics. Internet Explorer 5.1 (for Mac OS Classic and Mac OS X) and Internet Explorer 6 (for Windows) can be downloaded from www.microsoft.com. Netscape Navigator can be downloaded from www.netscape.com.

Required Hardware

Macintosh computer

Macintosh users need a G3 or G4 PowerPC processor, a minimum of 128MB of RAM, at least 320MB of free hard-drive space, and a color monitor that displays at least 800 x 600 resolution and is powered by a 16-bit or stronger color video card.

Windows computer

Windows users should have an Intel Pentium class III or 4 processor, a minimum of 128MB of RAM, at least 280MB of free hard-drive space, and a color monitor with at least 800 x 600 resolution and a 16-bit color video card.

CD-ROM drive

You'll need an internal or external CD-ROM drive to use the files and software on the CD-ROM that accompanies this book. The CD-ROM and its files can be read on both Macintosh and Windows platforms.

Optional digital still camera; optional scanner

Neither a digital camera nor a scanner is necessary to work through the tutorials in this book. However, if you have access to either, you can use it to bring images into Photoshop as resource material for supplemental projects.

Required Operating system

Macintosh OS

Mac OS 9.1 or 9.2, or Mac OS X.

Windows OS

Microsoft Windows 98, Windows 98 Second Edition, Windows Millennium Edition, Windows NT with Service Pack 6a, Windows 2000 with Service Pack 2, or Windows XP.

Using This Book with Different Operating Systems

The main instructions and figures in this book illustrate Photoshop 7 on a Macintosh running OS X, but the instructions work just as well in Windows and the other Macintosh operating systems that support Photoshop 7.

Why have I chosen to write this book in the Macintosh OS X environment? It's not because I'm a Mac fan (although I will admit to loving my PowerBook). It's because Macs are disproportionately popular in the design community and because one of the most significant features of Photoshop 7 is that it has been rewritten (carbonized) to run natively in Mac OS X. Until the release of Photoshop 7, many designers, educators, and students had no reason to switch to OS X. Now they do. This book will help them learn how to use Photoshop 7 in the new OS X environment.

What if you are a Windows user or a Macintosh user who's decided not to make the switch to Mac OS X? You're in luck! Photoshop 7, like its predecessors, is designed to work the same way across platforms and operating systems. This means that virtually all the instructions in this book apply without modification if you're using Photoshop 7 on a Windows system or on a Macintosh running Mac OS 9 directly or Mac OS 9 Classic. If there are any relevant and noteworthy cross-platform or cross-operating system differences, I will bring them to your attention.

Required Files

The CD-ROM at the back of the book contains a folder called Tutorial Files. That folder holds the prebuilt files that you'll use as starting points for many of the tutorials in the book. Before you start work on any tutorial, open the Tutorial Files folder on the CD-ROM, find the folder for the current tutorial, and copy that folder to your computer, following the instructions in Appendix A. Use the files copied to your computer, rather than those on the CD-ROM, as you do the tutorial.

I've explained that in each tutorial you'll work on a piece of the final project, a program guide for a film festival. In the course of working through the tutorials and sessions, you'll be creating collaged artwork for the pages of the brochure. The Tutorial Files subfolder for each session contains one file that contains the word _end in the filename. The _end file is an example of the collage that you'll be working on in that session, showing the collage as it will look at the end of the session. (You may work on the same collage for more than one consecutive session.)

You'll also find iteration files in some of the Tutorial Files subfolders. These are fresh versions of the files as they look at intermediary points in the session. The text instructs you when you have a choice of using an iteration file or the file you've been building as you work through the session. These iteration files give you some breathing room in case you mess up the file that you've been working on in a particularly long session or if you decide to skip one or more tutorials in a session.

See Appendix A for more instructions on how to use the CD-ROM files.

As you work through the tutorials, you'll make changes to the prebuilt tutorial files you copied from the CD-ROM to your hard drive. When you're prompted to save a file, I suggest that you save right over the version you copied to your computer. That way, you'll always know where the latest version of the file is located. If you need to start over with a clean copy of a file, just go back to the CD-ROM and copy the file again.

Stepping through the Project Stages

The Photoshop 7 Complete Course is divided into parts, sessions, and tutorials. The parts are general subject matter categories that contain chapters called *sessions.* The tutorials in each session are the heart of the book. Each tutorial focuses on a handful of related Photoshop features. It walks you through the steps of using those features to create part of the brochure project that you'll be developing throughout the book.

Each tutorial builds on and assumes that you know the skills taught in the preceding tutorials. So if you're a beginning Photoshop user, I strongly suggest that you work through the tutorials in order. At the same time, each session can stand on its own. So if you already have Photoshop's basics under your belt, you may be comfortable approaching the sessions on a piecemeal basis (although you won't end up with all the printable pieces of the brochure project).

I've become a true believer in the tutorial method after teaching Photoshop to hundreds of students. I've found that most people learn better with their hands on a keyboard, trying out the features of the program, rather than just reading about them. To get the most out of this book, I recommend that you do the same. I don't mind if you cozy up with the book in bed, but in the morning please take it with you to your computer and actually work through the tutorials.

I hope that you'll make this book yours by giving it a real workout. I'd like to picture your copy of *Photoshop 7 Complete Course* fondly dog-eared and worn, a familiar companion on your way to learning Photoshop.

Part II
Getting to Know Photoshop

Session 1

Customizing Photoshop

Session Introduction

Photoshop is a flexible program that you can customize to suit your own needs. In this session, you'll be introduced to Photoshop's work area, learning how to access the basic tools and commands, which are located in the toolbox, Options bar, menu bar, and palettes. Then you'll find out how to make the program your own by changing preferences, arranging palettes to your liking, saving reusable workspace configurations, and creating and saving tool presets.

TOOLS YOU'LL USE
Menu bar, toolbox, Options bar, palettes, Preferences, custom workspaces, and Tool Presets

CD-ROM FILES NEEDED
01_oldcamera.psd and 01_velvetrope.psd

TIME REQUIRED
90 minutes

Tutorial
» Accessing Tools and Commands

Take a tour of the Photoshop 7 work area to see how to access the program's tools and commands, which are located in the menu bar, the toolbox, the Options bar, and the palettes. You'll be amazed at how it easy it is to find what you need in this economical workspace.

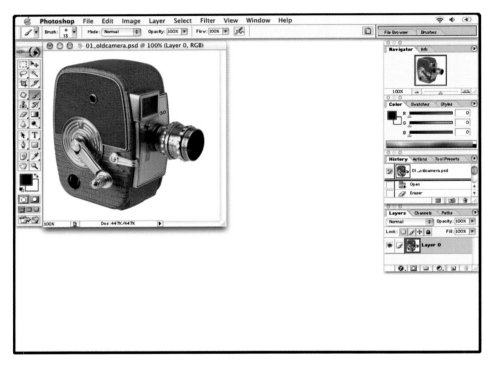

1. **Make sure that the Session 01 Tutorial Files folder from the CD-ROM that accompanies this book is on your hard drive.** See Appendix A for information about working with the CD-ROM files.

2. **Double-click the Adobe Photoshop program icon inside the Adobe Photoshop 7 application folder on your hard drive to launch Photoshop.**

New Photoshop Menu for Macintosh OS X Users

Macintosh OS X users will see a new menu labeled *Photoshop* on the left of the menu bar. Click it, and you'll see that Photoshop Preferences, Color Settings, Quit Photoshop, About Photoshop, and About Plug-In have all moved to this menu. It's not hard to find those commands in their new location, but if you're an old Photoshop user like me, you may find it hard to retrain your hand to move to the right one notch when you're reaching for the File menu. Old habits die hard, but because all OS X programs have an application menu like this one, this should feel natural soon. Windows and Macintosh OS 9 users won't see a Photoshop menu in Photoshop 7. In Windows, Preferences and Color Settings are in the Edit menu, Quit is in the File menu, and About Photoshop and About Plug-In are in the Help menu. The same is true in Mac OS 9 except that About Photoshop and About Plug-In are in the Apple menu.

3. **Choose File→Open from the menu bar at the top of your screen.**
   The menu bar contains a series of menus that have commands for executing tasks in Photoshop. You'll work with many of these commands in this book.

4. **Navigate to the Session 01 Tutorial Files folder on your hard drive. Choose** 01_oldcamera.psd **and click OK in the Open window.**
   Click Don't Show Again and OK if you get a warning about unreadable information when you open this or any file from the CD-ROM. You can safely ignore all such warnings.

5. **Move your cursor over the Eraser tool in the Photoshop toolbox to see that icon light up.**
   This tool rollover effect, which is new to Photoshop 7, works with all the tools in the toolbox, and on all platforms.

6. **Leave your cursor hovering over the Eraser tool to reveal a ToolTip that tells you the name of that tool.**
   Most of the ToolTips also display a letter, which is a keyboard shortcut that you can click for quick access to a tool. If you're a beginning Photoshop user, I don't suggest that you bother learning lots of keyboard shortcuts, but they can be real time-savers for more advanced users. I'll point out the shortcuts that I think are most valuable throughout the book.

7. **Click once on the Eraser tool in the toolbox to make that tool active.**

8. **Click and drag on the white background of the image to erase some pixels.**
   After you make a tool active in the toolbox, you can use it to affect an open image, as you did here. By the way, the gray-and-white checkerboard pattern you now see in the image indicates that the erased area is transparent.

9. **Click the Eraser tool to reveal a menu of extra eraser tools.**

<NOTE>
Any tool that has an arrow in its bottom-right corner is hiding extra tools. Try clicking some other tools that display such an arrow to see for yourself.

10. **Click the Magic Eraser tool in the menu of extra tools.**
    The extra tool menu disappears, and the Magic Eraser icon appears in the toolbox.

11. **Click anywhere on the white background of the image to apply the Magic Eraser tool.**

    The Magic Eraser deletes all pixels that are similar in color to the pixel that you clicked. This is a great tool for eliminating solid color backgrounds, such as this one, with a single click. You'll work more with the Magic Eraser tool in future tutorials.

12. **Click the Dodge tool in the toolbox and keep your eye on the Options bar near the top of the screen.**

    You'll see that the content of the Options bar changes as you switch tools. Each tool has its own options, which determine how the tool behaves. You'll work with many tool options as you go through the tutorials in this book.

13. **Change the Dodge tool options so that they match those in the illustration.**

    To make those changes, click the Brush option to open the Brush Picker, and drag the Master Diameter slider in the Brush Picker to set the tip of the brush that you'll be using to 50 px. Click the Range option and choose Midtones from that menu. Click inside the Exposure option and type **80%**.

    < T I P >

    You'll see some of the same options in the Options bar for more than one tool. For example, the Brush option appears in the Option bar for the Clone Stamp, Pattern Stamp, Eraser, Magic Eraser, Background Eraser, Blur, Sharpen, Smudge, Brush, Pencil, History Brush, Art History Brush, Dodge, Burn, and Sponge tools.

14. **Click once in the image inside the camera viewfinder to lighten that area with the Dodge tool settings that you just chose.**

    The Dodge tool in Photoshop acts just like an exposure dodging tool in a photographic darkroom; it lightens the dodged area.

15. **Locate the History palette among the palette groups on the right side of the screen. If you don't see it there, choose Window→History from the menu bar.**

16. **Click the arrow at the top right of the History palette to display a menu of palette options. Choose New Snapshot from the menu and click OK in the dialog box that appears.**

    This creates a snapshot of the image as you've edited it to this point. You can go back to this state at any point in the future by clicking this snapshot. Don't worry about understanding all the details of the History palette now. You'll learn more about it in the next session. The point of this step is to let you know about palette option menus.

17. **Choose File→Close from the menu bar and click Don't Save at the prompt.**

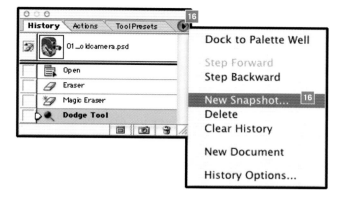

Contextual Menus

Hidden contextual menus are another place from which you can access certain Photoshop commands. To view a contextual menu, Ctrl+click (Windows: right-click) on a palette or an image. For example, Ctrl+click (Windows: right-click) on any state in the History palette to see a contextual menu with some of the options related to that palette. The trick is knowing where and when to click to find a contextual menu. I'll let you know about the contextual menus I recommend as they come up in the course of tutorials.

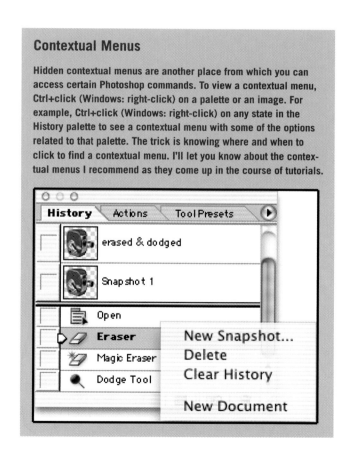

Tutorial
» Setting Preferences

Photoshop offers several Preference settings that you can use to customize the way your copy of the program runs. This tutorial isn't intended to be an exhaustive look at all of the Photoshop Preferences. Instead, I'll show you those that deserve special attention when you're doing a print project, like the project in this book. The remaining tutorials assume that you've made the changes suggested here, but whether you change these permanently in your copy of Photoshop is, of course, your preference.

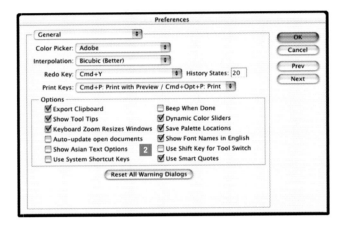

1. **Choose Photoshop→Preferences→General (Windows, Macintosh OS 9: Edit→Preferences→General) from the menu bar.**
   This takes you to the General Preferences set, the first of eight sets.

2. **Click the Use Shift Key for Tool Switch check box to remove the check mark.**
   This Preferences change makes it easier to find a particular hidden tool in the toolbox. Now you can cycle through a group of hidden tools by repeatedly clicking the keyboard shortcut for that group (without having to hold the Shift key).

3. **Click the Preferences Set button (currently labeled General) at the top of the Preferences dialog box and choose File Handling to reveal that set of preferences.**

4. **Click the Always Maximize Compatibility for Photoshop (PSD) Files check box to remove its check mark. Click Yes at the prompt.**
   The reason that you may want to turn off this preference is to keep the files you save in Photoshop's native PSD format as small as possible. Otherwise, when you save a layered file as a PSD, Photoshop creates and saves a flattened version of the file along with the layers — which increases file size.

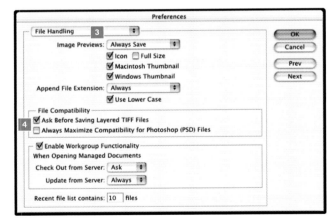

<**W A R N I N G**>
Do not turn off Always Maximize Compatibility for Photoshop (PSD) Files in the File Handling Preferences box if you are preparing PSD files for use in a page layout application, such as QuarkXPress. That and other applications can't read the layers in a PSD file and require the flattened composite that's created when this preference is left on.

Adobe also warns that "turning off maximize PSD compatibility may interfere with the use of PSD files . . . with future versions of Photoshop." This means that if a future version of Photoshop were to interpret Layer Blending modes, Layer Styles, or some other feature in a different way than Photoshop 7 does, the appearance of the layered image could be different in that future version. A flattened composite could act as a safeguard against that possibility. This all sounds pretty speculative. But to be safe, a compromise approach is to turn off the Maximize Compatibility preference when you're making working saves of a document, but turn it back on when you save a final PSD file for archival purposes.

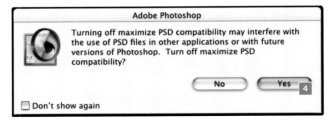

5. Click the Preferences Set button and choose Displays & Cursors to reveal that set of preferences.

I suggest that you leave all the Displays & Cursors preferences at their defaults, as shown here. Leaving the Painting Cursors set to Brush Size displays the exact size of any brush tip that you use with the Brush tool, Eraser tools, and other painting tools. Leaving Other Cursors set to Standard displays an icon of the tool that you're using. You can change any cursor temporarily to Precise (a cross-hair through which you can see the image) while you're working by clicking the Caps Lock key.

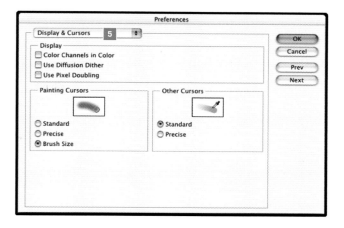

6. Click the Preferences Set button and choose Transparency & Gamut.

This is another preference pane to leave at its defaults. The Transparency Settings are responsible for the way transparent pixels are displayed in an image — as a checkerboard of gray-and-white squares by default.

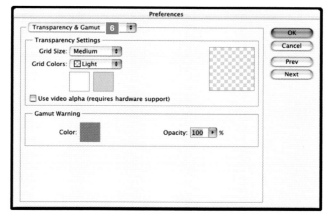

7. Click the Preferences Set button and choose Units & Rulers.

If you're working on a print project, as you are for most of this book, leave these settings as they are so that the unit of measurement in the document window rulers and in dialog boxes is inches. However, if you're creating images for the Web or the screen, change the Rulers setting from inches to pixels. New Document Preset Resolutions, which you can leave at their defaults, are new to Photoshop 7. They determine the default resolutions of document presets in the New file dialog box. You'll learn about document presets in the next session.

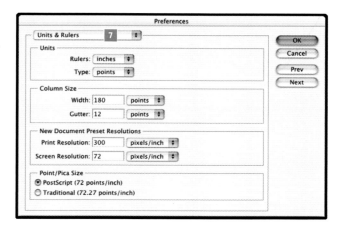

< T I P >

You can change rulers temporarily from inches to pixels when you're working on a document by choosing View➜Rulers to display rulers. Then Ctrl+click (Windows: right-click) in a ruler and choose pixels from the contextual menu that appears.

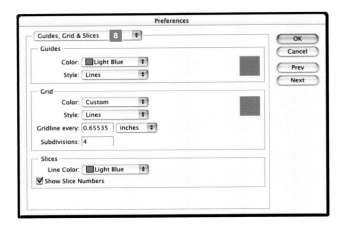

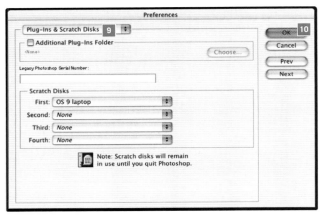

8. **Click the Preferences Set button and choose Guides, Grid & Slices.**

These are cosmetic preferences that you can leave at their defaults. The Slice Guides and Numbers settings have been moved from the Options bar in the last version of Photoshop to this preference set in Photoshop 7.

< T I P >

If you ever want to revert to the default preferences, quit Photoshop, relaunch, and just after launching, press Option+⌘+Shift (Windows: Alt+Ctrl+Shift). Click Yes when you're prompted to delete the Adobe Photoshop Settings file. This is something to try if Photoshop is behaving strangely, which sometimes is a result of damaged Preferences.

9. **Click the Preferences Set button and choose Plug-Ins & Scratch Disks. If you have an additional hard drive or a drive partition with lots of free space other than the one on which you're running Photoshop 7, click First and choose that drive or partition as your First scratch disk.**

If you have additional drives or partitions, you can set them as Second, Third, and Fourth scratch disks the same way.

10. **Click OK to close the Preferences dialog box.**

A final word of advice on changing preferences: I suggest that you change only those preferences you understand and are sure that you want to change, so you don't cause any unexpected modifications that may be hard to diagnose later.

< N O T E >

A *scratch disk* is what Photoshop uses as virtual memory if it runs out of RAM when you're working on a big file. By default, Photoshop uses the drive on which it's running as the first scratch disk.

< N O T E >

There is one more Preferences set — Memory & Image Cache (OS 9 and Windows: Image Cache). The only change that I recommend here is the one I suggested for Macintosh OS X users back in Part I's "Project Overview." There I recommended that Mac OS X users change the maximum available RAM allocable to Photoshop to 90% or lower. Check there for an explanation of this preference.

Tutorial

» Creating Custom Workspaces

Photoshop has several palettes, which you can arrange to meet your individual needs. In this tutorial, you'll learn how to close, collapse, move, and group palettes and how to store palettes in the Options bar. Then you'll practice using Photoshop 7's new Workspace feature, with which you can save multiple arrangements of palettes as reusable, custom workspaces.

1. **Open** 01_velvetrope.psd **from the Session 01 Tutorial Files folder on your hard drive.**
   If you get a warning dialog box about this file, click OK to ignore it.

2. **Choose Window→Workspace→Reset Palette Locations from the menu bar.**
   This reopens any palette that you may have closed and resets all palettes to their default locations. This command has moved to the new Workspace menu in Photoshop 7. It used to be in the main level of the Window menu.

3. **Locate the palette group that contains the Navigator palette. Click the Info tab to bring the Info palette to the foreground in that palette group.**
   This is the fastest way to switch between palettes that are grouped together.

4. **Click the red button at the top left (Windows: the Close button at the top right; Mac OS 9: the Close button at the top left) of the Info palette group to close that group of palettes.**

5. **Locate the History palette and click the green Zoom button at the top left of its palette group (Windows, Mac OS 9: the Minimize button at the top right of the palette group).**
   The palette group collapses so that only its title bar is showing. This is a good way to conserve screen real estate, while keeping all your palettes accessible. To re-expand the palette group, click the Zoom button (Windows, Mac OS 9: Minimize button) again.

6. **Locate the Layers palette, click the title bar of its palette group, and drag the palette group away from the edge of your screen.**

7. **Click the green Zoom button at the top left of the Layers palette group (Windows, Mac OS 9: the Minimize button at the top right of the palette group).**
   The Layers palette resizes to fit its existing content. As you can see, the Zoom button (Windows, Mac OS 9: Minimize button) has slightly different effects on different palettes. To collapse the Layers palette to just its title bar, you'd have to Option+click (Windows: Alt+click) this button.

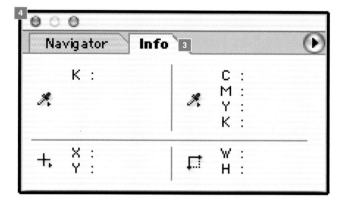

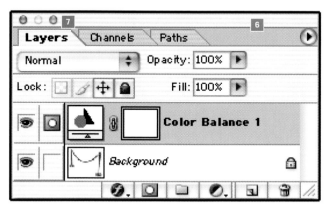

< T I P >

To reopen any closed palette, go to the Window menu in the menu bar and click once on the name of the palette. There may be times, as you work through this book, that you won't see a palette on your screen that's called for in a tutorial. In that case, try this to display the palette.

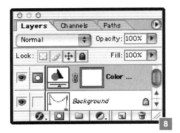

8. **Click and drag from the bottom-right corner (Windows: any corner) of the Layers palette to resize the palette by hand. You can make it narrower, wider, longer, or shorter.**

9. **Click and drag the Channels tab to separate the Channels palette from its palette group.**

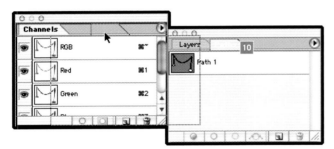

10. **Click and drag the Paths tab from its current palette group into the Channels palette group. Release the mouse button when you see a black box around the inside perimeter of the Channels palette.**

    This adds the Paths palette to the Channels palette group.

11. **Click and drag the Layers tab from its current palette group to just below the title bar of the Paths/Channels palette group. Release the mouse button when you see a thin black box beneath the title bar.**

    This joins the Layers palette to the top of the Paths/Channels palette group. Now when you click and drag from the title bar of the joined palettes, all of them move together. I suggest that you join palettes you often use together so that you don't have to hunt for any of them.

    <WARNING>
    Joining palettes can be tricky. You have to release the mouse button when you see the thin black box, rather than the black box around the inside perimeter of the palette.

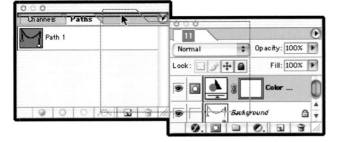

12. **Shift+click the title bar of the Layers palette group to snap the joined palette groups to the nearest edge of your screen.**

    This is a quick way to tidy up your workspace. Palettes also snap to any edge of the screen if you drag them near the edge.

13. **Click the title bar of the toolbox and drag the toolbox to the right side of your screen.**

    You can also drag the Options bar anywhere on your screen.

14. **Click the Color tab and drag it into the gray Palette well on the right side of the Options bar (which contains the Brushes palette and the File Browser by default).**

    The Palette well is a great place to store palettes that you use frequently. Another way to send a palette to the Palette well is to click the arrow at the top right of any palette and choose Dock to Palette Well from the palette options menu. Try this with the Swatches palette.

<**WARNING**>

You won't be able to see the Palette well if your computer's resolution is set to less than 800 pixels wide.

15. **Click the tab of the Color palette in the Palette well to open that palette. Click the tab again to close the palette.**

    To remove a palette from the Palette well, click and drag the palette by its tab.

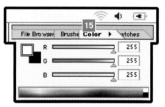

16. **Choose Window→Workspace→Save Workspace. Give this workspace a name in the Save Workspace window. (I chose the name** illustration **to represent the task for which I use this palette configuration.) Click Save.**

    This saves a custom workspace with your palettes, Palette well, Options bar, and toolbox arranged as you've set them.

17. **Rearrange and close some of the palettes on your screen. Then choose Window→Workspace→illustration to reuse your illustration workspace.**

    All your palettes snap back to the configuration that you saved as the illustration workspace.

<**NOTE**>

You can create and save multiple workspaces. I suggest that you make separate workspaces for each task you perform, such as collage, color correction, illustration, and type.

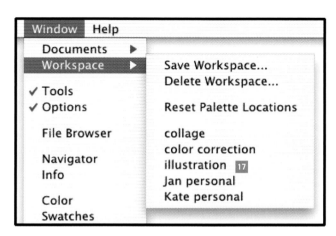

18. **Click Window→Workspace→Reset Palette Locations to restore the default palette configuration before moving on to the next tutorial.**

19. **Close** 01_velvetrope.psd **without saving.**

Tutorial
» Customizing Tools with Presets

In past versions of Photoshop, you could choose options for a tool, but there was no way to save those options for reuse. Adobe has filled that void in Photoshop 7. The new Tool Presets feature saves a copy of a tool with whatever tool options you choose, giving you the ability to create custom tools. In this tutorial, you'll create several Type tool presets, which you can use to quickly create headlines and text in a document.

1. **Click the Type tool in the toolbox.**
   The Options bar changes to display options for the Type tool.

2. **Click the Font option in the Options bar and choose Arial Black. Click the Size option in the Options bar and choose 36.**
   The fonts used in this tutorial are common ones, but if you don't have them in your computer, use fonts of your choice.

3. **Click the Type tool on the far left of the Options bar to open the Tool Preset picker.**

4. **Click the Create New Tool Preset icon on the Tool Preset picker.**

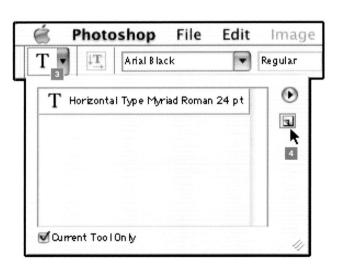

5. **Give your new tool preset a name and click OK in the New Tool Preset dialog box.**
   Photoshop suggests a name for the new tool preset that describes the tool options. You may prefer to give your tool preset a meaningful name that relates to the project in which you plan to use it (such as **Program Guide Headline 1**, which I suggest that you use here).

6. **Click the Size option in the Options bar and choose 18, leaving the Font option set to Arial Black.**

7. **Repeat steps 3 through 5 to create another tool preset. Name this one** Program Guide Subhead 2.

8. **Click the Font option in the Options bar and choose Arial. Click the Size option in the Options bar and choose 12.**

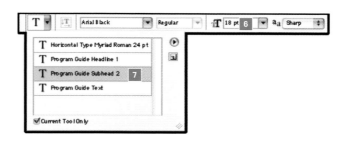

9. **Click the tab of the Tool Presets palette to bring that palette to the foreground in its palette group.**

   This is an alternative way to make a new tool preset. You can create and apply tool presets from either the Tool Presets palette or the Tool Presets Picker on the Options bar.

10. **Click the Create New Tool Preset icon at the bottom of the Tool Presets palette.**

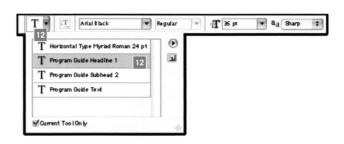

11. **Name this tool preset** Program Guide Text **in the New Tool Preset dialog box and click OK.**

    Another Type tool preset appears in both the Tool Presets palette and the Tool Presets Picker on the Options bar, along with all the other presets for the Type tool. If you ever want to delete a tool preset from this list, select it in either location, click the arrow on the top right of that palette or picker, and choose Delete Tool Preset.

12. **Make sure that the Type tool is still selected in the toolbox. Click the Type tool icon on the Options bar to reopen the Tool Presets Picker. Click the tool preset labeled Program Guide Headline 1 to select that tool preset for use.**

    This is all that you have to do to use a tool preset. If you were to type inside an image now, the type would appear with the options that you built into this custom tool preset. You can select a tool preset from the Tool Presets palette the same way.

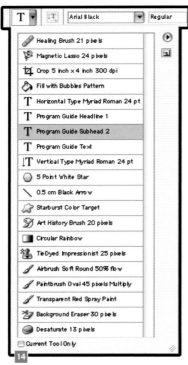

13. **Click the arrow on the top right of the Tool Presets Picker and choose Reset Tool from the menu.**

The Type tool is restored to its default settings — Helvetica, Medium, 12 pt — which will be displayed in the Options bar. You can also choose Reset All Tools from this menu to restore all tools to their default settings. Experienced Photoshop users may remember that Reset All Tools used to be located in the General Preferences window in previous versions of Photoshop.

<NOTE>

The Tool Presets menu also offers options for saving and loading sets of tool presets. For example, you can click Save Tool Presets to save your Type tool presets as a .tpl format file and share that file with other users. Or you can use tool presets that another user created and saved as a .tpl file by downloading that .tpl file to your computer and clicking Load Tool Presets. By the time you're reading this book, there will probably be Internet sites offering Photoshop 7 tool presets for free or for sale.

14. **Click the Current Tool Only check box in the Tool Presets Picker to remove the check mark.**

You'll see a list of the main set of tool presets that ship with Photoshop, as well as those you just created. Check some of these out when you have some free time.

15. **Click the arrow on the top right of the Tool Presets Picker, choose Text from the menu, and click OK at the prompt to replace the main set of tool presets with a set of Type tool presets that ships with Photoshop.**

Photoshop 7 also ships with sets of Art History, Brushes, Cropping, and Marquee tools that you can load from this menu.

16. **Repeat the previous step, but this time choose Reset Tool Presets to restore the main set of tool presets.**

» Session Review

This session introduces Photoshop's work area and shows how to access tools and commands using the Menu bar, the toolbox, the Options bar, and palettes. You also learned how to customize Photoshop 7 to suit your personal work habits by setting preferences, rearranging palettes, and using the new custom workspace and tool preset features. Use the following questions to review what you learned in this session. You'll find the answer to each question in the tutorial noted.

1. What does an arrow on the bottom right of a tool icon in the toolbox signify? (See "Tutorial: Accessing Tools and Commands.")

2. How do you access the menu of palette-related options associated with each palette? (See "Tutorial: Accessing Tools and Commands.")

3. How do you display a contextual menu? (See "Tutorial: Accessing Tools and Commands.")

4. Why would you turn off Use Shift Key for Tool Switch in General Preferences? (See "Tutorial: Setting Preferences.")

5. Which drive should you choose as the first scratch disk in Plug-Ins & Scratch Disks Preferences? (See "Tutorial: Setting Preferences.")

6. How do you resize a palette manually? (See "Tutorial: Creating Custom Workspaces.")

7. How do you separate a palette from its palette group? (See "Tutorial: Creating Custom Workspaces.")

8. How do you add a palette to a palette group? (See "Tutorial: Creating Custom Workspaces.")

9. How do you join palettes together? (See "Tutorial: Creating Custom Workspaces.")

10. How do you snap a palette group to the edge of the screen? (See "Tutorial: Creating Custom Workspaces.")

11. How do you save a custom workspace? (See "Tutorial: Creating Custom Workspaces.")

12. Can you save multiple custom workspaces? (See "Tutorial: Creating Custom Workspaces.")

13. How do you reuse a custom workspace? (See "Tutorial: Creating Custom Workspaces.")

14. How do you reset all the palettes to their default locations? (See "Tutorial: Creating Custom Workspaces.")

15. How do you create a new tool preset? (See "Tutorial: Customizing Tools with Presets.")

16. How do you apply a tool preset? (See "Tutorial: Customizing Tools with Presets.")

17. How do you reset all tools? (See "Tutorial: Customizing Tools with Presets.")

Managing Documents

Tutorial: **Creating Images**

Tutorial: **Saving Files**

Tutorial: **Viewing and Opening Images with the File Browser**

Tutorial: **Managing Files with the File Browser**

Tutorial: **Fixing Mistakes**

Session Introduction

This session teaches fundamental lessons about creating, managing, and saving files in Photoshop. You'll learn about bringing documents into Photoshop and saving them. You'll practice viewing, opening, rotating, ranking, sorting, organizing, and naming documents in Photoshop's most impressive new feature — the File Browser. Then you'll find out how to fix your Photoshop mistakes using the History palette and related features.

TOOLS YOU'LL USE
Open dialog box, Save dialog box, Save As dialog box, File Browser, Undo command, Revert command, Fade command, and History palette

CD-ROM FILES NEEDED
02_films.psd and the photos folder

TIME REQUIRED
90 minutes

Tutorial

» Creating Images

In this tutorial, you'll create a Photoshop file from scratch, learning important information about filenaming, image resolution, and color modes along the way. You'll also be introduced to other methods of getting images into Photoshop.

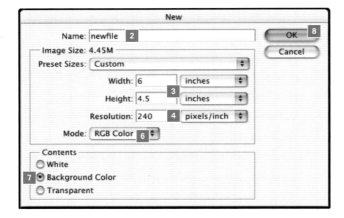

<NOTE>

Macintosh OS X, like Windows, supports long filenames. If you're naming a file in Photoshop 7 on those systems, you're not limited to 31 characters, as you are if you're naming a file in Photoshop 7 in Macintosh OS 9. However, regardless of the operating system that you're using when you create a document, it makes sense to name the file with 31 characters or less if there's a possibility it will be viewed in Macintosh OS 9. That's because in Mac OS 9, a longer filename appears truncated and displays meaningless characters before the dot, which can make it hard to identify.

<NOTE>

If you were creating an image for the Web or other on-screen delivery, rather than for print, you'd set the unit of measurement to pixels and type in the desired number of pixels of width and height. Then just ignore the Resolution field. It doesn't matter what number appears there when you set the physical dimensions of the image in pixels. Honest!

1. **Choose File→New.**
   This opens the New dialog box. The default settings that you see on your screen will be different than those shown here. They come either from your virtual Clipboard, which remembers the settings of the last image you copied, or if there's nothing in the Clipboard, from the last image you created.

<TIP>

If you want to make a series of images that are the same size and color mode, create one image with your desired settings. Then press Option (Windows: Alt) each time you choose File→New to bypass the contents of the Clipboard.

2. **Type a name for the new file in the Name field.**
   Don't bother adding a file extension (such as .psd or .tiff) to the name at this point. Photoshop does that for you automatically when you save the file.

3. **Click the button to the right of the Width and Height fields and choose inches as the unit of measurement. Type 6 in the Width field and 4.5 in the Height field.**
   This sets the physical dimensions of the image as it will print — 6 inches wide by 4.5 inches high.

4. **Check that the button to the right of the Resolution field is set to pixels/inch and type 240 in the Resolution field.**
   This tells Photoshop to put 240 pixels of information in every inch of width and height in this image.

Resolution Primer

Image resolution for print is one of the more difficult subjects you'll run into in this book. You don't have to know everything about resolution to work with Photoshop, but you'll feel more comfortable in the long run if you know the following terms and concepts.

A *pixel,* which stands for picture element, is a tiny rectangle of color information that is the basic building block of a bitmap digital image. Image resolution in Photoshop is the number of pixels that make up each printed inch of the image. The higher the resolution of an image, the more clear and detailed the image will look when it's printed, at least up to the limitations of the printer.

The downside of a high resolution is that it increases file size. An image with a large file size can be slow to edit in Photoshop and will take relatively longer to print and to transfer electronically. The larger the file size, the more storage space the file requires, but that's becoming less of an issue as storage becomes cheaper and easier.

Image resolution also affects the amount of space an image takes up on your computer screen. An image with a high resolution may take up more space than you can see all at once. For example, the image you just created is 1440 pixels wide by 1080 pixels high (240 pixels per inch x 6 inches = 1440 pixels, and 240 pixels per inch x 4.5 inches = 1080 pixels). If your computer monitor can display only 1024 x 768 pixels, you won't see the whole image on your screen when you're working on it in Photoshop. Although this may be uncomfortable, it isn't fatal because you can use the Hand

tool to scroll around the image or you can set Photoshop's magnification to less than 100% (which you'll learn to do in the next session).

So how do you pick a resolution setting when you're creating a new document in Photoshop or scanning? Aim for the highest resolution that your printer can reproduce, as long as you have enough RAM, scratch disk space, and monitor resolution to work on the image efficiently in Photoshop. There's no reason to go to a higher image resolution because it won't improve the printed image and it will inflate your file size and screen size. On the other hand, you don't want the resolution to be too low, or your printed image will look fuzzy, lack detail, and may look pixelated.

The best resolution for a color image destined for a current inkjet printer is between 240 and 300 pixels per inch (ppi). Don't be confused by the advertised resolution of your inkjet printer. The printer uses several dots of ink to create the color of each pixel, so you only need about one-third as much image resolution as the printer's advertised dots per inch (dpi). For example, the tutorial files for this book were created at 240 ppi, which is an optimal image resolution for printing on my 720 dpi inkjet.

Resolution for images that will be printed commercially is determined differently. Commercial printers usually use a halftone screen and measure screen frequency as lines per inch (lpi). Ask your print shop what lpi setting will be used to print your image and set a resolution in Photoshop that's no more than two times that lpi setting.

When to Use RGB Mode

RGB is the mode you'll use most often, whether you're creating an image in Photoshop's New dialog box or scanning an image yourself for editing in Photoshop. RGB is the way to go if you're preparing an image for output to an inkjet printer because most inkjet printers use RGB color drivers (even if they print with CMYK inks). Web graphics must be RGB because that's the only kind of image that can be seen on the Web. Images for other kinds of on-screen display should be RGB because color monitors always display all

images in RGB. Most images you'll bring into Photoshop from digital cameras and scanners (other than high-end, professional CMYK scans) are already RGB because that's the mode those devices generate. Even if you're making a grayscale image, you'll often get the best results by starting with an RGB image and converting to grayscale later using one of several methods (Image➡Adjustments➡Desaturate; Image➡Mode➡Grayscale; the Channel Mixer; or one of the channels from the Channels palette).

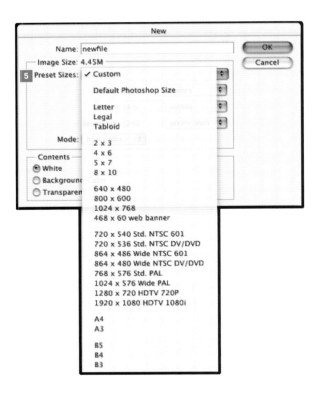

5. **Click the Preset Sizes button in the New dialog box and take a look at the list of preset document sizes, which is a new feature in Photoshop 7. You can close this menu without making a choice for now.**

   The Preset Sizes list offers presets for the physical dimensions and resolution of a new document.

6. **Click the Mode button and choose RGB Color.**

   The *mode* is the set of colors from which your image will be built. RGB Color mode offers 16.7 million colors. Each pixel in RGB mode is described by a combination of red, green, and blue color values.

7. **Click the Background Color radio button.**

   This creates a background for the image that's filled with whatever color is currently in the Background Color box in the toolbox. A background looks like a layer in the Layers palette, but it acts differently than a regular layer, as you'll find out in Session 8.

8. **Click OK.**

   A new document window opens containing an image with a plain background and the other settings that you chose.

<TIP>
To create a new image with a regular layer instead of a special background, choose Transparent as the image content, rather than Background Color or White. You'll be able to save the image at that point only in a format that supports layers — PSD, TIFF, or PDF — unless you flatten the image first (Layer→Flatten Image).

RGB or CMYK Mode for Commercial Printing?

CMYK mode simulates the cyan, magenta, yellow, and black inks used in commercial printing. Some Photoshop users prefer to edit in CMYK mode when they're preparing an image for a commercial printer. However, there are good arguments in favor of working in RGB rather than CMYK mode in that situation. Not all filters are available in CMYK mode. Other Photoshop features, such as layer blending, adjustments, and layer effects, often give better results when applied to an RGB image than a CMYK image. CMYK files are bigger than RGB files because they have four instead of three color channels. If you use CMYK mode, your monitor translates those colors to RGB for display anyway. And, as mentioned earlier, most digital photographs and nonprofessional scans are RGB in the first place. So it makes sense to edit in RGB mode, unless you are work-ing with a high-end CMYK scan and can handle the larger file size.

If you do work in RGB, you can soft proof an image to get an idea of how it will look in CMYK without permanently changing its

colors. Choose View→Proof Setup and select Working CMYK to see how your image will look in the CMYK working space defined in Photoshop's Color Settings (which you'll learn about in Session 4). Or choose Custom to load a custom proof setup for another printer. Turn the soft proof display off and on by choosing View→Proof Color. New In Photoshop 7 is the ability to set Photoshop's Info palette to display the color values of a soft proof. (Click the arrow on the top right of the Info palette, click one of the Readout Mode buttons, and choose Proof Color.)

You can convert an image to CMYK for printing after you finish editing it in RGB by choosing Image→Mode→CMYK Color. Remember to flatten the image first (Layer→Flatten Image), or layer blending may not work the way you intended. Be prepared to see a color change when you convert from RGB to CMYK.

9. **Leave the image open for the next exercise.**

   If you were to close the document at this point, you wouldn't find a trace of it on your hard drive. That's because a new document is not automatically saved at the time it's created. So it's smart to save each document soon after creating it and to resave often. You'll learn all about saving in the next tutorial. Creating an image from scratch has taught you about resolution, color mode, and other basic concepts of digital imaging. Making a new image is a fundamental Photoshop skill, but it's not the only way to get an image into Photoshop for editing. Table 2-1 introduces other ways to bring images into Photoshop. You'll use some of these methods, such as opening an existing image in Photoshop, many times in this course and as you work on your own. Others are more esoteric. So rather than walk you through each method, I offer this summary as a reference list.

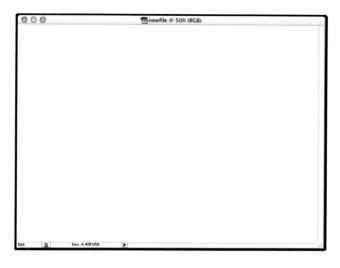

Table 2-1: Other Ways to Get Images into Photoshop

Method	Photoshop Command	Tips
Open an existing image in Photoshop	File→Open and navigate to the file in the Open window	Click Open or just double-click the filename in the Open window. To reopen a file you've opened recently, choose File→Open Recent. To locate and open files visually, use the File Browser, which you'll learn about in this session.
Scan an image into Photoshop	File→Import and choose Twain driver or File→Import→WIA Support (Windows XP and Me only)	Alternatively, scan using your scanner's software and open the resulting image in Photoshop.
Bring photographs from a digital camera into Photoshop	File→Import→WIA Support (Windows XP and Me only)	Alternatively, use your digital camera's software to bring photographs into your computer and open the photographs in Photoshop.
Bring an EPS or Illustrator file into Photoshop	File→Open or File→Place	Both methods rasterize the file (convert it from a mathematically defined, vector format into pixels, so you can no longer scale and edit it as vector data). Use Open to open the file as a new image in Photoshop at the resolution you choose. Use Place to bring the file into an open image in Photoshop at the resolution of that image.
Copy an object from an Illustrator file into an image in Photoshop	File→Paste→Paste As Pixels, Paths, or Shape Layer	Pasting as paths or as a shape layer keeps the artwork in vector format, so you can scale and edit it in Photoshop without degrading its appearance.
Open images contained in a PDF (Adobe Acrobat format) file in Photoshop	Import→PDF or File→ Automate→Multi-Page PDF to PSD	Use the Import method to bring a single image contained in a PDF into Photoshop. Use the Automate method to open multiple images from a PDF as new images in Photoshop.

Tutorial
» Saving Files

In this tutorial, you'll find out all about saving files, including how to save a new file for the first time, how to save a file as you work on it, how to save an open file in a new format, and how to save a file with layers. It's crucial to get in the habit of saving your work often. If your computer crashes or Photoshop freezes, you'll lose all the work you've done since the last save. So save frequently as you go through the tutorials in this book and as you work on your own projects.

1. **Check that your newfile image is still open from the last tutorial. If it's not, create a new document following the steps in the preceding tutorial, "Creating Images."**

2. **Try to choose File→Save. You'll see that that command is grayed out, meaning that it's unavailable.**
   You can't use the Save command if you haven't made a change to the image since you created or last saved it.

3. **Choose Layer→New→Layer and click OK to add a layer to this image.**

<NOTE>
You're adding a layer to this image so that you can see how to save a file with layers. Don't bother trying to figure out other aspects of layers now. You'll find out more about them in Session 8.

4. **Click the Paintbrush tool in the toolbox and draw on the image in the document window.**

5. **Choose File→Save.**
   Now that you've made some changes to the file, the Save command is available. This opens the Save As dialog box.

6. **Make sure that there's a filename in the Save As field.**
   Photoshop uses the name that you gave the image when you created it. If you didn't name the image then, type **newfile** over the portion of the default filename before the dot.

<NOTE>

Photoshop automatically adds a three letter extension to the filename to match the format of the file. That's because you left Append File Handling set to its default — Always — in Preferences➔File Handling.

7. **Click the Format button to see the formats in which you can save a file in Photoshop. Leave this file set to the default Photoshop format.**
   The Photoshop format (PSD) is Photoshop's and ImageReady's native format. It retains all the Photoshop features that you may add to an image — layers, masks, styles, and so on.

8. **Make sure that there's a check mark in the Layers check box.**
   This ensures that layers are saved with the file.

9. **Navigate to the Session 2 folder on your hard drive in the Save As dialog box.**

10. **Click the New Folder button. Type** saving files **as the name for this folder and click Create in the New Folder window. (Windows: Click the yellow New Folder icon at the top right of the Save As dialog box, and type the new folder name** — saving files — **over the default folder name.)**
    You don't have to create a new folder when you save a file. It's simply a way of organizing files.

11. **Click Save in the Save As dialog box. Click OK if a warning appears about maximizing compatibility (see the "Maximize Compatibility Warning" sidebar).**
    Your open file is now saved in PSD format. That's all there is to saving a new file for the first time.

12. **Make another change to your image (such as drawing some more with the Paintbrush tool). Then choose File➔Save.**
    Photoshop saves over the last-saved file, replacing it with the changed version. You'll use File➔Save, or its shortcut ⌘+S (Windows: Ctrl+S), often as you work on an image.

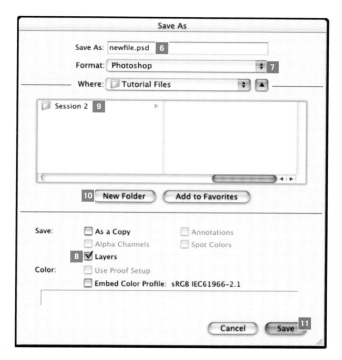

<TIP>

Whenever you create a file in PSD fomat, save it as a PSD before flattening, converting to another file format, or saving for the Web. Store the full-featured PSD version in a safe place. That way you'll always have a source file with all its layers and other Photoshop features intact to modify or use as a template in the future.

<NOTE>

There are only three formats in which you can save layers — PSD, TIFF, and PDF. You'll work with PSD and TIFF in this tutorial. PDF is Adobe's Portable Document Format for sharing and editing digital files, which you'll probably use less often than PSD or TIFF.

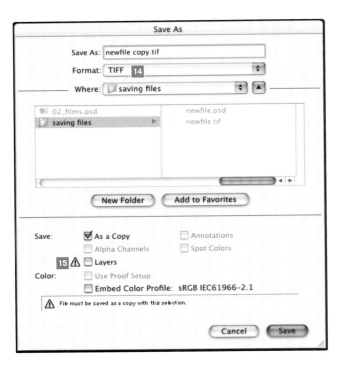

13. Choose File→Save As.

In the next steps, you'll learn how to use the Save As command to save an open file in a different file format.

14. Click the Format button in the Save As dialog box and choose TIFF.

This automatically changes the extension on the filename to .tif. TIFF is a robust file format that's commonly used in prepress workflows.

15. Uncheck Layers temporarily, to see what happens.

Layers is checked by default when you save a TIFF in Photoshop 7. If you uncheck Layers, you see a warning that the file must be saved as a copy, a check mark appears in the Save As a Copy check box, and Photoshop adds the word *copy* to the filename. If you were to click Save (but don't do so now), Photoshop would save a flattened TIFF as a copy, and the original layered file would remain open. This is what Photoshop does whenever you try to save a file in a format that doesn't support all the file's features.

<TIP>
Don't panic if you save over a file by mistake. As long as you haven't closed the file, you can go back to the saved-over version by clicking ⌘+Z (Windows: Ctrl+Z). You'll find out more about fixing mistakes later in this session.

Maximize Compatibility Warning

In Photoshop 7, a warning appears whenever you try to save a file in PSD format, if you previously unchecked Always Maximize Compatibility in Preferences→File Handling. Clicking OK in this warning causes your PSD file to be saved without an extra composite layer, as you probably intended when you set the preference. If you were to put a check mark in this Maximize Compatibility check box before clicking OK, a composite layer would be added to the file. This warning is an attempt to get you to rethink the choice you made when you set the Always Maximize Compatibility preference. If you're confused about the pros and cons of that choice, review the discussion of the Always Maximize Compatibility preference in Session 1. Unfortunately, the price of standing by that choice is having to see this warning every time you save a PSD file.

16. **Recheck the Layers box before continuing. Leave the other settings in the Save As dialog box as they are and click Save.**

A TIFF Options dialog box opens. Some, but not all, file formats display a dialog box like this with extra options.

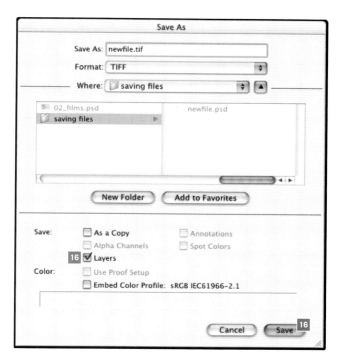

17. **Leave the settings in the TIFF Options dialog box at their defaults for purposes of this tutorial and click OK.**

<TIP>

Saving a TIFF looks more complicated in Photoshop 7 than in previous releases because the default behavior has changed. Photoshop 7 defaults to saving a TIFF with layers and to offering relatively advanced options for compressing TIFFs. If you're preparing a TIFF for commercial printing and you're not sure whether to save with layers or how to set TIFF Options, be sure to consult your printer.

18. **Click OK again when you see a warning that including layers will increase the file size.**

The open file is now saved in the same location as the PSD file you originally saved, but with a different file format. Notice that the currently open file is a TIFF.

19. **Choose File→Close.**

<TIP>

Another potential use for Save As is to save a file with the same format as the original but in a different location.

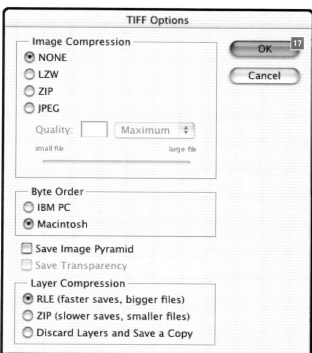

Tutorial

» Viewing and Opening Images with the File Browser

The File Browser is the hottest new feature in Photoshop 7. It's an image viewer, a source of file information, and a file organizer. The File Browser is great for organizing photos from a digital camera, which often come into your computer without thumbnails, with meaningless names, and with vertical images rotated the wrong way. It's just as good for managing any folder full of image files for print or Web. This tutorial introduces you to the File Browser and teaches you how to use it to view and open documents. In the next tutorial, you'll delve into the file management features of the File Browser — rotating, organizing, ranking, sorting, and renaming files.

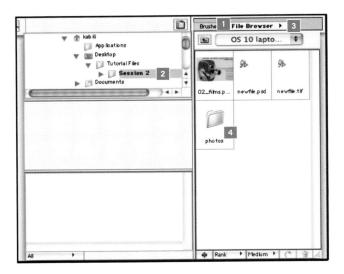

<NOTE>

These thumbnails are generated by the File Browser. This means that you can visually preview all your images even if image icons weren't generated by the software that comes with your digital camera or by the application in which you created an image. If you've ever been frustrated by the meaningless list of images with no previews that you used to get from your digital camera, you'll really appreciate the File Browser!

1. **Click the File Browser tab in the Palette well on the right side of the Options bar.**
   The File Browser opens in the Palette well. The default position of the File Browser is in the Palette well. If you don't see the File Browser tab there, choose Window→File Browser, and the File Browser will open as a standalone window.

2. **Navigate through the file tree on the top left of the File Browser to the Session 2 Tutorial Files folder that you transferred to your hard drive.**
   (Reminder: The instructions for transferring Tutorial Files folders to your hard drive are located in Appendix A.) You'll see thumbnails of the contents of the Session 2 folder on the right side of the File Browser. You can scroll down to see all the thumbnails or change the thumbnail view, as you'll do in the next step.

3. **Click the arrow on the File Browser tab and choose Medium Thumbnail.**
   You should see thumbnails of all the image files and one folder contained in the Session 2 folder. If you don't see the photos folder, click the arrow at the top right of the File Browser and choose Show Folders.

4. **Double-click the thumbnail of the photos folder on the right side of the File Browser.**
   The File Browser displays thumbnails of all the images in the photos folder.

5. **Click the thumbnail of the landscape photo on the right side of the File Browser.**

   A larger preview of that image appears on the left side of the File Browser, along with detailed information about the image.

6. **Click the diagonal lines at the bottom-right corner of the File Browser and drag down. Click and drag up on the borders above and below the larger preview to reveal more of the image information on the bottom left of the File Browser.**

   The File Browser can display EXIF information from a digital camera, as well as information from the image itself. EXIF information can include anything from image resolution to whether the camera's flash fired when the picture was taken. If you want to see only the EXIF information, click the arrow at the bottom left of the File Browser and choose EXIF.

7. **Double-click the landscape thumbnail in the File Browser to open the full image in a document window.**

   This is a feature that I use often to open images. It's the quickest way of identifying which image I want to open.

Double-clicking a File Browser thumbnail to open an image causes the docked File Browser to close back into the Palette well. If you want the File Browser to stay open when you open an image, Option+double-click (Windows: Alt+double-click) the image thumbnail. However, if you then click on the image, or anywhere outside of the File Browser for that matter, the File Browser closes again. The only way to leave the File Browser open while you work on an image is to remove the File Browser from the Palette well, as you'll do in the next tutorial.

8. **Leave the File Browser open and move on to the next tutorial.**

Tutorial
» Managing Files with the File Browser

Now that you're familiar with the File Browser and know how to use it to view and open images, you'll find out how to use its file management features — rotating, organizing, ranking, sorting, and renaming images — all from one convenient window and with visual feedback.

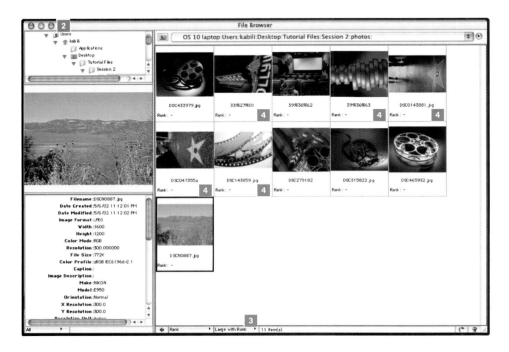

1. **Click on the File Browser tab and drag the File Browser out of the Palette well.**

2. **Click the Maximize button at the top left (Windows: top right) of the free-standing File Browser.**
   Alternatively, you can resize the free-standing File Browser horizontally, vertically, and diagonally by clicking and dragging the diagonal lines on the bottom-right corner.

   <NOTE>
   If you want to see the entire maximized File Browser window, close the palettes that cover it. When you open the File Browser outside the Palette well, it acts like a Photoshop window, sliding under palettes and menu bars. By contrast, when the File Browser is open in the Palette well, it acts like a Photoshop palette, covering the neighboring palettes.

3. **Click the View By arrow at the bottom of the File Browser and choose Large with Rank as the thumbnail size.**
   Alternatively, you can click the arrow at the top right of the File Browser and make the same choice from the menu that appears.

4. **⌘+click (Windows: Ctrl+click) each of the image thumbnails that is rotated the wrong way to select them all.**

   <NOTE>
   ⌘+click (Windows: Ctrl+click) selects noncontiguous thumbnails. Shift+click selects thumbnails that are next to one another. Ctrl+click (Windows: right-click) any thumbnail and choose Select All to select all thumbnails in the File Browser.

5. **Click the Rotate icon (the curved arrow) at the bottom right of the File Browser to rotate the selected thumbnails 90° and mark the image to be rotated upon opening. Click OK at the prompt.**
   Vertical photographs usually are rotated horizontally when they come into your computer from a digital camera. The File Browser's rotate feature saves you all the time that you used to spend opening, rotating, and resaving photos one at a time.

<NOTE>
Another way to rotate selected images is to ⌘+click (Windows: Ctrl+click) one of the selected images and choose rotate 180°, 90° CW (clockwise), or 90° CCW (counterclockwise).

6. **⌘+click (Windows: Ctrl+click) the thumbnails of your four favorite images to select them. Then Ctrl+click (Windows: right-click) one of the selected files and choose Rank A from the menu that appears.**
   All the selected thumbnails display the label *Rank A.* This is a quick way to give multiple thumbnails the same rank for sorting.

7. **Click in the rank field of the landscape image and type** reject. **Click in the Rank field of each of the remaining thumbnails and type the number** 2.
   You can give individual thumbnails any name or number up to 15 digits as a custom rank. This enables you to sort images by any category that you find relevant.

8. **Click the Sort By button at the bottom of the File Browser and choose Rank.**
   This sorts the thumbnails, and the corresponding files on your hard drive, numerically and then alphabetically by rank.

<NOTE>
Rank enables you to sort by your own criteria. Alternatively, you can sort by any of the categories in the Sort By menu — File Size, File Type, Date Created, and so on.

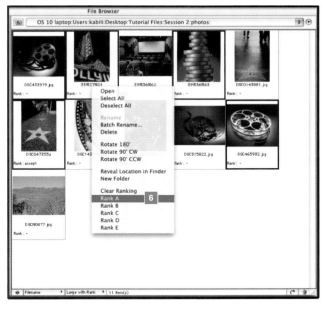

9. **Click and drag the landscape image to the Trash icon at the bottom right of the File Browser. Click Yes at the prompt.**
   This deletes the corresponding file from your hard drive. Be sure before you invoke this command!

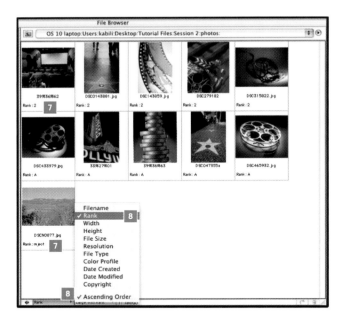

10. **Click the arrow on the top right of the File Browser and choose New Folder.**
This creates a new folder on your hard drive.

11. **Click the label Untitled Folder under the new folder thumbnail, and type** best photos **to rename the folder.**
This names the new folder on your hard drive.

12. **Shift+click all the thumbnails labeled Rank A and drag them onto the thumbnail of the best photos folder.**
This moves the actual files into the best photos folder on your hard drive.

13. **Shift+click all the thumbnails labeled 2. Click the arrow on the top right of the File Browser and choose Batch Rename.**

14. **Click Rename in Same Folder in the Batch Rename dialog box.**

15. **Click the first button in the File Naming area of the dialog box and choose 2 Digit Serial Number.**
This adds a different two digit serial number as part of the new name of each selected thumbnail and corresponding file. Serial Number is the only choice that changes automatically from file to file. For example, if you chose document name and didn't include one of the Serial Number options in part of the filename, all the selected files would have the same name.

16. **Click the next button in the File Naming area and choose extension. Click OK.**
This renames each of the selected thumbnails and corresponding files with the two variables that you chose. You could have added more information to each filename by clicking the other buttons in the File Naming area and choosing from the same menu of variables. If you've ever slogged through a folder of files from a digital camera, manually changing meaningless filenames one by one, you'll love what the File Browser's Batch Rename feature can do for you.

17. **Open the photos folder on your hard drive to see that your files have been moved, sorted, and renamed to reflect all the changes that you made to the thumbnails in the File Browser.**

<TIP>

A quick way to open the photos folder on your hard drive is to select one of the thumbnails in that folder in the File Browser, click the arrow on the top right of the File Browser, and choose Reveal Location in Finder (Windows: Reveal Location in Explorer).

18. **Click the arrow on the top right of the File Browser and choose Export Cache.**

If you move or rename the photos folder before you export the cache, all the rotating and ranking instructions that you applied in the File Browser will be lost. Exporting the cache copies that information into the photos folder, so it stays with the affected files. After the cache is exported, you can move the photos folder or even burn it onto a CD-ROM to give to a coworker or client without losing the work that you did to the files in the File Browser.

19. **Click the arrow on the top right of the File Browser and choose Purge Cache.**

    This deletes the cache that was originally created by the File Browser in your system files, so thumbnails will load faster the next time you access the photos folder in the File Browser.

Purging the cache eliminates all the rotating and ranking data in the original cache. So don't purge the cache until you've clicked Export Cache.

20. **Click the arrow on the top right of the File Browser and choose Dock to Palette Well.**

    This returns the File Browser to its default location in the Palette well. You can't drag the File Browser back into the Palette well, as you can with regular palettes.

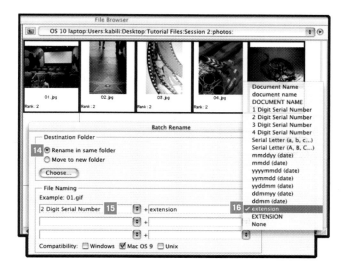

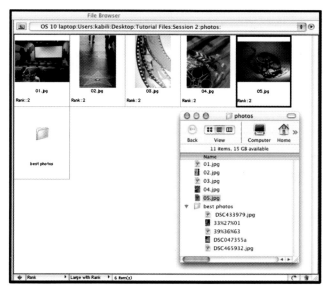

Tutorial
» Fixing Mistakes

This is one tutorial that you won't want to skip. You'll learn several different ways to go back in time to change what you've done to an image in Photoshop, using the Undo, Revert, and Fade commands and the History palette.

1. **Choose File→Open and navigate to** 02_films.psd **in the Session 2 Tutorial Files folder on your hard drive. Click Open.**

2. **Make sure that the Layers palette is showing. If it's not, choose Window→Layers.**

3. **Click in the empty box in the column of eye icons to the left of the film schedule layer.**
   This adds an eye icon to that box and makes the artwork on the film schedule layer visible in the image.

4. **Choose File→Save and click OK at the prompt.**
   Note the way the image looks at this point. You'll revert to this point later in this tutorial.

5. **Make sure that the Background layer is selected in the Layers palette. Select the Paintbrush tool in the toolbox and draw three lines anywhere in the image.**

   Say that you change your mind and want to eliminate these brush strokes. The simple solution is to use multiple undo's, as you'll do in the next few steps.

6. **Press ⌘+Z (Windows: Ctrl+Z).**

   This takes you back one step to the condition of the image as it was before your last action. This is commonly known as an *undo*. You'll use this shortcut so often that I used it as the instruction in this step, rather than the longhand command, which is Edit→Undo Brush Tool.

<NOTE>

⌘+Z (Windows: Ctrl+Z) undoes your last action even after you save or print a document, as long as you don't close and reopen the document.

7. **Choose Edit→Step Backward twice.**

   All three of your brush strokes are now gone from the image. Thank goodness Photoshop offers multiple undo's. The shortcut for each undo after the first one is ⌘+Option+Z (Windows: Ctrl+Alt+Z).

<NOTE>

If you change your mind again, choose Edit→Step Forward to reapply your last action.

8. **Draw some more on your image, using lots of individual brush strokes.**

   Don't spend too much time on this drawing because you're going to eliminate the result shortly.

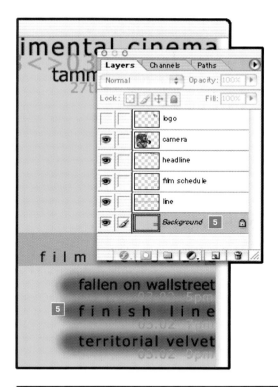

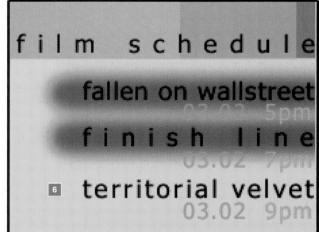

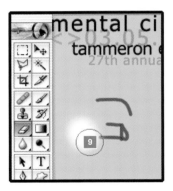

9. **Select the Eraser tool and try to erase what you just drew.**
   Notice that the Eraser tool erases back to the color that's currently in the Background Color box in the toolbox. The Eraser is not always the best choice for fixing mistakes because it doesn't really move your image back in time. The History palette, which you'll practice using shortly, does a better job. It's the most precise and flexible method of correcting mistakes in Photoshop.

10. **Choose Edit→Fade Eraser. In the Fade dialog box, move the Opacity slider to the left and notice that the erasure diminishes in your image.**
    If you moved the slider all the way to 0%, all trace of the erasure would be gone from your image. This is another way of correcting mistakes in Photoshop.

11. **Make sure that the History palette is showing. If it's not, choose Window→History.**
    Notice that each action you've taken since your multiple undo's is recorded as a state in this palette.

12. **Click one of the Brush Tool states in the History palette. Notice that your image changes to the condition it was in at the time you made that brush stroke.**
    Alternatively, move the slider on the left side of the palette up to this state.

< N O T E >

The History palette records 20 states by default. To increase that amount, go to Preferences→General and type a different number in the History States field. Theoretically, you can have up to 1,000 history states in an image in Photoshop 7, but use some restraint here because each additional history state in an image increases file size.

13. **Click the state at the very top of the History palette, labeled** 02_films.psd.
    This returns your image to the condition that it was in when you first opened it, as it appeared back in step 1.

14. **Choose File→Revert.**
    This takes you all the way back to the condition of the image as it was the last time it was saved, back in step 4. This is the most heavy-handed way to fix mistakes. Sometimes it takes you back in time farther than you'd like to go, so use it judiciously.

15. **Choose File→Save As. Rename the file** 02_films_end.psd. **Make sure that the format is set to Photoshop and Layers is checked. Navigate to the Session 2 Tutorial Files folder on your hard drive and click Save.**
    This saves over the version of 02_films_end.psd that I provided for you. If you ever find that you want my version of 02_films_end.psd, you can always get a new copy of it from the CD-ROM.

Take a Snapshot for Later

Sometimes, as you're working on an image, you get to a point to which you may want to return later. You can take a snapshot of the condition of the image at that point by clicking the arrow at the top right of the History palette and choosing New Snapshot, and then clicking OK. The snapshot appears near the top of the History palette. You can click it any time to return your image to that condition.

» Session Review

This session covers getting images into Photoshop, saving images out of Photoshop, using the File Browser, and fixing mistakes using the History palette and the undo, revert, and fade commands. Use the following questions to help you review the materials in this session. You'll find the answer to each question in the tutorial noted in parentheses.

1. Is a new file saved automatically when it's created? (See "Tutorial: Creating Images.")

2. What does the number that you put in the Resolution field in the New dialog box mean? (See "Tutorial: Creating Images.")

3. Why don't you want to set image resolution higher than the resolution your printer can reproduce? (See "Tutorial: Creating Images.")

4. Why don't you want to set image resolution too low? (See "Tutorial: Creating Images.")

5. Which color mode will you use most often when you're creating a new image? (See "Tutorial: Creating Images.")

6. Name the three file formats in which you can save a file with layers. (See "Tutorial: Saving Files.")

7. How do you get the File Browser to stay open when you open an image from the File Browser? (See "Tutorial: Viewing and Opening Images with the File Browser.")

8. How do you select and rotate multiple image thumbnails in the File Browser? (See "Tutorial: Managing Files with the File Browser.")

9. How do you rank and sort thumbnails by your own criteria in the File Browser? (See "Tutorial: Managing Files with the File Browser.")

10. How do you rename multiple files at once in the File Browser? (See "Tutorial: Managing Files with the File Browser.")

11. Which variable from the File Browser's Batch Rename dialog box should you include to make sure that multiple files are given different names? (See "Tutorial: Managing Files with the File Browser.")

12. What is the function of the Export Cache feature in the File Browser? (See "Tutorial: Managing Files with the File Browser.")

13. What is the shortcut for undo in Photoshop? (See "Tutorial: Fixing Mistakes.")

14. What happens to an image when you click a state in the History palette? (See "Tutorial: Fixing Mistakes.")

15. What's the most extreme way of fixing mistakes in Photoshop? (See "Tutorial: Fixing Mistakes.")

tammeron international experimental cinema

03.02.03<>03.05.03

tammeron england

27th annual festival

2003

film schedule

fallen on wallstreet
03.02 5pm

f i n i s h   l i n e
03.02 7pm

territorial velvet
03.02 9pm

arising to the end
03.03 7pm

four large squares
03.04 7pm

frozen with steak
03.05 7pm

reason to cry
03.05 9pm

Viewing Documents

Session Introduction

The Photoshop document window is the heart of the Photoshop interface. This session covers many aspects of viewing and handling an image that's open in the document window. You'll learn how to change your view of an image, move around in an image, access document information, display a document in different screen modes, change the size of an image and its canvas, and crop an image. Knowing how to use these features will make you a more adept and efficient Photoshop user.

TOOLS YOU'LL USE
Zoom tool, Hand tool, Navigator palette, New Window command, Patch tool, title bar, file information menu, Info palette, Eyedropper tool, Move tool, Measure tool, Notes tool, Screen Mode buttons, Canvas Size dialog box, Crop tool, and Image Size dialog box

CD-ROM FILES NEEDED
03_films.psd and 03_films_end.psd

TIME REQUIRED
90 minutes

Tutorial
» Controlling Image Magnification

There will be times when you'll want to change the magnification at which you view an image you're working on in Photoshop. You can zoom in, increasing magnification, to get a close-up of part of an image for detail work. You can zoom out, decreasing magnification, to see the big picture. In this tutorial, you'll find out how to control image magnification using the Zoom tool, zoom settings on the Options bar, and some keyboard shortcuts.

1. **Choose File→Open and navigate to** 03_films.psd **in the Session 3 Tutorial Files folder on your hard drive. Click Open.** 03_films.psd is a replica of the finished file 02_films_end.psd that I asked you to save into your Session 2 Tutorial Files folder at the end of Session 2. If you completed all the tutorials in Session 2, feel free to use your own file instead of 03_films.psd.

2. **Look at the title bar at the top of the document window, or the zoom field at the bottom left of the document window, to see the magnification at which the image is displayed.**
   Photoshop has some preset magnifications (such as 25%, 33.3%, 50%, 66.7%, and 100%). An image opens at the largest of the preset magnifications that fits on your screen between any open palettes, the toolbox, and the menu bar. On my screen, the image opened at 33.3%, although yours may be different. 33.3% magnification means that you're viewing the image at one-third of its actual size in pixels.

Do not confuse image magnification with image size. Magnification changes only the way you view the image; it has no effect on the actual size of the image. You'll learn how to change image size later in this session.

<TIP>
If you look closely at the figure, you'll see that the text in the image appears degraded. That's because it's being viewed at a magnification other than one of Photoshop's round-numbered presets. If you ever have an image that looks degraded on-screen, try changing the magnification to one of those round presets — such as 25%, 50%, or 100%. Chances are that it will look a lot better.

3. **Double-click the Zoom tool in the toolbox to view the image at 100% magnification.**

   This changes the image magnification to 100%. Notice that there's no image distortion at this magnification. You won't be able to see this whole image at 100% without moving it around in the document window, which you'll learn to do in the next tutorial.

4. **Make sure that the Zoom tool is selected in the toolbox.**

   This causes the Options bar to display Zoom tool options.

<TIP>

Clicking the Actual Pixels button in the Options bar is another way to zoom to 100% magnification. I suggest that you ignore the other large buttons on the Options bar (Fit On Screen and Print Size) in favor of the control offered by the Zoom In and Zoom Out buttons and their shortcuts, which you'll try out in the next steps.

5. **Select the Zoom Out button (the one with the minus symbol) on the Options bar. Then click several times in the document window until you see in the title bar that the image magnification is 25%.**

   The Zoom Out button tells Photoshop to reduce the size at which the image is displayed. There's empty space around the image because the document window doesn't resize to match the image by default. You'll change this behavior in the next step.

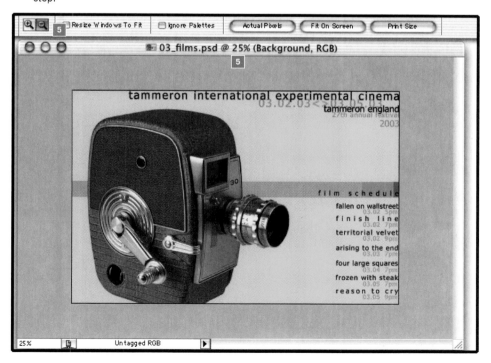

<TIP>

A quick way to switch between zooming in and zooming out is to press the Option (Windows: Alt) key with the Zoom tool selected. If the Zoom In button is selected in the Options bar, you'll see the icon on the cursor change from + to −, and vice versa.

6. **Click in the Resize Windows To Fit box on the Options bar to add a check mark. Select the Zoom In button (the one with the plus symbol) on the Options bar. Click in the document window to increase magnification to 33.3%.**
   With the Resize Windows To Fit option checked, the document window grows or shrinks as necessary to fit the magnified image.

7. **Click in the Ignore Palettes box on the Options bar to add a check mark. Then click once more in the document window to increase magnification to 50%.**
   The Ignore Palettes option allows the enlarged document window to slip under any open palettes. Otherwise the document window would expand no farther than the left edge of the palettes.

<NOTE>

This setup (50% magnification, with the document window resized and palettes ignored) is the way I suggest that you view the tutorial files as you work through this book. You'll be able to see the entire contents of each file on most screens, and the images won't look degraded. If open palettes get in your way at any time, you can close them temporarily.

<TIP>

You'll often need to zoom in or out when you're using another tool. The quickest way to do that is to hold the ⌘ (Windows: Ctrl) key and press the plus (+) key to zoom in or the minus (−) key to zoom out. In Windows, the document window doesn't resize itself with these shortcuts.

8. **Click and drag a selection around the number 30 on the camera in the image. Release the mouse button, and the selected portion of the image increases to the highest magnification that fits on your screen.**

This technique is useful for doing detail work, such as painting in a mask.

<NOTE>

An image can be magnified to as high as 1600% and reduced as low as .05%, although I can't imagine why you'd go to those extremes.

9. **Leave this image open for the next tutorial.**

Tutorial
» Navigating the Document Window

Sometimes you can't see an entire image in your document window, as you just learned. Knowing how to move an image around in the document window is crucial in that situation. Here you'll practice using the Hand tool, its keyboard shortcuts, and the Navigator palette to navigate inside the document window.

1. **Check that** `03_films.psd` **is still open from the last tutorial. If it's not, open** `03_films.psd` **from the Session 3 Tutorial Files folder on your hard drive.**

2. **Select the Hand tool in the toolbox.**
   This changes the Options bar to options for the Hand tool.

3. **Click the Actual Pixels button to return the image to 100% magnification.**

4. **Move your cursor over the image and notice that the cursor changes to a hand. Click and drag the image around in the document window.**

<NOTE>

You can access the Hand tool temporarily when you have another tool selected by holding the spacebar down and dragging in the image. This comes in handy when you're painting, drawing, or selecting inside a large image and need to move beyond the area that you can see in the document window.

5. **Choose Window→Navigator if you can't see your Navigator palette.**
   The Navigator palette acts like a combination Hand tool and Zoom tool to help you zero in on a specific part of an image. Notice there's a red box in the Navigator palette that defines the visible area of the image in the document window.

6. **Click inside the Navigator palette and drag the red box so that it's centered around the camera lens.**
   Notice that the image in the document window moves in sync with the red box in the Navigator palette, so the camera lens is now centered in the document window, too.

7. **Click the larger of the two mountain icons on the Navigator palette.**
   This magnifies to 200% the part of the image in the document window that corresponds to the area inside the red box on the Navigator palette. Clicking the smaller mountain icon reduces the corresponding area in the document window. You can accomplish the same thing by moving the slider on the Navigator palette.

8. **Leave this image open for the next tutorial.**

Tutorial
» Displaying an Image in Multiple Windows

You can display an open image in more than one document window. This is useful when you've zoomed in to work on an area and want to see the results from a larger perspective as well. Any editing you do in one window appears in the other window too. Photoshop 7 adds a new wrinkle. You can now automatically position multiple document windows in tiled or cascading arrangements. In this tutorial you'll work with multiple windows, and you'll get a sneak preview of the new Patch tool.

1. **Make sure that** `03_films.psd` **is still open from the last tutorial. If it's not, open** `03_films.psd` **from the Session 3 Tutorial Files folder on your hard drive and zoom in to 200%.**

2. **Choose Window→Documents→New Window to create a second window that displays the same image.**
   This command is just like the View→New View command that you may remember from Photoshop 6.

3. **Select the Zoom tool in the toolbox and the Zoom Out button in the Options bar. Click several times in the new window to zoom it out to 25%.**

4. **Select the Hand tool, click inside the larger window, and move the image until you see the words** *MADE IN U.S.A.* **on the camera.**
   Making the larger window active caused it to obscure the smaller window. You'll fix that in the next step.

5. **Choose Window→Documents→Tile.**
   Use the tile view to see multiple windows regardless of their size. If you ever want to go back to your original multiple window arrangement, choose Window→Documents→Cascade.

6. **Click the Healing Brush tool (the one with the bandage icon) in the toolbox and select the Patch tool from the hidden menu that appears. Select the camera layer in the Layers palette. In the larger of the two image views, click and drag a selection around the words** *MADE IN U.S.A.*

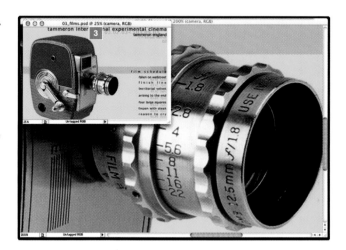

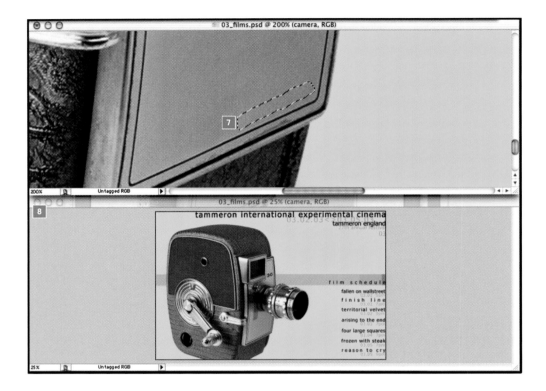

7. **Click inside the selection that you just made, drag it just above the words _MADE IN U.S.A.,_ and release the mouse button.**
Wow! The words _MADE IN U.S.A._ have disappeared in both document windows. After you get over your amazement at how well the Patch tool works, focus on the fact that the change you made in the larger view also appears in the smaller view.

<NOTE>
You're probably itching to know more about the Patch tool, which is new to Photoshop 7. You'll find out all about it in Session 13.

<TIP>
Another good use for multiple document windows is to display the image in more than one color mode. For example, if you're preparing an image for commercial printing, you can work on it in RGB mode in one window and soft proof it in CMYK in another window at the same time. (If you don't remember how to soft proof, turn back to Session 2 and take another look at the "RGB or CMYK Mode for Commercial Printing?" sidebar.)

8. **Click the Minimize button at the top left (Windows: top right) of the smaller document window.**
This sends the minimized document window to the dock in OS X and to the bottom of the application window in Windows XP. Click its icon or tab whenever you want to reopen it. This is a new feature for Macintosh users. It isn't available if you're running Photoshop 7 in OS 9.

9. **Use the Zoom tool and the Zoom Out option to reduce the magnification of the larger document window back to 50% and leave that window open for the next tutorial.**

Tutorial

» Viewing Image Information

You can get all kinds of information about an image from Photoshop. Session 2 covers the image information available in the File Browser. After an image is opened, use the title bar, the file information menu at the bottom of the document window, and the Info palette to find out more about an image. Add your own information to the image with the Notes tool. You'll use all of these features in this tutorial.

1. **Check that** 03_films.psd **is still open from the last tutorial. If it's not, open** 03_films.psd **from the Session 3 Tutorial Files folder on your hard drive and zoom out to 50%.**

2. **Take a look at the title bar at the top of the document window to get some basic information about the open document.**
   The title bar reveals the name of the file, the image magnification (50%), the layer that's selected in the Layers palette (the camera layer), and the color mode of the image (RGB).

3. **Click the arrow in the bottom border of the document window (Windows: the application window) to reveal the file information menu. Choose Document Sizes if it isn't already selected.**
   Document Sizes reveals two pieces of information in the information field to the left of the menu. The number on the left tells you that this file would contain 6.18 megabytes of information if you were to flatten its layers and save it. The number on the right tells you the true file size of this image — 13.3 megabytes — which takes into account all the layers and channels in this image.

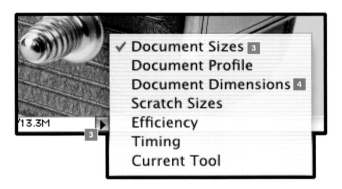

<NOTE>
The number of layers that you add to a file has a big impact on file size. The artwork, as well as the transparent pixels on each layer, affects file size.

4. **Click the arrow again and choose Document Dimensions.**
   You'll see that this image is 6 inches by 4 inches. This is the actual physical size of the document and has nothing to do with image magnification.

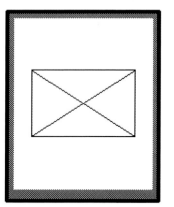

Width: 1800 pixels (6 inches)
Height: 1200 pixels (4 inches)
Channels: 3 (RGB Color)
Resolution: 300 pixels/inch

5. Click the arrow again and choose Current Tool.
This tells you which tool is currently selected in the toolbox. It's useful if you've closed your toolbox to gain more screen real estate or if you've moved your toolbox to a second monitor.

6. Choose Window➜Info to display the Info palette.

< T I P >

Option+click (Windows: Alt+click) the information field, and a pop-up menu tells you fundamental information about the image — its width and height, the number of channels it has, and the image resolution in pixels per inch. Although you can get this information from the file information menu, this is a handy shortcut.

< T I P >

Click the information field, and you'll see a diagram of the position and orientation of the image as it will print. You can change these settings in the Print dialog box, which you access by choosing File➜Print with Preview.

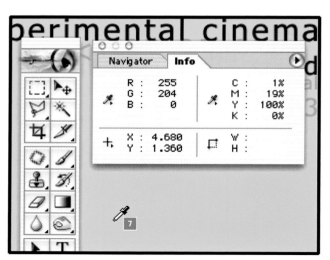

7. Click the Eyedropper tool in the toolbox and move your cursor anywhere in the open image, keeping an eye on the Info palette.
The Info palette displays different information depending on which tool you're working with. With the Eyedropper tool selected, the Info palette tells you the RGB and CMYK values of the color directly under the cursor.

< N O T E >

You can change the color mode for either of the two mode readouts in the Info palette by clicking the arrow at the top right of the Info palette and choosing Palette Options. Click either of the Mode buttons, choose a color mode, and click OK. For example, you can choose Web Color if you're creating a Web graphic and want to know the hexadecimal code for a color in your image. Or you may choose Proof Color if you're soft proofing an image and have chosen a proofing mode under View➜Proof Setup. The proof color values are displayed in the Info palette in italics to distinguish them from the actual color values.

8. **Click in the empty Visibility box to the right of the logo layer in the Layers palette to make the artwork on that layer visible. Click the logo layer to select it.**
An eye icon appears in the Visibility box on the logo layer, indicating that that layer is now visible. You'll see a camera logo in the image.

9. **Select the Move tool in the toolbox. Click and drag in the image to move the artwork on the selected layer so that it's in line with the left edge of the list of films. Keep your eye on the Info palette as you do so.**
At the top right of the Info palette, you'll see how far you've moved the artwork from its original location and the angle of movement. At the bottom left of the Info palette, you'll see the location of your cursor, measured from the top-left corner of the image.

<TIP>
You'll run into lots of reasons to create individual pieces of artwork on separate layers as you work through this book. You just experienced one of those reasons. It's easiest to move pieces of artwork around if you have the foresight to create them on separate layers.

10. **Click the Eyedropper tool in the toolbox and select the Measure tool from the hidden menu that appears. Click and drag from one side of the camera to the other, while observing the Info palette.**
The Info palette displays the distance that you just measured — 3.7 inches. If you ever want to replace the camera with another image, you'll know exactly how big to size that image.

11. **Click any other tool in the toolbox to hide the measured line in the image.**

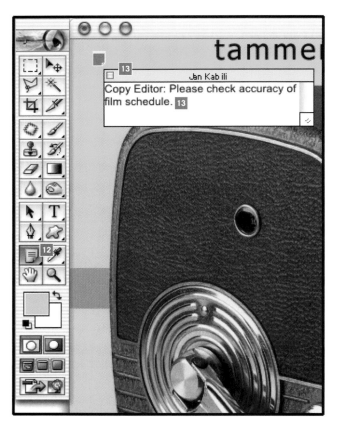

12. **Select the Notes tool in the toolbox. Click and drag in the image to create an annotation.**

    With the Notes tool, you can add your own information to an image — to remind yourself of something or share information with someone else.

13. **Type a message inside the annotation box. Then click the close box at the top-left corner of the annotation.**

    This leaves a note icon in the document. To read the annotation, double-click that icon.

    < N O T E >

    To hide all the note icons in a document, choose View→Show→ Annotations to remove the default check mark. To delete an annotation, Ctrl+click (Windows: right-click) its note icon, choose Delete Note, and click OK at the prompt.

14. **Choose File→Save As. In the Save As window, make sure that the format is set to Photoshop and Save Annotations is checked. Click Save. (You can save over the** 03_films.psd **that you copied to your hard drive.)**

    You have to save the file as a Photoshop or Portable Document Format (PDF) file to retain the annotation. A person who receives your file can read the annotation if he or she opens the file in either Photoshop or Adobe Acrobat.

15. **Leave this image open and continue to the next short tutorial.**

Tutorial
» Changing Screen Display Modes

In this tutorial, you'll learn how to display an image in Photoshop without any distracting interface elements. Try this when you want to impress a client.

1. **Make sure that** 03_films.psd **is open from the last exercise.**

2. **Choose View→Show→Annotations to hide the note icon.**

3. **Press F on your keyboard to display your image with a plain gray background.**
   Alternatively, click the middle of the three screen mode buttons near the bottom of the toolbox.

4. **Press F a second time to display the image with a black background.**
   Or click the rightmost screen mode button in the toolbox.

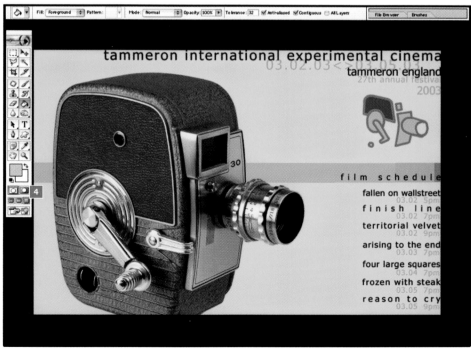

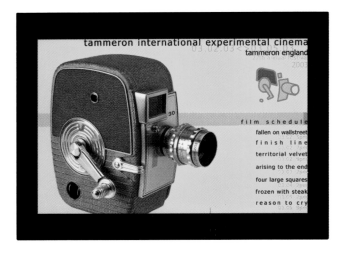

5. **Press the Tab key to hide the toolbox and menu bar.**
   This is an elegant way to display an image without distractions. However, at this point, the only way you could work on the image would be with keyboard shortcuts. So unless you're a Photoshop power user, click the Tab key again to bring back the toolbox and menu bar.

6. **Press F again to return to the gray background mode.**

7. **Select the Eyedropper tool and click on the brown part of the camera in the image.**
   This sets the Foreground Color box in the toolbox to brown.

8. **Click the Gradient tool in the toolbox and select the Paint Bucket tool from the hidden menu that appears. Hold the Shift key and click in the gray area that surrounds the image.**
   This fills the gray area with whatever color is in the Foreground Color box. It's another nice effect for displaying an image. Keep in mind that the brown border you see is not part of the image. It's the empty area of the document window.

9. **Click the leftmost screen mode button to return to regular screen mode.**

10. **Leave the image open for the next tutorial.**

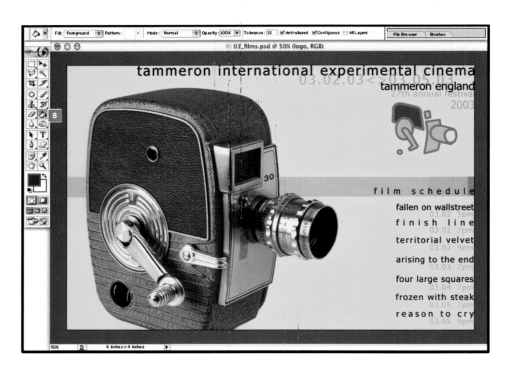

Tutorial
» Changing Canvas Size

The canvas is an important part of a Photoshop image. Increasing canvas size adds to the image area without stretching the image itself. Decreasing canvas size can cut off part of the image without shrinking the whole image. Photoshop 7 introduces a new method for changing canvas size. You can now modify the canvas size relative to the existing canvas. Work through this tutorial to see what I mean.

1. **Make sure that** 03_films.psd **is open from the last tutorial.**

2. **Select the Eyedropper tool in the toolbox. Hold the Option key (Windows: Alt key) and click in the yellow area of the image.**
   This sets the Background Color box in the toolbox to yellow.

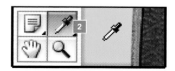

3. **Choose Image→Canvas Size.**

4. **Type .5 into both the Width and Height fields and leave the Relative box checked.**
   This tells Photoshop to add .5 inches to both the width and height of the canvas. This increases the canvas from its current 6 inches by 4 inches to 6.5 inches by 4.5 inches. If you were to uncheck the Relative box, you would type 6.5 into the Width box and 4.5 into the Height box to get the same result.

<TIP>
To decrease canvas size with the Relative box checked, type negative numbers into the Width and Height fields.

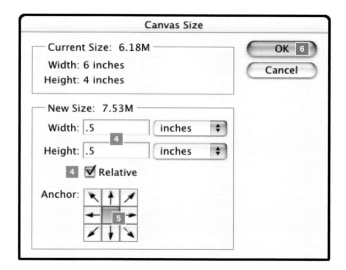

5. **Click the center anchor tile in the diagram in the Canvas Size dialog box.**
   This tells Photoshop where to position the image when it increases the canvas — in the center of this canvas. This causes .25 inches to be added to each side of the canvas.

6. **Click OK.**
   This increases the canvas and fills it with the yellow in the Background Color box in the toolbox.

7. **Save the image. Leave it open for the next tutorial.**

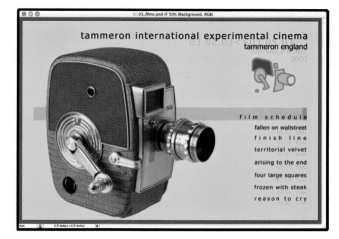

Tutorial

» Cropping an Image

Cropping is similar to changing canvas size. In this tutorial, you'll practice using the Crop tool.

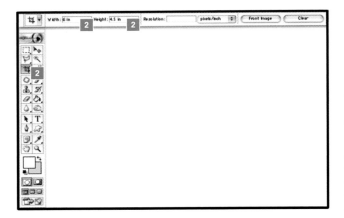

1. **Make sure that** `03_films.psd` **is open from the last tutorial.**

2. **Select the Crop tool in the toolbox. In the Options bar, type** 6 in **in the Width field and** 4.5 in **in the Height field. Leave the other options at their defaults for now.**

<TIP>
If you don't know the size to which you want to crop an image, you can drag out a bounding box to define the cropping area manually.

<NOTE>
The Hide option in the Crop tool Options bar gives you the chance to hide, but not completely eliminate, the cropped areas. Hide is the option to choose if you think you may change your mind about the crop.

3. **Click in the image and drag out the bounding box that defines the area to be cropped.**
   The dark areas outside of the bounding box are the areas that will be cropped off. The Shield option in the Options bar causes them to look screened back so that you can evaluate how the rest of the image will look after cropping.

4. **Adjust the bounding box that defines the area to be cropped so that its position matches that shown here.**
   To move the bounding box, click inside it and drag. You can also change the shape of the bounding box by clicking an anchor point and dragging. To rotate the bounding box, move the cursor outside of the box until it changes to a double-pointed area and drag.

<TIP>
You can use the Crop tool to extend the canvas, which is similar to increasing canvas size as you did in the last tutorial. Draw a bounding box inside the image, click its anchor points, and drag the box out into the empty area of the document window (the brown area in this case).

5. **Click the big check mark icon at the right of the Options bar to commit the crop.**

6. **Resize the document window to fit the image. Save and leave the image open for the next tutorial in this session.**

Tutorial
» Changing Image Size

There are two ways to change the actual size of an image. You can change the number of pixels in the image, which is called *resampling*. It's okay to resample down, but resampling up (increasing the amount of information in an image) is usually a bad idea. The other way to change the size of an image is to leave the total amount of information the same and just trade off a change in physical dimensions for a change in resolution. You'll learn how to do both in this tutorial.

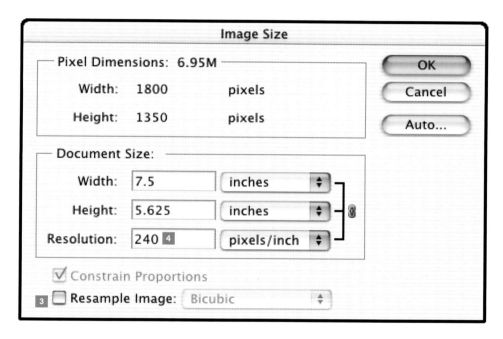

1. **Check that** `03_films.psd` **is open from the last tutorial.**

2. **Choose Image→Image Size.**

3. **Click the Resample Image check box to remove the check mark.**

4. **Type** 240 **in the Resolution field.**
   This resolution field is just like the one in the New file dialog box that you used in Session 2. It tells Photoshop to include 240 pixels per inch in the printed image.

< N O T E >

Notice that when you decrease the Resolution field in the Image Size dialog box from 300 to 240, the physical dimensions of the image in the Width and Height fields increase (from 6 x 4.5 inches to 7.5 x 5.625 inches). However, the file size reported at the top of the dialog box remains the same (6.95M). All this is because you unchecked Resample Image, which told Photoshop not to change the total number of pixels in the image. That number is a function of physical dimensions and resolution, so changing one of those factors (changing resolution from 300 to 240) necessitated an automatic change in physical dimensions. However, in this case, you want the width and height to stay at 6.5 x 4 inches, and you want to reduce the resolution to 240, based on the assumption that that's the best resolution for your printer. (Turn back to the "Resolution Primer" sidebar in Session 2 if you need a refresher on choosing print resolution.) In the next steps, you'll learn how to accomplish this.

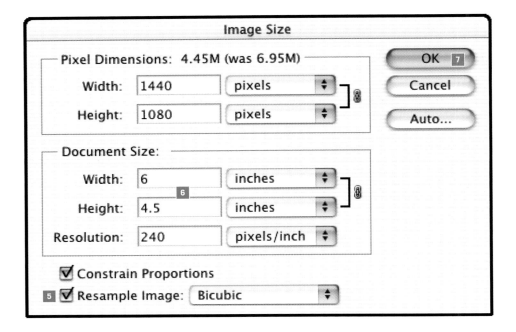

5. **Click the Resample Image check box to add a check mark.**

6. **Type** 6 **in the Width field and** 4.5 **in the Height field. Leave the Resolution field at 240.**
   Notice that the total file size has changed. The dialog box tells you that it's now 4.45 megabytes, but it was 6.95 megabytes.

7. **Click OK.**

When the Resample Image box is checked, avoid increasing width, height, or resolution. If you add pixels, Photoshop has to make up image information for those pixels, and the result is almost always a degraded image. The rule is that it's okay to resample down, but not up.

Don't uncheck Constrain Proportions in the Image Size dialog box, unless you deliberately want to distort the shape of your image.

8. **Choose File→Save As, rename the file** 03_films_end.psd, **navigate to the Session 3 Tutorial Files folder on your hard drive, and click Save.**
   This saves over the version of 03_films_end.psd that I provided for you. If you ever find that you want my version of 03_films_end.psd, you can always get a new copy of it from the CD-ROM.

» Session Review

This session covers the many aspects of viewing documents in Photoshop. It includes lessons on zooming in and out to adjust image views, moving around an image with the Hand tool and the Navigator palette, displaying an image in multiple windows at once, viewing information about the image in the image information field and the Info palette, changing the screen display mode, adjusting canvas size, cropping, and changing image size. Here are some questions to help you review the information in this session. You'll find the answer to each question in the tutorial noted in parentheses.

1. Does image magnification affect actual image size? (See "Tutorial: Controlling Image Magnification.")

2. At what magnifications is your image least likely to appear degraded? (See "Tutorial: Controlling Image Magnification.")

3. What does double-clicking the Zoom tool do? (See "Tutorial: Controlling Image Magnification.")

4. What does the Actual Pixels button do? (See "Tutorial: Controlling Image Magnification.")

5. What tool would you use to navigate around an image in the document window? (See "Tutorial: Navigating the Document Window.")

6. What does the red box in the Navigator palette do? (See "Tutorial: Navigating the Document Window.")

7. What does the slider in the Navigator palette do? (See "Tutorial: Navigating the Document Window.")

8. When you're viewing one image in multiple windows, do changes you make to the image in one window appear in the other window? (See "Tutorial: Displaying an Image in Multiple Windows.")

9. What does the Notes tool do? (See "Tutorial: Viewing Image Information.")

10. What two formats can you save an image in if you want to preserve an annotation that you've made with the Notes tool? (See "Tutorial: Viewing Image Information.")

11. How do you display an image in Photoshop without any menu bars, toolbox, or other distracting elements? (See "Tutorial: Changing Screen Display Modes.")

12. When you're changing canvas size, what is the function of the anchor tile in the Canvas Size dialog box? (See "Tutorial: Changing Canvas Size.")

13. When you're changing image size, what is the effect of unchecking the Resample Image check box in the Image Size dialog box? (See "Tutorial: Changing Image Size.")

14. When you're changing image size, is it best to resample an image up or down, and why? (See "Tutorial: Changing Image Size.")

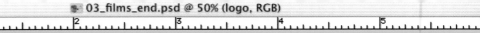

tammeron international experimental cinema

tammeron england

03.02.03<>03.05.03

27th annual festival

2003

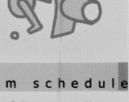

f i l m   s c h e d u l e

fallen on wallstreet
03.02 5pm

f i n i s h   l i n e
03.02 7pm

territorial velvet
03.02 9pm

arising to the end
03.03 7pm

four large squares
03.04 7pm

frozen with steak
03.05 7pm

r e a s o n   t o   c r y
03.05 9pm

Part III
Painting and Drawing

Choosing and Using Color

experimental cinema
.02.03<>03.05.03
tammeron england
27th annual festival
2003

Session Introduction

This session is all about color. You'll be introduced to Photoshop's color management system and learn how to set it up to keep the color of an image as consistent as possible as it moves from your screen to your printer. Then you'll practice using Photoshop's features for choosing colors — the Foreground and Background Color boxes, the Eyedropper tool for sampling colors, the Color Picker, the Color palette, and the Swatches palette.

TOOLS YOU'LL USE
Color Settings dialog box, Eyedropper tool, Foreground and Background Color boxes, Color Picker, Color palette, and Swatches palette

CD-ROM FILES NEEDED
04_films.psd and 04_films_end.psd

TIME REQUIRED
40 minutes

Tutorial
» Managing Color for Print

Color management is a subject that makes many Photoshop users cringe. It's a complex, technical area that can be difficult to understand, so I've tried to make it as simple as possible for you. In this tutorial, I'll show you one way to approach color management when you're working in RGB color mode preparing an image for print on an inkjet printer. In the process, you'll get a handle on what color management is and the steps to take to use Photoshop's color management system.

Color Management Simplified

The goal of Photoshop's color management system is to keep the colors in your images as consistent as possible from screen to print. This is no easy task because each piece of hardware takes the raw values that describe color and interprets them differently. You can do several things to help the process.

First, characterize your monitor, creating a monitor profile that describes to Photoshop how your monitor reproduces color. In Windows, you can use the Adobe Gamma utility that is installed with Photoshop 7 for Windows. Go to the Program Files→Common Files→Adobe→Calibration folder on your hard drive, click on the Adobe Gamma Control Panel, and choose the Step by Step Wizard that will take you through the process. Photoshop 7 for Macintosh operating systems no longer comes with Adobe Gamma. On a Mac, you can use the Apple Display Calibration utility, which has an assistant that walks you through the process. To access it in Macintosh OS X, go to System Preferences→Displays, select the Color tab, and click the Calibrate button. In Macintosh OS 9, go to Control Panels→Monitors, click the Color button, and click the Calibrate button. These utilities create a custom monitor profile for you. If you save the profile where the utility suggests, Photoshop will be able to access it automatically.

Second, choose the color management settings that your copy of Photoshop 7 will use when you create or open a file in Photoshop. Access these settings by choosing Photoshop→Color Settings (Windows and Macintosh OS 9: Edit→Color Settings). You can choose a preset bundle of settings, such as the U.S. Prepress Defaults settings you'll use in this tutorial, which are generally useful for print work. Or you can set the fields individually. The Working Spaces fields define how Photoshop interprets and displays color data in an image. Adobe RGB is a good all-around working space choice for print work, as you'll see in this tutorial. The Color Management Policies fields dictate how Photoshop handles

images that have been tagged with color management settings that don't match yours. In this tutorial, these will be set automatically to warn you when there's a mismatch. If you find this bothersome, you can uncheck the Ask When Opening and Ask When Pasting check boxes.

Third, when you save a document in Photoshop, embed the color profile of its working space by checking the Embed Color Profile check box in the Save As dialog box. Profiles are the heart of Photoshop's color management scheme. They tag an image with information about the working space in which the image was created. Printers that read color profiles can use that information to try to match the print output to the colors you see on-screen. If the image is opened on another computer in Photoshop or in some other program that reads color profiles, that program can use the profile to display the image as it looked when you created it. You can convert an open image to a different color profile at any time by choosing Image→Mode→Convert Profile.

Fourth, when you're ready to print your image, go to File→Print with Preview, click the Output button, and choose Color Management. Make sure that Document is selected as the source. Under Print Space, click the Profile down arrow and choose your printer's profile from the menu. This converts the colors in the image temporarily to the device-specific color space that your printer uses. Note that these color management print settings are in a new location in Photoshop 7.

Caveat: Keep in mind that the color management setup recommended in this tutorial is not the only way to go. It assumes that you're preparing images in RGB for an inkjet printer. If you're working on files for commercial CMYK printing, consult your printer about choosing color management settings and embedding profiles. If you want to know more about color management, read the Photoshop 7 Help files, which have a pretty good explanation.

1. **Choose Photoshop→Color Settings (Windows and Macintosh OS 9: Edit→Color Settings).**

   In the Color Settings dialog box, the Settings field defaults to Web Graphics Defaults. In the next step, you'll use this field to choose a package of presets that are more appropriate for print work.

2. **Click the Settings button and choose U.S. Prepress Defaults.**

   This changes all the settings in the Color Settings dialog box. U.S Prepress Defaults is the best choice if most of your work is preparing images for print output according to U.S. printing standards. Table 4-1 briefly explains these settings.

3. **When you're done choosing color settings, click OK.**

4. **Open** 04_films.psd **from the Session 4 Tutorial Files folder on your hard drive.**

   04_films.psd is a replica of the finished file 03_films_end.psd that I asked you to save into the Session 3 Tutorial Files folder on your hard drive at the end of Session 3. You can use your file, 03_films_end.psd, in this session instead of 04_films.psd if you completed all the preceding tutorials.

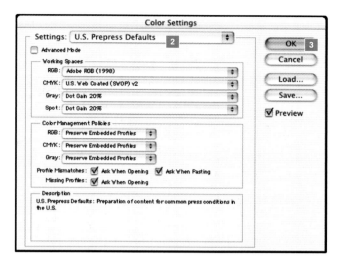

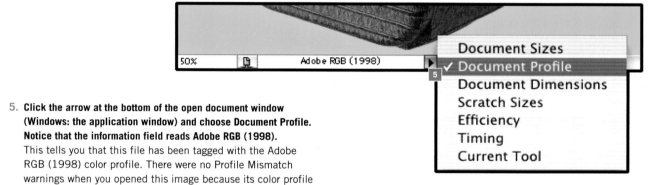

5. **Click the arrow at the bottom of the open document window (Windows: the application window) and choose Document Profile. Notice that the information field reads Adobe RGB (1998).**

   This tells you that this file has been tagged with the Adobe RGB (1998) color profile. There were no Profile Mismatch warnings when you opened this image because its color profile matches the Adobe RGB (1998) color environment that you chose as your working space in step 2.

6. **Leave this file open for the next tutorial.**

Table 4-1: Color Management Settings

Field	U.S. Prepress Default Setting	Explanation
RGB (in the Working Spaces area)	Adobe RGB (1998)	A working space is a color environment that determines how Photoshop interprets the raw color values in an image when it displays them on your screen. The most important working space setting for your purposes here is the RGB working space because the files that you're using in these tutorials are RGB files. Adobe RGB (1998) is generally the best RGB working space setting for images destined for print because it contains a wide range of colors. Therefore, it matches the *gamut* (which means the range of reproducible colors) of most RGB printers, and it converts well to CMYK color mode if necessary. If you're interested in a description of the other RGB color spaces, select each color space from the Working Spaces RGB menu in the Color Settings dialog box and read the description that appears at the bottom of the dialog box.
Profile Mismatches	Ask When Opening	This instructs Photoshop to warn you when an image you're opening contains an embedded profile that's different than your working space. The best choice usually is to accept the default behavior — preserve embedded profile — which maintains the color integrity of the image as it was created. You can choose to convert the colors to your working space, which will change the colors, but may be useful if you plan to collage the image with other images created in your working space. Or you can discard the embedded profile entirely. Doing so creates an untagged image that doesn't carry a profile to tell other devices how you intended the colors to look. I don't recommend this option unless you're creating images for the Web. (Web browsers can't read color profiles anyway.)
Profile Mismatches	Ask When Pasting	This tells Photoshop to warn you when you're pasting a selection from one image into another image that has a different embedded profile. You'll be offered options for how to deal with that selection.
Missing Profiles	Ask When Opening	This instructs Photoshop to warn you when an image you're opening contains no embedded profile. The default choice is to leave the document as is (don't color manage). In that case, the image is left untagged, but will be interpreted according to your working space while it's open. Alternatively, you can choose to convert the image to your working space or assign another color profile.

Tutorial

» Setting Foreground and Background Colors

The Foreground and Background Color boxes in the toolbox are like paint wells that hold the colors that you'll use as you work on an image. You can select the colors that appear in these boxes several different ways. This short tutorial teaches you how to set Foreground and Background colors by sampling colors from an open image, and how to return the Foreground and Background Color boxes to their black and white defaults. In the tutorials that follow, you'll learn other ways to choose color: with the Color Picker, the Color Palette, and the Swatches palette.

1. **Select the Eyedropper tool in the toolbox and click a color in the image.**
   This fills the Foreground Color box in the toolbox with the sampled color from the open image. The color in the Foreground Color box is used whenever you apply the painting tools, the Type tool, one of the Shape tools, or the Edit→Stroke command. You'll work with all these features in upcoming sessions.

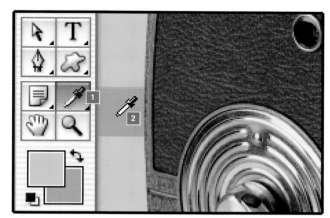

<TIP>
Photoshop's Eyedropper tool can sample colors from any place on your screen. This means that you can sample a color from a document that's open in another program, from a Web page that's open in a Web browser, or even from image thumbnails in Photoshop's File Browser. To try this, click inside the Photoshop document window, keep the mouse button held down, and move the Eyedropper outside the Photoshop document window. Notice the Foreground Color box change as you move over colors anywhere on your screen. Release the mouse button to sample whatever color is under the cursor.

2. **Option+click (Windows: Alt+click) inside the image to sample another color.**
   This fills the Background Color box in the toolbox with this sampled color. The Background color appears when you erase a bottom layer with the Eraser tool, and it fills the blank area of the canvas when you increase the canvas size.

3. **Click the Default Colors icon (the small black and white squares) in the toolbox.**
   This changes the Foreground color to black and the Background color to white. The keyboard shortcut for this operation is the D key on your keyboard. This is a shortcut that you'll use often.

4. **Click the double-pointed arrows in the toolbox.**
   This switches the two color boxes, so that the Foreground color is now white and the Background color is black. The keyboard shortcut for this operation is the X key on your keyboard. This is another shortcut worth memorizing.

5. **Leave this image open for the next tutorial.**

Tutorial
» Choosing Colors with the Color Picker

The Color Picker is one of several features you can use to select colors in Photoshop. It's my favorite because it offers lots of different ways to view color. You'll learn how to use the Color Picker in this tutorial.

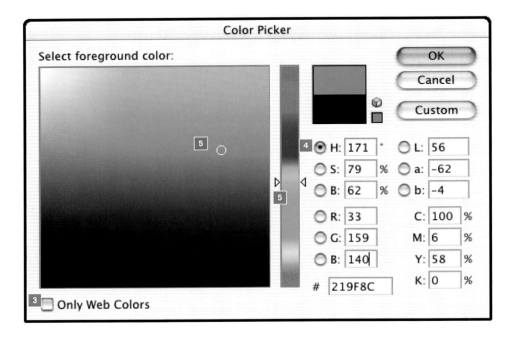

1. Make sure that 04_films.psd is open from the last tutorial.

2. Click the Foreground Color box to open the Color Picker.

3. Uncheck Only Web Colors if that box has a check mark in it.
   This box limits the display of colors in the Color Picker to 216 Web-safe colors. There's no reason to limit your color choices this way when you're designing for print.

4. Click the H radio button to display colors by hue.
   The slider in the middle of the Color Picker now shows a rainbow of hues. The color area on the left of the Color Picker shows the hue that's selected in the slider at different combinations of brightness (from top to bottom) and saturation (from right to left).

5. Move the slider to the blue-green area of the spectrum. Then click inside the color area to select a blue-green that you like.
   The new color and the last selected color appear in the square at the top of the Color Picker. If you like the new color, you could click OK at this point, but hold off for now so that I can show you some more features of the Color Picker.

6. Click again in the color area, until you see a triangular alert icon to the right of the new color square.

This is an out-of-gamut warning, indicating that the color you've chosen is beyond the range of printable colors on a CMYK printer. The small square under the alert icon contains the closest color that's printable with CMYK inks.

7. Click the triangular alert icon to change your selection to the nearest printable color.

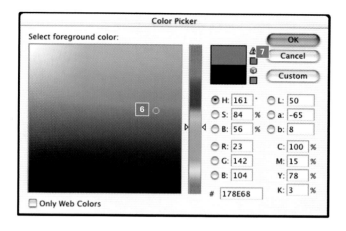

<NOTE>

You may be wondering about the cube icon just below the out-of-gamut warning. That indicates that you've chosen a non-Web-safe color and isn't relevant when you're creating an image for print. Another Web-only feature is the # field at the bottom of the Color Picker, where you can enter the hexadecimal code for a color if you want to match a color in a Web graphic to a color identified in the hexadecimal numbering system in a Web page's HTML code.

8. Click the S radio button to display colors by saturation.

9. Click the first B radio button to display colors by brightness.

All of these different displays show the same colors, but they're just arranged in different ways to help you select colors that go well together.

10. Click the R, G, or B radio button to display colors by amount of red, green, and blue.

<TIP>

If you know the exact RGB color value that you're after, you can type it into the R, G, and B boxes. For example, 0, 0, 0 are the RGB values for black, and 255, 255, 255 are the RGB values for white.

11. Click the L, a, or b radio button to display colors by luminosity.

These displays suggest some nice color combinations that you may use when you're trying to come up with a palette for an image.

<TIP>

If you're ever trying to select a Pantone color, click the Custom button and explore the options there.

12. When you've finished exploring the Color Picker, click the OK button.

You'll see the color that you selected in the Foreground Color box in the toolbox.

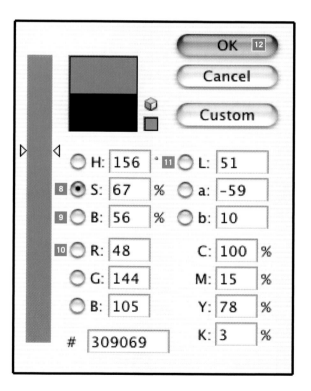

13. **Select the Brush tool in the toolbox, click the Brush Preset Picker in the Options bar, and select the Logo layer in the Layers palette. Then have some fun coloring in the handle of the camera logo in the image.**

<TIP>

You may want to zoom in, as you learned how to do in Session 3, to make it easier to see where you're painting.

14. **Choose File→Save As. Navigate to the Session 04 Tutorial Files folder, and click Save, writing over the document of the same name that's already there. Leave the image open for the next tutorial.**

<NOTE>

Notice the Embed Color Profile command at the bottom of the Save window. It's set to Adobe RGB (1998), which is the RGB working space you chose in your color management settings at the beginning of this session. It's checked by default, which causes Photoshop to embed this profile in the document when you click Save.

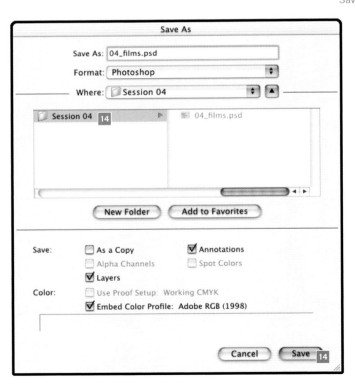

Tutorial
» Choosing Colors with the Color Palette

The Color palette is an alternative way of choosing colors. It offers the same colors as the Color Picker, arranged in a different interface. You may prefer the Color palette if you like to mix colors visually or if you don't have room on your screen for the bulky Color Picker. Try out the Color palette in this tutorial.

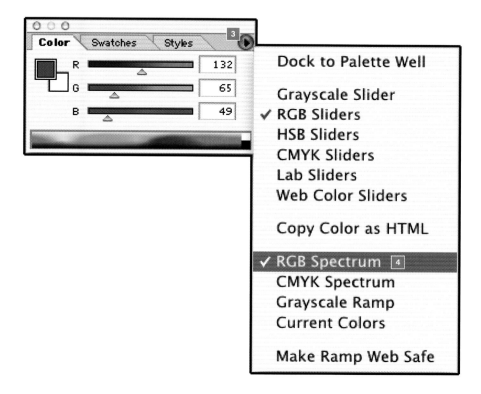

1. Make sure that 04_films.psd is open from the last tutorial.

2. Choose Window→Color if the Color palette is not already displayed on your screen.

3. Click the arrow at the top right of the Color palette to reveal a menu of options.

4. Choose RGB Spectrum.
   This sets the color bar at the bottom of the Color palette to RGB colors. You can set the color bar and the color sliders at the top of the palette to separate color modes.

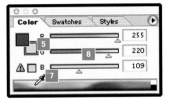

5. Click in the Background Color box on the Color palette.

The Color palette has a Foreground and Background Color box, just like the toolbox.

6. Move your cursor over the color bar.

Notice that the cursor changes to an eyedropper.

7. Click to sample a color from the yellow area of the color bar.

Use the color bar as a starting point to get to the general color area that you want.

8. Move the R, G, and B sliders to fine-tune your color selection to a light yellow.

Notice in the figure that the Color palette has a triangular alert icon for out-of-gamut colors, just like the Color Picker. It also has a non-Web-safe color alert and small black and white default icons, like the Color Picker.

<NOTE>

Whatever color you choose as the Background color in the Color palette also will appear in the Background Color box in the toolbox.

9. Select the Eraser tool in the toolbox, select the Background layer in the Layers palette, and erase inside the lens of the camera logo.

The Eraser tool erases to the background color when you have the bottom-most layer selected in the Layers palette. You'll find out more about layers in Session 8.

10. Make a new folder on your hard drive and name it collages.

This is where you'll store each final collage as you finish working on it in the tutorials. Keep this folder safe so that you can print its contents as the final project at the end of the book. Keep your collages folder on your desktop or anywhere else in your file system that's easy for you to find.

11. Choose File→Save As and save the file as 04_films_end.psd **in the collages folder.**

12. Close the image. You don't need an open image for the next tutorial.

Tutorial

» Choosing Colors with the Swatches Palette

The Swatches palette is yet another source of colors in Photoshop. Using the Swatches palette is similar to working with a painter's palette. You can limit your colors by loading preset swatches or swatches that you create yourself and see those colors in front of you as you work. Small custom palettes are handy for creating a series of images with the same colors. In this tutorial, you'll learn how to load a preset swatch and create and load your own color swatch.

1. **Click the Swatches tab next to the Color palette or choose Window→Swatches to bring the Swatches palette to the foreground.**

2. **Click the arrow on the top right of the Swatches palette and choose PANTONE Solid Matte from the menu of preset Swatches. Click OK at the prompt.**
   This replaces the default swatch with a swatch made up entirely of Pantone solid matte colors. If none of the preset swatches suit you, you can make your own, as you'll do shortly.

3. **Move the cursor over any color in the Swatches palette to view the name of that color.**

4. **Click any color in the Swatches palette to set the Foreground Color box to that color.**

5. **Click the arrow on the top right of the Swatches palette and choose any of the smaller palettes, such as HKS E. Click OK at the prompt.**
   You'll use this preset palette as a starting point for creating your own custom palette.

6. **Option+click (Windows: Alt+click) any color in the Swatches palette to change the cursor to scissors and eliminate that color from the palette. Repeat this until you've deleted all the colors that you don't want to include in your custom swatch.**
   Alternatively, click any color and drag it to the Trash icon at the bottom of the Swatches palette to delete it from the palette.

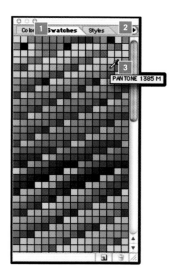

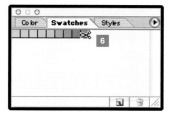

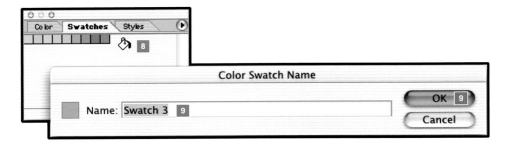

7. **Use any of Photoshop's color selection methods (such as choosing a color from the Color Picker or Color palette) to select another color that you want to include in your custom swatch.**
   This places the selected color in the Foreground Color box in the toolbox.

8. **Move your cursor over the blank area of the Swatches palette until it changes to a Paint Bucket icon and click.**

9. **Type a name for your new swatch color in the Color Swatch Name dialog box and click OK.**
   This adds the Foreground color to your custom swatches. Alternatively, click the New Color icon at the bottom of the Swatches palette and name your new color.

10. **Repeat steps 7 through 9 until the Swatches palette contains all the colors that you want to include in your custom swatch.**

11. **Click the arrow at the top right of the Swatches palette and choose Save Swatches.**

12. **In the Save dialog box, name your new swatches file** filmfest.aco, **making sure to keep the** .aco **extension, and save it to the default location (the Color Swatches folder in the Presets folder inside the Photoshop Application folder on your hard drive).**

13. **Click the arrow at the top right of the Swatches palette and choose Reset Swatches.**

    This loads the default swatch into the Swatches palette. In the next steps, you'll find out how to replace this swatch with your custom swatch so that it's ready to use on any image.

14. **Click the arrow at the top right of the Swatches palette again and choose Replace Swatches.**

    This opens the Load window, displaying all the swatches in the Color Swatches folder, including your custom swatch, `filmfest.aco`.

15. **Choose** `filmfest.aco` **in the Load window and click Load.**

    This replaces the default swatches in the Swatches palette with your custom-built swatches.

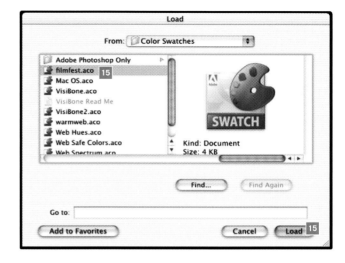

<NOTE>

Your custom swatches are now displayed in the Swatches palette, ready to use on any open image.

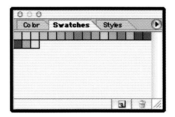

» Session Review

This session covers how to choose and use color in Photoshop. You were introduced to Photoshop's color management system and practiced selecting colors for image editing using a variety of methods — the Eyedropper tool, the Color Picker, the Color palette, and the Swatches palette. Work through these questions to review what you learned in this session.

1. What is the purpose of Photoshop's color management system? (See "Tutorial: Managing Color for Print.")

2. Does Photoshop 7 for Macintosh include the Adobe Gamma utility? (See "Tutorial: Managing Color for Print.")

3. What does the RGB Working Space color management setting do? (See "Tutorial: Managing Color for Print.")

4. How do you embed a color profile into a document? (See "Tutorial: Managing Color for Print.")

5. What does a color profile do? (See "Tutorial: Managing Color for Print.")

6. How do you convert the colors in an image to the color space that your printer uses? (See "Tutorial: Managing Color for Print.")

7. What does checking the Profile Mismatches Ask When Opening check box in the Color Settings dialog box instruct Photoshop to do? (See "Tutorial: Managing Color for Print.")

8. What tool do you use to sample a color from an image to fill the Foreground Color box? (See "Tutorial: Setting Foreground and Background Colors.")

9. How do you set the Background Color box in the toolbox to a sampled color? (See "Tutorial: Setting Foreground and Background Colors.")

10. What does clicking the Default Colors icon in the toolbox do? (See "Tutorial: Setting Foreground and Background Colors.")

11. Name four alternative tools/features that you can use to choose a color in Photoshop. (See all tutorials except "Managing Color for Print.")

12. What does the triangular alert in the Color Picker tell you about a selected color? (See "Tutorial: Choosing Colors with the Color Picker.")

13. What is the purpose of the color bar in the Color palette? (See "Tutorial: Choosing Colors with the Color Palette.")

14. How do you select a color to apply to an image from the Swatches palette? (See "Tutorial: Choosing Colors with the Swatches Palette.")

15. Are preset swatches the only kind of swatch that you can load into the Swatches palette? (See "Tutorial: Choosing Colors with the Swatches Palette.")

tammeron international experimental cinema

03.02.03<>03.05.03

tammeron england

27th annual festival

2003

film schedule

fallen on wallstreet
03.02 5pm

finish line
03.02 7pm

territorial velvet
03.02 9pm

arising to the end
03.03 7pm

four large squares
03.04 7pm

frozen with steak
03.05 7pm

reason to cry
03.05 9pm

Session 5

Painting and Filling with Pixels

Session Introduction

You'll get your creative juices flowing in this session, as you learn about Photoshop's pixel-based filling and painting features. You'll find out how to fill with color, pattern, and gradient. You'll try out Photoshop 7's new Brushes palette, learning how to use preset brushes, edit preset buttons using Photoshop's many brush options, and define a new brush of your own. You'll paint away color with the Eraser, Magic Eraser, and Background Eraser, and you'll accent your collage by stroking with pixels.

TOOLS YOU'LL USE
Fill command, Lock Transparency button, Rectangular Marquee tool, Paint Bucket tool, Pattern Stamp tool, Define Pattern command, Pattern Maker, Gradient tool, Gradient Editor, Brush tool, Brushes palette, Brush pop-up palette, Define Brush command, Options bar, Stroke command, Eraser tool, Magic Eraser tool, and Background Eraser tool

CD-ROM FILES NEEDED
05_sponsors.psd, 05_sponsors_patt.psd,
05_sponsors_grad.psd, 05_sponsors_brush.psd,
05_camera.psd, and 05_brush.psd

TIME REQUIRED
120 minutes

Tutorial
» Filling a Layer

This session begins on a simple note with this tutorial, which teaches how to use Photoshop's Fill command to fill a whole layer with a solid color.

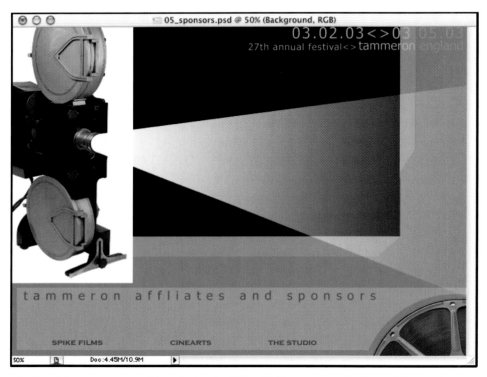

1. **Open** 05_sponsors.psd **from the Session 5 Tutorial Files folder on your hard drive.**

   05_sponsors.psd is a barebones image that you will develop into a page for your film festival program guide over the course of this and the following session.

2. **Choose Window→Layers to open the Layers palette if it isn't already visible on your desktop.**

An Introduction to Layers

The files that you'll use in this session have several layers, each of which contains separate pieces of artwork. Structuring an image this way makes it easy to fill and paint individual items. Don't worry that you haven't yet studied the subject of layers in detail. For now, it's sufficient to know that each layer in a PSD file can contain pixels of artwork, as well as transparent pixels. When you look at a layered image on your screen, it's as if you were looking down through the stack of layers from top to bottom. So you can see through transparent areas on a layer to the layers below. In addition, each layer and its artwork can be made temporarily visible and invisible, can be edited separately, and can be moved up or down in the stack of layers. You'll experiment with these and other qualities of layers when you get to Session 8.

3. **Click the Background layer in the Layers palette to select that layer.**

4. **Click the Foreground Color box in the toolbox to open the Color Picker, and then select a yellow-green color in the Color Picker and click OK.**

   If you want to use the exact same color that I did, type its RGB values in the RGB fields in the Color Picker. Those values are R: 199, G: 181, B: 20.

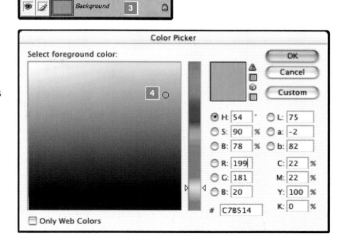

5. **Go to the menu bar at the top of the screen and choose Edit→Fill.**
   This opens the Fill dialog box.

6. **Check that the Use setting in the Fill dialog box is set to Foreground Color.**
   This instructs Photoshop to use the contents of the Foreground Color box in the toolbox as the fill color. Leave the other fields at their default settings for now, as shown here.

7. **Click OK to fill the Background layer with yellow-green.**

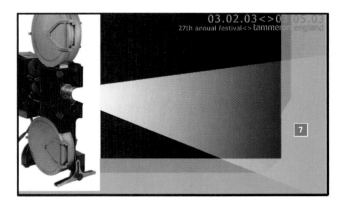

<NOTE>

Another way to fill an image with a solid color is by applying a Fill layer (choose Layer→New Fill Layer→Solid Color and select a color from the Color Picker that opens). The advantage of using a Fill layer is that it can be easily modified without disturbing the original artwork, and its content can be quickly changed from a solid color to a pattern or gradient. Fill layers are addressed in Session 8.

8. **Option+click (Windows: Alt+click) the eye icon in the Visibility box to the left of the Background layer in the Layers palette.** This hides the eye icons on all the layers except the Background layer, leaving only the contents of the Background layer showing in the document window. Now you can see that you've filled the entire Background layer with yellow-green. In the next tutorial, you'll learn how to restrict a fill to the artwork on a layer, leaving transparent pixels on that layer unfilled.

9. **Option+click (Windows: Alt+click) the eye icon on the Background layer again.** This makes all layers visible again.

10. **Choose File→Save and leave this document open for the next tutorial.**

Working with Pixels and Bitmapped Images

When you fill an area with color, as you did in this tutorial, you are modifying pixels in a bitmapped image. The same is true when you use Photoshop's painting tools and many of its other features and commands. This session focuses on filling and painting with pixels, so you'll find it useful to have a basic understanding of what the terms *pixel* and *bitmapped image* mean.

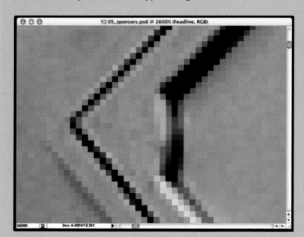

A *pixel* is a tiny rectangle that contains information about the color at a particular location in an image. A *bitmapped image* (sometimes called a *rasterized image*) is made up of pixels arranged on a grid. You can actually see image pixels and their grid-like arrangement if you zoom in on an image that's open in Photoshop, such as the one shown here.

A bitmapped image can display gradual changes between colors and subtle blends between foreground and background elements. This makes bitmapped images ideal for photographs, soft-edged graphics, and continuous tone artwork. On the downside, a bitmapped image contains a finite number of pixels. Therefore, the image won't look very good if you try to make it bigger. Scaling up a bitmapped image in a page layout program such as QuarkXPress or a drawing program such as Illustrator just stretches the existing pixels, creating a pixelated image. You learned in Session 3 that in Photoshop you can increase the number of pixels in an image by checking Resample Image and increasing the resolution or dimensions in the Image Size dialog box. However, that requires Photoshop to generate image information to fill in the gaps, which usually causes the printed image to look blurry. (*Tip:* If you must resample up, apply Photoshop's Unsharp Mask filter afterwards to increase contrast, which can make the image look more focused.)

Photoshop is best known for its prowess at creating and editing bitmapped images. In addition, Photoshop 7 has some useful vector-based features. Vector objects are quite different than bitmapped artwork because they are mathematically defined rather than pixel-based. Vector objects are used for graphic art that requires crisp edges and may need to be resized for different uses without degradation. This session focuses on some of Photoshop's many bitmapped-image editing capabilities. In the next session, you'll learn how to create and edit vector objects in Photoshop.

Tutorial
» Filling the Artwork on a Layer

In this tutorial, you'll learn how to confine a color fill to the artwork on a layer, leaving transparent pixels on the layer unfilled. This is a useful technique for changing the color of all the artwork on a layer at once, without having to do any selecting.

1. **Make sure that** 05_sponsors.psd **is open from the preceding tutorial.**

2. **Click the main box layer in the Layers palette to select that layer.**

3. **Click the Lock Transparency button at the top left of the Layers palette.**
   The Lock Transparency button darkens, and a hollow lock icon appears on the main box layer, indicating that you can't paint, fill, or otherwise edit any transparent pixels on that layer.

4. **Select the Eyedropper tool in the toolbox. Click the thin dark green polygon on the right side of the image.**
   This sets the Foreground Color box in the toolbox to dark green. You already practiced this technique in Session 4.

5. **Choose Edit→Fill, leave the Use field in the Fill dialog box set to Foreground Color, and click OK.**
   This fills the rectangle on the main box layer with dark green.

<NOTE>
There are three other lock buttons in the Layers palette. The Lock Image button (with the paintbrush icon) prevents you from filling, painting, or otherwise changing existing artwork on a layer. The Lock Position button (with the arrows icon) prevents you from moving the artwork on a layer. The Lock All button (with the lock icon) freezes all these layer properties.

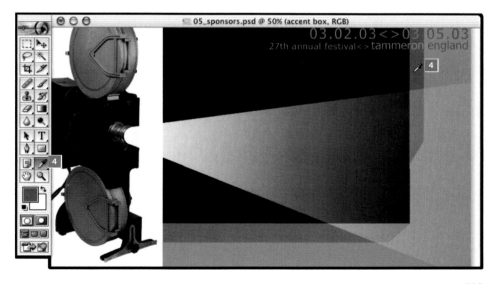

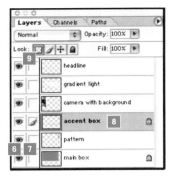

If you filled the entire layer with yellow by mistake, it's because you forgot to click the Lock Transparency button, which is a common oversight. Fix it by clicking ⌘+Z (Windows: Ctrl+Z) to undo, and try the last few steps again.

<NOTE>
Protecting transparent pixels while filling changes the color of all the artwork on a layer. To color just part of the artwork on a layer, you have to isolate that area before filling, as you'll do in the next tutorial.

6. **Option+click (Windows: Alt+click) the eye icon on the main box layer in the Layers palette.**
This makes all layers except the main box layer invisible. Notice that you've filled the artwork, rather than the entire layer, with dark green. The transparent pixels on the main box layer (represented by the gray checkerboard pattern) were protected from the fill by the transparency lock feature. In the next steps, you'll try this again on another layer, using an efficient shortcut for the Fill command.

7. **Option+click (Windows: Alt+click) the eye icon on the main box layer again.**
This makes all layers visible again.

8. **Select the accent box layer in the Layers palette.**

9. **Click the Lock Transparency button to protect the transparent pixels on the accent box layer.**

10. **Click the Foreground Color box in the toolbox to open the Color Picker, choose yellow (R: 255, G: 204, B: 0), and click OK.**

11. **Click Option+Delete (Windows: Alt+Delete).**
This is a useful shortcut for filling with the foreground color. The artwork on the accent box layer is now filled with yellow.

12. **Choose File→Save and leave this image open for the next tutorial.**

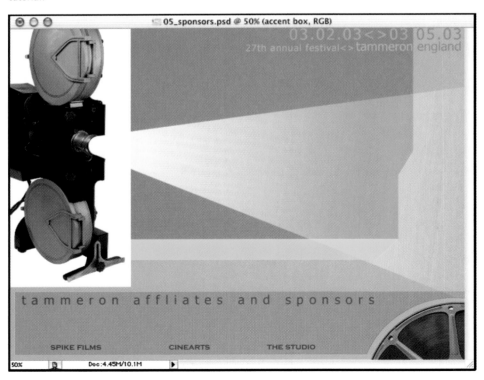

Tutorial

» Filling Selected Artwork

In the preceding tutorial, you learned how to fill all the artwork on a layer. There will be times when you'll want to limit the extent of a fill even further so that only part of the artwork on a layer is affected by the fill. You'll do that in this tutorial.

1. **Check that** 05_sponsors.psd **is still open from the last tutorial.**

2. **Click the Foreground Color box in the toolbox to open the Color Picker. Choose a bright blue-green (R: 153, G: 204, B: 153) and click OK.**

3. **Select the headline layer in the Layers palette.**

4. **Click the Lock Transparency icon.**
   This prevents the transparent pixels on the headline layer (all the pixels except the text) from being filled.

5. **Click the Rectangular Marquee tool in the toolbox. If it's not visible, click whichever marquee tool is showing in the toolbox and choose Rectangular Marquee Tool from the hidden menu.**
   The Rectangular Marquee is one of Photoshop's selection tools. You'll learn all about selection tools in Session 7.

6. **Click and drag a selection around the phrase "festival < >tammeron" in the document window.**
   This limits the area that you're about to fill to just the selected phrase on the headline layer.

<NOTE>
The headline layer isn't a type layer. If it were, you couldn't isolate and change the color of words on the layer the same way. (In Part V, you'll learn how to change the color of a type layer.) This is just a regular layer that contains artwork in the shape of text. The technique that you learned here would work the same way if this layer contained images rather than words.

7. **Option+click (Windows: Alt+click) to fill the selected phrase "festival < > tammeron" with blue-green.**

8. **Click anywhere outside the selection to deselect.**
   This causes the marching ants to disappear.

9. **Choose File→Save. Leave the image open.**

<NOTE>
The animated broken lines around the selection are called *marching ants.*

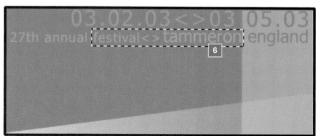

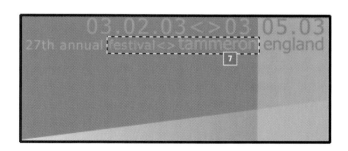

Tutorial
» Filling with the Paint Bucket Tool

The Paint Bucket tool offers another method of filling that's different than the Fill command or fill shortcut. Those methods are useful for filling an area of solid color or an area that you've defined. The Paint Bucket tool comes in handy when you want to fill pixels of a related color. Try it in this tutorial.

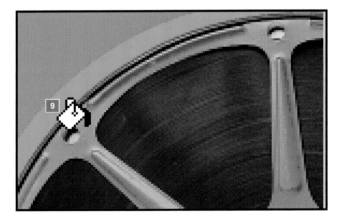

1. **Make sure that** 05_sponsors.psd **is open from the last tutorial.**

2. **Click the reel layer in the Layers palette.**

3. **Click the Lock Transparency button in the Layers palette.**

4. **Click the Eyedropper tool in the toolbox and click in the purple box at the bottom of the image to set the Foreground Color to purple.**

5. **Click the Paint Bucket tool in the toolbox. If you don't see it, click the Gradient tool to reveal a hidden tool menu and choose Paint Bucket Tool from that menu.**
   The Options bar changes to display options for the Paint Bucket tool.

6. **Click in the Tolerance field in the Options bar and type** 40.
   The Paint Bucket fills all pixels that have color values sufficiently similar to the pixel on which you click with that tool. Increase tolerance if you want to expand that range to fill a larger area; decrease tolerance if you want to fill a smaller area. This is one of those settings that demands experimentation. I found that 40 worked fine here.

7. **Click in the Mode field in the Options bar and choose Overlay.**
   The mode determines how the Paint Bucket's fill blends with the underlying image. I found that Normal produced a fill that was too solid for my taste. Overlay allows the tones in the underlying image to show through. Many tools have blending mode options, and they usually require lots of experimentation.

8. **Make sure that Contiguous and Anti-aliased are checked in the Options bar.**
   The Contiguous option tells the Paint Bucket to fill only pixels that are touching. The Anti-aliased option gives your fill a graduated edge that blends nicely into surrounding pixels. You'll see these options on the Options bar for other tools too.

9. **Click in the metal part of the film reel in the document window to fill that area.**
   You may have to try several times, clicking in different spots, to get the look you want.

10. **Choose File→Save and leave** 05_sponsors.psd **open if you want to use it in the next exercise. You'll have the option of starting the next exercise with a fresh prebuilt file.**

Tutorial
» Filling with a Pattern

You can fill a layer, artwork, or a selection with a pattern, instead of a solid color. Both the Fill command and the Paint Bucket give you the option of filling with a pattern. In this tutorial, you'll use the Fill command to fill the artwork on a layer with a pattern.

1. **Check that** 05_sponsors.psd **is still open from the last tutorial. Alternatively, you can open** 05_sponsors_patt.psd **from the Session 5 Tutorials folder on your hard drive.**
   05_sponsors_patt.psd is a replica of how 05_sponsors.psd should look if you've completed all the preceding tutorials in this session. If you skipped any of the tutorials in this session or if you messed up your file along the way, feel free to start with this fresh file.

2. **Select the pattern layer in the Layers palette.**

3. **Click the Lock Transparency button in the Layers palette.**
   This protects the transparent pixels on the pattern layer from filling with a pattern.

4. **Choose Edit→Fill. In the Fill dialog box, choose Pattern from the Use menu.**

5. **Click in the Custom Pattern sample in the Fill dialog box to open the Pattern Picker.**
   The pattern picker displays a default set of patterns that ship with Photoshop.

6. **Click the arrow on the top right of the Pattern Picker and choose Patterns 2.**

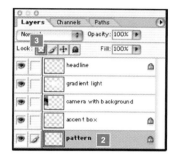

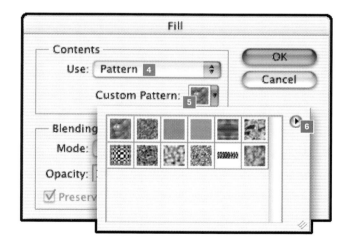

7. **At the prompt, click OK.**
   This replaces the default set of patterns with another set of patterns.

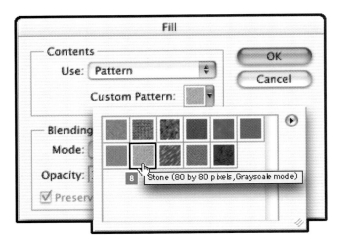

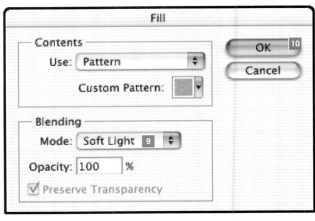

8. **Select the Stone pattern in the Pattern Picker and click anywhere inside the Fill dialog box to close the Pattern Picker.**

9. **Click in the Mode field under Blending in the Fill dialog box and choose Soft Light from the menu.**
   The blending mode determines how the pattern fill blends with pixels on other layers. The Soft Light blending mode creates a combination of the gray stone pattern and the colors on other layers, darkening some pixels and lightening others. The result is a textured green-gray appearance.

<NOTE>
It's difficult to predict the outcome of different blending modes on different artwork. The best method for choosing a blending mode is trial and error.

10. **Click OK in the Fill dialog box to apply the pattern fill to the pattern layer.**

11. **Click the eye icon on the gradient layer to get a better view of your pattern fill. Leave the gradient layer hidden.**

<TIP>
Patterns are potential attention-grabbers that can overpower an otherwise balanced design. To protect against this, consider using subtle patterns and keeping patterned areas small, as in this example.

12. **Choose File➔Save As. Save the file as**
   05_sponsors_patt.psd **(whether you used your own file or the fresh file provided for you for this tutorial). Leave the file open for the next exercise.**

<NOTE>
Another way to fill an image with a pattern is to use a Fill layer, as you'll learn how to do in Session 8.

Tutorial
» Defining and Applying a Custom Pattern

If you have a creative spirit, you're likely to prefer your own custom-made pattern over the canned patterns that come with Photoshop. The traditional way of creating a pattern in Photoshop is with the simple Define Pattern command, which you'll use in this tutorial. You can fill an area with a custom-made pattern using the Fill command or the Paint Bucket tool. Another option, which you'll try here, is to paint with your pattern, using the Pattern Stamp tool.

1. **Make sure that** `05_sponsors_patt.psd` **is open from the last tutorial.**

2. **Double-click the Zoom tool in the toolbox to magnify the image to the 100% view.**

3. **Select the Rectangular Marquee tool in the toolbox.**

4. **Click and drag a small selection around the design on the movie projector in the image.**
Be sure not to feather, expand, or otherwise modify your selection.

5. **Choose Edit→Define Pattern.**

6. **Give your pattern a name (such as** my triangle**) and click OK.**

7. **Click anywhere in the image to deselect.**

<NOTE>
That's all there is to defining a custom pattern. The pattern now appears in the Pattern Picker, which is accessible from the Fill command and from the Paint Bucket tool Options bar. You could use either of those methods to fill an area with your pattern. The pattern will repeat itself in a grid pattern. In the following steps, you'll learn another, more controlled way to apply your pattern — painting it into your image with the Pattern Stamp tool.

8. **Click the Clone tool in the toolbox to display a hidden tool menu. Select the Pattern Stamp tool from that menu.**

9. **Click the camera with background layer and click the New Layer button at the bottom of the Layers palette.**
This creates a new layer on which to draw with the Pattern Stamp tool. Drawing on a separate layer protects the existing artwork and makes it easy to delete your drawing if you don't like it.

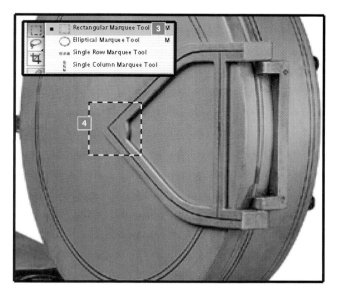

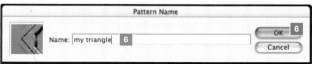

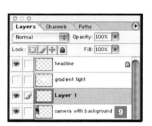

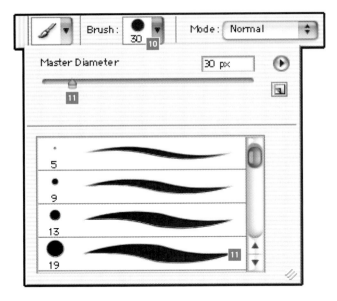

10. **Click the Brush sample in the Options bar to open the Brush pop-up palette.**

<NOTE>
The Brush pop-up palette is one place to select a brush style and size for any of Photoshop's brush tools (which include the Paint Brush tool, the Pencil tool, the Healing Brush tool, the Clone tool, the Stamp tool, the Eraser tools, the History brushes, and the Darkroom tools). It's sufficient when you want quick access to one of the preset brush tools that come with Photoshop. But if you want to vary brush options to create a custom brush, use the new Brushes palette, which you'll learn about later in this session.

11. **Select a hard-edged brush from the Brush pop-up palette. Then move the Master Diameter slider until your brush tip is around 30.**
You can change the size of the brush tip as you paint, which is a very useful new feature in Photoshop 7.

12. **Click anywhere in the Options bar to close the Brush pop-up palette.**

13. **Choose Layer→New→Layer. Name the new layer pattern stamp in the dialog box that appears and click OK.**
You could paint directly on an existing layer, but I suggest that you make a new layer so that you can easily throw your paint job away if you decide that you don't like it.

14. **Click and drag in the image to paint the camera reel with your custom pattern.**

15. **Click your pattern stamp layer in the Layers palette and drag it to the Trash icon.**
This is one reason that it makes sense to create different pieces of artwork on different layers. It makes it so easy to change your mind! By the way, if you really like the pattern that you just drew and want to keep it in your image, you can skip this step.

16. **Choose File→Save and leave the image open for the next tutorial.**

Tutorial

» Using the Pattern Maker

Photoshop 7 has a new feature for creating custom patterns — the Pattern Maker. The Pattern Maker has its own interface (like the Extract tool or the Liquify feature), but it's not as complicated as it may look at first. What the Pattern Maker does is create pattern tiles from rectangular selections of artwork and arrange those tiles in repeating patterns. It attempts to make those patterns look seamless, with more or less success depending on the source material. In this tutorial, you'll use the Pattern Maker to create a pattern and automatically apply it to your collage.

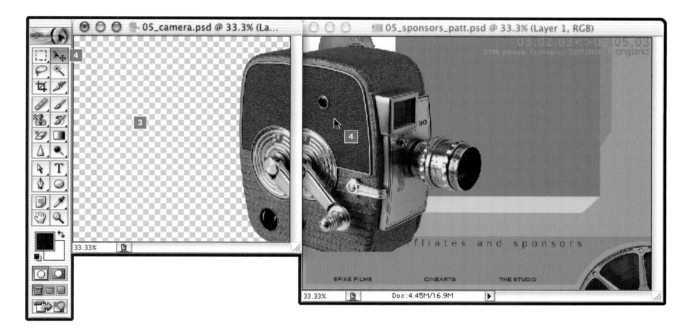

1. **Make sure that** 05_sponsors_patt.psd **is still open from the last tutorial.**

2. **Click the top layer of the image in the Layers palette.**

3. **Open a second image,** 05_camera.psd, **from the Session 5 Tutorial Files folder on your hard drive.**

4. **Select the Move tool from the toolbox and click and drag the single layer of artwork from** 05_camera.psd **into** 05_sponsors_patt.psd.
   The camera image appears in your collage, on a new layer called Layer 1. It doesn't matter where the camera lands in the collage or whether it is centered.

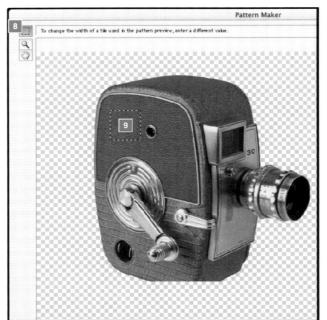
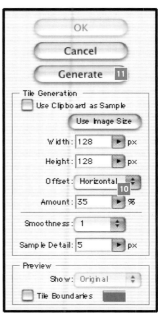

5. **Click on** 05_camera.psd **and choose File→Close.**
   You won't need this file any longer.

6. **Click the Layer 1 layer in the Layers palette and drag it down to just above the Background layer. Release the mouse button when a black line appears between the Background layer and the sponsors box layer just above it.**
   Layer 1 is now located just above the Background layer in the Layers palette.

<TIP>
If you're creating a pattern from a layer you want to keep, make a copy of that source layer before you open the Pattern Maker (by dragging the layer onto the New Layer icon at the bottom of the Layers palette). The Pattern Maker will completely fill the source layer with a pattern, obliterating any artwork on that layer. In this case, it isn't necessary to make a copy of the source layer because you won't be using it in this collage.

7. **Choose Pattern Maker from the Filter menu at the top of your screen.**
   This opens the Pattern Maker dialog box.

8. **Select the Rectangular Marquee tool at the top left of the Pattern Maker dialog box.**

9. **Click and drag a small rectangle around part of the brown leather on the camera in the preview area of the Pattern Maker.**
   This defines the tile from which your pattern will be built. Choose a relatively uniform part of the leather so that you don't get repeating lines in the pattern.

10. **Click the Offset button in the Pattern Maker and choose Horizontal. Type any number except for 50 into the Amount field.**
    This offsets the tiles from one another in the pattern. You'll see this for yourself when you turn on Tile Boundaries after generating a pattern shortly.

11. **Leave the other settings as they are for now and click Generate.**
    Photoshop generates a large preview of a pattern on the left side of the Pattern Maker.

12. **Click the Tile Boundaries check box to see an overlay of the grid of tiles in the pattern.**

    The tile boundaries preview where the edges of each tile are in the pattern. Although you can see some irregularities in the pattern, offsetting helps avoid obviously symmetrical patterns.

13. **Click the Smoothness button and increase that field to 3.**

    In some cases, this makes the transition between tiles less obvious.

14. **Click Generate Again.**

    Photoshop makes a second pattern preview.

15. **Click the Tile Boundaries check box to remove the check mark.**

    Now you can evaluate patterns without the boundaries obscuring your view.

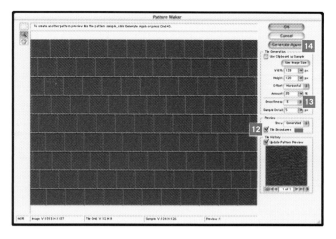

16. **Click the arrows at the bottom of the Tile History preview on the right of the Pattern Maker to scroll through the previews that you just made.**

    The pattern previews on the left will change as you scroll if Update Pattern Preview is selected. If you come across a tile that you're sure you don't want, you can delete it by dragging it to the Trash icon at the bottom of the Tile History Preview area.

17. **Stop scrolling when you get to the tile that you want to use and click OK.**

    Photoshop fills Layer 1 in your image with a pattern made from this tile. The Pattern Maker closes automatically.

<NOTE>

You can treat Layer 1 like any other layer. Try changing its opacity and blending mode from the controls at the top of the Layers palette. Or click the Move tool to reposition the layer in the image. I tried all of that and was still not satisfied with the look of this pattern layer. So I deleted it, as I recommend you do.

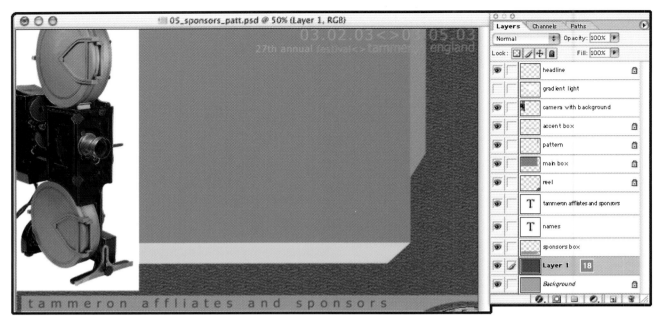

18. **Click Layer 1 in the Layers palette and drag it to the Trash icon at the bottom of the Layers palette.**

    Some settings in the Pattern Maker dialog box are probably new to you. Table 5-1 contains a summary of what each does.

19. **Leave** 05_sponsors_patt.psd **open for the next tutorial if you want to use it (instead of a fresh prebuilt file) in the next exercise.**

    I didn't tell you to save again here because you haven't made any changes since the last time that you were instructed to save.

Table 5-1: Pattern Maker Settings

Setting	Function
Generate or Generate Again	Creates a pattern preview based on your settings.
OK	Fills the selected layer with a pattern made from the selected tile and closes the Pattern Maker.
Cancel	Closes the Pattern Maker without making a pattern.
Use Clipboard as Sample	Used when you've copied a selection from another image to use as a pattern tile.
Use Image Size	Makes a single pattern tile as big as the entire source image.
Width and Height	Determine the size of the pattern tile.
Offset	Offsets tiles from one another in the pattern.
Smoothness	Increasing this sometimes makes the edges between tiles in a pattern less obvious.
Sample Detail	Increasing this sometimes helps unify graphic details broken up by a pattern.
Show	Displays the original image or a pattern preview in the preview area.
Tile Boundaries	Indicates the location of tile edges in a pattern preview.

Creating Pattern Tiles with the Pattern Maker

In this tutorial, you've learned how to use the Pattern Maker to create a pattern and apply it, all in the same image. You can also use the Pattern Maker to create and save a small tile to be made into a pattern elsewhere. After you've generated several tiles as you did in this tutorial, choose one to save and click the Save button at the bottom left of the Tile History preview in the Pattern Maker. That tile will automatically appear in the Pattern Picker that's accessible from the Fill command, the Paint Bucket tool, and the Pattern Stamp. You can apply it from any of those features, just like the prebuilt patterns that you used in the preceding tutorials. You may wonder why you need the Pattern Maker, when you already know how to make a pattern tile using the Define Pattern command. The main advantage of the Pattern Maker is that it attempts to blend the edges of the tiles it makes so that the resulting pattern appears relatively seamless.

Tutorial

» Using the Gradient Tool

A gradient is a special kind of fill that is a gradual blend of colors and opacities. Photoshop offers several features that you can use to create gradients — the Gradient tool, the Gradient Fill layer, and the Gradient Overlay layer style. Fill layers and layer styles are special features that are addressed later in this book. In this tutorial, you'll get to know the basic Gradient tool, using it to replace a selected area of solid color with one of the many preset gradients that ships with Photoshop 7.

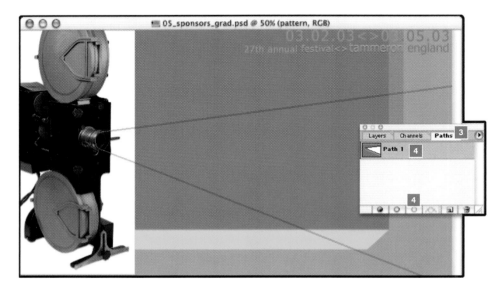

1. **Check that** 05_sponsors_patt.psd **is still open. Alternatively, you can open** 05_sponsors_grad.psd **from the Session 5 Tutorials folder on your hard drive.**
   05_sponsors_grad.psd is a replica of how 05_sponsors_patt.psd looks if you completed all the preceding tutorials in this session. If you haven't done that, start with this fresh file.

2. **In the Layers palette, select the gradient light layer. Choose Select→All from the menu at the top of the screen. Then choose Edit→Clear.**
   You'll be replacing this gradient with one of your own in this tutorial.

3. **Click the Paths tab to display the Paths palette.**
   You'll find the Paths tab in the same palette group as the Layers tab. Alternatively, you can access the Paths palette by choosing Window→Paths.

4. **Select Path 1 in the Paths palette. Then click the Load Path as Selection icon at the bottom of the Paths palette.**
   You'll learn more about paths in the next session. So don't worry about understanding how they work now. This step is necessary because you can't recolor the transparent pixels in this semitransparent gradient using the lock transparency approach that you learned earlier. Instead, you need a selection to shape the area that you're going to fill with a new gradient. Photoshop just made that selection for you from the vector outlines with which the projector light was originally drawn.

5. **Click Foreground Color box in the toolbox to open the Color Picker. Choose a yellow (such as R: 255, G: 204, B: 0) in the Color Picker and click OK.**

    This sets the foreground color to yellow.

6. **Click the Paint Bucket tool in the toolbox to display another hidden tool menu. Select the Gradient tool.**

7. **Click the drop-down arrow to the right of the gradient sample in the Options bar.**

    This opens the Gradient Picker, which displays some of the preset gradients that ship with Photoshop 7.

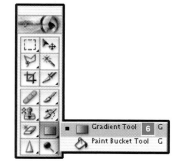

<TIP>

Photoshop ships with more preset gradients than you see here. To replace this default set of gradients, click the small arrow at the top right of the Gradient Picker and choose any of the eight sets of gradient presets listed at the bottom of the drop-down menu (Color Harmonies, Metals, Noise Samples, and so on). Click OK at the prompt to replace the current group of preset gradients, or Append to add more presets to this group.

8. **Select the Foreground to Transparent thumbnail in the Gradient Picker.**

    This thumbnail is yellow to transparent, because you set the Foreground Color to yellow in step 5.

9. **Click anywhere in the Options bar to close the Gradient Picker.**

    Your selected gradient appears in the gradient sample field of the Options bar.

10. **Type 75% in the Opacity field in the Options bar. Leave the other options at their defaults.**

    This lowers the opacity of the whole gradient.

    Try out the other Gradient tool settings on the Options bar when you get a chance. Table 5-2 is a rundown of what each does.

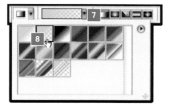

<NOTE>

Don't confuse lowering the opacity of a gradient in the Options bar with using opacity stops in the Gradient Editor to make some parts of a gradient more transparent than others (as you'll learn to do in the next tutorial). In fact, you can apply both features to the same gradient.

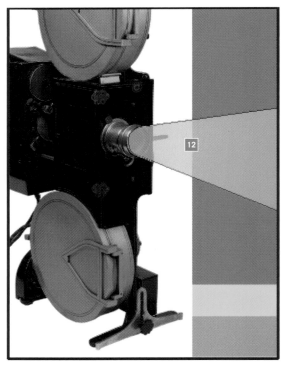

11. **Click inside the lens of the projector in the image and drag to the right edge of the document window.**

    As you drag, you'll see a blue line tracing your progress. The beginning point of that line represents the first color in this gradient (yellow) and the ending point of the line the last color in this gradient (transparency). The length and direction of the gradient depends on where you are in the image when you release the mouse button.

12. **Release the mouse button to fill the selected area with a yellow to transparent gradient.**

    If you didn't have an area selected, the gradient would have filled the entire layer. That's all there is to applying a preset gradient. In the next tutorial, you'll practice creating a custom gradient starting from one of the presets.

13. **Choose Select→Deselect from the menu bar at the top of the screen to turn off the marching ants.**

14. **Choose File→Save As. Save the file as** 05_sponsors_grad. psd **(whether you used your own file or the fresh file provided for you for this tutorial). Leave the file open for the next tutorial.**

Table 5-2: Gradient Tool Options

Option	Function
Style buttons	The buttons on the left of the Options bar determine the style of shading in a gradient (linear, radial, angular, reflected, or diamond). Linear is the default. It lays down bands of color starting with the first color you specify and ending with the last.
Mode	This determines how the gradient blends with other colors in the image, just like the Mode setting for the Fill command and other painting tools.
Reverse	This switches the starting and ending colors of a gradient. It is off by default.
Dither	This mixes adjacent pixels in a gradient in an attempt to reduce the appearance of separate bands of color. Banding is a common problem in gradients. Bands often appear when a gradient is printed, even if they're not terribly obvious on the computer monitor. Dithering can help.
Transparency	This must be checked to allow different levels of opacity at different points in a gradient. In this example, if you unchecked Transparency, you would lose the realistic effect of light falling off as it moves away from the projector.

Tutorial
» Creating a Custom Gradient

Photoshop's preset gradients are only a starting point for an infinite variety of custom gradients that you can create. In this tutorial, you'll learn how to custom build a gradient in the Gradient Editor.

1. **Make sure that** `05_sponsors_grad.psd` **is open from the previous tutorial.**

2. **Click the main box layer and drag it to the New Layer icon at the bottom of the Layers palette.**
   This creates a duplicate of the main box layer, called main box copy. You'll work on this duplicate layer so that you don't harm the underlying artwork. I'm a big fan of nondestructive editing like this because it keeps more options open.

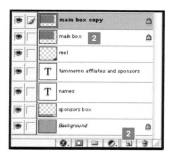

<NOTE>
The fact that the Gradient tool is destructive of original artwork is one reason to consider using one of the alternative methods when you want to apply a gradient. A Gradient Fill layer places a gradient on a Fill layer that is separate from the original artwork layer and is easily editable or removable. A Gradient layer style adds a gradient in the form of a layer style that can be easily removed from a layer of artwork. Or you can use the Gradient tool on a duplicate layer, as you did here, in order to preserve the original art.

3. **Click inside the gradient sample on the Options bar to open the Gradient Editor.**

Don't click the down arrow to the right of the gradient sample. That opens the Gradient Picker, not the Gradient Editor. You have to click right inside the gradient sample to open the Gradient Editor.

4. **Select one of the gradient thumbnails in the Gradient Editor as a starting point.**
   I chose the black to white gradient, which has only two defined colors, because I want to show you how to add color points to a gradient.

5. **Make sure that Gradient Type is set to Solid.**
   This is the setting for making a smooth gradient, as opposed to the choppy gradient that you get if you choose Noise from this menu.

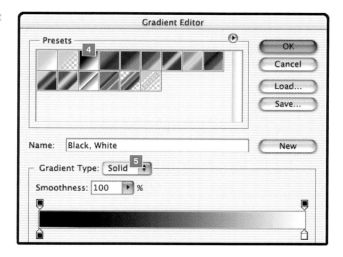

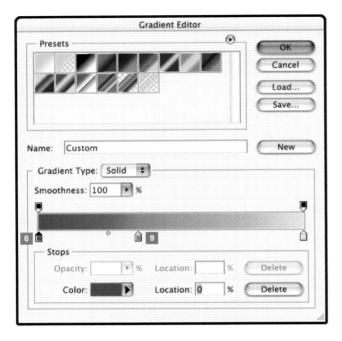

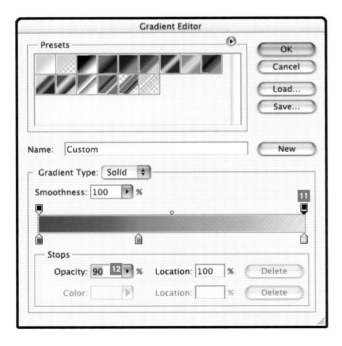

6. **Select the color stop located underneath and to the far left side of the gradient preview bar in the Gradient Editor. Then click in the Color field at the bottom of the Gradient Editor to open the Color Picker.**

   A *color stop* is a device for setting a color at a designated point in a gradient. When a stop is selected, its triangular top turns black.

7. **Choose purple (R: 109, G: 79, B: 158) in the Color Picker and click OK.**

   This fills the selected color stop with purple and colors the nearby pixels in the gradient purple.

8. **Repeat the preceding two steps for the color stop on the right, choosing light yellow (R: 243, G: 235, B: 171) as its color.**

9. **Click the bottom edge of the gradient preview bar to add a third color stop to your gradient.**

   Adding color stops to a gradient enables you to define and control more colors.

10. **Move your cursor out of the Gradient Editor and over the purple box at the bottom of the open image. The cursor turns to an eye-dropper. Click to fill your new color stop with that purple.**

    Pulling colors from the image in which you plan to use a gradient is a good design strategy.

11. **Select the opacity stop that is located above and on the far right side of the gradient preview bar.**

    An *opacity stop* is used to vary the opacity of the colors in a gradient. It enables you to increase or decrease the opacity of the colors that are near that stop.

12. **Click the Opacity field at the bottom of the Gradient Editor and move its slider to 90%.**

    This reduces the opacity of the light yellow colors in this gradient. You can partially see through those colors on the right side of the gradient preview bar, down to the gray-and-white checkerboard pattern that indicates transparency.

13. **Click any of the color or opacity stops and drag them to the right or left on the gradient preview bar to adjust the arrangement of colors in the gradient.**

    You can also move the small diamonds on the gradient preview bar. They represent midpoints between colors and opacities.

14. **Type a name** (sponsors) **for your custom gradient in the Name field and click the New button.**

    This adds a thumbnail of your sponsors gradient to the Gradient Editor. However, that thumbnail isn't fixed there permanently. It will disappear if you replace this gradient set with another.

15. **Click Save in the Gradient Editor and save into Photoshop's Gradients folder on your hard drive a new gradient preset that includes the custom gradient you just made.**

    This safeguards your new custom gradient. You can now access it at any time by clicking the arrow at the top of the Gradient Editor, choosing Replace Gradients, and selecting this custom gradient set.

<NOTE>

You can customize this gradient set, eliminating those gradients you don't like and keeping those you do, by opening and editing the set in the Preset Manager.

16. **Click OK to close the Gradient Editor.**

17. **Make sure that the main box copy layer is selected in the Layers palette and click the Lock Transparency button at the top of the palette.**

18. **Click and drag in the image to apply your custom gradient to the box in the middle of the image.**

    I dragged from the top of the box to the bottom to create the gradient on the box, behind the projector light.

19. **After you've admired your overlapping gradients, delete the gradient you just made by clicking on the main box copy layer in the Layers palette and dragging that layer to the trash.**

    Sorry, but this gradient isn't part of the final design of this collage.

20. **Choose File→Save and leave** 05_sponsors_grad.psd **open if you want to use it in the next exercise. (You'll have the option of starting with a fresh prebuilt file.)**

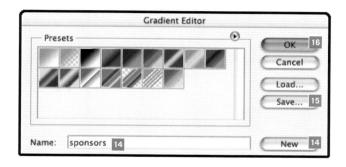

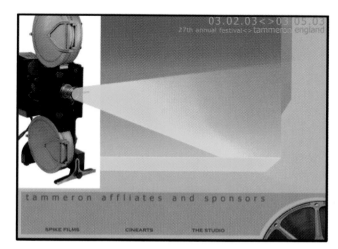

Tutorial
» Exploring the New Brushes Palette

Photoshop 7 has a number of new painting features that put it in the big leagues as a professional painting program. These include a revamped Brushes palette that you'll explore in this tutorial. You'll learn how to view and select brushes in the Brushes palette. You'll use the new Master Diameter slider to resize brushes, and you'll have a chance to try out some of the many preset brushes that ship with Photoshop 7.

1. **Use** 05_sponsors_grad.psd **from the last tutorial or open the fresh file** 05_sponsors_brush.psd.
   The fresh file mimics 05_sponsors_grad.psd as it should look at this point if you've done all the tutorials.

2. **Select the main box layer in the Layers palette and choose Layer→New→Layer to create Layer 1. Double-click Layer 1 and rename it** painting.
   You'll use this new layer to practice using some brush tools without destroying any existing artwork. This is another example of using layers for nondestructive editing.

3. **Select the Paint Brush tool in the toolbox.**
   If you open the Brushes palette before you've selected one of the painting tools in the toolbox, the contents of the Brushes palette will be grayed out and unavailable.

4. **Click the Brushes tab, which is docked in the Palette well at the right side of the Options bar.**

   This opens the Brushes palette, but leaves it docked in the Palette well.

<NOTE>

If your monitor resolution is set to fewer pixels than 1024 x 768, you probably can't see the Palette well on your screen. I suggest that you increase your monitor resolution to 1024 or higher. If you don't know how to do that, consult the Help files or user guide for your particular operating system. If you can't do that, you can open the Brushes palette by choosing Window➜Brushes.

<TIP>

When the Brushes palette is left docked in the Palette well, it will close every time you click anywhere outside of it, including when you click in an image to paint. If this bothers you, click the tab at the top of the Brushes palette and drag the Brushes palette out of the Palette well. The result is that the Brushes palette now stays open until you close it. On the other hand, it's more likely to get in your way.

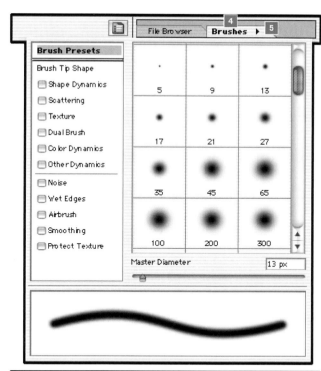

5. **Make sure that your Brushes palette matches the figure. If your palette is displaying only brush tips, click the arrow on the right side of the Brushes tab and choose Expanded View.**

   Expanded View displays the currently loaded preset brushes on the right, a preview of the stroke that a selected brush will draw on the bottom, and a list of brush options on the left.

6. **Click the arrow on the Brushes tab and choose Stroke Thumbnail from the Brushes palette menu.**

   This changes the view of currently loaded preset brushes on the right side of the palette, showing a stroke sample for each brush in addition to the brush tip. There are basically three ways to view brushes in the Brushes palette — by stroke sample, by thumbnail, and by list. All are accessible from the Brushes palette menu.

7. **Move your cursor over any stroke sample on the right side of the palette and wait a moment.**

   A larger preview of that stroke appears in the bottom pane of the Brushes palette, as well as a ToolTip with the name of the brush.

8. **Click any stroke sample on the right side of the palette to select a brush. Click and drag the Master Diameter slider to change the size of the brush.**

   You can change the diameter of any brush in Photoshop 7, including specialty brushes and custom brushes that you create yourself (which you'll learn to do shortly).

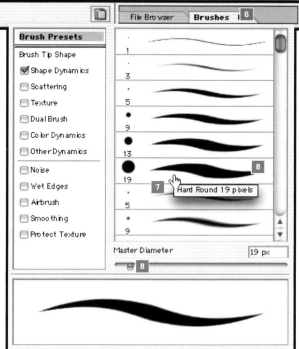

9. **Make sure that the painting layer is still selected in the Layers palette. Click and drag in the document window to try out your selected brush.**

Don't worry about making a mess. You're going to throw out this painting layer shortly anyway. It's just a place to practice.

10. **Click the arrow on the right side of the Brushes tab and choose any of the other sets of preset brushes at the bottom of the Brushes palette menu. Click OK at the prompt to replace the current set of brushes with the new set that you've chosen.**

This is how you load sets of brushes.

11. **Try some of these other preset brushes by selecting them and drawing in the image. When you're done, click the eye icon to the left of the painting layer to hide what you've drawn for now.**

<NOTE>

Many of the new preset brushes are designed to help you paint with the look and feel of natural media. There are wet and dry brushes and natural brushes with which you can digitally simulate traditional art techniques. Give them a try.

12. **Choose File→Save As. Save the file as**
05_sponsors_brush.psd **(whether you used your own file or the fresh file provided for you for this tutorial). Leave the file open for the next tutorial.**

<TIP>

If all you need to do with a brush at any time is what you've learned here — select, resize, and perhaps load a preset brush — you're just as well off using the simple Brush pop-up palette as the more elaborate Brushes palette. You learned how to use the Brush pop-up palette with the Pattern Stamp tool earlier in this session. It works just the same way with any of the painting tools. You can access the Brush pop-up palette by selecting one of the painting tools and clicking the Brush sample on the left side of the Options bar.

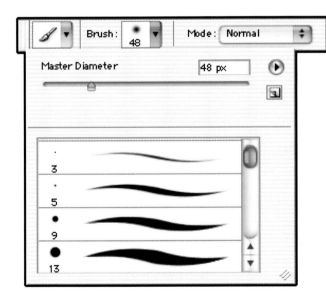

Tutorial
» Using Brush Options

The Brushes palette offers several options that you can use to modify and customize a preset brush. In this tutorial, you'll use some of those options to create new brushes, which you can save for reuse as tool presets. You'll also use brush options from the Options bar.

1. **Make sure that** 05_sponsors_brush.psd **is open from the last tutorial.**

2. **Choose Layer→New→Layer. Double-click your new Layer 1 in the Layers palette and rename it** roses**. Click and drag the roses layer to just below the gradient light layer in the Layers palette.**

3. **Click the Paths tab and select Path 1 in the Paths palette. Click the Load Path as Selection icon at the bottom of the Paths palette.** You've created a selection in the shape of the projector light in your image, just as you did in a previous tutorial in this session. Your roses layer should still be selected.

4. **Select the Paint Brush tool in the toolbox. Click the Palette button on the far right side of the Options bar to open the Brushes palette.** This is an alternative to clicking the Brushes tab to open the Brushes palette. The Palette button appears on the Options bar for all the painting tools.

5. **Click the arrow on the right of the Brushes tab and choose Special Effects Brushes. Click OK at the prompt to replace the current brush set with the Special Effects preset brushes.**

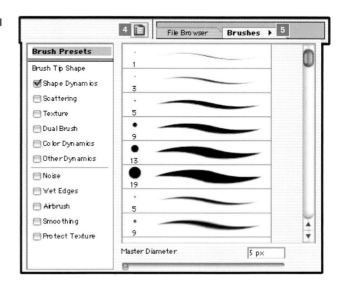

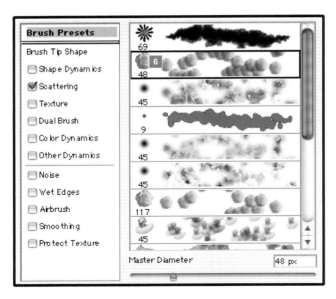

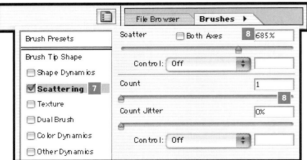

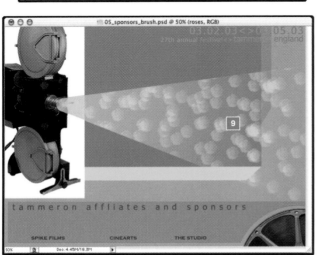

6. **Select the Scattered Roses brush from the Brushes palette.**

   Notice that there is a check mark next to the Scattering option on the left side of the Brushes palette. This indicates that the Scattering option is active for this brush, but you can't see the settings for the Scattering option until you select that option, as you'll do in the next step.

7. **Click the Scattering option on the left side of the Brushes palette.**

   The Scattering option is highlighted, and the Scattering option settings appear on the right side of the Brushes palette.

   < N O T E >

   When Scattering is activated, a brush makes more than one mark with each brush stroke. You control the number and placement of those marks with the Scattering settings, which you'll access in the next step.

8. **Click the Scatter slider on the right side of the Brushes palette and move it up to around 685%. Leave Count at 1 and jitter at 0% to match this figure.**

   This increases the scattered placement of marks and instructs Photoshop to put one mark at each spacing interval. *Jitter* is a word that you'll see in many of the Brush options. Whenever you increase the jitter of a setting, you increase the random variation in the setting. Notice that the preview at the bottom of the settings area shows you what a stroke will look like with these settings.

9. **Paint a few brush strokes in your image.**

   Notice how the roses are applied in a scattered pattern when you paint. If you're wondering why your strokes are confined to the shape of the projector light, remember that you selected this area back in step 3.

10. **Choose Select→Deselect.**

11. **Select the sponsors box layer in the Layers palette. Choose Layer→New→Layer to make another new layer. Double-click the new layer and name it** logos.

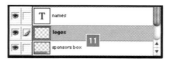

12. **Click Brush Presets at the top of the Brushes palette.**
This returns the right side of the palette to a view of brush presets.

13. **Click the arrow on the Brushes tab and choose Reset Brushes. Click OK at the prompt.**
This replaces the current set of brushes with the default preset brushes.

14. **Select the Fuzzball brush from the brush presets.**

<NOTE>

This brush comes with lots of options activated. Shape Dynamics control the size and shape of brush marks. Scattering controls the placement and number of brush marks. Color Dynamics allow variation in color in a brush stroke. Other Dynamics control opacity and flow in brush strokes. There is so much jitter in many of the option settings that each brush stroke you make in an image will produce different combinations of color, size, opacity, and other attributes. So it's unlikely that copying the settings used in this example will give you the same result that you see here. It's up to you to experiment! I suggest that you leave all the options at their defaults and concentrate on the Color Dynamics setting, as covered in an upcoming step. Consult your Photoshop User Manual if you want to know more about any of the other options.

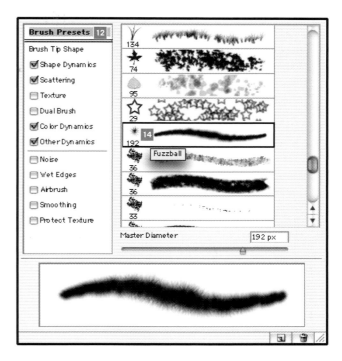

15. **Click in the Foreground Color box in the toolbox and set the foreground color to aqua. Click in the Background Color box and set the background color to purple.**
Don't worry about matching my colors in this case.

16. **Click the Color Dynamics option.**

<NOTE>

Try increasing the amount of Foreground/Background Jitter and set Control for that option to Fade. This varies the color in a brush stroke between the foreground and background colors. Leave the level of Hue Jitter low to avoid lots of random colors in your brush strokes. Increase Saturation and Brightness Jitter to get some variation in saturation and brightness within a brush stroke. Leave Purity at 0% so that the colors you're using keep their normal saturation.

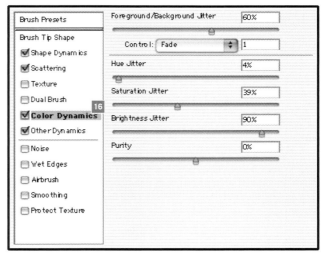

17. **Click in your image and draw a small logo. If you don't like the results, choose Edit→Step Backward and try again.**

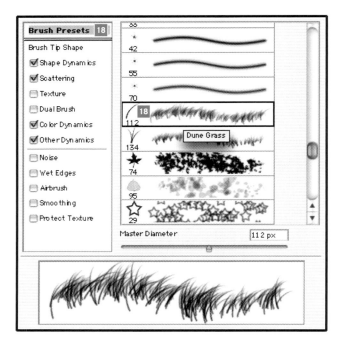

18. **Click Brush Presets in the Brushes palette. Select the Dune Grass brush in the Brushes palette. Experiment with drawing a logo with that brush, varying some of the brush options.**

19. **Click Brush Presets again and select a hard round brush.**

20. **Click the Brush Tip Shape option on the left side of the Brushes palette.**

    This opens a set of options for modifying the shape of any brush tip.

21. **Increase the Diameter of the brush to 30 px and increase the Spacing to 200%. Set Brush Roundness to 84%, Angle to 25°, and Hardness to 95%.**

    Spacing is a very useful setting. Use it to increase the amount of space between brush strokes to simulate a dotted line with a round brush.

22. **Set the foreground color in the toolbox to yellow and the background color to aqua. Click the Color Dynamics brush option in the Brushes palette. Increase Foreground/Background Jitter and set Control to Fade. Click and drag to draw a third logo in your image.**

<N O T E>

You can save any brush you create with brush options as a reusable tool preset. Take a look back at Session 1 to remind yourself how to make a new tool preset.

23. **Choose File→Save and leave** 05_sponsors_brush.psd **open for the next tutorial.**

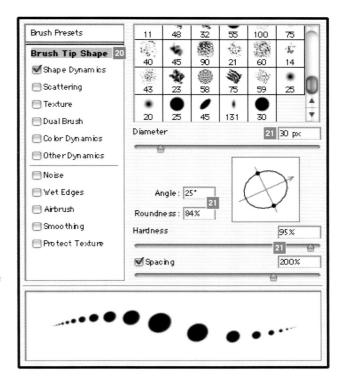

Tutorial

» Defining a Brush

You aren't limited to using the preset brushes that ship with Photoshop or even brushes you make yourself by modifying those presets. You can create your own brush from scratch from a drawing or other image, as you'll do in this tutorial.

1. **Open** 05_brush.psd **from the Session 5 Tutorial Files folder on your hard drive.**
   Use this image as the source of your brush or draw your own image of the same size (50 x 50 pixels) with black paint on a white background.

   <TIP>
   In most cases, you'll want to define a brush from a black-and-white line drawing. This results in a solid, opaque brush. You could use a color or grayscale image as the basis for a brush, but that brush would paint with semitransparency rather than solid outlines.

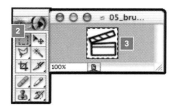

2. **Select the Rectangular Marquee tool in the toolbox. If it's not showing, click on the marquee that is displayed and select the Rectangular Marquee tool from the hidden menu that pops out.**

3. **Draw a selection around your image.**
   Draw your selection tight to the image. Don't leave extra white space surrounding your selection or that too will be part of the brush.

4. **Choose Edit→Define Brush from the menu bar at the top of the screen.**

5. **Type** 50 cut **in the Brush Name dialog box that appears and click OK.**

6. **Click the Paint Brush tool in the toolbox.**

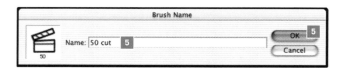

7. **Click the Brushes tab to open the Brushes palette. Scroll to the bottom of the brush previews. Your new brush should be there, ready to use!**

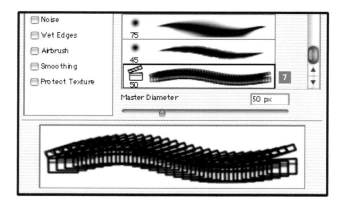

8. **Click the Scattering option on the left side of the Brushes palette to display the Scattering settings.**

9. **Click the Scatter slider at the top of the right side of the Brushes palette and increase it to around 500%. Decrease the Count slider to 1.**

10. **Click the Foreground Color box in the toolbox and choose a light yellow color.**

11. **Click the Paths tab to display the Paths palette. Click Path 1 and then click the Load Path as Selection button at the bottom of the Paths palette.**
    This selection limits the area in which you'll paint to the shape of the projector light.

<NOTE>

If you see a small number 01 at the top left of the image, you can ignore it. It is a slice number and won't print with the image. If it bothers you, choose View→Extras to uncheck Extras.

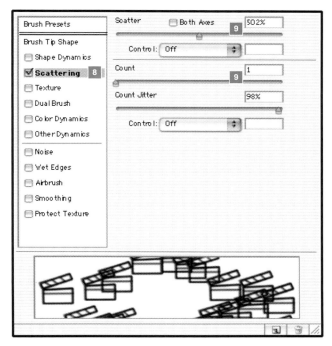

12. **Click the roses layer in the Layers palette and drag it to the Trash icon at the bottom of the palette.**

13. **Choose Layer→New→Layer in the Layers palette. Double-click the new layer and name it** cuts. **Drag it to just below the gradient light layer.**

14. **Type** 50% **in the Opacity field.**
    You'll learn in the next tutorial that this reduces the density with which your brush will paint.

15. **Click and drag in the image** 05_sponsors_brush.psd **to paint with your new brush in the area of the projector light.**

16. **Choose Select→Deselect to eliminate the marching ants. Click the Paths tab and click off Path 1 in the Paths palette to eliminate the blue paths.**

17. **Choose File→Save and keep** 05_sponsors_brush.psd **open for the next tutorial. Close the small image** 05_brush.psd **without saving.**

Tutorial
» Using Brush Settings on the Options Bar

Given the variety of brush options available in the Brushes palette, it's hard to believe that there are more brush settings to consider. However, the Options bar has some important brush settings that you can use alone or in combination with options from the Brushes palette. You'll use some of them in this short tutorial.

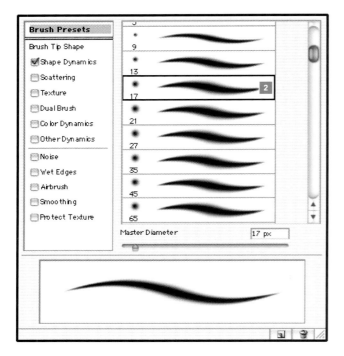

1. **Use** 05_sponsors_brush.psd **from the last tutorial.**

2. **Select the Paint Brush tool in the toolbox and select a 17 px soft-edged brush in the Brushes palette.**

3. **Click the Mode button on the Options bar and choose Behind from the list of brush blending modes.**
   You've run into blending modes several times already in the context of other tools and fill features. You'll also find blending modes in the Layers palette. The blending modes for the Paint Brush tool determine how the color applied by that tool interacts with the artwork on other layers. The Behind blending mode causes a brush to apply color only where there are transparent pixels on a layer. That will create a nice contour when you paint along the semitransparent pixels of the gradient light layer.

4. **Click the arrow on the Opacity field on the Options bar and drag the slider to the left to decrease Opacity to around 40%.**
   Opacity is the density with which a brush adds color. Lowering opacity this much will give a very transparent look to the painted area.

5. **Click the arrow on the Flow field on the Options bar and drag the slider to around 40%, too.**
   Flow is the speed with which paint is delivered by a brush. Reducing this parameter softens the stroke.

<NOTE>
The Airbrush has been demoted from a tool in the last version of Photoshop to a setting on the Options bar. The Airbrush offers a softening effect, but it also makes paint pool if you hold your cursor in one place, just like a real airbrush. That's an effect you don't want here, so don't click on the Airbrush option.

6. **Select the Eyedropper tool from the toolbox and click on a semi-transparent yellow area of the projector light in the image.**

This sets the foreground color to a mustard yellow.

7. **Hold the Shift key down. Then click on the beginning of the top edge of the projector light in the image. (The edge of the shape should intersect your brush.) Click on the end of that edge (again with the edge intersecting the brush).**

This draws a straight line down the top edge of the projector light, adding a subtle contour to that edge.

<TIP>

Knowing how to draw a straight line in any direction will come in handy. You must hold the Shift key down before the first click and keep it held down through the second click, as you just did.

8. **Choose File→Save and leave** 05_sponsors_brush.psd **open for the next tutorial.**

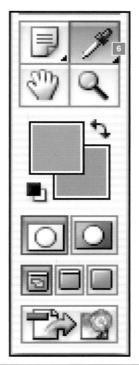

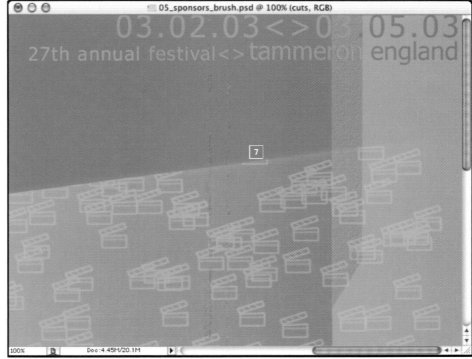

Tutorial

» Stroking

Stroking places a border around isolated artwork. It qualifies as a painting technique because it deposits color by way of pixels. In this short tutorial, you'll use the Stroke command along with the transparency lock to put a stroke around the artwork on a layer. You can also use this command to stroke a selection.

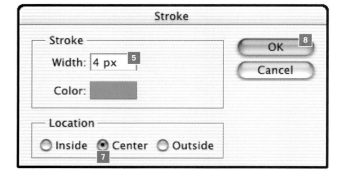

1. **Use** `05_sponsors_brush.psd` **from the preceding tutorial.**

2. **Select the accent box layer in the Layers palette.**

3. **Click the Lock Transparency button at the top left of the Layers palette if there isn't already a lock symbol in the accent box layer.**

4. **Choose Edit→Stroke from the menu bar at the top of the screen.**

5. **In the Stroke dialog box, type** 4 px **in the Width field.**

6. **Move your cursor out of the Stroke dialog box; it becomes an eyedropper. Click in the green-blue text at the top of the page to set the Color field in the Stroke dialog box.**

7. **Choose Center as the location of the stroke.**
   This centers the stroke over the edge of the selected area.

8. **Click OK to create a green-blue stroke around the yellow accent box.**

9. **Select the Paint Brush tool in the toolbox and a 5 pixel hard brush from the Brush pop-up palette.**

10. **Hold the Shift key and click in the top-left corner of the accent box, just inside the blue stroke. Keep the Shift key pressed and click straight across in the top-right corner of the accent box, inside the blue stroke.**
    This is a way to make one leg of the stroke look thicker than the others, in order to add some perspective. You have to click inside the blue stroke because the Lock Transparency button is still on, making it impossible to paint outside of the yellow accent box.

11. **Choose File→Save and keep this image open for the next tutorial.**

Tutorial
» Erasing

There are tools other than the Paint Brush tool that are technically brush tools, in that they paint with pixels and use brushes accessed from the Brush palette. The Eraser tools are a hybrid. The main Eraser tool acts like a brush. It paints with pixels and uses brushes just like the Paint Brush and other painting tools. The Magic Eraser is like a selection tool. It selects pixels and deletes them in one fell swoop. The Background Eraser distinguishes foreground elements from their surroundings and erases only the surroundings. You'll use all three Eraser tools in this tutorial.

1. **Make sure that** 05_sponsors_brush.psd **is open from the last tutorial.**

2. **Select the Eraser tool from the toolbox. It's the one with the plain eraser icon. If it's not showing, click whichever eraser tool is showing and select the Eraser tool from the hidden tool menu.**

3. **Select the cuts layer in the Layers palette.**

4. **Choose a medium-sized brush (such as a 19-pixel hard round one) from the Brush pop-up palette.**

5. **Click and drag over any of the cut designs that you want to eliminate from your image.**
   The Eraser tool paints out pixels on a layer so that you can see what's on the underlying layers.

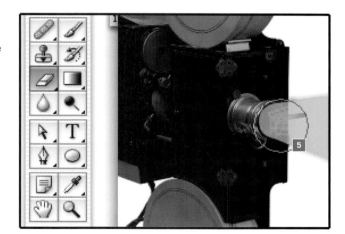

<NOTE>
If you erase on a Background layer, the Eraser erases to the background color identified in the toolbox.

6. **Select the camera with background layer in the Layers palette.**

7. **Click the Eraser tool in the toolbox and select the Background Eraser tool (the one with the Scissors icon).**

8. **Make sure that the settings in the Options bar match those shown here.**

<NOTE>

There are quite a few settings in the Background Eraser's Options bar. Choosing Contiguous in the Limits field instructs the Background Eraser to only erase colors that touch the color that's at the center of the Background Eraser. Adjust Tolerance up to erase more pixels and down to erase fewer pixels. If there's a color you do not want erased, choose it as the foreground color in the toolbox and check Protect Foreground Color in the Options bar. Setting Sampling to Once tells the Background Eraser that it only has to decide what the background color is one time, which works here because the background is all one color.

9. **Zoom in to 100% with the Zoom tool.**

10. **Position the cursor so that the cross at its center is very near, but not touching, the camera. Move the cursor around the outside edge of the camera, being careful not to let the cross touch the camera.**
The Background Eraser is smart enough to erase the white background, but not the camera, letting you see through to green pixels on the layer below!

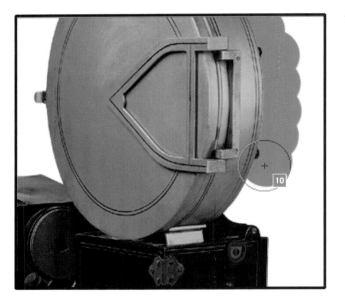

11. **Click the Background Eraser tool in the toolbox and select the Magic Eraser (the one with the asterisk) from the hidden menu.**

12. **Make sure that the settings in the Options bar are the same as the ones shown here.**

13. **Click anywhere in the white area that surrounds the camera, and the entire white background will disappear at once!**

14. **Choose File→Save As. In the Save As dialog box, name this image** `05_sponsors_end.psd`. **Make sure that Layers and Embed Profile are checked. Save it in a safe place. You'll be working on this collage further in the next session.**

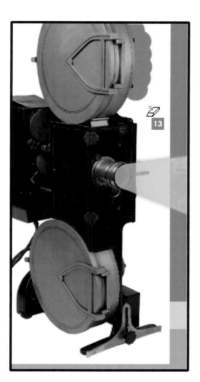

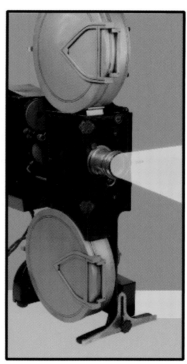

» Session Review

This session covers how to fill and paint with pixels. You learned to fill with the Fill command, the Paint Bucket tool, and the Pattern Stamp. You defined your own pattern using the Define Pattern command, and you learned how to use the new Pattern Maker to create a fill from artwork tiles. You filled an area with a prebuilt gradient, and you learned how to make a custom gradient in the Gradient Editor. Then you were introduced to Photoshop 7's new Brushes palette, which has lots of preset natural media brushes and many options from which you can create custom brushes. You learned how to stroke artwork, and you were introduced to the three Eraser tools — the Eraser, the Background Eraser, and the Magic Eraser. There's a lot to remember from this session. Use these questions to jog your memory about what you learned here.

1. What is a pixel? (See "Tutorial: Filling a Layer.")

2. Why doesn't a bitmapped image look good if you try to make it bigger by resampling in Photoshop? (See "Tutorial: Filling a Layer.")

3. How can you confine a fill to the artwork on a layer and leave the transparent pixels on the layer unfilled? (See "Tutorial: Filling the Artwork on a Layer.")

4. If you want to fill only part of the artwork on a layer, what do you have to do? (See "Tutorial: Filling Selected Artwork.")

5. What command would you use if you wanted to fill an entire layer with color? (See "Tutorial: Filling the Artwork on a Layer.")

6. What is the shortcut for the command that you would use if you wanted to fill an entire layer with color? (See "Tutorial: Filling the Artwork on a Layer.")

7. Name two features that you could use to fill an entire layer with a pattern. (See "Tutorial: Filling with a Pattern.")

8. Name two features that you could use to create a pattern. (See "Tutorial: Defining and Applying a Custom Pattern" and "Tutorial: Using the Pattern Maker.")

9. What is a gradient? (See "Tutorial: Using the Gradient Tool.")

10. What feature do you use to create a custom gradient? (See "Tutorial: Creating a Custom Gradient.")

11. Name three ways that you can view brush presets in the Brushes palette. (See "Tutorial: Exploring the New Brushes Palette.")

12. Other than the Brushes palette, what feature can you use to select preset brushes? (See "Tutorial: Exploring the New Brushes Palette.")

13. In what two places are brush options located? (See "Tutorial: Using Brush Options" and "Tutorial: Using Brush Settings on the Options Bar.")

14. What command do you use to define a brush from another image? (See "Tutorial: Defining a Brush.")

15. What does the Magic Eraser do? (See "Tutorial: Erasing.")

16. What does the Background Eraser do? (See "Tutorial: Erasing.")

17. What feature do you use to put a border around artwork? (See "Tutorial: Stroking.")

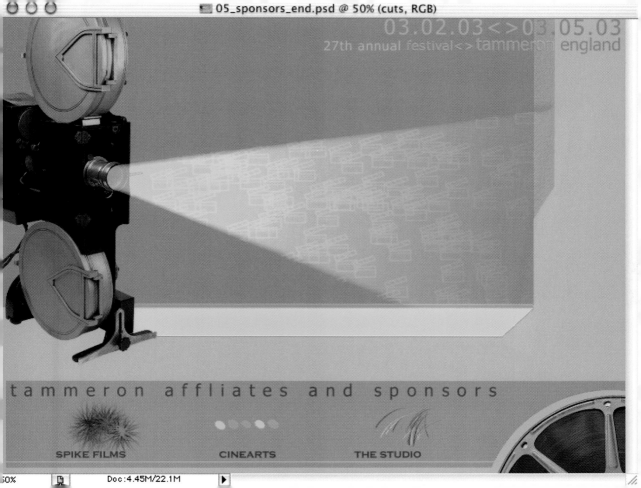

Session 6

Drawing with Vectors

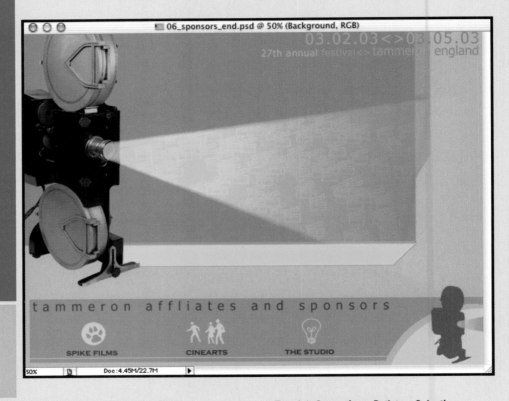

06_sponsors_end.psd @ 50% (Background, RGB)

03.02.03<>03.05.03
27th annual festival<> tammeron england

tammeron affliates and sponsors

SPIKE FILMS   CINEARTS   THE STUDIO

50%   Doc :4.45M/22.7M

Session Introduction

Photoshop isn't just a bitmapped image-editing program. It also includes vector-based drawing tools — the Pen tools and Shape tools — which you'll try out in this session. You'll be introduced to drawing and editing vector paths with the Pen tools. You'll see how easy it is to create a vector logo, resize it for use in another document, and color it by filling and stroking its path. You'll also practice converting a path to a selection so that you can further embellish it with bitmap editing features. Then you'll learn all about the Shape tools, which you can use to create geometric shapes or variations on the many prebuilt graphic shapes that ship with Photoshop 7.

TOOLS YOU'LL USE
Pen tools, Paths palette, Path Selection tool, Direct Selection tool, Shape tools, shape layers, and Custom Shape tool

CD-ROM FILES NEEDED
06_camera_paths.psd, 06_camera_edit.psd, 06_camera_magnet.psd, 06_camera_fill.psd, 06_camera_move.psd, 06_sponsors_move.psd, 06_sponsors_select.psd, 06_sponsors_shape.psd, and 06_sponsors_end.psd

TIME REQUIRED
90 minutes

Tutorial
» Drawing with the Pen Tool

Paths are lines and curves that make up the outlines of vector graphics. The Pen tool is the most precise method of creating paths in Photoshop. In this tutorial, you'll learn the basics of using the Pen tool to draw and edit paths. If you're an illustrator, you'll love the flexibility and precision this tool offers. But if you're handier with a camera than with a sketch pad, you may not take to the Pen tool right away. You can look forward to the tutorials at the end of this session, where you'll learn an easier way to make vector graphics using the Shape tools.

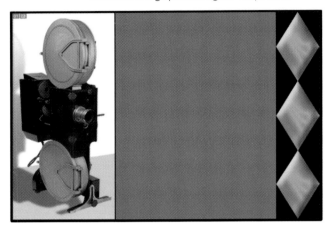

1. **Open** 06_camera_paths.psd **from the Session 6 Tutorial Files folder on your hard drive.**

<NOTE>
This isn't one of the collages for your final film festival guide project. It's merely a source document in which you'll practice drawing and editing paths and from which you'll trace and copy a path for use in a final collage that you'll complete later in this session.

2. **Select the Pen tool in the toolbox. If one of the Pen tool variations is showing in the toolbox, click the tool that is displayed and choose the Pen tool from the hidden menu.**

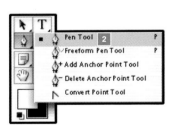

An Introduction to Vector Graphics

You learned about bitmapped images, which are composed entirely of pixels, in the last session. You'll remember that bitmapped images are resolution dependent and are best-suited for continuous tone images, such as photographs and soft-edged graphics.

Vector graphics, which are the subject of this session, are very different than bitmapped images. Vector graphics consist of mathematical instructions rather than pixels. They can be resized and reshaped without damaging image quality because they are resolution independent. Vector objects are easy to select and recolor even if they aren't located on separate layers. And vector objects have crisp edges if they are printed on a PostScript printer, saved as a PDF file, or exported to another vector program, such as Adobe Illustrator. All of this means that vector objects are useful for commercial graphics, and particularly for items such as logos that you may want to reuse at different sizes.

There are a couple ways to work with vector graphics in Photoshop — as paths created with Pen tools and managed in the Paths palette or as shapes created with Shape tools and located on shape layers — both of which are covered in this session. (You'll also find paths or shapes located in vector masks, which are used to reveal or hide portions of an image. Vector masks are covered in Session 9.)

3. **Click once in the image to create a point. Release the mouse button and click again in another place to draw a path in the shape of a straight line. ⌘+click (Windows: Ctrl+click) anywhere else in the image to end the path that you just created.**

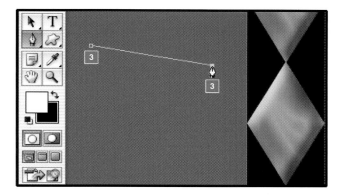

4. **Repeat the preceding step to draw another line, but this time don't end the path. Instead, click several more times to draw four connected straight lines that form a polygon. To close the polygon, move your cursor over the first point that you drew and click when you see a tiny circle that indicates you're back where you started.**

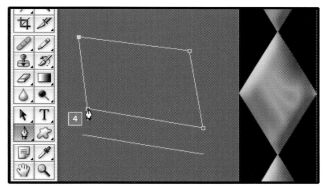

<NOTE>

The lines that you've drawn so far look jaggedy. That's because they aren't drawn at 45° angles to conform to the invisible grid of pixels on your screen. (Even vector lines can look jaggedy on a computer screen because the screen has to use pixels to represent them.) If you hold the Shift key while you click, your lines will be constrained to 45° angles and will look straight and clean on-screen.

Paths Primer

The outline of a vector graphic is called a *path*. A path consists of straight and curved line segments connected with points. You can leave a path open-ended to form a straight or curved line, or you can close a path to form a shape.

Paths are independent of any particular layer. So you can use a path to define shapes on more than one layer in a document, or you can copy and use a path in other documents, as you'll do in this session.

Paths are created and edited with Photoshop's Pen tools and are managed from the Paths palette. In the Paths palette, you can convert a temporary work path into a saved path that stays with the image. You can activate a path so that it can be stroked with color or filled with color, a pattern, or a history state. You can convert a path to a selection so that it can be edited further as a bitmapped graphic. Or you can convert a selection to a path so that you can resize it or distort its shape. You'll learn how to do all of this as you work through this and the following tutorials.

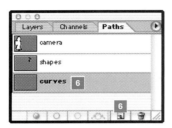

5. **Choose Window→Paths to open the Paths palette. Notice that it contains a path labeled *Work Path.* Double-click Work Path in the Paths palette to open the Save Path dialog box. Type the name** shapes **and click OK.**

You've converted a temporary work path, containing the objects you just drew, to a permanent saved path that will remain with the image unless the path is deliberately deleted. The work path was created automatically when you began drawing with the Pen tool.

If you click off a work path in the Paths palette and then draw even one more point, the current work path will be replaced, and you will lose all the objects you've drawn to that point. So it's wise to convert a work path to a saved path as soon as you've drawn a path that you want to keep.

6. **Click the Create New Path button at the bottom right of the Paths palette to create a new path called Path 1. Double-click Path 1 and rename it** curves**. Make sure that the curves path is selected.**

Creating and selecting a permanent path before you start drawing is the way to avoid drawing on an automatically created work path, which is temporary and can be inadvertently replaced.

7. **Choose View→Show→Grid.**

Turning on the grid eases the job of drawing curves with the Pen tool because the points that you draw will snap to the intersections of the grid and the grid lines will help you judge the length and angle of your direction lines, as you'll see in the next steps.

<NOTE>

I've changed the color of the grid lines in Photoshop's Grids, Guides & Slices Preferences to make the grid more noticeable for you.

8. **Select the Pen tool in the toolbox. Click the Options arrow in the Options bar and put a check mark next to Rubber Band in the Options menu.**

The Rubber Band option previews each path segment for you as you're drawing.

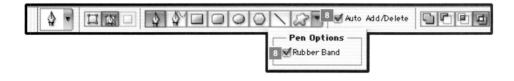

9. **Click an intersection of the grid to begin drawing a curve. Drag in the direction that you want the curve to bow (to the left in this case).**
   As you drag, a direction line appears. Follow the horizontal line of the grid as you drag if you want to keep your curves uniform.

10. **Release the mouse button when you reach the intersection one square to the left of the beginning point.**

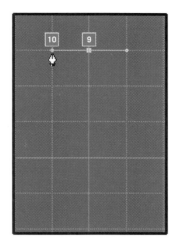

11. **Click an intersection of the grid where you want your curve to end (try one square down from the beginning point).**

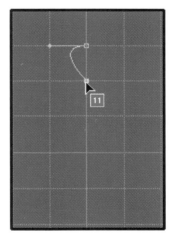

12. **Drag a direction line to the right, away from the bow of the curve.**

13. **Release the mouse button when you reach the intersection one square to the right of your ending point.**
    You could close the path at this point by ⌘+clicking (Windows: Ctrl+clicking) off the path. Instead, in the next steps you'll draw some more curves that are connected to this path.

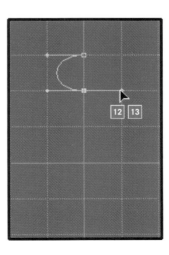

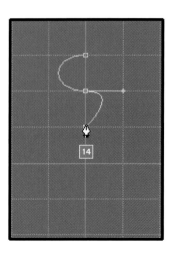

14. **Click the intersection one square below the ending point of the first curve.**

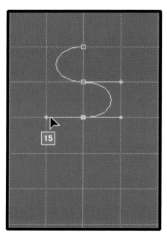

15. **Drag to the left. Release the mouse button at the intersection one square to the left.**

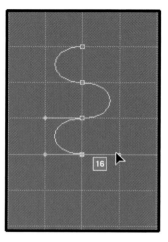

16. **Click the intersection one square below the beginning point of the curve that you're currently drawing. Drag to the right. Release the mouse button at the intersection one square to the right.**

<TIP>

When drawing a single curve with the Pen tool, place your first point where you want the curve to start. Also, drag from the start point toward the direction that you want the curve to bow. Place your second point where you want the curve to end, rather than in the middle of the curve. And finally, drag from the end point away from the bow of the curve.

17. **Option+click (Windows: Alt+click) the end point of the last direction line you drew.**

18. **Drag the direction line down and around to the left.**
    This changes the direction so that the next curve you draw will bow out to the left (the way the direction line is now pointing).

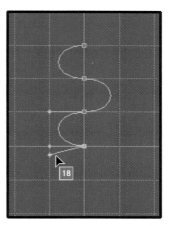

19. **Click the intersection one square below the beginning point of this curve. Drag to the right. Release the mouse button at the intersection one square to the right. ⌘+click (Windows: Ctrl+click) anywhere in the image to close the path.**

20. **Choose File→Save and leave** 06_camera_paths.psd **open if you want to use it for the next tutorial. You'll have the option of starting the next tutorial with a fresh prebuilt file.**

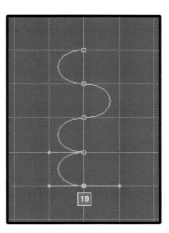

Tutorial
» Editing Paths

In the preceding tutorial, you learned the basics of drawing paths with the Pen tool. In this tutorial, you'll learn how to move and adjust paths.

1. **Check that** `06_camera_paths.psd` **is open from the last tutorial or open the fresh file** `06_camera_edit.psd` **from the Session 6 Tutorial Files folder on your hard drive.** `06_camera_edit.psd` is a replica of how `06_camera_paths.psd` should look at the end of the last tutorial.

2. **Select the shapes path in the Paths palette.**

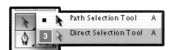

3. **Select the White Arrow tool from the toolbox. If you don't see it, click the Black Arrow tool to reveal a hidden menu and choose the White Arrow tool from that menu.**

<NOTE>
The official name of the White Arrow tool is the Direct Selection tool, and the official name of the Black Arrow tool is the Path Selection tool. To make things easier, I call them by their generic names.

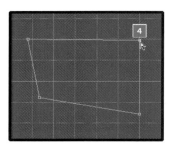

4. **Click one of the corner points in the polygon-shaped path in the image and drag to reshape the attached line so that it's straight up and down. Repeat this on the other corner points to try to straighten all the lines so that the polygon becomes a rectangle.**

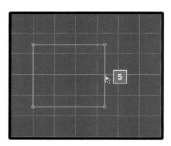

5. **Click any of the line segments in the shape and drag to reposition that line. Try to change the shape into a square.** Don't worry if you don't succeed in creating a perfect square. The point is for you to see that the White Arrow tool is used to select, reshape, and move individual line segments.

6. **Click the White Arrow tool in the toolbox and select the Black Arrow tool from the hidden menu.**

7. **Click anywhere inside the square and drag to move the whole shape to another location on the screen.**

   The Black Arrow tool is used for selecting and moving whole objects, rather than line segments like the White Arrow tool. More than one object can exist in the same path, such as the square and the line you drew in this path. To select multiple objects in a path, hold the Shift key while you click those objects.

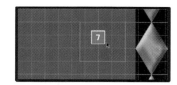

8. **Click the Pen tool and select the Add Anchor Point tool from the hidden menu.**

9. **Click the top line of the square to add a point to that line segment.**

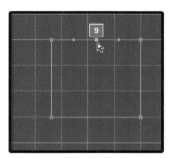

10. **Click the point that you added and drag to change the shape of the line segment on which the point is located.**

   The Add Anchor Point tool acts like the White Arrow tool when you click a point (enabling you to reshape a line segment just as you can with the White Arrow tool).

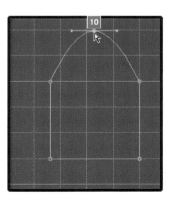

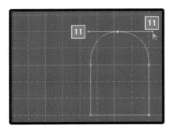

11. **Click each end of the direction lines on the point you added and drag to further change the shape of the line segment.**

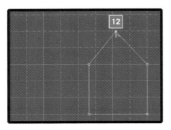

12. **Click the Add Anchor Point tool in the toolbox and choose the Convert Point tool from the hidden menu. Click the point that you added.**
    The Convert Point tool changes a curve from smooth to sharp.

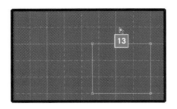

13. **Click the Convert Point tool in the toolbox and choose the Delete Point tool from the hidden menu.**
    Click the point you added to eliminate that point. The line segment returns to its original shape.

14. **Select the Black Arrow tool from the toolbox. Draw a marquee around all the shapes on the path and press the Delete key.**

15. **Choose File→Save As. Save the file as** 06_camera_edit.psd **(whether you used your own file or the fresh file provided for you for this tutorial). Leave the file open for the next tutorial.**

Tutorial

» Tracing a Path with the Freeform Pen Tool

You can use the path drawing and editing skills you learned in the preceding tutorials to create a vector graphic from scratch, or you can cut a few corners by tracing a path around an existing image. In this tutorial, you'll use the Freeform Pen tool, with its magnetic option activated, to trace around a photograph. A few tweaks with the path editing tools, and you'll have a crisp-edged vector shape that looks like it took you hours to draw.

1. **Make sure that** 06_camera_edit.psd **is open from the last tutorial or open the fresh file** 06_camera_magnet.psd **from the Session 6 Tutorial Files folder on your hard drive.**
   06_camera_magnet.psd is a copy of
   06_camera_edit.psd as it should look after the last tutorial. You can use either file.

2. **Choose View→Show→Grid to turn off the grid if it's still showing.**

3. **Click the camera path in the Paths palette to see a prebuilt version of the path that you'll be drawing in the image. Click in the blank area of the Paths palette when you're done looking at this path.**
   Notice that this path hugs the contours of the image. You could draw this path by hand, using all the methods that you learned in the preceding tutorials. But a faster way to trace a path like this is to use the Freeform Pen tool with its magnetic option turned on, as you'll do in the next steps.

4. **Select the Zoom tool from the toolbox and click in the document window to zoom in to 200%.**

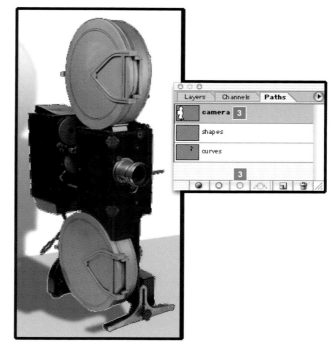

5. **Click whichever pen tool is showing in the toolbox and choose the Freeform Pen tool from the hidden menu.**

<TIP>
Another way to access the Freeform Pen tool, if the Pen tool is active, is from the Freeform Pen tool icon on the Options bar.

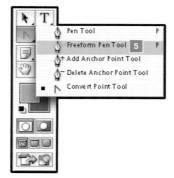

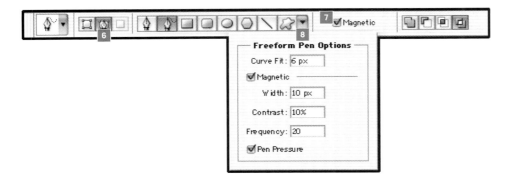

6. **Make sure that the Path button is selected in the Options bar.**
   This ensures that you are drawing a path, as opposed to a shape or a bitmapped graphic, which are the other two choices in this area of the Options bar.

7. **Put a check mark next to Magnetic in the Options bar.**
   This changes the Freeform Pen tool into a Pen tool with magnetic properties, so it creates a path that automatically finds and snaps to the edge of any image. You'll see how this works in the next steps.

8. **Click the arrow to the right of the Shape tool icons on the Options bar to display the Freeform Pen options. Leave these options at their defaults for now.**

Freeform Pen Options

If the Magnetic Pen doesn't work the way you'd like it to on a particular image, reopen the Freeform Pen Options menu and experiment with these options:

Curve Fit: This controls how closely the path fits the image you're tracing, within a range of 0.5 to 10 pixels. If you'd like a closer fit than you're getting, decrease this value. The result will be more points and a less smooth path. If you'd like a smoother path than you're getting, increase this value. The result will be less points and a less exact fit.

Width: This determines how many pixels the Magnetic Pen takes into account when it looks for the edge of an image, within a range of 1 to 256 pixels. Press the Caps Lock key on your keyboard to see a visual representation of this parameter. If you're working on an edge that has lots of turns and crevices, decrease this number. If you want more latitude to trace farther away from the edge when you're working on an larger, uncluttered edge, increase this number. You can change this parameter on-the-fly while you're drawing by clicking the left bracket key on your keyboard to decrease the width and the right bracket key to increase the width. If you're drawing with a stylus tablet, your pen pressure will affect Width if there's a check mark in the Pen Pressure box on this Options menu.

Contrast: Contrast is what the Magnetic Pen uses to find the edge of an image. If you're working on a low contrast image, increase this value, which ranges between 1 and 100 percent.

Frequency: This value, which ranges between 5 and 40, determines how often the Magnetic Pen sets a point as you move around the image. The lower the value, the more frequently the tool will lay down points. The more points in the path, the rougher the path will look.

9. **Click anywhere on the edge of the camera to begin the path. Move, but don't drag, your cursor around the edge of the camera.** As you move, you'll see a path form, snapping to the edge of the camera. Points will automatically appear on the path. If you don't like where Photoshop added a point, follow the instructions in the next step.

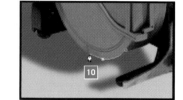

10. **Press the Delete or Backspace key on your keyboard and notice that the last point on the path disappears. You can delete more points if necessary. Then back up and continue forward again to redraw the path.**

11. **Click to add a point manually, if the Magnetic Pen doesn't add a point where you want it to.**

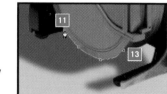

12. **If the path jumps away from the edge, press the left bracket key on your keyboard to decrease the width of the area the Magnetic Pen uses to locate an edge, as described in the sidebar "Freeform Pen Options."**

13. **Click the beginning point of the path, after you've gone all the way around the image, to close the path.**

14. **Clean up the path, using the techniques that you learned in the preceding tutorial.**
    Use the White Arrow tool to select points that are too far a field and tuck them into the edge. Use the Add Anchor Point tool to add and drag a point when necessary and the Delete Anchor Point tool to delete a point that's distorting part of the path.

15. **Double-click Work Path in the Paths palette to save your work path as a permanent path. Name the path** my camera **and click OK.**

16. **Choose File→Save As. Save the file as** 06_camera_magnet.psd **(whether you used your own file or the fresh file provided for you for this tutorial). Leave the file open for the next tutorial.**

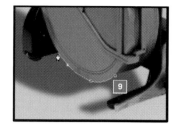

Tutorial
» Stroking and Filling a Path

You may have wondered what you can do with a path after you've created it. You can turn that path into a logo or other graphic by stroking its outline with color or filling it with color, a pattern, or an image from a previous history state. In this tutorial, you'll learn to stroke and fill a path.

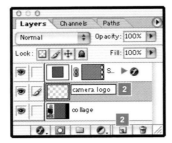

1. Use `06_camera_magnet.psd`, **which you saved from the last tutorial, or open the fresh file** `06_camera_fill.psd` **from the Session 6 Tutorial Files folder on your hard drive.**
   `06_camera_fill.psd` is a replica of `06_camera_magnet.psd` as it should look at the end of the last tutorial. You can use either file.

2. **Click the Create New Layer button at the bottom of the Layers palette, double-click Layer 1, and rename that layer** camera logo.
   This is where the fill and stroke that you create with the path outline will be located. The path itself remains independent of any particular layer. If you try to fill a path without first selecting a layer, you'll find the Fill command unavailable.

3. **Select a Brush tool and a small brush (try 3 pixels) from the Brush pop-up palette on the Options bar.**

4. **Click the Foreground Color box in the toolbox and choose an olive color from the Color Picker. (I chose R: 207, G: 143, B: 3.)**

5. **Make sure that the my camera path is selected in the Paths palette.**

6. **Click the arrow at the top right of the Paths palette and choose Fill Path.**
   This opens the Fill Path dialog box.

7. **Make sure that the Use field is set to Foreground Color, Blending Mode is set to Normal, Opacity is set to 100%, and Rendering is set to Anti-aliased. Click OK.**
   This fills the selected path with the foreground color.

<NOTE>
The Fill Path dialog box has several options, most of which are probably familiar to you from other contexts, like options for brushes and layers. Blending Mode determines how the fill pixels blend with colors on other layers. Opacity controls the density of the fill. You'll usually want to leave Anti-aliased checked to ensure that your fill has gradual rather than jaggedy edges. Increasing the Feather Radius blurs the fill on both sides of the path, creating a soft watercolor effect. (See the discussion of anti-aliasing and feathering in Session 7.) There's no need to check Preserve Transparency because there are no transparent areas in the camera image encompassed by the path. If there were, checking Preserve Transparency would keep those transparent areas from being filled. The Use field gives you the option to fill with various colors, a pattern, or imagery from a prior history state. Experiment with these fill options on your own.

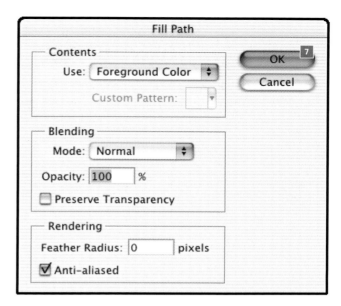

8. **Click off the my camera path in the Paths palette and turn the collage layer's eye icon off in the Layers palette so that you can get a better view of your filled path.**

<TIP>
You may want to separate and dock together your Layers and Paths palettes, as shown here, so that you can see them both. You learned how to do that in Session 2.

9. **Select the Brush tool in the toolbox. Select a brush in the Brushes palette. (I loaded the Natural Brushes brush set into the Brushes palette and selected a brush called Stipple 12 pixels. See Session 5 if you need to review how to use the Brushes palette.)**

10. **Click the Default Foreground and Background Color icons in the toolbox to set the foreground color to black.**

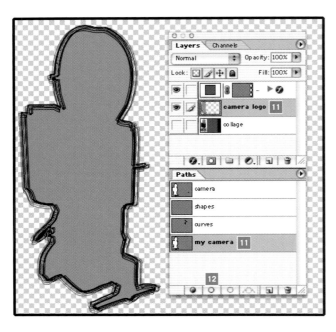

11. **Select the my camera path in the Paths palette and the camera logo layer in the Layers palette again.**

12. **Click the Stroke Path button at the bottom of the Paths palette.**

<NOTE>
Try stroking a path with a tool other than the Brush tool. Click the arrow on the top right of the Paths palette and choose Stroke Path from the menu. In the Stroke Path dialog box, choose Tools and try some of the options there. Try Dodge or Burn for some interesting effects.

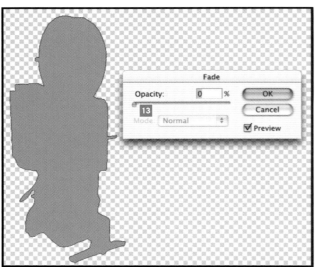

13. **Choose Edit→Fade Stroke Path, lower the Opacity in the Fade dialog box, and click OK to decrease the intensity of the stroke effect. Lower the Opacity all the way to 0 to eliminate the stroke.**

14. **Choose File→Save As. Save the file as** `06_camera_fill.psd` **(whether you used your own file or the fresh file provided for you for this tutorial). Leave the file open for the next tutorial.**

Tutorial
» Copying a Path between Documents

Now that you've created a vector graphic by tracing it from a source document, how do you get it into one of the collages that you're making for the final project? In this tutorial, you'll learn how simple it is to copy a path from one document to another.

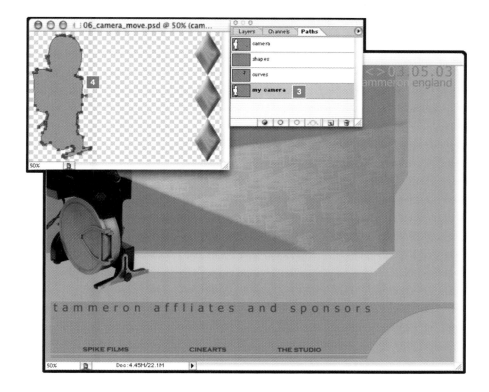

1. **Make sure that** `06_camera_fill.psd` **is open from the last tutorial or open the fresh file** `06_camera_move.psd` **from the Session 6 Tutorial Files folder on your hard drive.**
   `06_camera_move.psd` is a copy of `06_camera_fill.psd` as it should look if you completed the preceding tutorial. This is the source document for the path that you're about to copy.

2. **Open** `06_sponsors_move.psd` **from the Session 6 Tutorial Files on your hard drive. Alternatively, if you prefer to use your own file, open** `05_sponsors_end.psd` **that you saved from the last session and click the eye icons on the gradient light, reelblue, and logos layers to hide those layers.**
   This is the target document.

3. **Select the my camera path in the Paths palette in the source document.**

<**N O T E**>
The source and target documents are set to 50% in this figure so that you can see both.

4. **Select the Black Arrow tool in the toolbox and click the path around the camera in the source document.**

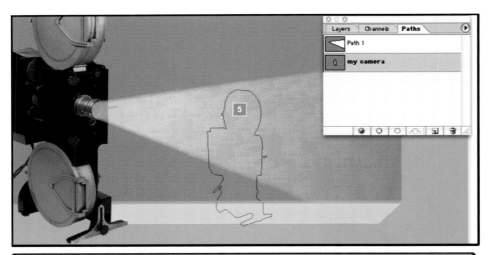

5. **Drag the path into the target document and release the mouse button.**
This pastes the my camera path into the Paths palette of the target document and drops the path outline in the middle of the target document. Notice that only the path, not its fill, was copied.

6. **Close the source document without saving.**

7. **Select the path in the target document and drag it to the lower-right corner.**

8. **Put a check mark next to Show Bounding Box in the Options bar.**

9. **Hold the Shift key to constrain the proportions of the path, click one of the corners of the bounding box, and drag to resize the path to match the figure.**
Resizing a path doesn't degrade the path.

10. **Select the accent box layer in the Layers palette. Click the Create New Layer button at the bottom of the palette. Double-click the new Layer 1, rename it** camera graphic**, and leave that layer selected.**

11. **Double-click the Foreground Color box and choose a dark olive-green color (try R:128, G:119, B:5) from the Color Picker. Click OK.**

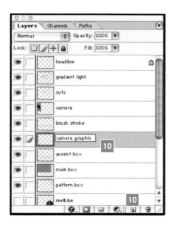

12. **Make sure that the my camera path is selected in the Paths palette of the target document and click the Fill Path button at the bottom of the Paths palette.**

13. **Click off the my camera layer in the Paths palette to see the results — a detailed, smooth-edged logo!**

14. **Choose File→Save As. Save the target document as** 06_sponsors_move.psd **(whether you used your own file or opened a fresh file in step 2). Leave the file open for the next tutorial.**

Tutorial
» Converting a Path to a Selection

In this tutorial, you'll draw a simple triangular path for a projector light. In order to fill this area with a gradient, you must convert the path to a selection, as you'll learn to do in this tutorial.

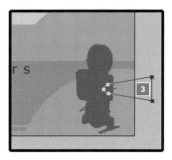

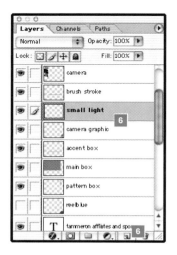

1. **Use** `06_sponsors_move.psd` **from the last tutorial or open the fresh file** `06_sponsors_select.psd` **from the Session 6 Tutorial Files folder on your hard drive.**
   `06_sponsors_select.psd` is a replica of `06_sponsors_move.psd` as it should look after the last tutorial.

2. **Select the Pen tool in the toolbox and click the Path icon on the left of the Options bar.**

3. **Draw a small triangular shape with a small curve on one end, in the shape of a projector light, as illustrated here. Close the shape.**
   This is easiest if you expand the canvas by clicking and dragging its bottom-right corner. You can draw into the canvas, as shown in the figure.

4. **Double-click Work Path in the Paths palette to save the path and name the path** light.

5. **Click the Load Path as Selection button on the bottom of the Paths palette.**
   You have to convert this path to a selection in order to fill it with a gradient because there is no direct way to fill a path with a gradient.

6. **Make sure that the camera graphic layer is selected in the Layers palette and click the Create New Layer button at the bottom of the palette. Name the new layer** small light.

7. **Select the Gradient tool in the toolbox. Create a lavender to light yellow gradient in the Gradient Editor. (If you need to review how to create a gradient, see Session 5.)**

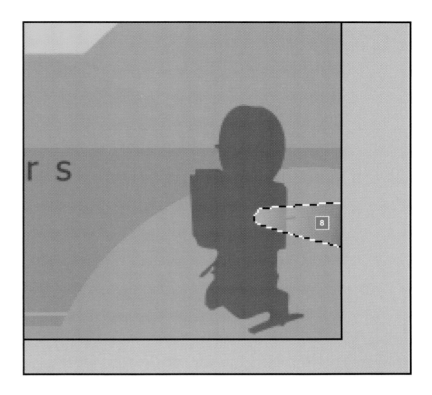

8. **Click and drag to fill the selection with the gradient.**

<NOTE>
You can go the other way and convert a selection to a path by clicking the Make Work Path from Selection button on the bottom of the Paths palette.

9. **Choose Select→Deselect from the menu bar at the top of the screen to deselect the filled area.**

10. **Choose File→Save As. Save the file as** `06_sponsors_select.psd` **(whether you used your own file or opened the fresh file provided for you). Leave the file open for the next tutorial.**

Tutorial

» Drawing a Geometric Shape with a Shape Tool

The last version of Photoshop introduced the Shape tools, which are a godsend for Photoshop users who prefer not to draw graphics from scratch. In this tutorial, you'll practice using one of the geometric Shape tools (which come in five flavors — Rectangle, Rounded Rectangle, Ellipse, Polygon, and Line).

1. **Open the fresh file** `06_sponsors_shape.psd` **from the Session 6 Tutorial Files folder on your hard drive, or you can use** `06_sponsors_select.psd` **that you saved from the last tutorial.**
   `06_sponsors_shape.psd` is a replica of `06_sponsors_select.psd` as it should look at the end of the last tutorial.

2. **Double-click the Foreground Color box to open the Color Picker and choose a light purple. (Don't worry too much about the color. You're going to change it in a minute.)**

3. **Click the Shape tool that is showing in your toolbox and choose the Ellipse tool from the hidden menu.**

4. **Click the Shape Layer icon on left side of the Options bar.**
   If you leave this control the way it was set in preceding tutorials, you'll end up drawing a work path rather than a shape on a shape layer.

5. **Click the down arrow to the right of the shape icons on the Options bar. Enter the diameter of the circle that you want to draw (585 pixels) in both the Width and Height fields.**

< TIP >

If you're drawing a circle from scratch, click Circle to constrain the ellipse to a circle. It's also helpful to click From Center in order to draw the circle from the center, rather than from one side.

6. **Select the topmost layer in the Layers palette.**
   This causes the shape layer that you're creating to be located just above the selected layer, so you can see it clearly for the purposes of this tutorial.

7. **Click in the document to create a circle shape.**

   If you hadn't chosen a fixed size, you would click and drag to create the circle shape.

8. **Select the White Arrow tool in the toolbox and click the thin vector outline around the circle. When you click that outline with the White Arrow tool, you'll see points. Click any of those points and drag to reshape the circle. When you're done, choose Edit→Step Backwards until your circle is restored. To hide the vector outline, click the vector mask thumbnail in the Layers palette.**

   Are you noticing similarities between the vector mask on a shape layer and paths? They are edited the same way because they are both vector shapes. The difference is that the vector shape on a shape layer is located on a mask.

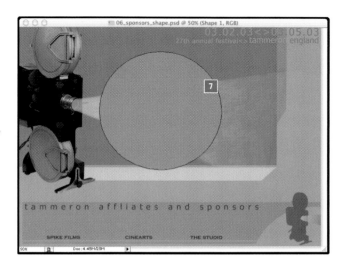

The Anatomy of a Shape Layer

Take a look at the new layer, labeled Shape 1, that was created in the Layers palette when you drew with the Shape tool. It has two thumbnails, representing the two components of a shape layer. The thumbnail on the left is a fill layer, which contains pixels of color. The thumbnail on the right is a vector mask, which contains a vector-based circle shape. That shape acts as a mask, hiding all the fill layer pixels outside of the white area of the mask. The link in between the thumbnails ties the fill layer to the vector mask layer. Clicking that line icon would unlink the two components of the shape layer.

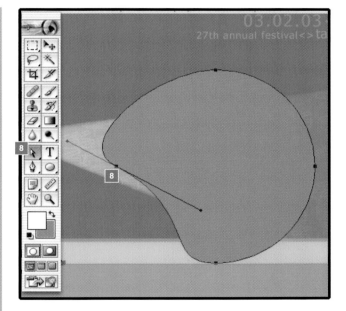

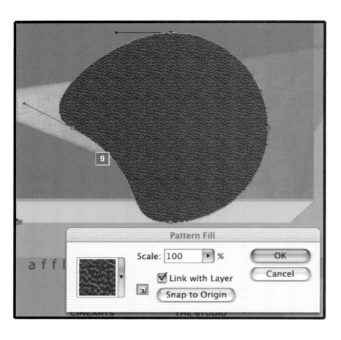

9. **Choose Layer→Change Layer Content→Pattern or Gradient to change the fill side of the shape layer from a solid color to a pattern or gradient. When you're done, choose Edit→Step Backwards until your circle is a solid color again.**

10. **Select a Shape tool in the toolbox. Click the Color field on the right of the Options bar to open the Color Picker. Choose bright gold (try R: 255, G: 204, B: 0).**
    This is how you change the color of a shape. It's an improvement over the method in the last version of Photoshop.

<NOTE>
Notice that the icon in the Style field contains a red slash. This means that no layer styles are applied to the shape you're drawing. You'll learn about layer styles in Session 10. For now, know that you can choose a layer style from the Options bar to draw a shape with a special effect. The gold diamonds on the right side of the source file that you used earlier in this session are shapes created with a satin layer style.

11. **Select the Move tool or the Black Arrow tool. (Either works to move a shape on a shape layer.) Drag the now gold circle to the lower-right side of the document window, aligning it with the edge of the curve on the purple bar. Position it so that only part of it is inside the image boundaries, as shown here.**

12. **Double-click the Shape 1 layer and name it** circle shape.

13. **Drag the circle shape layer to just above the sponsors box layer in the Layers palette so that the circle isn't obscuring other items in the image.**

14. **Choose File→Save As. Save the file as** 06_sponsors_shape.psd **(whether you used your own file or opened the fresh file provided for you). Leave the file open for the next tutorial.**

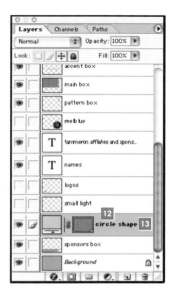

Tutorial

» Using Custom Shapes

Photoshop 7 ships with a whole slew of new custom shapes. These are exactly like the geometric Shape tools that you just mastered, except they are in the shape of icons, frames, and borders. They can be resized and modified as much as you like because they are vector-based.

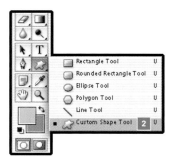

1. Use 06_sponsors_shape.psd, **which you saved from the last tutorial.**

2. **Select the Custom Shape tool from the hidden menu of Shape tools in the toolbox or from the Options bar.**

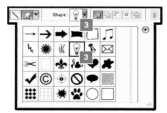

3. **Click the Shape sample down arrow to open the Custom Shape Picker. Click the light bulb icon to select it.**

4. **Click in the image and drag to draw this shape to approximately the size shown here.**
   You can make a custom shape as big or small as you'd like without harming it.

5. **Open the Custom Shape Picker again and click the arrow on its upper right. Choose All from the drop-down list and OK at the prompt.**
   This replaces the small default set of custom shape icons with all the custom shapes that come with Photoshop.

6. **Click the bottom-right corner of the Custom Shape Picker and drag to see all the Custom Shapes. Select single pedestrian.**

7. **Click and drag in the image to the size shown here.**

8. **Click the Add to Shape Area button in the Options bar.**
   If these shape combination buttons are grayed out, make sure that the proper shape layer is selected in the Layers palette.

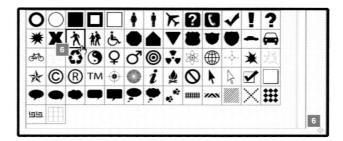

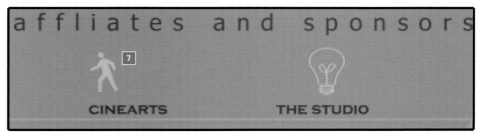

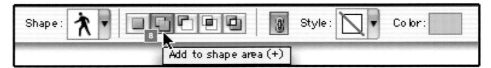

9. **Open the Custom Shape Picker again and select the two pedestrians. Click and drag in the image.**
   All three pedestrians are now located on the same shape layer. So if you were to change the nature or color of the fill, all would be affected.

10. **Click the Ellipse Shape tool on the Options bar. Click the arrow to the right of the Shape icons in the Options bar and change the Options so that there is no fixed size and Circle is checked. Click and drag a small circle in the image.**

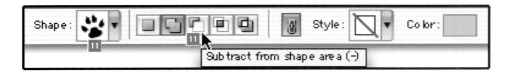

11. **Select the Custom Shape tool in the Options bar. Choose the dog print shape from the Custom Shape Picker. Click the Subtract from Shape Area button.**

12. **Click and drag on top of the small yellow circle to create a negative shape in that circle.**

13. **Choose File→Save As, name the image** `06_sponsors_end.psd`**, and save this image in your collages folder.**
    This is one of the final collages that you'll be including in the film program guide you're creating in this course.

» Session Review

This session covers how to work with vector-based objects in Photoshop. You learned to create and edit paths with the Pen tools, how to fill and stroke paths, and how to copy a path between documents. Then you learned all about Shape tools and shape layers, including the geometric Shape tools and the Custom Shape tool. These questions will help you review this session.

1. What is a path? (See "Tutorial: Drawing with the Pen Tool.")

2. What are vector graphics made up of? (See "Tutorial: Drawing with the Pen Tool.")

3. Can you resize a vector graphic without damaging its image quality? (See "Tutorial: Drawing with the Pen Tool.")

4. What is the tool to use to draw a vector graphic? (See "Tutorial: Drawing with the Pen Tool.")

5. Name three things that you can use as a fill for a path. (See "Tutorial: Drawing with the Pen Tool.")

6. How do you end a straight path? (See "Tutorial: Drawing with the Pen Tool.")

7. How do you end a closed path? (See "Tutorial: Drawing with the Pen Tool.")

8. Why is it important to convert a work path to a saved path? (See "Tutorial: Drawing with the Pen Tool.")

9. What does the Pen tool's Rubber Band option do? (See "Tutorial: Drawing with the Pen Tool.")

10. What are the functions of the White Arrow tool (officially the Direct Selection tool)? (See "Tutorial: Editing Paths.")

11. What are the functions of the Black Arrow tool (officially the Path Selection tool)? (See "Tutorial: Editing Paths.")

12. What does the Convert Point tool do? (See "Tutorial: Editing Paths.")

13. How do you make the Freeform Pen tool act like a magnetic tool? (See "Tutorial: Tracing a Path with the Freeform Pen Tool.")

14. When you're using the Freeform Pen tool with its magnetic options, do you click and drag to move around the image? If not, what do you do? (See "Tutorial: Tracing a Path with the Freeform Pen Tool.")

15. How do you convert a path to a selection? (See "Tutorial: Converting a Path to a Selection.")

16. Describe what the two thumbnails on a shape layer represent. (See "Tutorial: Drawing a Geometric Shape with a Shape Tool.")

17. Can you resize custom shapes? (See "Tutorial: Using Custom Shapes.")

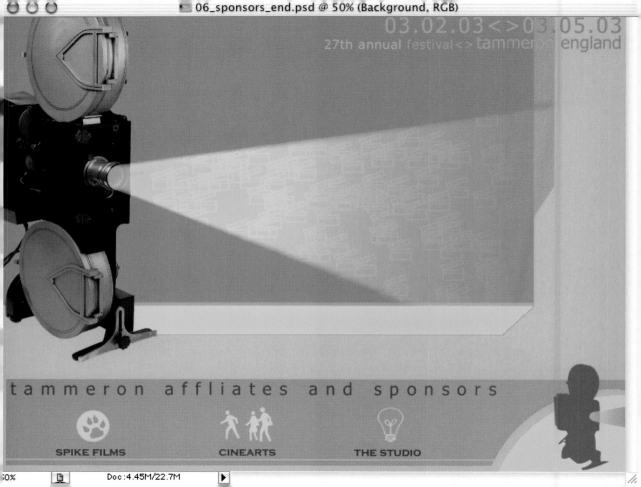

Part IV
Image Editing

tamme
03.02
27th

Session 7

Selecting

film festival tickets

ticket locations
ticket max
box office
web site

Session Introduction

Selecting is a prerequisite for almost all bitmapped editing tasks in Photoshop. You have to select pixels in an image in order to fill, move, copy, cut, transform, adjust, or otherwise edit those pixels. There are many different tools for selecting in Photoshop, including Marquee selection tools for making geometric selections, Lasso tools for drawing selections, the Magic Wand tool and the Color Range command for selecting by color, the Extract feature for selecting complex images such as hair or foliage, and the Quick Mask feature for cleaning up selections. This session teaches how to use these tools and offers ideas about which selection tool to use when. You'll also learn how to save and reuse a selection, how to make aliased, anti-aliased, and feathered selections, and how to move, copy, hide, invert, modify, and transform selections. There's a lot to learn, but it's all pretty straightforward, as you'll see in the tutorials that follow.

TOOLS YOU'LL USE
Marquee tools, Lasso tools, Quick Mask feature, Magic Wand tool, Color Range command, Extract feature, Select menu, anti-aliasing, feathering, and Transform commands

CD-ROM FILES NEEDED
07_tix.psd, 07_fox.psd, 07_tix_copy.psd, 07_tix_wand.psd, 07_tickets.psd, and 07_tix_end.psd

TIME REQUIRED
90 minutes

Tutorial
» Selecting Geometric Forms with the Marquee Tools

It's relatively simple to recolor, transform, adjust, style, or filter artwork that is isolated on its own layer, as you've learned elsewhere in this course. However, you'll frequently be confronted with an image in which pieces of artwork that you want to treat separately are located on the same layer. That's when you'll have to use one or more of Photoshop's selection techniques to isolate the areas you want to affect. When the areas to select are geometric forms, Photoshop's Marquee selection tools are the tools to reach for first. In this tutorial, you'll learn how to use the Rectangular and Elliptical Marquee tools.

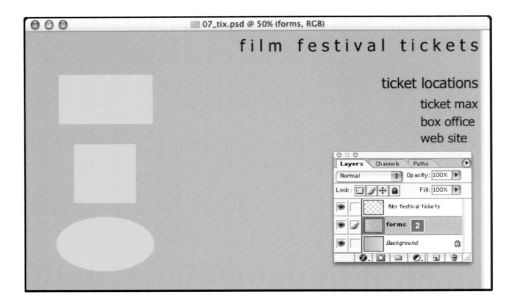

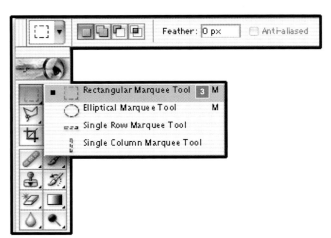

1. **Choose File→Open, navigate to** `07_tix.psd` **in the Session 7 Tutorial Files folder on your hard drive, and click Open.**
   Notice that this image contains geometric forms merged with a color fill on the forms layer. In the next steps, you'll learn how to select each of these forms with a Marquee selection tool.

2. **Make sure that the forms layer is selected in the Layers palette.**

3. **Select the Rectangular Marquee tool from the toolbox. If it's not showing, click whichever Marquee tool is displayed there and choose the Rectangular Marquee tool from the hidden menu.**
   Leave the settings in the Options bar at their defaults for now.

4. **Click the top-left corner of the yellow rectangular shape and drag a rectangular selection around that shape.**
   Your selection is defined by an animated boundary of marching ants.

5. **Fill the selected rectangle with your foreground color, using any of the fill methods that you learned back in Session 5.**
   Don't worry about how the fill looks because this rectangle won't be part of your final collage. Now that the rectangle is selected, you can do any number of things to it without affecting the rest of the Background layer. You can fill the shape, as you did here, or copy it, cut it out, move it, transform it, add a layer style to it, filter it, and more.

6. **Choose Select→Deselect from the menu bar at the top of the screen to eliminate your selection.**
   Remember to deselect whenever you finish an operation on a selected area. If you don't, your next operation will be limited to that area, or, in some cases, Photoshop will refuse to perform the next operation.

7. **Hold the Shift key, click a corner of the yellow square, and drag with the Rectangular Marquee tool.**
   This constrains your selection to a square.

<NOTE>
Holding the Shift key doesn't constrain a selection to a square if there is another selection in the image. In that case, holding the Shift key has another function. It adds the second selection to the first, just like the Add Selection combination button, which you'll learn about later in this session.

8. **Click the Rectangular Marquee tool and select the Elliptical Marquee tool from the hidden menu.**
   Leave the Options bar set to its defaults, as in this figure.

<NOTE>
Deselecting is something that you'll do frequently. So it's worth remembering two shortcuts for Deselect: The keyboard shortcut for deselecting is ⌘+D (Windows: Ctrl+D), and the physical shortcut for deselecting is to click anywhere else in the document (as long as none of the combined selection buttons, which you'll learn about in the next tutorial, are activated in the Options bar).

<NOTE>
If you change your mind after deselecting and want your last selection back, you can choose Select→Reselect. This restores the last selection that you made, even if you've made other kinds of edits to your image in the meantime.

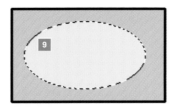

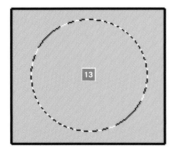

<NOTE>

If you find that drawing a circular selection with the aid of the modifier keys, as you did in step 13, seems to require an extra pair of hands, you may prefer setting the Style button in the Options bar to Fixed Aspect Ratio and entering the same number in both the Width and Height fields (try 1). This constrains the Elliptical Marquee to a circle, freeing you from holding the Shift key. You can still use the Option (Alt) key and the spacebar with this feature. This trick also works to constrain a rectangular marquee to a square.

<NOTE>

If you know the dimensions of the Rectangular or Elliptical selection that you need in either inches or pixels, set the Style button in the Options bar to Fixed Size and type the dimensions, followed by in or px, in the Width and Height fields. Don't forget to change Style back to Normal when you're done so that your next selection isn't constrained.

<NOTE>

There are two more marquee tools, the Single Row and Single Column Marquee tools. These draw horizontal or vertical lines one pixel wide, respectively. They are useful for drawing or cutting out thin rules for design interest. Try selecting the Single Column Marquee tool and clicking in the document window to the right of the shapes. Press Option+Delete (Alt+Delete) to fill the thin line with color. Press ⌘+D (Windows: Ctrl+D) to deselect.

<TIP>

If you find that you're often switching between the Rectangular and Elliptical Marquee tools as you work, you'll like this shortcut. With either of the two tools selected in the toolbox, press Shift+M to toggle to the other tool.

9. **Click any edge of the ellipse and drag. Part way through your drag, press the spacebar and reposition the selection to match the artwork. Release the spacebar and continue to drag. Repeat this several times to fit the selection to the form.**

This creates an elliptical selection, beginning with one edge of the ellipse. This method can require quite a bit of fine-tuning with the spacebar to match the selection to the artwork.

10. **Click outside of the selection to deselect.**

In the next step, you'll try a method that's similar, except that it draws from the center of the ellipse out, which you may find easier.

11. **Hold the Option (Windows: Alt) key, click in the center of the ellipse, and drag to create an elliptical selection from the center out. Part way through the drag, with the Option (Alt) key still held down, press the spacebar and reposition the selection to match the artwork.**

This method usually requires less fine-tuning than the last method.

12. **Click outside of the selection to deselect.**

In the next step, you'll draw a circular selection. You won't always be selecting an existing object when you draw a selection. Sometimes you'll draw a selection from scratch, as you'll practice doing in the next step.

13. **Hold the Option (Windows: Alt) key to draw from the center out and at the same time hold the Shift key to constrain your selection to a circle. Click and drag in the green area beneath the ellipse to draw a circular selection. Release the mouse button before you release the Option (Alt) and Shift keys.**

14. **Press Option+Delete (Windows: Alt+Delete) to fill the circular selection with the foreground color.**

15. **Choose File→Save and leave** 07_tix.psd **open for the next tutorial.**

<NOTE>

Use the Marquee tools when the selection you're making is a square, rectangle, ellipse, or circle — for example, when you're creating buttons for a Web page layout or making frames to set off photos. The Marquee tools also come in handy when the color-based selection tools, such as the Magic Wand or Color Range command, won't work due to lack of contrast between colors. You can start with a Marquee tool selection and then expand it to other parts of the image with the Grow command, which is covered later in this session.

Tutorial
» Moving and Copying Selections

In the last tutorial, you learned how to move a selection as you drew it. It's more common that you'll want to move a selection after you've drawn it, which is what you'll learn to do in this tutorial. You'll also learn the important difference between moving a selection outline and moving the contents of a selection.

1. **Use** 07_tix.psd, **which should still be open from the last tutorial.**

2. **Make sure that the forms layer is still selected in the Layers palette.**

3. **Select the Elliptical Marquee tool from the toolbox. If one of the other Marquee tools is showing, select it and click Shift+M to cycle through the Marquee tools to the Elliptical Marquee.**

4. **Use any of the techniques that you learned in the last tutorial to drag a selection around the circle in the document. Don't bother pressing the spacebar to move the selection into place as you draw.**

5. **Leave the Elliptical Marquee tool selected, click inside the selection, and drag to move the selection into position over the circle graphic.**

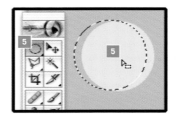

<NOTE>
The trick to moving a selection outline, rather than the contents of the selection, is to have one of the selection tools selected in the toolbox. Resist the temptation to use the Move tool for this purpose because it will move the contents of the selection, as you'll see in step 7.

6. **Press the arrow keys on your keyboard, with the Marquee tool still selected, to finish the job by nudging the selection into position one pixel at a time.**
   Hold the Shift key while pressing an arrow key to move the selection ten pixels at a time, when a selection tool is active.

7. **Select the Move tool in the toolbox. Click inside the selection and drag.**
   This causes the contents of the selection, the yellow circle, to move with the selection outline, leaving a hole in the fabric of the forms layer. (Your hole may not look as pronounced as the one shown here because you have a green layer underneath the forms layer.)

<TIP>
You can select the Move tool temporarily while another tool is active by clicking and holding the ⌘ key (Windows: Ctrl key).

8. **Choose Edit→Undo.**

<TIP>
If you want to move the yellow ellipse graphic without cutting a hole in the forms layer, you'll have to make a copy of the selected graphic. There are two ways to do this, and the first is only temporary:

● Hold the Option (Windows: Alt) key while dragging the selected graphic with the Move tool. This creates a temporary "floating" copy of the graphic that you'll be able to move without consequence until you deselect it. Then it will become part of the forms layer, and selecting and moving it again will cause a hole in the layer. If you're a Photoshop old-timer, you may remember floating selections like this from back in Photoshop 4.

● Choose Layer→New→Layer Via Copy, with the yellow ellipse selected. This creates a new layer above the forms layer that contains a copy of the selected graphic, which you can move as much as you want without damaging other layers.

<NOTE>
You can copy the content of a selection between images, as well as within an image. This is a skill that you'll use often as you build collages in Photoshop. You'll learn how to do this in the following steps.

9. **Click the eye icon on the forms layer to hide that layer for now, and select the forms layer.**
   You'll see the gradient background of the collage you're building in this session.

10. **Open a second image, 07_fox.psd, from the Session 7 Tutorial Files folder on your hard drive.**

11. **Make sure that 07_fox.psd is the active image and choose Select→All from the menu bar at the top of the screen.**
    A marching ants selection border surrounds the entire image.

<TIP>
The shortcut for Select→All is ⌘+A (Windows: Ctrl+A).

12. **Choose Edit→Copy from the menu bar at the top of the screen.**

13. **Click in** `07_tix.psd` **to make that the active image, make sure that the forms layer is selected, and choose Edit→Paste.**
This pastes the selection from `07_fox.psd` into `07_tix.psd` and creates a new layer for the pasted content above the selected layer.

<NOTE>
This technique would have worked the same way if the selection that you'd copied and pasted had been a portion of an image, rather than the entire image.

<NOTE>
Another way to copy a selection from one image to another is to click and drag the selection with the Move tool.

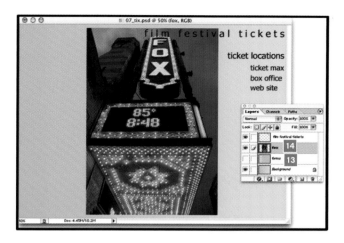

14. **Double-click the new layer in** `07_tix.psd` **and name it** fox.

15. **Select the Move tool in the Layers palette and click and drag the pasted content to the bottom-left corner of the document.**
By default, a selection is pasted into the center of the destination document, but you can move it wherever you like because it is automatically isolated on its own layer.

<TIP>
If you want a selected image to land somewhere other than the center of the destination document, make a selection elsewhere in the destination document and then choose Edit→Paste. The image will be centered on that selection, even if the selection is smaller than the image. Note that this is a different technique than the Paste Into technique discussed in the following sidebar.

16. **Click in** `07_fox.psd` **and choose Edit→Close.**

17. **Choose File→Save and leave** `07_tix.psd` **open if you want to use it in the next exercise. You'll have the option of starting the next tutorial with a fresh prebuilt file.**

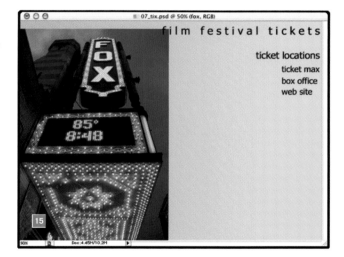

Pasting into a Selection

When you paste a copied selection into a document, you can paste into a space that's limited by another selection. This is a technique that's useful for creating vignetted images in a document.

To try it, select all or a portion of 07_fox.psd. Select the Rectangular Marquee tool and drag out a rectangular selection in your destination document 07_tix.psd. Choose Select→Feather and add about 20 pixels to blur the edges of the selection. Choose Edit→Paste Into. The image is pasted into a layer with a layer mask in the shape of your selection. Select the Move tool and move the image around in the selected area until you're satisfied with the part that's showing.

You can use a prebuilt shape instead of a feathered selection for another look. Select the Custom Shape tool in the toolbox. Click the Paths button on the left of the Options bar. Choose a custom shape from the Custom Shape Picker on the menu bar and click and drag in the image. Click the Load Path as Selection button at the bottom of the Paths palette. Choose Edit→Paste Into and position the image in the shape with the Move tool. When you're done, choose Edit→Step Backwards to delete these experiments from your collage.

Tutorial

» Using the Lasso Selection Tools

In this tutorial, you'll learn how to use the Lasso selection tools, including the freeform Lasso, the Polygonal Lasso, and the Magnetic Lasso.

1. **Make sure that** `07_tix.psd` **is open from the last tutorial or open the fresh file** `07_tix_copy.psd` **from your Session 7 Tutorial Files folder.**
   `07_tix_copy.psd` is a replica of the way `07_tix.psd` should look at the end of the last tutorial. You can use either file.

2. **Select the Lasso tool in the toolbox. If it isn't showing, click whichever Lasso tool is displayed and choose Lasso Tool from the hidden menu.**

3. **Click and drag a selection around the Fox sign in the image. Release the mouse button when you near the beginning of the selection.**
   Notice how difficult it is to draw a precise selection with the Lasso tool in its default mode, in which it acts like a freeform drawing tool. Notice also that as soon as you release your mouse button, the selection closes, which means that you can't release the mouse button until you've completed the selection. In step 5, you'll learn how to use the Lasso tool with the Option (Windows: Alt) key to address both of these problems.

4. **Press ⌘+D (Windows: Ctrl+D) to deselect.**

5. **Press and hold the Option (Windows: Alt) key. Click and drag with the Lasso tool around the top of the Fox sign in the image. When you get to a straight section of the sign, release the mouse button. Click again at the bottom of the straight section of the sign to create a straight segment of the selection. Then click and drag again. Repeat this until you get near the beginning of the selection. Release the mouse button and the Option (Alt) key to close the selection.**
   Holding the Option key as you used the Lasso tool enabled you to add straight lines to your selection and to release the mouse button during the selection without closing the selection. This works better than using the freeform Lasso tool, but an even easier way to do the same thing is to select with the Polygonal Lasso tool, as you'll do in the next steps.

6. **Press ⌘+D (Windows: Ctrl+D) to deselect.**

<TIP>
The Lasso tool isn't a great tool for making precise selections. You'll find it most useful for defining a rough area to limit the reach of other selection tools, such as the Magic Wand, that you can use in combination with the Lasso tool.

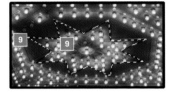

7. **Select the Polygonal Lasso tool from the toolbox. If it isn't show-ing, click whichever Lasso tool is displayed and choose Polygonal Lasso Tool from the hidden menu.**
This tool works just the opposite way from the Lasso tool. It defaults to drawing straight lines and enables you to draw freeform lines by pressing the Option (Windows: Alt) key, as you'll see in the next step.

8. **Click at the beginning of a straight section of the Fox sign. Release the mouse button (don't drag) and click again at the end of the straight section of the sign. Press and hold the Option (Windows: Alt) key and drag around the curved edge of the sign. Repeat this around the other side of the sign. When you're done, move your cursor over the beginning of the selection until you see a small circle. Then release the mouse button (and the Option key if you're holding it down) to close the selection.**

< T I P >
You'll probably find the Polygonal Lasso tool easier to use than the regular Lasso tool, particularly when your entire selection is made up of straight lines, as in the next step.

9. **Click with the Polygonal Lasso tool on one of the points in the star shape on the underside of the theater marquee. Click an inner corner to draw a straight line. Continue clicking around the star shape. Close the shape by clicking the beginning point of the selection when you see a small circle symbol.**

< T I P >
If you make a mistake while you're creating a selection with the Polygonal Lasso tool, press the Delete or Backspace key on your keyboard to remove the last segment of the polygon.

10. **Select the Zoom tool and click several times on the letter *X* in the Fox sign.**

11. **Select the Magnetic Lasso tool from the toolbox. If it isn't showing, click whichever Lasso tool is displayed and choose the Magnetic Lasso tool from the hidden menu.**

< N O T E >
The Magnetic Lasso tool works much the same way as the Freeform Pen tool with the Magnetic option, which was covered in detail in Session 6. Turn back to that session for information about the Width, [Edge] Contrast, and Frequency options, which apply equally to both tools. You'll find those settings on the Options bar for the Magnetic Lasso tool. You can change the Width setting as you're using the Magnetic Lasso tool to adjust how many pixels the Magnetic Lasso takes into account when it's looking for the edge of the image you're selecting. Click the left bracket key to decrease this number if you're working on an edge with tight turns and narrow crevices or if the selection you're making jumps away from the edge of the image you're selecting. Click the right bracket key if you're working on a larger, uncluttered edge. If the Magnetic Lasso tool is still not doing a good job of selecting, try increasing the Edge Contrast setting, which helps the tool find the edge of a low contrast image. You can also try increasing the contrast in your image temporarily by adding a brightness and contrast, curves, or levels adjustment layer.

12. **Click any edge of the letter *X* in the sign. Move, but don't drag, your cursor around the edge of the *X*.**

    The Magnetic Lasso tool draws a selection border for you, placing points along the way. All you have to do is move your cursor around the edge of the *X*, without dragging. Once in a while (for example, at the inner edges and corners of the *X*), you may have to click to set a point manually if the Magnetic Lasso tool skips a spot.

<NOTE>

If you don't like the selection the Magnetic Lasso tool is making, press the Delete key to eliminate the last point set by the Magnetic Lasso. Repeat this to delete more than one point if necessary. Move your cursor backward along the selection boundary and then move the cursor forward, without dragging, to continue the selection.

13. **Choose File➔Save As. Save the file as** `07_tix_copy.psd` **(whether you used your own file or the fresh file provided for you). Do not deselect. Leave this file open for the next tutorial, in which you'll use the Quick Mask feature to clean up this selection.**

Tutorial
» Refining a Selection in Quick Mask Mode

The Quick Mask is an invaluable feature for augmenting selection tools. You can use it to correct and refine any selection. As you can tell by its name, the Quick Mask is really a mask that represents a selection. You can edit the mask by painting with the Brush tools, adding to or subtracting from any areas that you missed with your selection tools. Then with the click of a button, you can convert the mask back to a selection.

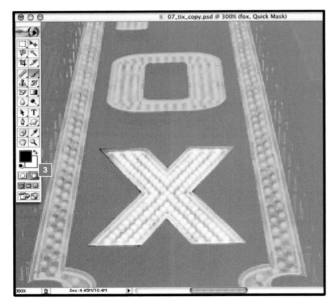

1. **Make sure that** `07_tix_copy.psd` **is open from the last tutorial and that there is a selection in the document. If for any reason there is not, repeat steps 10 through 13 of the preceding tutorial.**

2. **Zoom in to 300% magnification, if you have not already done so, so that you have a detailed view of the selection you made in the last tutorial.**
   Notice that the selection shown here doesn't reach all the way to the edges of the *X* in a few places. You'll fix that by painting in those areas in the Quick Mask in the following steps.

3. **Click the Quick Mask icon in the toolbox.**
   This puts the entire document into Quick Mask editing mode. The unselected portions of the document now appear covered with a semitransparent red (like the rubylith used in nondigital graphic design).

4. **Double-click the Quick Mask icon in the toolbox to open the Quick Mask Options dialog box. Change the Opacity to 70% to make the red mask less transparent so that there's more contrast between the mask and the selected image. Click OK.**

< N O T E >
If you're ever working with selected content that doesn't contrast sufficiently with the color of the mask for you to see the difference between them, you can change the color of the mask by clicking in the Color field in this Quick Mask Options dialog box. If you prefer having the colored mask cover the selected area of the image, rather than the unselected area, you can click the Selected Areas button.

5. **Select the Brush tool in the toolbox and choose a hard round small brush from the Brush pop-up palette on the left of the Options bar.**

6. **Click the Default Foreground and Background Colors icon at the bottom of the toolbox to set those colors to black and white, respectively. Then click the double-pointed Switch Foreground and Background Colors arrow to set the foreground color to white and the background color to black.**

It's important that you paint with black or white when working in Quick Mask mode in order to make pixels completely selected or deselected. Painting with a color results in partially selected pixels (such as the kind found in a gradual edge).

7. **Paint with white over all the areas in which the red mask infringes on the X, causing the mask to disappear from those areas.**

Use the Zoom tool to get in closer and the Hand tool to move the image around if necessary.

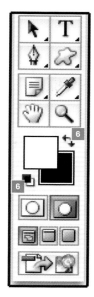

<TIP>

As you work in Quick Mask mode, you may have to reduce the brush size as low as 1 pixel to paint into corners and along edges. A shortcut for changing brush size on-the-fly is to click the left bracket key to reduce brush size and the right bracket key to increase brush size.

<NOTE>

If you make an error and paint too far into the red area, click the Switch Foreground and Background Colors arrow in the toolbox to change the foreground color to black and paint over your stray brush strokes, causing the red mask to reappear where you paint.

8. **Click the Standard Edit mode icon just to the left of the Quick Mask mode icon in the toolbox.**

This converts the mask (actually the inverse of the mask) back to a selection. The selection should now extend to all the corners and edges of the X. The following figure shows how clean the selection looks when filled with a gradient.

9. **Press ⌘+D (Windows: Ctrl+D) to deselect.**

10. **Leave the file open for the next tutorial.**

Tutorial
» Selecting by Color with the Magic Wand Tool and Color Range Command

The selection tools that you've used so far have selected based on shape and contrast. The Magic Wand tool and Color Range command are two selection methods based on the color of pixels. You'll learn how to use these features in this tutorial.

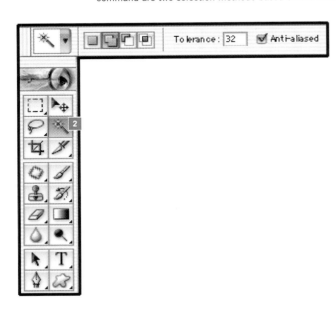

1. **Make sure that** `07_tix_copy.psd` **is still open from the preceding tutorial and that the fox layer is selected in the Layers palette.**

2. **Select the Magic Wand tool in the toolbox. Leave the settings in the Options bar at their defaults for now (Tolerance: 32, Anti-aliased checked, Contiguous checked, and Use All Layers unchecked).**

3. **Click the blue sky on the right side of the photograph to make your first selection.**
   It's unlikely that all neighboring pixels of sky will be selected, so in the next step you'll add to the selection.

Magic Wand Tool Options

When you click a pixel (or sample of pixels) with the Magic Wand tool, all pixels in the image that are similar in color to that pixel may be selected, depending on how you've set the following:

>> Checking Contiguous in the Options bar limits the resulting selection to pixels that touch one another. If you uncheck this option, the Magic Wand selects all pixels within the appointed range anywhere in the image.

>> The Tolerance setting in the Options bar determines the range of colors that are selected (based on brightness values in each of the RGB color channels). Higher Tolerance values result in a broader selection.

>> Checking Anti-aliased ensures that the selection has a soft edge. (You'll learn more about anti-aliasing later in this session.)

>> Leaving Use All Layers unchecked tells the Magic Wand to consider the color of pixels only in the selected layer.

>> The number of pixels the Magic Wand samples depends on the Sample Size selected in the Options bar for the Eyedropper tool. Point Sample (which means 1 pixel) is the default.

4. **Hold the Shift key and continue to click in different areas of the sky outside the metal sign supports, until all the sky outside the sign is selected.**
   If you select too much, use the Quick Mask to paint that area out of the selection, as you learned to do in the last tutorial.

<NOTE>
The Shift key enables you to make multiple selections, adding to the selected area. The selections don't have to be contiguous. You can get the same result by clicking the Add to Selection button on the Options bar. Adding selections together makes more sense than trying to select the whole sky by increasing the Tolerance settings because any Tolerance setting is unpredictable.

5. **Select the Lasso tool in the toolbox. Holding the Shift key, draw a rough selection around the black area at the bottom right of the photograph to add it to the selection. You can draw beyond the boundaries of the photograph because there is no content there on this layer.**
   It often makes sense to use other selection tools in combination with the Magic Wand to add areas that weren't selected or to subtract areas you don't want to include in the selection.

<NOTE>
At first glance, the Magic Wand looks like the easiest of the selection tools to use. However, this tool suffers from unpredictability. It's impossible to know with certainty what selection will result from any click of the Magic Wand.

<NOTE>
The Magic Wand works best when the area that you want to select differs in brightness from the surrounding areas.

6. **Choose Edit→Cut from the menu bar at the top of the screen.**
   This cuts all the selected content out of the fox layer.

7. **Select the Polygonal Lasso tool and draw a rough selection around the remaining area of sky on the left of the Fox sign. Double-click to close the selection. Click the Add to Selection button on the left side of the Options bar. Then draw a similar selection on the right.**
   These selections limit the area of the next Magic Wand selection. You may have tried to include these small inside areas of sky in your original selection and found that that caused other unwanted areas to be selected, too.

8. **Select the Magic Wand tool in the toolbox.**

9. **Uncheck Contiguous in the Options bar so that you can include the small isolated blue areas inside the sign supports in your next Magic Wand selection.**

10. **Click the Intersect with Selection button on the left side of the Options bar.**
    This button restricts combined selections to areas of selections that overlap. This stops a noncontiguous selection with the Magic Wand tool from spilling over the boundaries of your Polygonal Lasso selections. You'll see what I mean in the next step.

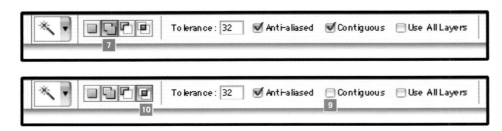

11. Click in the blue area of sky on either side of the sign.

This selects only the noncontiguous blue areas that are also surrounded by the Polygonal Lasso selections. Although the selection doesn't include every last bit of blue sky, it does a pretty good job.

12. Choose Edit→Cut.

The theater marquee is now free of sky and stands isolated against the gradient background on a lower layer.

<NOTE>

Another selection feature that selects by color values is the Color Range command, which you try out in the next steps.

13. Select the Polygonal Lasso tool in the toolbox and use it to draw a rough selection around the star shape under the marquee, as shown here.

This will isolate the effect of the Color Range command.

14. Choose Select→Color Range from the menu bar at the top of the screen.

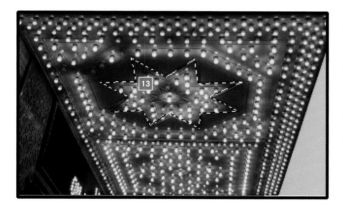

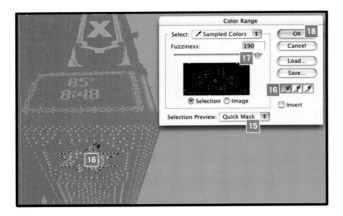

15. **In the Color Range dialog box, set Selection Preview to Quick Mask.**
    This lets you view the image through a mask, just like the Quick Mask feature you used earlier. The areas that you select with the Eyedropper tool will be clear. The unselected areas will be covered with a red mask.

16. **Click the Eyedropper tool in the Color Range dialog box and click one of the light bulbs inside the star selection in the masked image.**
    The selected area appears light inside the black mask in the dialog box.

17. **Click the Fuzziness slider in the Color Range dialog box and move it to the right.**
    As you do, the range of colors selected will become broader. You'll see a preview of which areas are selected in two places — in the black mask in the dialog box and in the document window.

<NOTE>

There are a number of useful options in the Color Range dialog box for you to try. The Select button gives you the choice of basing the selection on colors that you sample with the Eyedropper — predefined colors; shadows, midtones, or highlights; or even colors that are out of gamut for CMYK printing (so you can identify, select, and change those colors in advance of printing). The two other Eyedropper tools are for adding and removing colors from the sample on which the selection is based. The Selection Preview button gives you a choice of viewing the image as a quick mask, as a color image against a white background, as a color image against a black background, or in grayscale. You can also choose the kind of image that appears as a preview in the dialog box by toggling the radio buttons under that preview.

<NOTE>

The Fuzziness slider works similarly to the Magic Wand tool's Tolerance setting. Both determine a range of color values that will be selected. You'll find that you have more control over the outcome with the Color Range feature than with the Magic Wand because you can adjust and readjust the Fuzziness slider as you're selecting and because you can see a preview of the results.

18. **Click OK to close the Color Range dialog box and to make the selection.**

19. **Choose a foreground color (such as rose) with which to fill the selected light bulbs and press Option+Delete (Windows: Alt+Delete) to execute the fill.**

20. **Choose File→Save. Leave** 07_tix_copy.psd **open if you want to use it in the next tutorial. You'll have the option of starting that tutorial with a fresh file that is a replica of** 07_tix_copy.psd **as it should look now.**

Tutorial

» Modifying and Transforming Selections

After you've created a selection, you don't have to live with it as it is. In this tutorial, you'll learn how to reshape and modify a selection using commands in the Select menu, including Transform Selection, Grow, Expand, Contract, and Smooth.

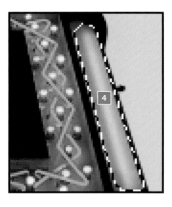

1. Use `07_tix_copy.psd`, **which you saved at the end of the preceding tutorial, or open the fresh file** `07_tix_wand.psd` **from the Session 7 Tutorial Files folder on your hard drive. Make sure that the fox layer is selected in the Layers palette.**

2. **Select the Magic Wand tool and set its options to Tolerance: 32, Anti-aliased, and Contiguous.**

3. **Click the purple light on the right side of the theater marquee, using the Magic Wand.**
   This partially selects the purple light.

4. **Choose Select→Grow several times, until the entire purple light is selected.**
   The Grow command selects neighboring pixels incrementally, based on the tolerance set for the Magic Wand tool.

<NOTE>
The Similar command in the Select menu is like the Grow command except that Similar selects pixels that are non-adjacent too. This is useful for selecting large areas that have variations on a color. If you want to try this command, open `07_fox.psd` again and make several small selections in the sky with the Rectangular Marquee tool. Then choose Select→Similar.

5. **Select the Polygonal Lasso tool from the toolbox and click around the polygon shape in the lights under the marquee, as shown here.**

6. **Choose Select→Modify→Expand, type** 15 **pixels, and watch the selection get larger.**

7. **Choose Select→Modify→Contract, type** 15 **pixels, and watch the selection get smaller.**

8. **Choose Select→Modify→Smooth, type** 20 **pixels, and watch the selection smooth out. Then choose Edit→Undo.**

9. **Choose Select→Modify→Border and type** 10 **as the width of the Border. Press Option+Delete (Windows: Alt+Delete) to fill the border with the foreground color.**

   The Border command creates a soft-edged selection. You'll learn how to hide the marching ants of a selection in the next step so that you can see that.

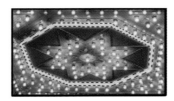

10. **Press ⌘+H (Windows: Ctrl+H) to hide the marching ants of this selection. Now you can see the soft edge of the border more clearly. Repeat this key command to make the marching ants visible again.**

    The marching ants that mark a selection often make it difficult to see the content of an image. It's very useful to be able to hide them, without dropping a selection.

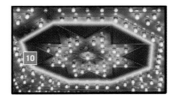

The trick when you hide a selection is remembering that there is a selection at all. If you don't remember that a hidden selection is active, you may be surprised that subsequent operations are limited to a particular area of your image. If something occurs in Photoshop that stumps you, press ⌘+H to see if there is a hidden selection at work.

11. **Choose File→Step Backward several times if you don't want to keep the border in your collage.**

12. **Select the Rectangular Marquee tool and draw a selection to encompass as much of the black box on the theater marquee as possible.**

13. **Choose Select→Transform Selection to display a bounding box around your selection. Ctrl+click (Windows: right-click) inside the bounding box to display a drop-down menu of transform commands. Choose Distort from that menu.**

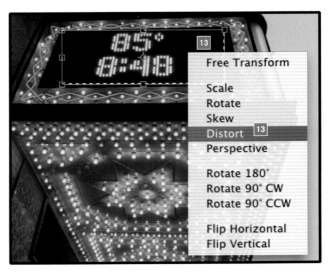

14. Click the points of the bounding box and pull them into position into the corners of the black box. Press Return or Enter to accept this transformation.

<NOTE>

To cancel a transformation, press the Esc key on your keyboard.

Do not confuse transforming a selection outline, which is the subject here, with transforming the contents of a layer (by using the Edit→Transform commands).

15. Choose File→Save As. Save the file as 07_tix_wand.psd (whether you used your own file or the fresh file provided for you). Leave the file open for the next tutorial.

Combining Selections

Another way to modify a selection is to combine multiple selections, which you've already done in preceding tutorials using a keyboard command (holding the Shift key to add to a selection) and using the combination buttons on the selection tools' Options bar. You've seen that one reason to combine selections is to limit the scope of a selection. Another is to resize or reshape a selection that isn't quite correct. For example, you may draw a selection that's too big. You can cut it down to size by choosing the Subtract from Selection combination button and drawing another selection that takes away part of the first selection. A more elaborate twist on that theme is the use of circular and rectangular selections in various combinations to build contoured shapes, such as Web navigation interfaces with rounded corners and cutouts.

Tutorial
» Creating Hard- and Soft-Edged Selections

Selections with hard jagged edges are called *aliased* selections. Selections with soft edges are either *anti-aliased* or *feathered* selections. In this tutorial, you'll practice making these different kinds of selections and learn what the differences are between them.

1. **Make sure that** `07_tix_wand.psd` **is still open from the last tutorial.**

2. **Select the forms layer and click its eye icon to make that layer visible in the document.**

3. **Select the Elliptical Marquee tool. Uncheck Anti-aliased in the Options bar. Click and drag an ellipse.**

4. **Click the Quick Mask button in the toolbox.**
   It's easiest to see the hard-edged and soft-edged nature of selections in Quick Mask editing mode. You can't really see the difference in an unfilled selection in Standard Editing mode.

5. **Select the Zoom tool and zoom in until you can see the jagged edge of the aliased selection that you drew.**

6. **Click the Standard Editing mode button in the toolbox.**
   In the next steps, you'll create an anti-aliased selection for comparison.

7. **Make sure that the Elliptical Marquee tool is still selected. Check Anti-aliased in the Elliptical Marquee tool's Options bar.**

8. **Click and drag an elliptical selection in the document.**

9. **Zoom in to see the relatively smooth edge of the anti-aliased selection (the selection on the bottom of the figure), as compared to the aliased selection (at the top of the figure).**
   Notice that there are partially selected pixels among the edge pixels of the anti-aliased selection. These pixels cause the edge to appear relatively smooth.

<N O T E>

An aliased selection is one with a jagged stair-stepped edge necessary to simulate a curved edge with rectangular pixels.

<W A R N I N G>

After you've drawn a selection with an aliased edge, there's no way to convert it into an anti-aliased selection.

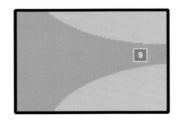

10. **Click the Standard Editing mode button in the toolbox and zoom back out to 50% magnification.**
In the next few steps, you'll make another sort of soft-edged selection — a feathered edge.

11. **Make sure that the Elliptical Marquee tool is still selected in the toolbox.**

12. **Type 7 in the Feather field in the Options bar.**

13. **Click and drag in the document to create a feathered selection.**

14. **Click the Quick Mask button in the toolbox and notice the difference between the blurry edge of the feathered selection at the bottom of the figure and the edge of the anti-aliased selection at the top of the figure.**

15. **Zoom in to the edge of this selection. If you look closely, you'll see that the blur goes both in and out from the edge of the selection.**

16. **Zoom back out to 50%. Click the Standard Editing mode button to exit Quick Mask mode.**

<NOTE>
Feathering creates a smooth-edged selection by blurring both the inside and outside of the edge of a selection.

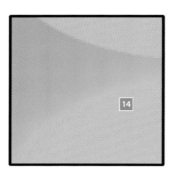

<NOTE>
Anti-aliasing is the gradual softening of an edge between a foreground and background element, achieved by the partial selection of some pixels along that edge. When you color a selection that has an anti-aliased edge, some pixels are only partially filled with color, which gives the illusion of a smooth edge. Anti-aliasing is the default behavior of all the selection tools, except the Rectangular Marquee tools and the One Pixel Vertical and Horizontal tools, which don't need anti-aliasing because they don't draw curved selections. You'll find an Anti-aliased option, which is checked by default, on the Lasso selection tools, the Magic Wand, and the Elliptical Marquee tool.

17. **Leave this file open for the next tutorial.**

<NOTE>
There are two ways to feather a selection. Enter a value between 1 and 250 (usually a low number is all you need) in the Feather field in the Options bar before drawing with a selection tool; or draw a selection, choose Select→Feather, and enter a value in the Feather Radius field of the dialog box and click OK.

Using Feathering to Vignette an Image

A classic effect that you can achieve with feathering is a vignette (which was often done in the old days with portraits). You can feather a selection to paste into, as you did in an earlier tutorial in this session, or you can feather the selected content. To do the latter, select the Elliptical Marquee tool and type a value (try 10) into the Options bar. Select the fox layer. Click and drag an ellipse over a portion of the photograph in the document. Choose Edit→ Copy and Edit→Paste. Select the Move tool and drag the copy to the right side of the document. That's all there is to creating a feathered vignette.

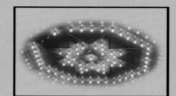

Tutorial

» Saving and Loading Selections as Alpha Channels

After you've gone to all the trouble of making a selection that you may use again, it makes sense to save it, rather than have to select it all over again. In Photoshop, you can save any selection as an alpha channel mask, which contributes little to file size and becomes a permanent component of the image. In this tutorial, you'll learn how to save a selection as an alpha mask and how to load it to use it again.

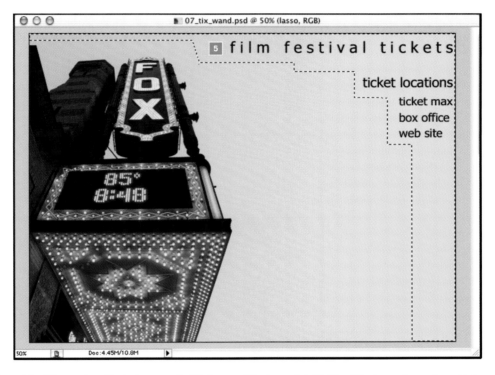

1. Make sure that `07_tix_wand.psd` is still open from the last tutorial.

2. Click the forms layer in the Layers palette and drag it to the Trash icon at the bottom of the Layers palette. Repeat this for Layer 1, which was created if you worked through the vignetting sidebar in the preceding tutorial.

3. Select the Polygonal Lasso tool in the toolbox. Make sure that Feathering is set to 0 and Anti-aliased is checked in the Options bar.

4. Drag the document window out so that it's larger than the image.

5. Click around the top and right side of the image to create a selection similar to the one shown here. (Yours doesn't have to match exactly.) Click the beginning point to close the selection.
   It will be easier to draw this selection to the edges of the document if you click outside of the document boundaries.

6. Select the Eyedropper tool in the toolbox and sample the yellow on the right side of the document.

7. Select the fox layer in the Layers palette, click the Create New Layer button, and make sure that the new layer is selected.

8. Press Option+Delete (Windows: Alt+Delete) to fill with the foreground color.

9. Choose Select→Save Selection.

10. **In the Save Selection dialog box, make sure that Channel is set to New and type** menubar **in the Name field. Click OK.**

11. **Click the Channels tab in the same palette group as the Layers palette.**
    You'll see your selection saved there as a mask in a channel. The channel, known as an *alpha channel,* is a grayscale image. It is just another way, other than marching ants, of visually representing a selection.

12. **Click in the Visibility box to the left of the menubar channel to make the mask visible in the document.**
    Notice that this mask looks just like the Quick Mask that you used to modify a selection in an earlier tutorial. The difference between this alpha channel mask and a Quick Mask is just that this one isn't temporary.

13. **Turn off the Visibility icon on the menubar channel to return to the normal view of the image.**

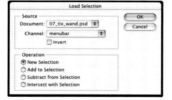

< N O T E >
To reuse this alpha channel mask as a selection, choose Select→ Load Selection from the menu at the top of the screen. In the Load Selection dialog box, choose the menubar channel by name and click OK. You'll find that each separate layer in a document has a separate listing in the menu as a transparency, making it easy to load a selection in the shape of all the artwork in any layer. You can fill or otherwise use that selection on any layer in the document because an alpha channel isn't tied to a particular layer.

14. **Choose File→Save and keep this file open for the next tutorial.**

Tutorial
» Using the Extract Feature

The Extract feature is useful for separating a foreground object from a background. It does a pretty good job of detecting other-wise hard-to-select wispy edges, such as hair, tree branches, and fibers, as long as there's lots of contrast between the foreground object and the background. In this tutorial, you'll learn how to use the Extract tool to separate an object from its background for use in your collage.

1. **Open** 07_tickets.psd **from the Session 7 Tutorial Files folder on your hard drive.**

2. **Choose Filter→Extract from the menu bar at the top of the page.**

3. **Select the Highlighter tool from the left side of the Extract dialog box.**

4. **Set the Brush Size on the right side of the dialog box to around 24.**
   The brush should be just big enough to cover the edge between the tickets and their background. Use a slightly big-ger brush when you come to the fibrous area at the top of the tickets by pressing the right bracket key on your keyboard to increase the size of the brush tip on-the-fly.

5. **Drag the highlighter around the tickets, making sure that the brush tip covers the edge of the tickets as you drag.**
   You can hold the Shift key and click from point to point on the straight edges if you prefer. Or try checking the Smart Highlighting box on the right side of the dialog box for help in finding the edges of the foreground item. Be sure to include the boundary of the document at the bottom of the image.

6. **Select the Paint Bucket tool from the left side of the dialog box and click inside the highlighted boundaries of the tickets.**
   If the paint runs out past the boundary of the highlighter, there's a hole in the boundary. Reselect the highlighter, fix the hole, and fill again.

7. **Click the Preview button at the top right of the dialog box.**

8. **Select the Cleanup tool from the top left of the dialog box. Hold the Option key (Windows: Alt key) and drag over areas in the tickets in which there are holes.**
   This restores any holes in the image caused by the extraction. If you restore part of the background by mistake, release the Option key and drag over that area with this same tool to delete the mistake.

9. **Select the Edge Touchup tool from the top left of the dialog box and drag along the edges of the tickets to sharpen those edges.**

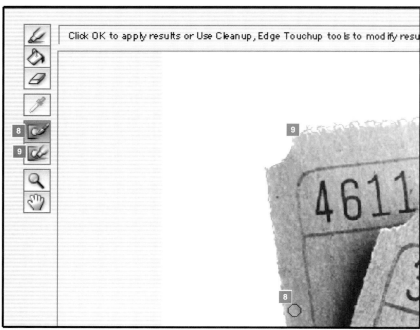

10. **Click OK in the Extract dialog box to perform the extraction of the tickets from the background. The result should look like what's shown here.**

    The Extract tool affects the original image. (So if you didn't have a clean copy of the image on the CD-ROM, it would have been a good idea to make a copy of the image before you started extracting.)

11. **Select the Move tool and drag the tickets into place in the open collage,** `07_tix_wand.psd`. **Name the new layer** tix **and move it above the menubar layer.**

12. **Make sure that the tix layer is selected in the Layers palette. Click the button on the top left of the Layers palette to see a menu of blending modes. Choose Luminosity.**

    This colorizes the grayscale tickets, using the yellow from the Background layer below.

13. **Choose File→Save As and name the image** `07_tix_end.psd`. **Save it in your collages folder for inclusion in your final project.**

    Now that you know all about selecting, you're ready for one of the most important sessions in the book, Session 8.

» Session Review

This session covers the many different selecting tools, options, and commands that you can use to select an area in an image.

1. Name any three things that you may want to do to an item in a document for which selecting is a prerequisite. (See "Tutorial: Selecting Geometric Forms with the Marquee Tools.")

2. How do you constrain a rectangular selection to a square? (See "Tutorial: Selecting Geometric Forms with the Marquee Tools.")

3. What do you press on your keyboard to reposition a selection while you're creating that selection? (See "Tutorial: Selecting Geometric Forms with the Marquee Tools.")

4. What kind of tool must be selected when you move a selection outline? (See "Tutorial: Moving and Copying Selections.")

5. How do you draw a selection with the Magnetic Lasso tool? (See "Tutorial: Using the Lasso Selection Tools.")

6. How do you enter Quick Mask Mode? (See "Tutorial: Refining a Selection in Quick Mask Mode.")

7. What colors should you paint with when you're working in Quick Mask Mode? (See "Tutorial: Refining a Selection in Quick Mask Mode.")

8. What does checking Contiguous do in the Magic Wand Options bar? (See "Tutorial: Selecting by Color with the Magic Wand Tool and Color Range Command.")

9. What does the Tolerance setting do in the Magic Wand Options bar? (See "Tutorial: Selecting by Color with the Magic Wand Tool and Color Range Command.")

10. Is transforming a selection the same thing as transforming layered artwork? (See "Tutorial: Modifying and Transforming Selections.")

11. What is an aliased selection? (See "Tutorial: Creating Hard- and Soft-Edged Selections.")

12. What is an anti-aliased selection? (See "Tutorial: Creating Hard- and Soft-Edged Selections.")

13. What is feathered selection? (See "Tutorial: Creating Hard- and Soft-Edged Selections.")

14. What is an alpha channel used for? (See "Tutorial: Saving and Loading Selections as Alpha Channels.")

Session 8

Using Layers

f i l m

f e s t i v a l

tammeron england
03.02.03<>03.05.03

27th annual festival
2003

Tutorial: **Creating Layers**

Tutorial: **Converting a Background Layer**

Tutorial: **Selecting Layers**

Tutorial: **Changing Layer Visibility**

Tutorial: **Locking Layer Properties**

Tutorial: **Changing Layer Opacity**

Tutorial: **Linking Layers**

Tutorial: **Organizing Layers in Layer Sets**

Tutorial: **Editing with Adjustment Layers**

Tutorial: **Using Fill Layers**

Session Introduction

I remember using Photoshop back in version 2.5, when layers were just a gleam in Adobe's eye. Now, if I had to pick one feature in Photoshop that I couldn't live without, it would be layers. Layers have revolutionized the way that images are edited because they enable you to work on one piece of artwork without affecting the rest of the image. After you've isolated artwork, it's easy to move, color, transform, filter, adjust, or apply effects to that item alone. In this session, you'll learn different ways to create layers. You'll practice working with the Layers palette — stacking, duplicating, deleting, locking, linking, and merging layers. You'll find out about layer visibility and how to move and transform the content of layers. You'll explore layer sets and learn how to use adjustment layers and fill layers. If you're a Photoshop novice, this session is a must-read because it covers the all-important layers basics. If you're more advanced, you'll find some tips in this session that will help you use layers more productively than you may have been doing.

Your exploration of layers doesn't end here. In Session 9, you'll explore more advanced layers features, including layer blending, layer masks, and vector masks. And you'll find out about layer styles and other features that breathe life into the content of layers in Session 10.

TOOLS YOU'LL USE
Layers palette, Layer sets, Auto Select Layer option, adjustment layers, and fill layers

CD-ROM FILES NEEDED
08_fest.psd, 08_fest_create.psd, 08_fest_eyes.psd, 08_fest_opacity.psd, 08_fest_links.psd, 08_fest_sets.psd, 08_logo.psd, and 08_fest_end.psd

TIME REQUIRED
60 minutes

Tutorial
» Creating Layers

There's more than one way to create a layer. In this session, you'll work through three ways to make a layer — from scratch, from a selection in another layer, and from another document. You've already seen some of the commands that you'll work with here in preceding tutorials, but this is where you'll pull it all together, along with details about each command and feature and a straightforward explanation of what layers are.

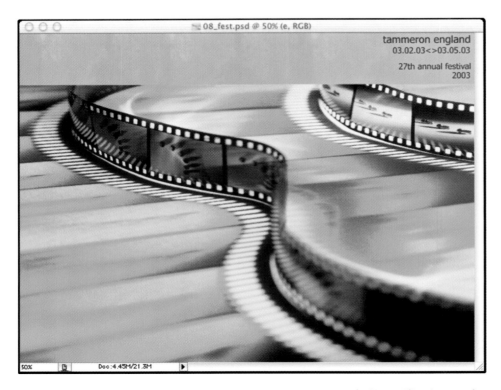

1. **Choose File→Open, navigate to** 08_fest.psd **in the Session 8 tutorial files on your hard drive, and click Open.**

2. **Choose Window→Show Layers to open the Layers palette if it isn't already open on your desktop. Click and drag the scroll bar to see all the prebuilt layers in this document.**

3. **Click the top layer in the Layers palette (labeled** *tammeron england*) **to select that layer.**
   This ensures that the layer you're about to create will be located above the tammeron england layer. When a new layer is created, it's always placed directly above the selected layer. Layer stacking order is important because it determines which artwork will be visible and which will be hidden behind other artwork.

What Are Layers?

Layers are individual images on transparent backgrounds stacked on top of one another. The analogy I like to use is that a document with layers is like a stack of sheets of glass. Imagine that each sheet in the stack starts out perfectly clear and that you add solid or partially transparent artwork to each sheet as you work.
If you looked down through the stack from above, you'd be able to see through to the sheets below wherever there was a clear or partially transparent area, but not where there was solid artwork. The same is true of a document with layers. Each layer starts out

as transparent pixels. You add solid and partially transparent pixels of artwork to individual layers. When you view the image on a computer screen, artwork on the top layers obscures lower layers. Where there is no artwork, you can see through to lower layers.

The beauty of using layers is that the artwork on each layer is isolated so that it can be edited, moved, styled, and adjusted independently of the content of other layers.

4. **Click the New Layer button at the bottom of the Layers palette.**
   This creates a new layer called *Layer 1*. That's how easy it is to make a new layer from scratch.

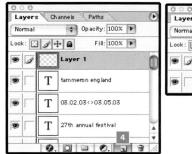
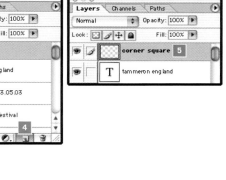

<NOTE>

The New Layer button creates an empty layer with default options (100% opacity and Normal blending mode). You can change these defaults to suit the content of the layer later. If you know which settings you want ahead of time (for example, if you're producing a series of similar images), you may prefer setting those options when you create the layer. Choose Layer➔New➔Layer to open the New Layer dialog box. Set your layer options, type a layer name there, and click OK to create a layer.

5. **Double-click directly on the Layer 1 name so that you can rename the layer. Type** corner square **as the new layer name and press Return (Windows: Enter) on your keyboard.**
   You have to click right on the layer name. Clicking anywhere else on the layer opens the Layer Style dialog box.

<TIP>

It's important to give your layers meaningful names so that you can identify them as you work. Don't put this step off; you'll regret it later.

<NOTE>

Adobe restored the double-click method of renaming layers in Photoshop 7, which is the way it always had been done until the last version of Photoshop. In Photoshop 6, you had to hold the Option (Windows: Alt) key while double-clicking. It's a relief to have the plain old double-click back again.

6. **Select the Rectangular Marquee tool in the toolbox. Click the Style button in the Options bar and choose Fixed Size from the menu. Type** 170 **in both the Width and Height fields of the Options bar.**

7. **Click inside the document window to create a square selection and drag the selection into position at the top-left corner of the image.**

Layer Transparency and Clipping Paths

You won't see anything in your document when you create a new blank layer because layers are transparent unless and until you fill them with content. If you look closely at the thumbnail on the layer that you created in the Layers palette, you'll see the telltale gray-and-white checkerboard that indicates transparency. Click the eye icons on all the layers to make those layers temporarily invisible, and you'll see the checkerboard in the document. Unfortunately, Photoshop transparency isn't recognized by object-oriented page layout programs and drawing programs, such as QuarkXPress, InDesign, Illustrator, or Freehand. If you import an image that has a transparent area in Photoshop into any of those programs, that area will be filled with a color. If you want to retain transparency so that the background of the document you're preparing in your page layout or illustration program shows through, add a clipping path to the artwork in Photoshop. This is most likely to come up if you want your artwork to appear nonrectangular. The alternative is to fill the background with pixels in Photoshop and bring the artwork into the object-oriented program as a rectangular, bitmapped image.

To practice adding a clipping path to an object, open 08_logo.psd from the Session 8 Tutorial Files folder. Choose Select→Load Selection. Click the Make Work Path from Selection button at the bottom of the Paths palette. (Turn back to Session 6 if you need a refresher on paths.) Double-click your work path in the Paths palette and click OK to save it as a path. Click the arrow at the top right of the Paths palette and choose Clipping Path. Leave the Flatness value blank for now and click OK. (Flatness determines the shape of the polygon that is used to approximate the curved image when printing. Ask your printer what value he recommends.) To import the document to a page layout or illustration program with the clipping path intact, you would save it as a Photoshop EPS file. For the purposes of this tutorial, just close the document without saving.

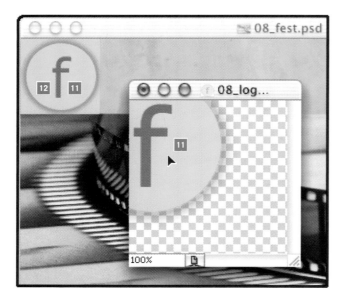

8. **Choose a yellow color (R: 246, G: 224, B: 56) in the Color palette. (If that palette isn't showing, choose Window→Color.)**

9. **Make sure that the corner square layer is selected in the Layers palette. If it's not, click that layer to select it. Press Option+Delete (Windows: Alt+Delete) to fill the square selection with yellow.**
   The gray highlight in a layer in the Layers palette indicates that that layer is selected as the active layer. When a layer is selected, almost any editing operation that you do will affect only that layer. Your yellow square is now isolated on the corner square layer. Any changes that you may make to it would not affect the artwork on other layers.

10. **Choose File→Open, navigate to 08_logo.psd in the Session 8 Tutorial Files folder, and click Open.**
    This source document contains artwork on a single transparent layer, the circle layer. If there were more than one layer in this document, you'd have to select the circle layer in the Layers palette before the next step.

11. **Select the Move tool in the toolbox. Click in the document window of the source document 08_logo.psd, drag to the document window of the destination document 08_fest.psd, and release the mouse button.**
    Alternatively, you can click the layer that you want to move in the Layers palette of the source document and drag to the document window of the destination document.

12. **Drag the logo into position on top of the yellow square.**

Layers and File Size

Each layer that you add to a document increases the file size of the document. This is true even of new transparent layers that have no artwork on them. Although the ability to isolate pieces of artwork on separate layers is invaluable, it has its price in file size. Too many layers can make editing sluggish, slow down printing, and require lots of storage space. What can you do about this? Merge layers together when you're done working on them. (Click the arrow on the top right of the Layers palette and choose Merge Down to merge a selected layer into the layer directly beneath it, or Merge Visible to merge all the visible layers into the bottom-most layer. You can also merge layers that are linked or layers you've put in a layer set.) Even better, juice up your computer with more RAM to increase performance while you're working and with a bigger hard drive for more storage space.

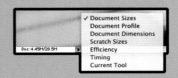

If you're curious about how much multiple layers add to file size, click the arrow at the bottom of the document window and choose Document Sizes from the pop-up menu. The number on the right (28.5 megabytes in the figure) is the size of the file with all its layers. The number on the left (4.45 megabytes) is an estimate of the size the file would be if all the layers were flattened into one.

13. **Take a look at the Layers palette and notice that there's a new layer, named circle, just above the corner square layer. The new layer was created automatically when you dragged content from the source document to the destination document.**

Where did the layer name *circle* come from? Photoshop was smart enough to take the new layer's name from the corresponding layer in the source document.

<NOTE>
Another source for a new layer can be an existing layer in the same document. In the next steps, you'll learn how to duplicate an entire layer and how to select and copy part of a layer.

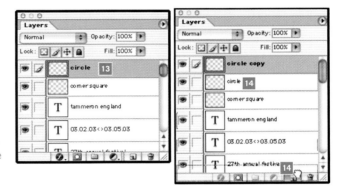

14. **Click the circle layer and drag it to the New Layer icon at the bottom of the Layers palette.**

This creates a new layer, called circle copy, which is a duplicate of the circle layer. You can't see both layers in the document window because the duplicate is located right on top of the original. Click and drag with the Move tool to view the duplicate.

15. **Click the circle copy layer in the Layers palette and drag it to the Trash icon at the bottom of the Layers palette to delete that layer.**

The Layer palette Trash can't be opened to retrieve deleted files like the regular Macintosh Trash or Windows Recycle Bin. After you've dragged a layer to the Trash in the Layers palette, the only way to get it back is with Edit→Undo or the History palette.

16. **Select the Polygonal Lasso tool in the toolbox and click repeatedly around the edge one of the film frames in the image to select that frame. Click the first point to close the selection.**

<TIP>
Duplicating a layer comes in handy when you're making similar-looking buttons for a Web site, as you'll do in Session 16. It's also useful for creating different pieces of text that have the same style. You can duplicate a text layer, select the duplicate text with the Type tool, and type different words that will have the same style as the source layer.

<TIP>
There's another way to make a duplicate layer that offers an additional useful option. Select the film layer in the Layers palette. Click the arrow at the top right of the Layers palette and choose Duplicate Layer. If you just clicked OK, you would get a duplicate layer in the same document, as you did in step 14. However, if you click Document and choose New, you'll get a separate document with a copy of the selected film layer. This would come in handy if you wanted to use this same layer to experiment with other collage ideas. For now, you can close this extra document.

17. **Ctrl+click (Windows: right-click) the film layer in the Layers palette to display a menu and choose Layer Via Copy.**
This creates a new layer above the film layer called Layer 1. Select the Move tool and click and drag in the document window to move the new Layer 1 away from the film layer so that you can see it.

18. **Click and drag Layer 1 from its current position in the Layers palette to just beneath the gradient layer. Wait until you see a black bar under the gradient layer to let go of the mouse button.**
That's all there is to reordering layers. If you ever lose the contents of a layer in the document window, it's probably because that layer is hidden under the artwork on another layer and needs repositioning in the stacking order of layers in the Layers palette.

19. **Drag Layer 1 to the Trash icon at the bottom of the Layers palette.**

20. **Choose File→Save. Leave** 08_fest.psd **open if you want to use it in the next tutorial. You'll have the option of starting that tutorial with a fresh prebuilt file that's a replica of how** 08_fest.psd **should look now.**

< N O T E >

There are a couple of other ways to create new layers, which you'll encounter elsewhere in this book. New layers are automatically created when you use the Type tool (see Session 11) and the Shape tools (see Session 6). Later in this session, you'll learn how to create two special kinds of layers — adjustment and fill layers.

Tutorial

» Converting a Background Layer

A Photoshop Background layer is a special kind of layer that has restrictions other layers do not. There will times, such as when you're trying to create a transparent GIF for the Web, that you'll want to eliminate the Background layer. This tutorial explains why and shows you how simple it is to convert a Background layer to a regular layer.

1. **Use the file that you saved at the end of the last tutorial,** 08_fest.psd**, or open the fresh file** 08_fest_create.psd **from the Session 8 Tutorial Files folder on your hard drive.**
   You have the option of using the fresh file so that you can continue on even if you didn't complete the last tutorial.

2. **Locate the bottom-most layer in the Layers palette, which is labeled** *Background* **in italics.**

3. **Double-click the Background layer. In the New Layer dialog box, you can accept the name that Photoshop suggests or type in a meaningful name, such as** texture. **Click OK.**
   That's all you have to do to convert a Background layer to a regular layer with none of the restrictions of a Background layer.

4. **Choose File→Save As. Save the file as** 08_fest_create.psd **(whether you used your own file or the fresh file provided for you at the beginning of this tutorial). Leave the file open for the next short tutorial.**

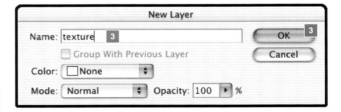

What Is a Background Layer?

When you create a new document in the New dialog box, you must choose white, background color, or transparent as the content of that document. If you choose either white or background color, Photoshop creates a special kind of layer at the bottom of the layer stack labeled *Background* layer. A Background layer acts differently than a regular layer. You can't add another layer beneath it in the Layers palette, change its opacity, or move its contents around in the document window. If you try to erase in the Background layer, you may be surprised that you don't see the gray-and-white transparency checkerboard beneath it, but rather the color in the Background Color box in the toolbox. The most significant restriction of a Background layer is that it doesn't support transparency. Transparent pixels on a Background layer are treated as white. So if you want to create a transparent graphic (for example, a transparent GIF for the Web), you'll have to delete the Background layer, turn off its visibility before you save a flattened file, or convert the Background layer to a regular layer.

<N O T E>

To convert a layer from a regular layer to a Background layer, choose Layer→New→Background from Layer.

Tutorial
» Selecting Layers

You've already learned that you have to select a layer in order to edit it. The trick is making sure that you've selected the right layer. More often than not, when you get stuck in Photoshop, it's because you're on the wrong layer. In this tutorial, you'll learn how to use the Auto Select layer features, which can help you avoid this problem.

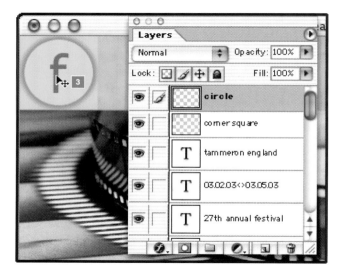

1. **Check that the file you saved at the end of the last tutorial,** `08_fest_create.psd`**, is still open.**

2. **Select the Move tool in the toolbox. Click to put a check mark next to Auto Select Layer in the Options bar.**

3. **Click the circle logo at the top left of the image.**
   The circle layer is selected automatically in the Layers palette. Activating Auto Select Layer causes Photoshop to select the topmost layer in the Layers palette that's under your cursor in the document. This can boost your speed and accuracy in selecting a layer. What if, though, you're looking for a layer that's not at the top of the stack at that location? Try using the contextual menu covered in the next step.

   If you turn on Auto Select Layer, remember to turn it off when you're done using it. Otherwise, you may not know what's happening the next time that you click in a document with the Move tool and find yourself automatically switched to a layer you don't want.

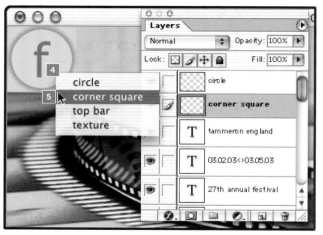

4. **Ctrl+click (Windows: right-click) the circle logo in the document.**
   You'll see a contextual menu that lists all the layers on which there are nontransparent pixels at the location under your cursor.

5. **Choose corner square from the contextual menu.**
   The corner square layer is selected automatically in the Layers palette.

6. **Leave this document open for the next tutorial. There's no need to save because you haven't changed any pixels in the image since the last time that you saved.**

Tutorial
» Changing Layer Visibility

The ability to make layers disappear temporarily from the document window is one of the most useful layer features. After you see how easy it is, you'll use it frequently for a variety of tasks, ranging from deconstructing an inherited file to isolating a layer to work on to creating rollover buttons for a Web page. In this tutorial, you'll learn how and when to make a layer invisible.

1. **Continue to use the file** 08_fest_create.psd.

2. **Click the eye icon to the left of the circle layer to make the layer temporarily invisible.**

3. **Click in the empty Visibility field on the circle layer again to make the eye icon and the contents of the layer reappear.**

4. **Click the eye icon on the tammeron england type layer and keep the mouse button held down as you run it over the eye icons on the three layers beneath that layer (down through the 2003 layer).**

5. **Click the empty Visibility field on the 2003 layer and slide back up the layer stack, turning on the eye icons up through the tammeron england layer.**

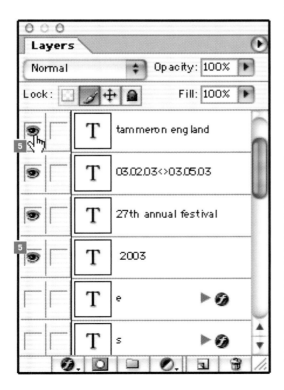

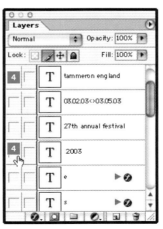

Why Change Layer Visibility?

There are several reasons to change layer visibility, including the following:

>> **To deconstruct a file:** When you first open a file that some-one else made, it's a good idea to hide all the layers and then make them visible again one by one as you keep an eye on the document window. This gives you a sense of what's on each layer and how the file was made, which will prove invaluable as you're working on the document.

>> **To isolate a layer to work on:** There are many times when you'll want to work on a layer unimpeded by the content of other layers. You can make all of the other layers invisible with one click using the Option+click (Windows: Alt+click) shortcut that you'll learn in this tutorial. It's just as easy to turn them all back on to see how the layer that you're work-ing on interacts with the other layers.

>> **To keep a layer in limbo:** The beauty of Photoshop is that it doesn't require you to make up your mind about the contents of an image until you're ready to save. You can make a layer invisible, but keep it in your document just in case you want to use it later. When you save in a non-layered format (any format other than PSD, PDF, and TIFF), your hidden layer will finally disappear for good.

>> **To make rollover buttons for the Web:** Layer visibility is one of several layer properties that you can manipulate in ImageReady to make rollovers for the Web. You can put different versions of an image on separate layers and make those layers visible or invisible on different rollover states. This makes the appearance of the image change as the viewer rolls the cursor over or clicks on a button. You'll learn how to do this in Session 16.

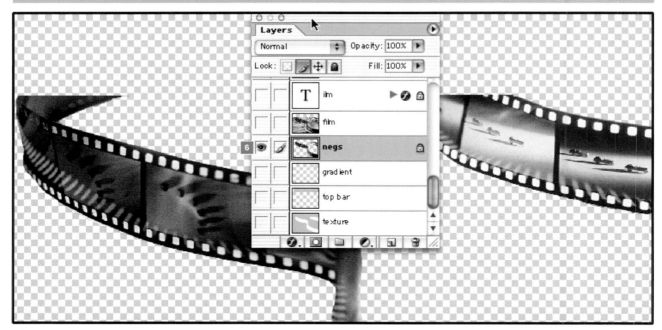

6. **Option+click (Windows: Alt+click) the eye icon on the negs layer.** This makes all the layers invisible except the negs layer. Leave the image like this for the next tutorial so that you can work on the negs layer unimpeded by the content of other layers.

7. **Choose File→Save. Leave** 08_fest_create.psd **open if you want to use it (instead of a fresh copy of this file) in the next tutorial.**

<N O T E>

Option+clicking (Windows: Alt+clicking) the eye icon on the negs layer a second time would make all the layers in the document visi-ble. Don't do that now, however, because you'll want to keep some layers hidden for later tutorials in this session.

Tutorial
» Locking Layer Properties

The Layers palette contains four buttons (Lock Transparency, Lock Pixels, Lock Position, and Lock All) that you can use to protect various properties of a layer from change. You'll explore these layer locks in this tutorial.

1. **Use the file that was open at the end of the last tutorial,** 08_fest_create.psd, **or open the fresh file** 08_fest_eyes.psd **from the Session 8 Tutorial Files folder.** 08_fest_eyes.psd is a replica of 08_fest_create.psd as it should look at the end of the last tutorial.

2. **Make sure that the negs layer is selected in the Layers palette and the visibility of all layers except the negs layer is off.**

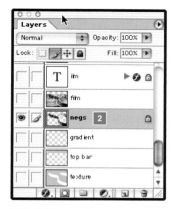

3. **Choose Filter→Distort→Polar Coordinates.**
   This filter normally distorts all the pixels on the layer, as you can see in the figure.

4. **Choose Edit→Undo.**

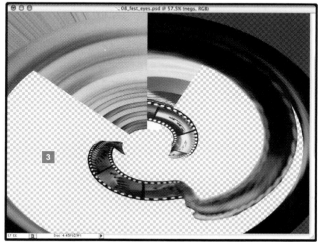

5. **Click the Lock Transparency button at the top of the Layers palette.**
   Notice the hollow lock icon that appears on the negs layer, indicating that this layer is partially locked.

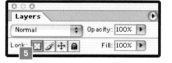

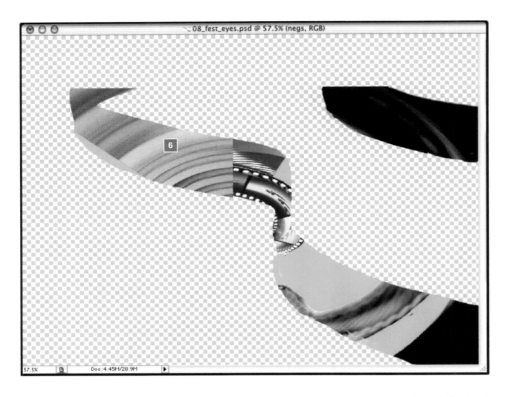

6. **Choose Filter→Polar Coordinates.**
   As you can see, the effect of the filter is now limited to the nontransparent pixels on the layer.

7. **Choose Edit→Undo.**

8. **Select the Brush tool in the toolbox and try to draw an *X* across one of the film frames and into the transparent area indicated by the gray checkerboard.**
   Notice that the paint only appears on the image, not in the transparent area.

9. **Choose Edit→Step Backwards until the *X* is gone.**

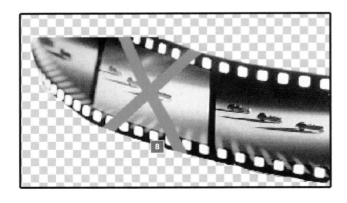

< T I P >

Another effect that you can achieve with the Lock Transparency button is custom-painted text. Use the Type tool and a thick font to type some words in a document. With the type layer selected, choose Layer→Rasterize→Type. (You'll find out more about rasterizing type in Session 12. For now, take my word for it that rendering is necessary because you can't paint on regular Photoshop type.) Activate the Lock Transparency button in the Layers palette. Then paint ribbons of color across the type. The color appears only on the letters and not on the transparent pixels between the letter forms.

10. **Click the Lock Pixels button at the top of the Layers palette.**
    This lock protects all pixels on a layer, nontransparent as well as transparent, from change. That's why the Lock Transparency button is also grayed out when you activate the Lock Pixels button.

11. **Try to paint anywhere in the document, and you'll get a warning that you cannot use the Brush tool because the layer is locked. Click OK in the warning box.**
    Although you can't modify any of the pixels on the layer, you can still move or transform the layer.

12. **Click the Lock Transparency and Lock Pixels buttons again to deactivate them.**

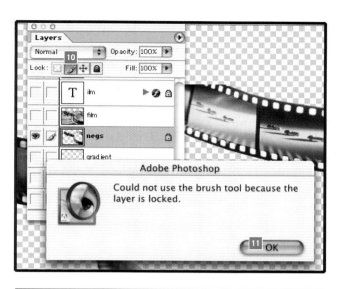

13. **Click the Lock Position button in the Layers palette.**

14. **Select the Move tool and try to move the content of the film layer. You'll get a warning that you can't because the layer is locked. Click OK in the warning box.**
    With the Layer Position lock on, you can make changes to pixels, but you can't move or transform the layer.

<TIP>
Instead of going to the toolbox to select the Move tool, you can press and hold the ⌘ key (Windows: Ctrl key) to switch to the Move tool temporarily. As long as you hold that modifier key down, you can use the Move tool.

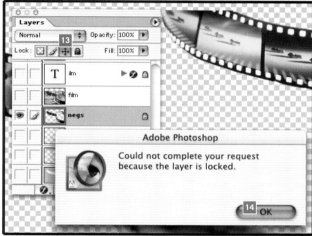

15. **Click the Lock All button at the top of the Layers palette.**

16. **Try to move the negs layer with the Move tool. Click OK in the warning box. Then try to paint on the layer with the Brush tool. Again, click OK in the warning box. Neither operation is successful.**
    Lock All activates all three of the other locks at once, causing them all to be grayed out in the Layers palette. Lock All protects all the pixels on a layer from movement, as well as from pixel-changing operations such as filling, painting, and filtering. Notice that the lock icon on the negs layer is now solid, as compared to the hollow icon that appeared when you activated any of the other three locks.

17. **Choose Edit→Undo.**

18. **Choose File→Save and close the file.**

Tutorial

» Changing Layer Opacity

Layer opacity, in simple terms, is how much you can see through the artwork on a layer. Lowering layer opacity makes a layer more transparent so that you can see through to artwork on the layers below. This tutorial shows you how and when to change layer opacity and introduces you to Photoshop 7's new Fill opacity slider.

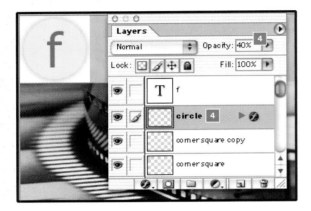

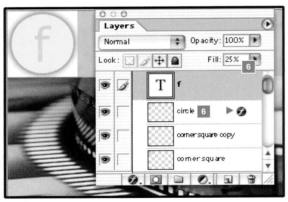

1. **Choose File→Open, navigate to** `08_fest_opacity.psd` **in the Session 8 Tutorial Files folder, and click Open.**

2. **Click the corner square layer and drag it to the New Layer icon at the bottom of the layers palette to create a copy of that layer.**

3. **Make sure that the corner square copy layer is selected in the Layers palette, choose Edit→Fill, and fill the layer with white.**

4. **Select the circle layer in the Layers palette. Click the arrow on the Opacity field at the top of the Layers palette and move the slider down to 40%.**
   This causes the yellow circle and the magenta glow around the circle to become more transparent.

   <NOTE>
   There's a great shortcut for changing layer opacity. Select the Move tool and type a number between **1** and **100**. The Opacity field in the Layers palette will automatically reflect that number.

5. **Return the Opacity slider to 100%.**

6. **Make sure that the circle layer is still selected. Click the arrow on the Fill opacity field at the top of the Layers palette and move that slider down to 25%. Leave the regular Opacity field set to 100%.**
   Notice that the yellow circle in the document window becomes more transparent, but the magenta glow around the circle remains full-strength. Fill opacity affects only the opacity of artwork on a layer; it doesn't affect the opacity of any layer style on that layer.

Why Change Layer Opacity?

There are several reasons to change layer opacity, including the following:

» **To composite layers:** You'll do this in the next session.

» **To position layers:** If you're trying to align the artwork on separate layers, it's often useful to lower the opacity of the top layer temporarily so that you can see through the artwork below.

» **To make rollovers and animations:** You can change the opacity of a layer on individual rollover states so that an image appears more or less opaque as the viewer interacts with it. When you're making an animation in ImageReady, you can create two frames in which you vary the opacity of a layer. Then have the program automatically create in-between frames with varying levels of opacity to make an image appear to fade in or out.

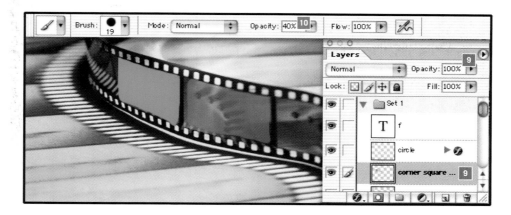

7. **Return the Fill opacity slider to 100%.**

8. **Select the Brush tool in the toolbox and choose a blue color in the Color palette.**

9. **Select the corner square copy layer in the Layers palette and make sure that Opacity is set to 100%. Paint in one of the frames in the image.**

10. **Click the Opacity field in the Brush tool Options bar and reduce that Opacity slider to 40%. Leave Opacity set to 100% in the Layers palette.**
    The Brush tool has its own opacity control that is separate from the Opacity slider in the Layers palette.

11. **Click the Opacity field in the Layers palette and reduce it to 25%.**
    This reduces the opacity of the whole corner square copy layer, so both painted frames are more transparent. Notice that the frame on the right is even more transparent than when it was created at 40% opacity. Both of the opacity controls have had an effect on this frame.

<NOTE>
You may be wondering which opacity control to use when. Use the Opacity field on the Layers palette when you want to affect the opacity of an entire layer. You can't restrict the effect of that Opacity field to just a portion of a layer (even if you select part of the layer, as you may imagine). If you want to affect the opacity of part of a layer, you have to do so when you're filling, painting, cloning, or erasing part of the layer. You'll find an Opacity control on the Options bar for the Brush tools (the Brush and Pencil, the History and Art History brushes, the Gradient and Paint Bucket, the Clone, and the Eraser tools) and in the fill dialog boxes.

12. **Click the corner square copy layer in the Layers palette and drag it to the Trash icon at the bottom of the Layers palette.**

13. **Don't save the file, but do leave it open for the next tutorial.**

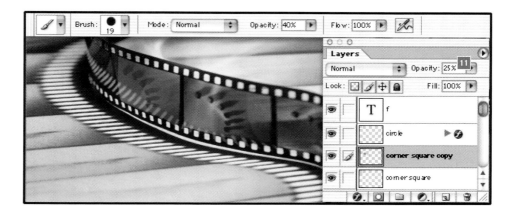

Tutorial
» Linking Layers

You can link layers together for the purpose of moving them together, transforming them together, and aligning them to each other or to the document. You'll try all of this in this tutorial.

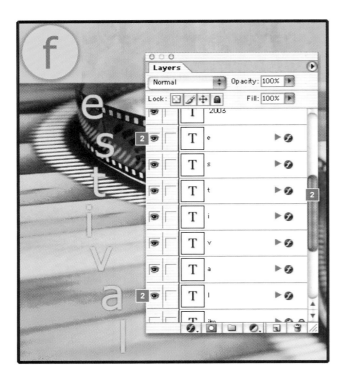
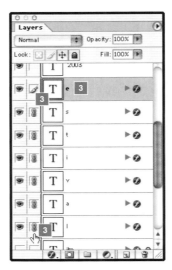

1. Use 08_fest_opacity.psd **from the last tutorial. If it's not open, open it again from the Session 8 Tutorial Files folder on your hard drive.**

2. **Click and drag the scroll bar in the Layers palette so that you can see the type layers labeled** *e, s, t, i, v, a,* **and** *l.* **Turn on the eye icons for each of these letter layers so that they are visible in the document.**

3. **Select the e layer in the Layers palette. Click in the Link field to the left of that layer and drag down through the link fields to the l layer.**
   This adds a link to each of the letter layers, linking them all to the selected e layer.

Be careful not to click in the link field next to any other layer, or you will include it in this group of linked layers. You'll know if you've inadvertently included another layer because you'll see it moving as you proceed through this tutorial. If that happens, click in the link field of that layer again and move it back to its original location.

4. **Select the Move tool in the toolbox and click and drag in the document window to move the letter** *e* **into position under the** *f* **logo in the document, as shown here.**
   Notice that all the other letters move with the *e* because they're linked to the selected e layer.

Why Link Layers?

There are several reasons to link layers, including the following:

>> To move multiple layers together.

>> To align objects on individual layers to one another, as you'll do in this tutorial. This is also useful for making multiple buttons for a Web page, as you'll see in Session 16.

>> To quickly create a layer set from linked layers, as you'll see in the next tutorial.

>> To transform the artwork on multiple layers at once.

>> To rasterize multiple layers at the same time (by choosing Layer→Rasterize→Linked Layers). You'll learn about rasterizing type layers in Session 12.

Aligning Linked Layers to the Document Window

The steps of this tutorial show you how to align and distribute objects on separate layers relative to one another, but what if you want to align layered artwork to the document? The secret is to select the whole document before aligning, which tells Photoshop to align to the selection. For example, to position these linked layers in the vertical center of the document window, choose Select→All from the menu bar at the top of the screen. Then click the Align Vertical Centers button on the Move tool Options bar. When you're done, deselect and choose Edit→Step Backward to send the letters back to the left side of the document.

5. **Make sure that the e layer is still selected in the Layers palette and the Move tool is still selected in the toolbox. Click the Align by Vertical Centers button in the Options bar.**
   This vertically aligns all the linked letters to the letter e.

6. **Click the Distribute by Vertical Centers button in the Options bar.**
   You'll see a slight movement in some of the letters in the middle of the group. This distributes the letters so that there is an equal amount of space between their centers

7. **Choose Edit→Transform→Skew.**
   This creates a bounding box with editable points around all the artwork on the linked layers.

8. **Click one of the corner points and drag to slant the linked letters. Press the Esc key on your keyboard to cancel the transformation.**
Experiment with some of the other transformation choices if you like — scale, rotate, distort, perspective, rotate, and flip. You can choose from the commands in the Transform menu or use Free Transform from the Edit menu if you're not sure what style of transformation you want. To accept a transformation and dismiss the bounding box, press Return (Windows: Enter) on your keyboard.

<NOTE>
You can transform either linked layers as you did here, a single layer (select that layer in the Layers palette and use the Edit→ Transform commands), the contents of a selection (create a selection and then use the Edit→Transform commands), or even a selection outline (create a selection and choose Select→Transform Selection).

9. **If you experimented with other transformations, as suggested in the comment following step 8, choose Edit→Step Backward to eliminate those transformations.**
The letters should look as they do in this figure when you're done.

10. **Choose File→Save. Leave** 08_fest_opacity.psd **open if you want to use it in the next tutorial, as opposed to a fresh copy of the file as it should look now.**

Each time that you accept a transformation, Photoshop resamples pixels, which can degrade the image. If you plan to do multiple transformations, do them all and then press Return or Enter.

Tutorial
» Organizing Layers in Layer Sets

Layer sets are great for organizing layers in the Layers palette, especially when you have lots of layers in a document. Layer sets are also useful for performing operations on multiple layers that you can't accomplish with linked layers, such as changing layer opacity, visibility, and blending modes. In this tutorial, you'll learn how to create and use layer sets.

1. **Use the file that you saved in the last tutorial,** 08_fest_opacity.psd**, or open the fresh file** 08_fest_links.psd **from the Session 8 Tutorial Files folder on your hard drive.**
   08_fest_links.psd is a copy of 08_fest_opacity.psd as the file should look at the end of the last tutorial.

2. **Check that the letter layers e, s, t, i, v, a, and l are still linked in the Layers palette. If they're not, run your cursor down the column of link fields on these layers to relink the layers.**

3. **Select any of the linked letter layers in the Layers palette. Click the arrow at the top right of the Layers palette and choose New Set from Linked.**

4. **In the New Set From Linked dialog box, type** festival set **in the Name field. Choose a color code to apply to the layer set and each of its layers for quick identification. Leave Mode set to Pass Through and Opacity set to 100% (see the "Layer Set Mode and Opacity" sidebar for an explanation of these items). Click OK.**
   This is the fastest way to create a layer set that contains multiple existing layers.

5. **Click the arrow on the festival set in the Layers palette to open that set. You'll see all the layers from which you made that set.**
   Notice that each of the layers in the set is indented and bears the color code that you chose for the set.

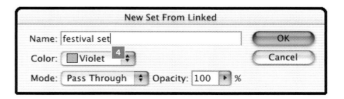

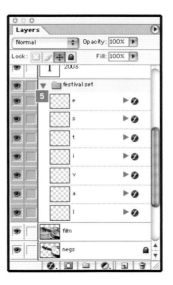

Layer Set Mode and Opacity

When you put layers into a layer set, you have the opportunity to apply a second round of layer blending and opacity. (You'll find out about layer blending in Session 9.) Photoshop first applies the opacities and blending modes that are set on the individual layers. In other words, the layers in the set are blended together according to their individual blending modes, and the opacity setting of each individual layer is taken into account. Then Photoshop blends the entire group with other layers in the image using the blending mode assigned to the layer set, and it applies the opacity of the layer set to the group as a whole. When you choose Pass Through as the layer set's mode, no additional blending is done. When you choose 100% as the layer set's opacity, there are no additional opacity changes.

6. **Click the empty Visibility field on the type layer labeled *ilm* to make that layer visible in the document. Click that layer in the Layers palette and drag it on top of the festival set to add the layer to that set.**

   This is how to add an existing layer to a layer set. Notice that the ilm layer is now indented under the festival set and bears the purple code of that set.

7. **Make sure that the festival set is open and any layer in the set, or the set itself, is selected. Click the New Layer icon at the bottom of the Layers palette.**

   This creates a new layer inside the layer set, called *Layer 1*.

8. **Click Layer 1 and drag it on top of the festival set to remove it from the set and place it directly below the set.**

   Another way to remove a layer from a set is to click and drag it elsewhere in the layer stack. I prefer the first way because I always know where to find the removed layer.

   Notice that even though you removed Layer 1 from the layer set, it retained its purple color code. This defeats the purpose of color coding to indicate assignment to a layer set. To remove the color code, Ctrl+click (Windows: right-click) Layer 1 and choose Layer Properties from the contextual menu. This opens the Layer Properties dialog box in which you can click the Color button and choose a new color or none.

9. **Click Layer 1 and drag it onto the Trash icon at the bottom of the Layers palette.**

10. **Click the arrow on the festival set to close that set and shorten your Layers palette.**

11. **Click the tammeron england layer in the Layers palette. Click the New Layer Set icon at the bottom of the palette to create a new set, Set 1, above the selected layer.**

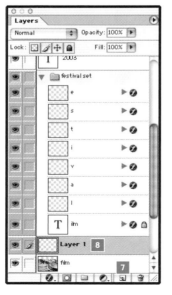

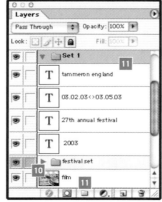

12. **Double-click Set 1 and rename it** headline set.

13. **Drag each of the four type layers located under the headline set in the Layers palette on top of that set to move them into the set. Then click the triangle on the headline set to close it.**
    If you want to give the headline set a color, Ctrl+click (Windows: right-click) the headline set and choose Layer Set Properties from the contextual menu. This opens the Layer Set Properties dialog box, in which you can click the Color button. When you're done, click the arrow on the headline set to close the set.

14. **Take a minute to create two more layers sets (a background set and a logo set) and organize the rest of the layers into those sets to match this figure.**
    This may not be the most exciting task in the world, but when you're done, you'll be happy to have a shorter, more manageable Layers palette.

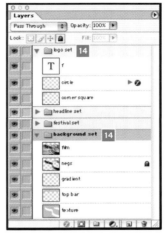

< N O T E >
The introduction to this tutorial mentioned that the benefit of using layer sets, other than organization, is its ability to affect multiple layers with an operation. In the next steps, you'll try some examples of what I mean. In addition to these operations, you can apply a layer mask to a layer set, you can alter the blending mode of a layer set, and you can transform a layer set.

15. **Select the logo set in the Layers palette. Select the Move tool and click and drag in the document window to move all the layers in this set around in the document window together. When you're done observing this, choose Edit→Undo.**

< N O T E >
The rest of the steps in this tutorial are for more advanced users, so don't worry if you don't completely understand them. The main point to take from them is that you can change the opacity of all layers in a layer set together, after Photoshop accounts for opacity levels assigned to individual layers.

16. **Option+double-click (Windows: Alt+double-click) the f layer in the logo layer set.**
    This opens the Layer Style dialog box.

17. **Move the Fill Opacity slider all the way to 0%. Then click the Knockout button and choose Deep.**
    This makes the fill on the f layer completely transparent, enabling you to see all the way down to the transparent pixels behind the image.

< N O T E >
In the next step, you'll see a neat trick you can do only when you're working on a layer that's in a layer set.

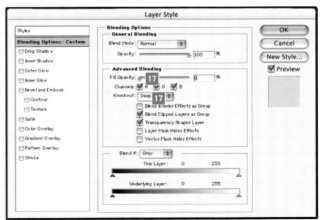

< N O T E >
This Fill Opacity slider is a copy of the Fill Opacity slider on the Layers palette, which you worked with earlier in this session. The only difference is that this copy of the slider comes with options.

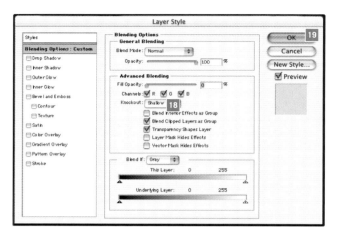

18. **Click the Knockout button again and choose Shallow.**
    Now you can see through the fill on the f layer only down to the bottom-most layer in the logo layer set (the orange patterned layer called *top bar*).

19. **Click OK to exit the Layer Style dialog box.**
    You'll learn more about the Layer Style dialog box in Session 10.

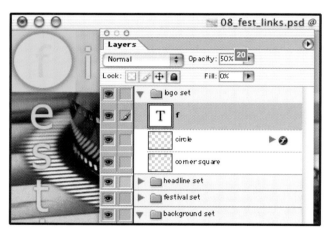

20. **Click the Opacity field on the Layers palette and move the Opacity slider to 50%.**
    Notice that this lowers the opacity of all the layers in the logo set and that the effect on the f layer is cumulative. This illustrates the point made earlier in this tutorial — that Photoshop first applies the opacities set for individual layers and then applies the opacity you assign to the layer set.

21. **Choose Edit→Step Backward several times until the f is purple and 100% opaque again. Click the arrows on all the layer sets to close them.**

22. **Choose File→Save As. Save the file as** `08_fest_links.psd`, **regardless of whether you used your own file or the fresh file provided for you at the beginning of this tutorial. Leave the file open for the next exercise.**

Tutorial

» Editing with Adjustment Layers

There are two special kinds of layers — adjustment layers and fill layers — with which you can make changes to an image without affecting the pixels of the original layers. This nondestructive editing is a real advantage because it gives you the flexibility to change your design decisions without having to start over. In this tutorial, you'll be introduced to adjustment layers, which you can use to make editable adjustments to image color and tone. In the following tutorial, you'll work with fill layers, which you can use to add editable color, pattern, or gradient to your image.

1. **Make sure that** 08_fest_links.psd **is open from the last tutorial or open** 08_fest_sets.psd **from the Session 8 Tutorial Files folder.**
   08_fest_sets.psd is a copy of 08_fest_links.psd, as the latter file should look at the end of the last tutorial.

2. **Click the arrow on the background set to open that set.**

3. **Select the top bar layer in the Layers palette. Choose Select→ Load Selection. In the Load Selection dialog box, make sure that the Channel button is set to top bar Transparency. Click OK.**
   You may remember this technique for selecting all the artwork on a transparent layer from Session 7.

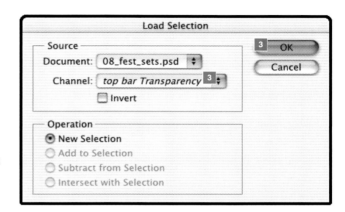

<NOTE>
You can apply an adjustment layer to a selected area or to the whole image. If you didn't want the adjustment to be limited to just a portion of the image, you would skip the step of making a selection before you create the adjustment layer.

4. **Click the New Fill or Adjustment Layer button at the bottom of the Layers palette and choose Hue/Saturation.**
   This opens the Hue/Saturation dialog box.

<NOTE>
There are many flavors of adjustments in this menu, including Levels, Curves, Variations, and some auto-adjustments. These are all different ways of adjusting the tonality and color of an image. You'll work with some of these other adjustments in Sessions 14 and 15.

<NOTE>
Don't confuse an adjustment layer with a regular adjustment (accessible from the Image→Adjustments menu). The difference is that a regular adjustment is applied directly to the selected layer, permanently altering the pixels of that layer. It's preferable to use the adjustment layer version of any of the adjustment commands because adjustment layers are nondestructive to the underlying image layers, as you'll see shortly.

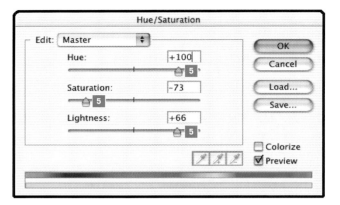

5. **Drag the Hue slider to +100 to change the hue of the selected portion of the selected area to green. Drag the Saturation slider to −73 to desaturate the color and drag the Lightness slider to +66 to lighten the color. Click OK.**

   There is nothing magical about these particular numbers. I arrived at them by watching the live preview in the document window as I moved the sliders until I got the color I wanted.

   < N O T E >

   Notice the new Hue/Saturation adjustment layer in the Layers palette. It contains a thumbnail on the left that represents the adjustment and a thumbnail on the right that represents a layer mask defined by the selection that you made in step 3. This mask limits the effect of the adjustment layer to the top bar in the image.

< N O T E >

An adjustment layer affects pixels on all the layers beneath it in the Layers stack, unless you specfically restrict its effect to the layer directly beneath the adjustment layer. To do that, hold the Option (Windows: Alt) key and move your cursor over the line between the adjustment layer and the layer beneath it. Click when the cursor changes to an icon of two circles. This groups the two layers and limits the adjustment to the layer that's been grouped with the adjustment layer. Repeat this to ungroup these layers.

6. **Turn the eye icon off on the adjustment layer, to see that none of the pixels of the underlying top bar layer have been changed. When you're done observing, turn the eye icon back on.**

   This illustrates the nondestructive nature of adjustment layers, which is one of the main advantages that they offer over other methods of correcting tone and color.

7. **Double-click the thumbnail on the left side of the adjustment layer in the Layers palette to reopen the Hue/Saturation dialog box. Click the Hue slider and move it to −161 to change the color of the adjustment to blue. Click OK.**

   You can reopen and make changes in this dialog box as many times as you want without harming the original artwork. The ability to edit your adjustments is the other major benefit of using adjustment layers to control tone and color.

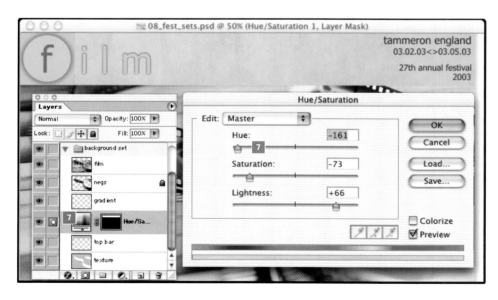

8. **Select the Rectangular Marquee tool in the toolbox. Click and drag to create a vertical selection on the left side of the document like that shown here.**

9. **Click the New Fill or Adjustment Layer button at the bottom of the Layers palette and choose Hue/Saturation. Set Hue to +173, Saturation to –83, and Lightness to +44. Click OK.**
   This creates a vertical bar in the image made entirely of adjusted color in a second Hue/Saturation adjustment layer.

10. **Choose File→Save As. Save this file as** 08_fest_sets.psd, **regardless of whether you used your own file or the fresh file provided for you at the beginning of this tutorial. Leave the file open for the next tutorial.**

Tutorial
» Using Fill Layers

Fill layers are similar to adjustment layers in that they don't permanently change the existing image and they are easily edited. Fill layers offer a means of adding editable solid colors, patterns, and gradients in selected areas of an image or across an entire image. Try them out in this tutorial.

1. **Make sure that** `08_fest_sets.psd` **is open from the last tutorial.**

2. **Select the film layer in the Layers palette.**

3. **Select the Polygonal Lasso tool in the Layers palette and click around the edges of one of the frames in the image to select that frame.**

4. **Choose Select→Feather and choose 1 pixel as the Feather Radius to soften the edges of the selection.**

5. **Click the New Adjustment or Fill Layer button at the bottom of the Layers palette and choose Pattern from the menu.**

6. **In the Pattern Fill dialog box, click the pattern sample down arrow to open the Pattern Picker.**

7. **Click the arrow on the Pattern Picker and choose Nature Patterns. Click OK at the prompt to replace the current patterns. Select the leaves pattern and click OK in the Pattern Fill dialog box.**
   This fills the frame with the pattern and creates a new fill layer in the Layers palette.

<NOTE>
Leaving the Link with Layer option checked in the Pattern Fill dialog box makes the pattern move when you move the layer. Clicking Snap to Origin returns the pattern to its original location. Scale transforms the pattern so that it appears bigger or smaller in the image. You can leave all of these Pattern Fill options at their defaults for now.

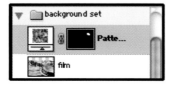

<NOTE>
A fill layer, like an adjustment layer, has two thumbnails. The thumbnail on the left represents the fill, and the thumbnail on the right represents the mask that determines where the fill is visible in the image.

8. **Double-click the pattern thumbnail on the left of the Pattern Fill layer to reopen the Pattern Fill dialog box. This time, choose the blue daisies pattern from the Pattern Picker. Click OK.**

   That's how easy it is to edit a Pattern Fill layer.

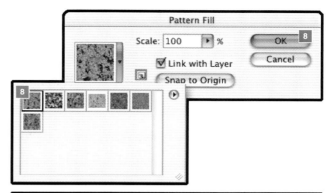

9. **Click the Layer Blending Mode button at the top left of the Layers palette and choose Multiply to blend the pattern with the underlying image.**

   You'll learn more about layer blending modes in Session 9.

10. **Repeat steps 2 through 7 on another frame in the image. Then choose Layer→Change Layer Content→Gradient.**

    This changes the nature of the fill from a pattern to a gradient and opens the Gradient Fill dialog box.

11. **Click the gradient bar in the Gradient Fill dialog box to open the Gradient Editor. Create a magenta (R: 111, B: 41, G: 109) to yellow (R: 248, G: 229, B: 50) gradient. (If you've forgotten how to create your own gradient in the Gradient Editor, turn back to Session 5.) Click OK in the Gradient Editor and OK in the Gradient Fill dialog box.**

12. **Click the Layer Blending Mode button in the Layers palette and choose Overlay to blend the gradient fill with the image.**

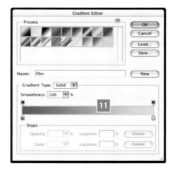

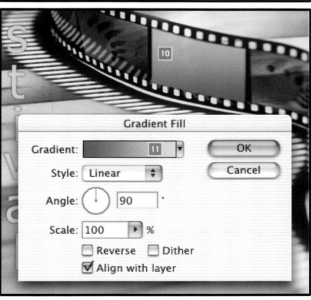

13. **Repeat steps 2 through 5 on a new frame in the image, except this time choose Solid Color from the menu that appears when you click the New Adjustment or Fill Layer button on the Layers palette.**
    This opens the Color Picker.

14. **Choose a light orange (try R: 255, G: 210, B: 128) in the Color Picker and click OK.**

15. **Click the Layer Blending Mode button in the Layers palette and choose Color to blend the solid color fill with the image.**

16. **Choose File→Save As and rename the file** 08_fest_end.psd. **This is a final collage for your complete course project, so navigate to your collages folder and click Save to save it there.**

» Session Review

This session covers layers. You learned to create layers from scratch, from another layer, and from another document. You practiced selecting layers with Auto-Select features. You learned how and when to change layer visibility, to lock layer properties, to work with layers, and to link layers. Then you created layer sets to manage your layers and work with multiple layers at once. Finally, you learned about two special kinds of layers — adjustment and fill layers. These questions will help you review this session.

1. Why is it important to give layers meaningful names? (See "Tutorial: Creating Layers.")

2. How do you rename a layer in Photoshop 7? (See "Tutorial: Creating Layers.")

3. When would you add a clipping path to an object on a layer? (See "Tutorial: Creating Layers.")

4. Do empty layers contribute to file size? (See "Tutorial: Creating Layers.")

5. Name one of the limitations a Background layer has. (See "Tutorial: Converting a Background Layer.")

6. How do you convert a Background layer to a regular layer? (See "Tutorial: Converting a Background Layer.")

7. What does the Auto Select Layer option do? (See "Tutorial: Selecting Layers.")

8. How do you turn off the visibility of a layer? (See "Tutorial: Changing Layer Visibility.")

9. How do you turn off the visibility of all layers except one? (See "Tutorial: Changing Layer Visibility.")

10. Name two reasons that you may want to change layer visibility. (See "Tutorial: Changing Layer Visibility.")

11. Name the four layer lock buttons on the Layers palette. (See "Tutorial: Locking Layer Properties.")

12. What does the Lock Transparency button on the Layers palette do? (See "Tutorial: Locking Layer Properties.")

13. Name one reason that you may want to change layer opacity. (See "Tutorial: Changing Layer Opacity.")

14. What's the difference between fill opacity and regular layer opacity? (See "Tutorial: Changing Layer Opacity.")

15. Name two reasons that you may want to link layers together. (See "Tutorial: Linking Layers.")

16. Name two benefits of using layer sets. (See "Tutorial: Organizing Layers in Layer Sets.")

17. Name one advantage of using an adjustment layer rather than a regular adjustment to edit tone or color. (See "Tutorial: Editing with Adjustment Layers.")

18. What is a fill layer? (See "Tutorial: Using Fill Layers.")

film

festival

tammeron england
03.02.03<>03.05.03

27th annual festival
2003

Session 9

Compositing Images

screenings

thursday 8 pm
friday 7 pm
saturday 8 pm
saturday 10pm
sunday 12 pm
sunday 4 pm

Session Introduction

Putting images together is what Photoshop is all about, but you'll find that it isn't as easy as it looks. To do it right requires understanding some of the more advanced Photoshop features, such as layer masks, vector masks, Blending sliders, and layer blending modes. In this session, you'll be introduced to those features, and you'll learn how to use some tools — rulers, guides, and the Crop tool — that will help you composite images. This session pulls together many of the skills that you've learned in previous sessions.

TOOLS YOU'LL USE
Crop tool, layer mask, vector mask, Blending sliders, Measure tool, rulers, guides, and blending modes

CD-ROM FILES NEEDED
09_screening.psd, 09_curtain.psd,
09_screening_mask.psd, 09_screening_blend.psd,
09_screening_mode.psd, 09_screening_end.psd,
09_lens.psd, and 09_vintage.psd

TIME REQUIRED
60 minutes

Tutorial
» Making Images Compatible

You'll make your job easier and have better results if you take some time before you start compositing to make your images compatible in terms of size and style. In this tutorial, you'll change the magnification of two images to view their relative size, crop one of the images to match the other, and adjust color before beginning to collage the images.

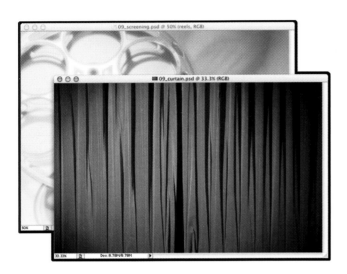

1. **Open two files from the Session 9 Tutorial Files folder on your hard drive** — 09_curtain.psd **and** 09_screening.psd. Depending on the size of your monitor, the two images may open at different magnifications that make them look, at first glance, approximately the same size. However, this is deceptive. You can't get a true picture of the relative size of two documents on-screen unless they are set to the same magnification. You'll fix this in the next steps.

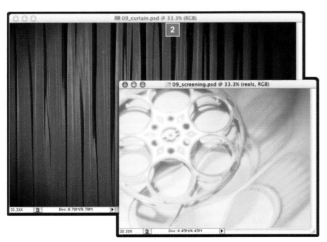

2. **Select the Zoom tool, set the tool to zoom in, and click one or both documents to set both to 33% magnification.**
Now you can see that 09_curtain.psd is bigger than 09_screening.psd.

3. Click the arrow at the bottom of either document window and choose Document Dimensions from the pop-up Information menu.
You'll see the dimensions in pixels of both of the documents, confirming that 09_curtain.psd is the bigger document.

<NOTE>
The relevant unit of measurement when you're comparing images on-screen is pixels.

<NOTE>
09_screening.psd has been sized to fit on a page of your final project, so you'll have to match the size of 09_curtain.psd to 09_screening.psd (1440 pixels x 1080 pixels). This sounds like it might require some serious math, but it doesn't at all. Photoshop will match the two images for you with just a click of the Crop tool, as you'll see in the next steps.

4. Select the Crop tool from the toolbox.

5. Click the Clear button on the Options bar to clear the option fields.
This deletes any Crop tool settings that you may have made previously.

6. Make sure that 09_screening.psd **is the active image and click Front Image.**
This inserts the pixel dimensions and resolution of 09_screening.psd in the Crop tool Options bar. This information will be applied when you use the Crop tool to crop another image.

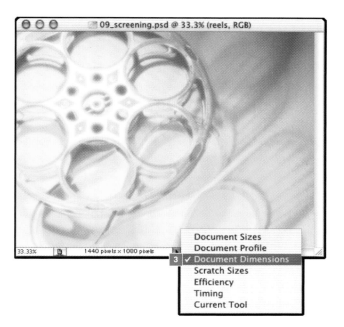

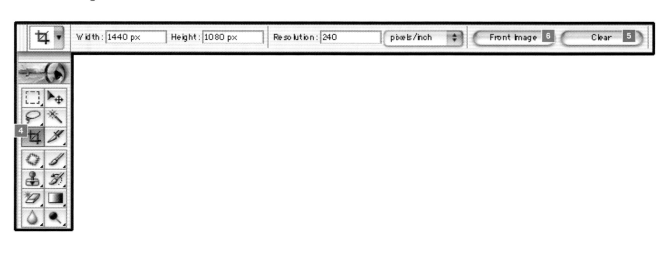

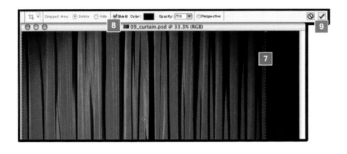

7. **Click and drag in the** 09_curtain.psd **document window to drag the crop boundary.**
A crop boundary looks just like a selection boundary. It's a little hard to see in the figure, but it is there.

8. **Uncheck Shield on the Options bar so that you can get a better view of the area to be cropped away.**
You can click and drag to reposition or rotate the crop outline. Accept the default position for now.

9. **Click the Check Mark icon on the Options bar to accept your crop settings and initiate the crop.**
Alternatively, you can press Return or Enter on your keyboard.

<N O T E>
Photoshop not only crops the curtain image, but also resamples the image so that it is the same size in pixels as 09_screening.psd. This feature is a real time-saver!

<N O T E>
Another way to resize images to make them compatible for collaging is to use the Transform→Scale command. You'll try that in the tutorial "Using Blending Sliders to Composite" later in this session.

10. **Click inside** 09_curtain.psd **and drag it into the** 09_screening.psd **document window.**
This copies the curtain image into the main image and creates a new layer in the Layers palette.

11. **Double-click the new Layer 1 in** 09_screening.psd **and rename it** curtain.

12. **You can close** 09_curtain.psd **without saving.**

<N O T E>
There are a lot of design considerations to take into account when you're choosing images to put together, ranging from the direction of shadows and light sources to texture, perspective, and point of view. An important design element that can make or break a composite image is color. In the next steps, you'll adjust the rich color of the curtain image to bring it into line with the softer gold theme of the main image.

13. **Select the curtain layer in the Layers palette. Choose Layer→New Adjustment Layer→Hue/Saturation.**
This opens the New Layer dialog box.

14. **Click the Group With Previous Layer check box and click OK.**
    Normally an adjustment layer affects all the layers below it.
    Group With Previous Layer restricts the effect of an adjust-
    ment layer to the layer immediately below it. In the last ses-
    sion, you learned another way to do this — by Option+clicking
    (Windows: Alt+clicking) the border between layers after, rather
    than before, creating an adjustment layer.

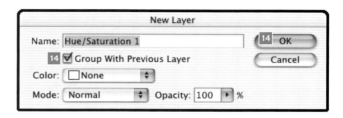

15. **In the Hue/Saturation dialog box, change the Hue to +40 and the
    Lightness to +3 and click OK.**

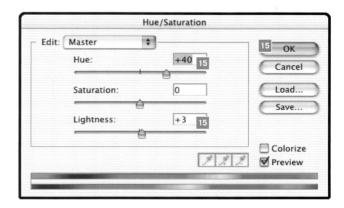

16. **Select the curtain layer in the Layers palette and click and drag
    the curtain image in the document window to move it into position
    over the main layer.**

17. **Choose File→Save and leave** 09_screening.psd **open for the
    next tutorial.**

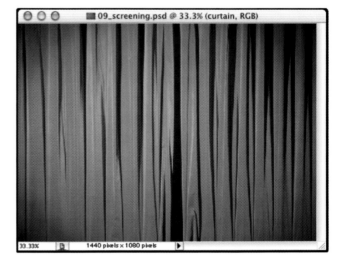

Tutorial

» Joining Images with Layer Masks

A *layer mask* is a bitmapped grayscale image that you can attach to a layer of artwork. You can paint on a mask with black, white, or shades of gray to hide and reveal artwork on the attached layer. One popular use for layer masks is to gradually fade one layered image into another. You can accomplish this by painting on the mask with feathered fills, soft brushes, or gradients, as you'll do in this tutorial.

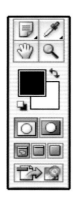

1. Use 09_screening.psd, which should be open from the last tutorial.

2. **Make sure that the curtain layer is selected in the Layers palette and click the Add Layer Mask icon on the bottom of the palette.**
   This adds a white thumbnail on the right side of the curtain layer. Another way to add this same kind of mask is to choose Layer→Add Layer Mask→Reveal All.

3. **Press the keyboard shortcut D to set white as the foreground color and black as the background color in the toolbox. Then press X to switch those colors so that black is the foreground color.**
   These shortcuts come in particularly handy when you're working with masks because you'll generally use only black, white, and shades of gray on a layer mask. You'll use these shortcuts throughout this session.

4. **Select the Gradient tool in the toolbox. Click the Gradient bar in the Options bar to open the Gradient Editor.**

<NOTE>

The right thumbnail represents the layer mask, the left thumbnail represents the regular layer, and the link symbol is the tie between the two. When the link is showing, moving either the mask or the layer will cause the other to move with it. If you deactivate the link (by clicking on it), the two components of this layer will move separately. You can use this feature to reposition a layer mask or to animate a mask to create different frames for an animated GIF in ImageReady.

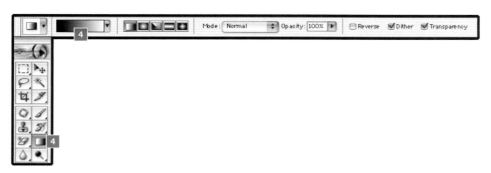

5. **Select the Foreground to Transparent gradient.**
   The icon for this gradient is black to transparent.

6. **Move the black stop on the gradient in the Gradient Editor to the far right so that there is just a small area of opaque pixels on the right side of the gradient. Click OK.**

7. **Make sure that the layer mask thumbnail is selected on the curtain layer in the Layers palette.**
   A black border around that thumbnail indicates that it is selected.

If the layer thumbnail rather than the layer mask thumbnail is selected, you'll end up painting on the image, rather than on the mask. This is difficult to undo, short of using the History palette, so try to avoid this common mistake.

8. **Click at the far right of the document window and drag to just before the left edge.**
   This draws a black to transparent gradient on the layer mask, hiding most of the image on the curtain layer. Where the mask is black, you can see through the curtain layer to the reels layer below. Where the mask is white (where the transparent part of the gradient lies), you'll see the curtains layer. Where the mask fades to gray, the two images gradually fade together.

<TIP>
The effect of drawing this gradient in the layer mask depends on the length and direction of your gradient line. If you don't like the gradient that you get, try drawing another gradient line over the first one until you're happy with the result.

<NOTE>
You could accomplish nearly the same thing by drawing a selection with the Rectangular Marquee tool to cover almost all the document except the area on the left edge. Choose Select→Feather and type a relatively large number in the feather radius field (try **40**). Press Option+Delete (Windows: Alt+Delete) to fill the selection on the layer mask with black. The heavily feathered left edge provides a soft transition between images, much like the gradient.

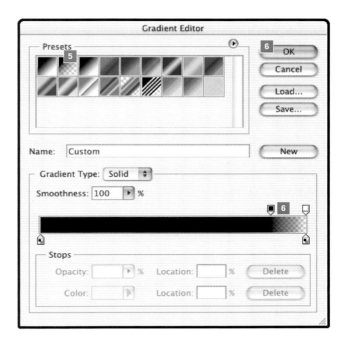

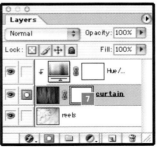

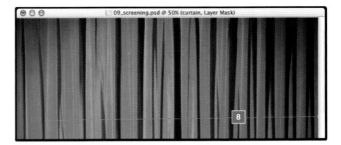

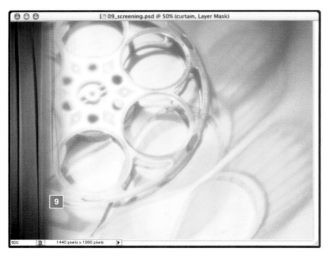

9. **Select the Brush tool in the toolbox and choose a big soft-edged brush from the Brush pop-up palette on the Options bar. Make sure that the layer mask thumbnail is still selected in the Layers palette. Paint with black wherever you want to paint away more of the curtain. Paint with white if you want to restore some of the curtain.**

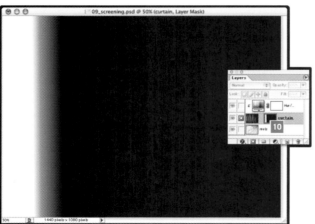

10. **Option+click (Windows: Alt+click) the layer mask thumbnail in the Layers palette to see the actual layer mask.**
    This illustrates the point that a layer mask is a bitmapped image composed entirely of shades of gray. You can see the black area that normally hides the image on the attached curtain layer, the white area that reveals that image, and the gradual gray edge between the two through which that image is partially visible.

11. **Option+click (Windows: Alt+click) the layer mask thumbnail again to return the document window to the normal view.**

12. **Shift+click the layer mask thumbnail in the Layers palette to temporarily disable the layer mask, revealing the image on the attached curtain layer. Shift+click again to reactivate the layer mask.**
    This feature comes in handy when you're trying to reposition a layer mask and need to see what's beneath it. When the layer mask is disabled, you'll see a red *X* across the layer mask thumbnail in the Layers palette.

13. **Choose File→Save. Leave** 09_screening.psd **open for the next tutorial, if you want to use it instead of the fresh file that has been provided for you to use there.**

Tutorial

» Combining a Vector Mask and a Layer Mask

Photoshop 7 offers a powerful vector mask feature that you can use to add a crisp scalable vector object to a layer of soft-edged pixel-based artwork. You can even combine a vector mask with a layer mask, as you'll do in this tutorial. This is an advanced technique, so feel free to skip this tutorial if your brain is full.

1. **Make sure that** `09_screening.psd` **is still open from the last tutorial or open** `09_screening_mask.psd` **from the Session 9 Tutorial Files folder on your hard drive.**
   `09_screening_mask.psd` is a replica of how `09_screening.psd` should look at the end of the last tutorial. Use `09_screening_mask.psd` if you didn't finish the last tutorial or if you messed up the file that you were using in that tutorial.

2. **Select the reels layer in the Layers palette. Click the New Layer button at the bottom of the Layers palette. Double-click the new layer and rename it** clouds**.**

3. **Click the eye icon on the curtain layer to hide that layer temporarily while you work on the layer beneath it.**

What's the Difference between a Vector Mask and a Layer Mask?

On a layer mask, the grayscale pixels that you add to the mask with Photoshop's regular painting and fill tools are what hide or reveal the image on the attached layer. You can paint soft-edged areas on a layer mask to create gradual transitions in the image, using the techniques that you learned in the last tutorial. On a vector mask, vector objects that you create with the Pen, Path, or Shape tools are what hide or reveal the image on the attached layer. Vector objects have smooth edges, as you may remember from Session 6. So vector masks create designs that have crisp edges in your image. Another unique feature of vector masks is that their shape is malleable. You can scale the shape of a vector mask with Transform commands or change the shape of the mask with the Pen tools, just as you can with any vector object. You can use a vector mask to mask out smooth shapes in the artwork on a layer, so you can see through to the layer below. If you want to get really fancy, you can use a vector mask in combination with a layer mask, as you'll do in this tutorial.

The contents of a vector mask are vector objects, which can come from a few different sources. The objects that you add to a vector mask can be objects created with the Shape tools (as in this tutorial), paths that you draw with the Pen tools, or vector objects that you create in another program, such as Illustrator, and copy and paste into the vector mask.

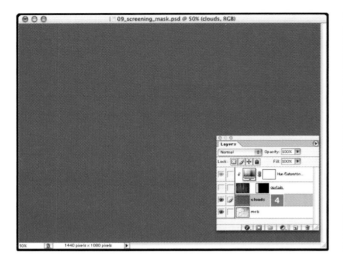

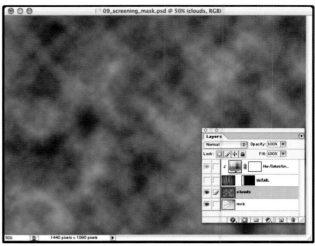

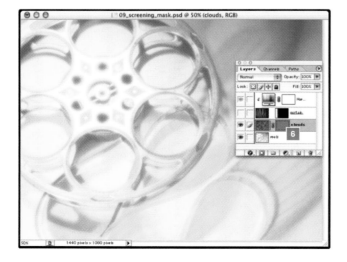

4. **Make sure that the clouds layer is still selected. Double-click the Foreground Color box in the toolbox to open the Color Picker. Choose a dark orange color (R:153, G:51, B:0). Press Option+Delete (Windows: Alt+Delete) to fill the clouds layer with this color.**

5. **Choose Filter→Render→Difference Clouds. Then choose Edit→Fade and move the slider to 86%.**
   This is a quick way to make a textured background. Although it looks "Photoshopped," most of this layer will be hidden from view by the vector mask that you'll be adding, so it will work fine here. You'll learn more about filters in Session 10.

6. **Make sure that the clouds layer is selected and choose Layer→Add Vector Mask→Hide All.**
   This creates a mask that hides all the content of the clouds layer, so you see only the layer below. Notice that the layer mask thumbnail on the clouds layer is filled with gray indicating it is a "hide" mask, rather than a "reveal" mask.

7. **Click the Shape tool that is displayed in the toolbox and choose the Custom Shape tool from the hidden tools menu.**

8. **Click the Paths button on the left side of the Options bar.**
   This causes the Custom Shape tool to draw a path, rather than create a shape layer, which is its default behavior.

9. **Click the Add to Path combination button on the right side of the Options bar.**
   If you don't choose the correct combination button, this tutorial won't work because the path will be inverted.

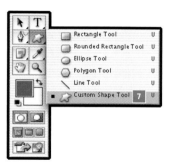

10. **Click the Custom Shape field's down arrow on the Options bar to open the Custom Shape Picker. Click the Grid shape at the bottom of the Custom Shape Picker. Click anywhere in the Options bar to close the Custom Shape Picker.**
    If you don't see the Grid shape in the Custom Shape Picker, click the arrow on the top right of that Picker, choose All from the menu of shapes, and click OK at the prompt.

11. **Press the keyboard shortcuts D and then X to set the foreground color in the toolbox to white.**

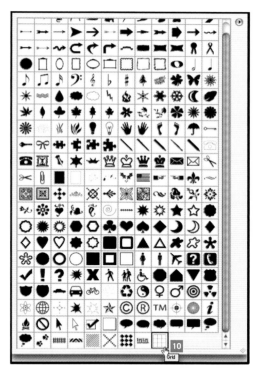

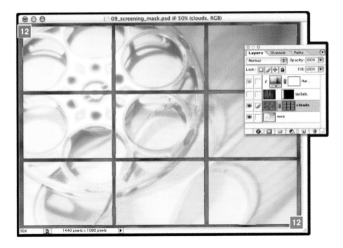

09_screening_mask.psd @ 50% (clouds, RGB)

12. **Click in the very top-left corner of the document window and drag across the image to the bottom-right corner.**

Drag carefully to make sure that the edges of the shape just fit against the boundaries of the document window. This particular shape is made up of multiple paths, so it would be hard to modify later with the Black and White Arrow tools (although it is possible, which is one of the benefits of a vector mask).

13. **Take a minute to play. First go to the History palette and click the Camera icon to make a snapshot of the current state. Then draw some more custom shapes in the grid to make sure that you really understand how this works. Click a shape with the Black Arrow tool to select and move it. Click a point in a shape with the White Arrow tool to modify the shape (like the double note in the figure). When you're done, click the snapshot that you made in the History palette to return to the state with the grid shape.**

If you're familiar with Photoshop 6, you may notice that the vector mask feature is similar to the layer clipping path feature in the last release of the program.

< N O T E >

That's all there is to adding a vector mask. Notice that the edges of the masked shapes are smooth. You can see the outlines of the vector shapes along the edges of the shapes. To hide those outlines, click another layer in the Layers palette. In the next steps, you'll add a layer mask to the same layer.

14. **Make sure that the clouds layer is selected in the Layers palette. Click the Add Layer Mask icon at the bottom of the palette.**

This adds a third thumbnail to the clouds layer. This is a layer mask, like the kind you worked with in the last tutorial. It's not a vector mask.

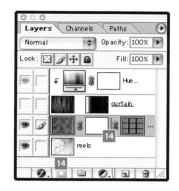

15. **Select the Rectangular Marquee tool in the toolbox. Click and drag around the inside of the four-square on the top left of the document window, as shown here. Try to make the selection butt sharply against, but not cut into, the edges of the bars that surround the selection.**

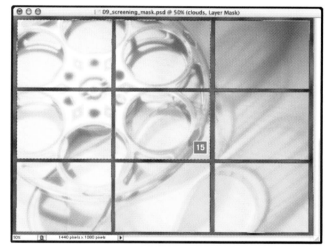

16. **Click the new layer mask thumbnail on the clouds layer in the Layers palette.**

It's very important that you click the right thumbnail. You'll see a black border around the layer mask thumbnail when it's selected.

17. **Press the keyboard shortcuts D and X to set the Foreground Color box in the toolbox to black.**

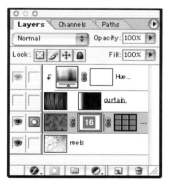

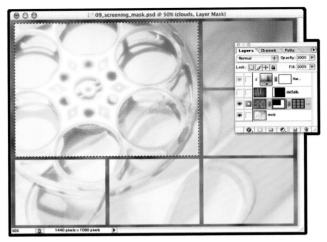

18. **Press Option+Delete (Windows: Alt+Delete) to fill the selection on the layer mask with black. Press the shortcut ⌘+D (Windows: Ctrl+D) to deselect the filled selection.**

    This hides the clouds image on the clouds layer that was previously visible through the vector mask, enabling you to see through this area of the grid to the reels layer below.

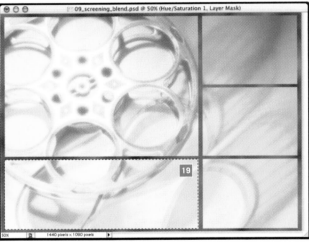

19. **Repeat steps 15 through 18 on the two-square on the bottom left of the document window, to match this figure.**

    < N O T E >

    Comprehending the way multiple masks interact can be mind-bending. So if you don't understand all the twists and turns yet, just remember that a vector mask and a layer mask can interact on the same layer, determining which part of an image is visible or invisible.

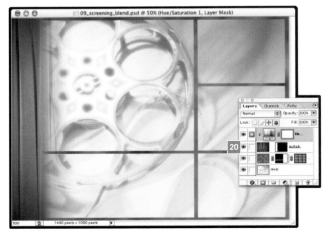

20. **Click the eye icon on the curtain layer in the Layers palette to redisplay that image and its layer mask.**

    As you can see, you can have multiple layers with masks, all of which interact.

21. **Choose File→Save and close the file.**

Tutorial
» Using Blending Sliders to Composite

The Blending sliders in the Layer Style dialog box offer a quick and easy way to blend images on separate layers based on the brightness of pixels in both images. This feature can be used to completely knock out bright or dark pixels in a layer. This makes it easy to eliminate the white backgrounds that you often see in studio photographs like the one you'll use in this tutorial. You'll also use the Transform feature to scale images to match as you composite.

1. **Open** 09_screening_blend.psd **from the Session 9 Tutorial Files folder.**

2. **Open a second file,** 09_vintage.psd, **from the Session 9 Tutorial Files folder.**
   If you get a message about missing file information, ignore it and click OK. It's irrelevant to what you're working on here.

3. **Select the topmost layer, the Hue/Saturation layer, in** 09_screening_blend.psd.

4. **Click and drag** 09_vintage.psd **from its document window into the** 09_screening_blend.psd **document window. (If you get a warning about missing file information, ignore it and click OK.)**
   This creates a new layer in the destination document (09_screening_blend.psd) called Layer 1.

5. **Close** 09_vintage.psd.

6. **Double-click Layer 1 and rename it** camera.

7. **Double-click the thumbnail on the camera layer to open the Layer Style dialog box.**

<NOTE>
The Layer Style dialog box can be intimidating at first. It has several different controls and takes up almost the whole screen on a laptop! Fortunately, you only have to focus on one small part of this monster for now — the Blend If section at the bottom of the Blending Options panel. You'll find out more about other features of this dialog box in Session 10.

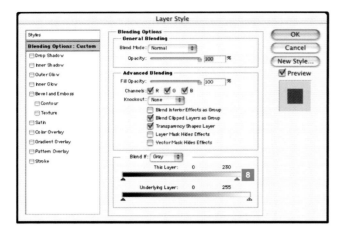

8. Click the white slider on the right side of the bar labeled This Layer and drag it to around 230.

The white area around the vintage camera disappears.

<NOTE>

You're probably wondering what made the white background of the camera disappear. That requires some further understanding of the Layer Style dialog box. Blending Options determine how the pixels in the selected layer (here the camera layer) will blend with pixels in the layers below. The This Layer slider controls which pixels are included in and excluded from that layer blend. The bar represents 255 brightness values with dark on the left and bright on the right. Photoshop blends only those tones between the dark and light sliders. Any tones that fall outside of those sliders are excluded, so they won't be visible in the blended image. When you moved the white slider to the left, you excluded all the bright tones to the right of the slider. That's why the bright whites disappeared from the image. They are actually still there; you just can't see them.

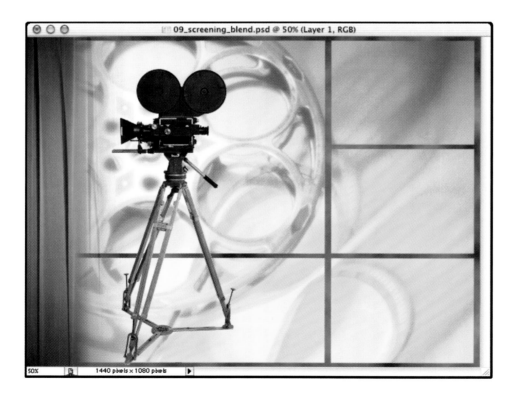

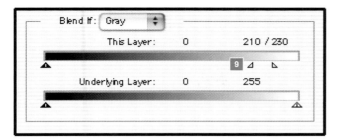

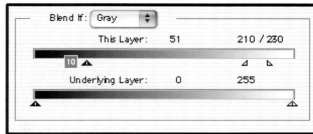

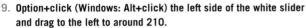

9. **Option+click (Windows: Alt+click) the left side of the white slider and drag to the left to around 210.**

   This should eliminate some of the stray white pixels that were still hanging around the edges of the image.

<NOTE>

Splitting the sliders like this when you move them is a good idea. It helps with the stray pixel problem and gives you a softer, blended edge around an object. That's because Photoshop partially blends any pixels that contain tones that fall between the two parts of the white slider or between the two parts of the black slider.

10. **Drag the black sliders on the This Layer bar to the right to see what they do. Then pull them back to their original position.**

    These sliders work like the white sliders on the This Layer bar, but in the opposite direction. Pulling them to the right causes all darker pixels in the camera layer (those to the left of 51) to disappear from the image.

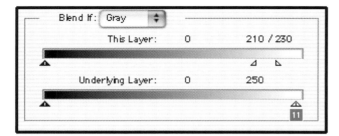

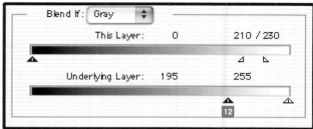

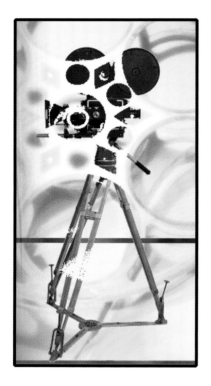

11. **Drag the white sliders on the Underlying Layer bar to the left. When you're done, pull them back to their original position.**

The sliders on the Underlying Layer bar are somewhat different than the sliders on the This Layer bar. Moving the white Underlying Layer sliders to the left causes all brighter tones in the reels layer (those to the right of 250) to break through the selected camera layer.

12. **Drag the black sliders on the Underlying Layer bar to the right. Then pull them back to their original position.**

Moving the black Underlying Layer sliders to the right causes all darker tones in the reels layer (those that are darker than 195) to show through the selected camera layer.

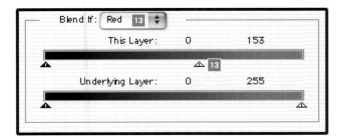

13. **Click the Blend If button and change it from Gray to Red. Move the white This Layer slider to the left. When you're done, return the slider to its original position.**

    The bright reds in the camera legs start to disappear. That's because you're now working in one of the color channels in the image and taking the color of pixels, rather than just their brightness, into account. The ability to exclude pixels on the basis of color gives you even more compositing options.

14. **Click OK in the Layer Style dialog box to close it.**

    You can reopen it at any time to make further modifications to a layer by double-clicking on the layer thumbnail.

<NOTE>

You brought the camera into this collage without resizing or cropping. Now that you can see the camera in place, you may agree that it needs to be scaled down a bit. For that task, you'll use the Transform command. This is just one more way to make images compatible when you're compositing.

15. **Make sure that the camera layer is selected and choose Edit→Transform→Scale from the menu bar at the top of the screen.**

16. **Hold the Shift key, click one of the corner points of the bounding box, and drag to make the camera image slightly smaller to match the figure. Press Return (Windows: Enter) on your keyboard to accept the transformation and eliminate the bounding box.**
If the camera is in a different position than the camera shown here, select the Move tool and reposition it.

17. **Choose File→Save and leave** 09_screening_blend.psd **open for the next tutorial.**

Tutorial
» Using the Measure Tool, Rulers, and Guides

Photoshop has some tools that I think of as handy utilities. They don't do anything fancy, but they're integral to getting the job done efficiently, and they're useful in lots of situations. Rulers, guides, and the Measure tool are that kind of flexible, reliable utility. In this tutorial, you'll practice using them to position artwork in a composite.

1. **Make sure that** `09_screening_blend.psd` **is still open from the last tutorial.**

2. **Click the Eyedropper tool in the toolbox to display a hidden menu of tools and choose the Measure tool.**
   This is a relatively unknown tool that's useful for measuring distances and angles.

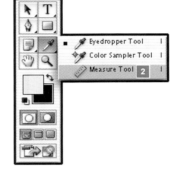

3. **Click the top line made by the vector shape in the right corner of the document window and drag down to the next line of the vector shape to measure the number of pixels of height in that space. Take a look at the H field in the Options bar, which reads approximately 352 pixels.**

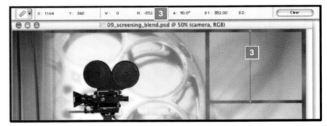

<NOTE>
The Measure tool has another feature that comes in really handy if you have an image that needs to be straightened, like a scan that came out a little crooked (as often happens). Locate a portion of the image that should be straight and click and drag across that area with the Measure tool. Click the end points of the line drawn by the Measure tool to adjust the line. Then choose Image→Rotate→Arbitrary. Photoshop compares the angle of the Measure tool's line to the angle of the image and rotates the image to make it straight.

<TIP>
When you're finished with a measure line, remove it from the visible portion of the document by clicking and dragging it off the side of the document. If you expand your canvas, you'll see that it's still sitting out there, but it won't print with the document.

Another way to measure is with the rulers and guides, which you'll try out in the next steps.

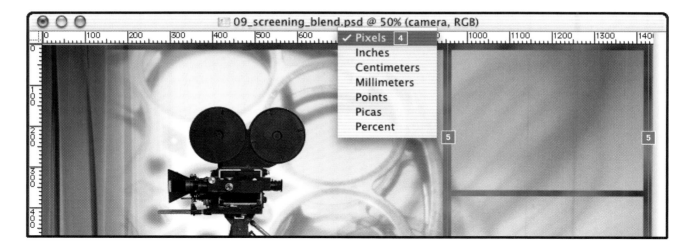

4. **Choose View→Rulers to make the vertical and horizontal rulers around the document visible. If your rulers display inches, change them by Ctrl+clicking (Windows: right-clicking) directly on a ruler and choosing Pixels from the menu that pops up.**

5. **Select the Move tool in the toolbox. Click inside the vertical ruler on the left of the screen and drag to the right to bring out a vertical guide. Position the guide in the middle of the bar made by the vector shape at the far right of the document ruler. Drag out a second vertical ruler and position it in the next vector shape bar to the left.**

   The guides are hard to see on the blue bars in the figure, but they are there.

<NOTE>

To reposition a guide, select the Move tool and move the cursor over the guide until the cursor becomes a double-pointed arrow. Then click and drag.

<NOTE>

There's an invisible grid underlying the document window, which helps position objects symmetrically on the screen. You can see the grid if you choose View→Show Grid. (Dismiss the grid by repeating that command.) Objects snap to the intersections of the grid lines if the Snap To feature is activated. To deactivate Snap To, choose View→Snap To→Grid to uncheck that option.

6. **Click in the top-left corner of the document window, where the two rulers meet, and drag to the first guide in order to reposition the 0, 0 point of the rulers. Take a look at the horizontal ruler on the top of the screen and note that the width of the space between the two guides is about 475 pixels.**

< T I P >

Keep track of the measurements that you've made (width = 475 px and height = 352 pixels) for the next tutorial.

7. **Choose View→Clear Guides to dismiss all the guides.**
   Alternatively, you can drag each guide off the edge of the document window using the Move tool. Or you can leave the guides where they are because guides don't print with a document.

8. **Double-click in the small box where the rulers meet at the top left of the document window to return the 0, 0 point of the rulers to its default.**

9. **Choose File→Save and close** 09_screening_blend.psd.

Tutorial

» Applying Blending Modes

Blending modes are a collection of prebuilt formulas that control how pixels in a layer will interact with pixels in the layers below. You can do some nice work with minimal effort using blending modes. You'll try some of my favorites in this tutorial.

1. **Open** 09_screening_mode.psd **from the Session 9 Tutorial Files folder.**

2. **Open a second document,** 09_lens.psd, **from the Session 9 Tutorial Files folder.**

<NOTE>

Your task is to put the lens image into the box formed by the grid at the top right of 09_screening_mode.psd. When both images are magnified to the same percentage, it's obvious that the lens image is way too big. In the next steps, you'll use the Crop tool to bring it down to size.

3. **Select the Crop tool from the toolbox. Type the dimensions that you measured in the last tutorial — Width:** 475 px, **Height:** 352 px **— into the respective fields on the Options bar. Leave the resolution at 240, which is the resolution of the destination document.** Photoshop needs the resolution to resample the image; otherwise, it just crops out part of the image with the specified dimensions.

4. **Click and drag in the document window of** 09_lens.psd, **reposition the cropping selection as you feel necessary, and press Return or Enter.**

5. **Make sure that the topmost layer — the camera layer — is selected in the Layers palette of** 09_screening_mode.psd.

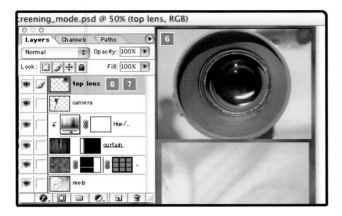

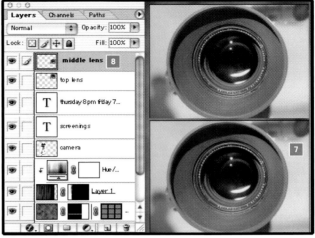

6. **Select the Move tool in the toolbox and click and drag the single layer from the** `09_lens.psd` **Layers palette (or document window) into the** `09_screening_mode.psd` **document window. Position the lens image in the rectangle at the top right of the image.**
   This creates a new layer in the destination document.

7. **Double-click the new layer and name it** top lens. **Then hold the Option key (Windows: Alt key), click the lens image in the document window, and drag down to the next grid box.**
   This creates a copy of the image and a new layer in the Layers palette called *top lens copy*.

8. **Double-click the top lens copy layer and rename it** middle lens. **Hold the Option key (Windows: Alt key), click the middle lens image in the document window, and drag down to the bottom grid box.**
   This creates yet another layer in the Layers palette called *middle lens copy*.

9. **Double-click the middle lens copy layer in the Layers palette and rename it** bottom lens.

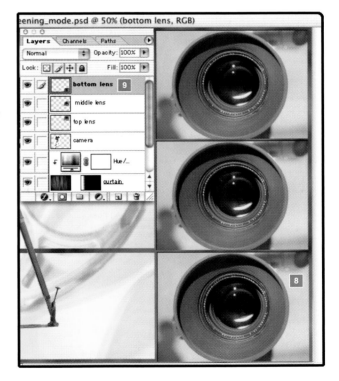

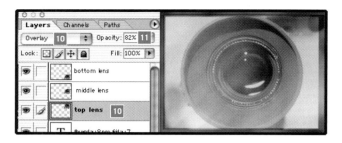

10. **Select the top lens layer in the Layers palette. Click the Blending Mode button on the top left of the palette and choose Overlay.**
The Overlay mode is one of my favorites. It darkens some pixels in the selected layer and lightens others depending on the pixels in the underlying layer. This often results in a painterly image that doesn't look too distorted.

11. **Click the Opacity field in the Layers palette and lower the opacity of the layer to around 82%.**
Lowering the opacity makes the effect of the blending mode more subtle.

12. **Repeat steps 10 and 11 on the middle lens layer, but choose the Exclusion blending mode. Lower the opacity to around 55%.**

What's New in Blending Modes

The blending modes menu has been reorganized in Photoshop 7 — which is a good thing. Blending modes are now grouped into more logical categories, which proves useful when you're trying out different blending modes but have only a general idea of the result that you're looking for. There is a group of modes that always darkens (Darken through Linear Burn), a group that always lightens (Lighten through Linear Dodge), and a group that darkens or lightens depending on the colors involved

(Overlay through Pin Light). There are also some new blending modes in Photoshop 7 — Linear Burn, Linear Dodge, Vivid Light, Linear Light, and Pin Light. If you'd like to read a technical explanation of each blending mode, take a look at the Photoshop 7 Help Files. My view is that this is a feature you have to use to understand. Each blending mode offers different results in different situations. So I suggest that you try out a few on the same image and compare the results, as shown in this tutorial.

13. **Repeat steps 10 and 11 on the bottom lens layer, but choose the Difference blending mode. Lower the opacity of the layer to around 63%.**

<TIP>

You may be wondering why I chose these particular blending modes and opacities. Unfortunately, there is no secret formula that I can share. I suggest that you experiment like crazy and see what works, keeping basic principles of good design and your own artistic style in mind. For example, in this case I looked for blending modes that honored the color palette of the image, and I tried to put the heavier, more dramatic effect on the bottom image to avoid creating imbalance.

14. **Select the Type tool. In the Options bar, set Font to Tahoma, Size to 18 pt, Anti-aliasing to Smooth, and Color to a burnt orange (R:172, G:77, B:46). Type** screenings**. Select the Move tool and drag the type into place.**

Selecting the Move tool also serves to accept the type, so you don't have to click the Check Mark icon on the Options bar.

15. **Change Size to 12 pt in the Options bar. Click in the document again and type a few more lines of text to match those shown here.**

If you get stuck, jump ahead and scan Session 11.

16. **Choose File→Save As, navigate to your collages folder, and rename the document** 09_screening_end.psd**. Save it as a final collage for your program guide project.**

» Session Review

In this session, you learned some techniques for compositing images. You used the Crop tool to make images compatible. You applied layer masks and a vector mask to hide and reveal artwork on layers. You learned how to use the blending sliders in the Layer Style dialog box and blending modes in the Layers palette. You also got a taste of Photoshop's utility tools — rulers, guides, and the Measure tool. These questions will help you review this session.

1. What tool can you use to resample and match the size of one image to another? (See "Tutorial: Making Images Compatible.")

2. What do you have to do to two documents to get a true picture of their relative size on-screen? (See "Tutorial: Making Images Compatible.")

3. What kind of image is a layer mask? (See "Tutorial: Joining Images with Layer Masks.")

4. What would you use a layer mask for when compositing? (See "Tutorial: Joining Images with Layer Masks.")

5. What does pressing the keyboard shortcuts D and then X accomplish? (See "Tutorial: Joining Images with Layer Masks.")

6. What colors should you usually use to paint on a layer mask? (See "Tutorial: Joining Images with Layer Masks.")

7. Name two ways to create a soft edge on a layer mask. (See "Tutorial: Joining Images with Layer Masks.")

8. Can you have more than one mask on a layer? (See "Tutorial: Combining a Vector Mask and a Layer Mask.")

9. Name one difference between a layer mask and a vector mask. (See "Tutorial: Combining a Vector Mask and a Layer Mask.")

10. Name two different tools that you can use to put a vector object on a vector mask. (See "Tutorial: Combining a Vector Mask and a Layer Mask.")

11. How can you change the scale or shape of an object on a vector mask? (See "Tutorial: Combining a Vector Mask and a Layer Mask.")

12. How do you make a Shape tool draw a path, rather than create a shape layer? (See "Tutorial: Combining a Vector Mask and a Layer Mask.")

13. What does sliding the white slider on the This Layer bar in the Layer Style dialog box accomplish? (See "Tutorial: Using Blending Sliders to Composite.")

14. How do you turn on rulers? (See "Tutorial: Using the Measure Tool, Rulers, and Guides.")

15. How do you change the units of measurement used by the rulers? (See "Tutorial: Using the Measure Tool, Rulers, and Guides.")

16. How do you create a guide? (See "Tutorial: Using the Measure Tool, Rulers, and Guides.")

17. What's the Measure tool used for? (See "Tutorial: Using the Measure Tool, Rulers, and Guides.")

18. What does the blending mode of a layer do? (See "Tutorial: Applying Blending Modes.")

screenings

thursday 8 pm
friday 7 pm
saturday 8 pm
saturday 10pm
sunday 12 pm
sunday 4 pm

Filters, Layer Styles, and Special Effects

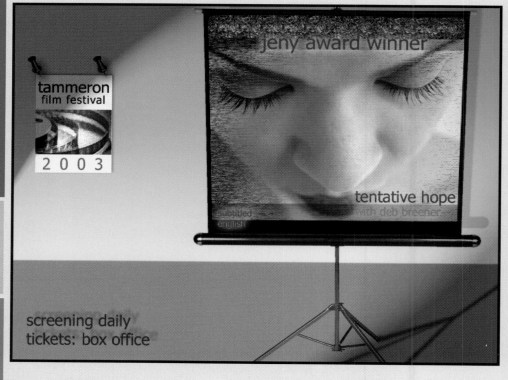

Session Introduction

Photoshop has a number of features that you can use to add special effects to images and text. In this session, you'll practice using filters to add special effects to the entire contents of a layer and to a selection of artwork on a layer. You'll also learn to use layer styles, with which you can add effects that are customizable and editable and do not destroy the underlying artwork. You'll create a customized layer style, save it in the Styles palette, and see how easy it is to reapply to another layer or image. You'll also try your hand at creating interesting effects with the History and Art History brushes, which you can use to paint with pixels from previous states, and with the Liquify feature, which you'll use to distort an image.

TOOLS YOU'LL USE
Gaussian Blur filter, Fade command, Mezzotint filter, Lighting Effects filter, Layer Style dialog box, Drop Shadow layer style, Color Overlay layer style, shape layers, Gradient Overlay layer style, Outer Glow layer style, Styles palette, Liquify feature, History palette, and History Brush tool

CD-ROM FILES NEEDED
10_effects.psd and 10_effects_end.psd

TIME REQUIRED
45 minutes

Tutorial
» Using Filters

Photoshop 7 ships with dozens of filters that apply prebuilt special effects to an image or text on a layer. In this tutorial, you'll use one of many image correction filters — the Gaussian Blur filter — to soften a shadow so that it looks more realistic. Along the way, you'll learn some filter basics, including how to preview filter effects and reapply a filter to intensify its effect.

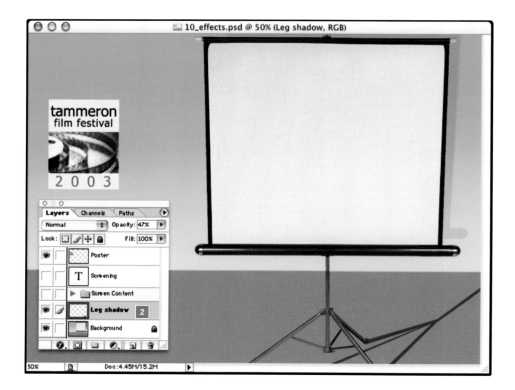

1. **Choose File→Open, navigate to** `10_effects.psd` **in the folder of Session 10 tutorial files on your hard drive, and click Open. Click Update if you see a warning that some text layers may need to be updated.**

    <NOTE>
    This is an RGB color image. Many filters (such as the Lighting Effects filter, which you'll use later in this session) are only available for use on RGB color images and don't work on CMYK images. If you want to use these filters on an image destined for a commercial printer, you can edit in RGB mode and then convert to CMYK mode (Image→Mode→CMYK).

2. **Select the Leg shadow layer in the Layers palette (Window→Layers).**

    You must select a layer before you apply a filter because a filter affects the active layer only, not the entire image.

3. **Choose Filter→Blur→Gaussian Blur.**

   The Gaussian Blur dialog box opens. The area filled with a checkerboard pattern is a preview pane in which you can view the effect of various filter settings before you apply a filter. You won't see a preview of the movie screen legs' shadow here without adjusting the view in the preview pane, as you'll do in the next steps.

4. **Move your cursor into the document window so that it changes to a square and click the shadow of the movie screen legs.**

   This centers the view in the preview pane on the shadow.

<TIP>

Another way to change the view in a filter's preview pane is to click and drag inside the preview pane to scroll to other parts of the image. The cursor automatically changes to a hand icon.

5. **Click the minus icon in the Gaussian Blur dialog box to zoom out so that you can see more of the shadow in the preview pane.**

6. **Make sure that there's a check mark in the Preview box in the Gaussian Blur dialog box so that you can see a live preview of your filter settings in the document window.**

   The live preview gives you a better view of the final result than the preview in the Gaussian Blur dialog box. However, the live preview takes a lot of processing power. If previewing filter effects on your computer is slowing you down, uncheck the Preview box.

<NOTE>

Not all filters offer a live image preview in the document window.

7. **Type 2 in the Radius field in the Gaussian Blur dialog box. Click OK.**

   The Radius setting determines the amount of blur. You can also use the slider to set this field. Although the current setting does soften the shadow, more softening is required to make the shadow look real. In the next step you'll learn a quick way to reapply the Gaussian Blur filter to intensify the blur effect.

8. **Click Filter and choose Gaussian Blur from the top of the menu.**

   This reapplies the Gaussian Blur filter with the same Radius setting that you chose in the last step. Photoshop saves the most recent filter settings as the top entry in the Filter menu.

<TIP>

The keyboard shortcut to repeat a filter is ⌘+F (Windows: Ctrl+F).

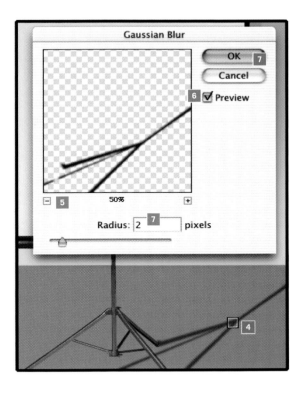

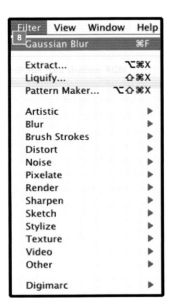

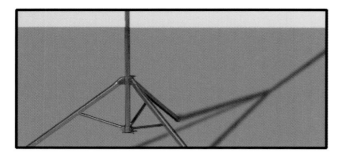

9. Repeat step 7.

The Gaussian Blur filter has now been applied three times in total. The shadow should look similar to the one shown here.

< N O T E >

The results of your successive applications of the Gaussian Blur filter could have been accomplished in one step by specifying a higher radius number when the filter was first applied. However, there are times when it is better to work in small steps. When you lightly apply a filter and then repeat to intensify the effect, you can experiment until you get to just the right amount of filtering.

10. Choose File→Save and leave the document open for the next tutorial.

Using Filters Wisely

Photoshop's filters can create some striking and useful effects, but you should be aware of their downsides. For one thing, filters produce standardized effects that can make your images look like everyone else's if you're not careful. Don't let this stop you from using filters, but do think about whether applying a filter will serve a real purpose. One legitimate purpose for which you'll use certain filters is to correct flaws in an image. For example, you've seen in this tutorial that the Gaussian Blur filter is useful for softening the look of hard-edged artwork. Along the same lines, you'll find the Dust & Scratches filter (in the Noise filter submenu) useful for eliminating small spots and imperfections and the Unsharp Mask filter (in the Sharpen filter submenu) great for sharpening scanned and retouched images.

Another problem with filters is that they permanently change the pixels of artwork that they affect. That leaves you little room for changing your mind after you've applied a filter to a layer, other than one chance at the Fade command (which you'll practice using in the next tutorial) or backing up to a previous state in the History palette. One way around this is to make a copy of a layer before you apply a filter. You can use layer blending modes to blend the filtered copy with the unfiltered original, and you'll always have the original to return to if you change your mind. A similar solution is to create a layer filled with a shade of black that is neutral in a particular blending mode and apply the filter to that layer, as you'll do in a tutorial later in this session. Another alternative is to create effects with layer styles, which are always editable, rather than filters. You'll learn about layer styles later in this session.

Tutorial
» Filtering Selected Areas

You won't always want to apply a filter effect to an entire layer. Photoshop selections provide the ideal solution. You can use any of Photoshop's selection tools to restrict the area to which a filter is applied. In this tutorial, you'll create a decorative effect using the Mezzotint filter on a selected part of a layer, without affecting the rest of the artwork on that layer. You'll also learn how to fade the intensity of a filter effect right after applying a filter.

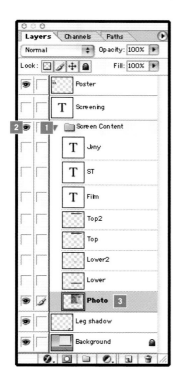

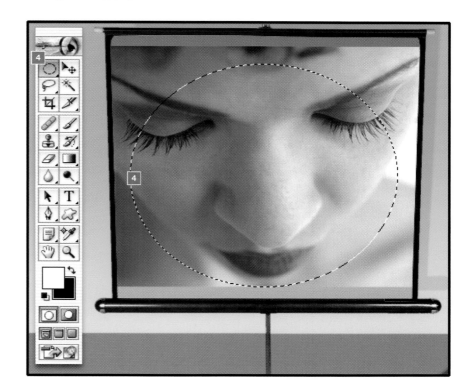

1. **Make sure that** `10_effects.psd` **is still open from the last tutorial. Click the triangle on the Screen Content layer set to expand that layer set in the Layers palette.**

2. **Click in the empty Visibility field of the Screen Content layer set.**
   This makes the one visible layer inside that layer set — the Photo layer — appear in the document window. You'll use the other layers in this layer set in later tutorials. All layers except the Photo layer in this set should have visibility turned off for now.

3. **Select the Photo layer.**

4. **Select the Elliptical Marquee tool in the toolbox. Click and drag in the woman's photo in the document window to select the center of her face (an area that includes most of the eyes and all of the nose and mouth, like the one shown here).**
   The easiest way to draw this selection is to hold the Option key (Windows: Alt key) to draw from the center outward. Without releasing the mouse button or the Option (Alt) key, press the spacebar to reposition the ellipse as you draw. When you're done, release the mouse button and then the Option (Alt) key.

5. **Choose Select→Feather from the menu bar at the top of the screen.**

   The Feather Selection dialog box opens.

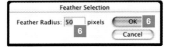

6. **Type** 50 **in the Feather Radius field. Click OK.**

   Feathering the selection provides a smooth transition between the woman's face, which won't be filtered, and the surrounding artwork on the layer, to which you will apply a decorative filter.

7. **Choose Select→Inverse.**

   This reverses your original selection so that now what's selected is everything except the woman's face. The filter that you're about to apply will affect only what is within the inverted selection boundaries on the selected layer.

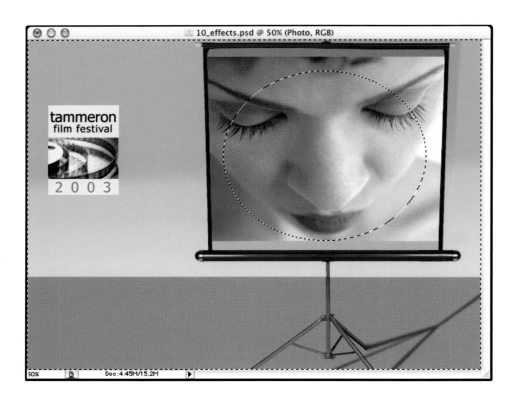

8. **Choose Filter→Pixelate→Mezzotint.**

   The Mezzotint dialog box opens, with a menu of types of mezzotint patterns and a preview pane.

9. **Choose Short Lines from the Type list. Click OK.**

   A strong filter effect appears in the document. The next step will reduce the intensity of the effect.

10. **Choose Edit→Fade Mezzotint.**

    The Fade dialog box opens. This command enables you to scale back the intensity of a filter effect, but it must be used immediately after the filter is applied. If you do anything else before making this choice, this command won't be available.

11. **Drag the Opacity slider in the Fade dialog box to 35%. Click OK.**

    You can preview the fade effect in the document window.

12. **Press ⌘+D (Windows: Ctrl+D) to deselect.**

13. **Choose File→Save and leave the document open for the next tutorial.**

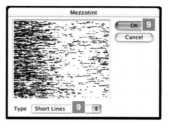

Tutorial

» Applying a Lighting Effect

Light is one of the most difficult effects to draw. Luckily, Photoshop provides a full lighting toolbox with its Lighting Effects filter. The Lighting Effects filter offers many adjustable attributes. In this tutorial, you'll create a custom spotlight effect to add drama and interest to the scene. You'll also learn how to apply a filter to a neutral-colored layer so that the filter doesn't alter the pixels of the layer that it affects. This gives you the option of deleting the filter effect at any time.

1. **Make sure that** `10_effects.psd` **is still open from the last tutorial. Select the Poster layer in the Layers palette.**

2. **Choose Layer→New→Layer.**
   The New Layer dialog box opens.

3. **Type** Lighting **for the name of the new layer in the New Layer dialog box. Choose Multiply from the Mode menu and put a check mark in the Fill with Multiply-Neutral Color (White) check box. Click OK.**
   This creates a new layer above the Poster layer that is filled with white and will blend with the underlying layer using the Multiply layer blending mode. In this blending mode, white is a neutral color, which means that it disappears, leaving only the filter effect that you're about to add to this layer.

<NOTE>
The method described in the preceding step shortens and takes the guesswork out of creating a neutral layer for a filter. You can get the same result by clicking the New Layer icon at the bottom of the Layers palette, setting the foreground color to the neutral color for the blending mode that you plan to use (which you'd have to determine by trial and error), pressing Option+Delete (Windows: Alt+Delete) to fill the layer with the foreground color, and setting the layer's blending mode.

4. **Check that the Lighting layer is selected in the Layers palette. Choose Filter→Render→Lighting Effects.**

   The Lighting Effects dialog box opens, which has several options for controlling lighting.

5. **Make sure that the Preview option is checked in the Lighting Effects dialog box.**

   This enables you to see a preview of your lighting effect in the Lighting Effects dialog box. Unfortunately, you can't see the underlying image in this preview, and there is no live image preview in the document window for this filter. This means that you have to use trial and error to get just the right lighting effect when you are working on a neutral color layer. (If you were working directly on an image layer, the image would be visible in the preview pane of this dialog box.)

6. **Choose Flood Light from the Style drop-down list.**

   Each preset style in this list sets the other controls in the Lighting Effects dialog box. You can modify these settings further to get the effect that you want, as you'll do in the next steps.

7. **Choose Spotlight from the Light Type drop-down list.**

   Spotlight creates a beam of light that is bright at its source and tapers off.

8. **Drag the slider bars to set each of the following attributes for Light Type: Focus: 100, Intensity: 21.**

   Focus controls the reach of the spotlight's beam. Intensity controls the brightness of the spotlight. The color field in the Light Type section enables you to change the color of the spotlight. Leave it white for now.

9. **Drag the slider bars in the Properties section of the dialog box to match the following settings: Gloss: 0, Material: 69, Exposure: 45, Ambience: 18.**

   Gloss and Material control how the light appears to reflect off the underlying image. Exposure affects the brightness of all the lights in the image, including the general ambient light. Ambience controls the level of that general light. The color field in the Properties section enables you to change the color of the ambient light. Leave it white for now.

10. **Leave Texture Channel set to None.**

    Texture Channel can be used to make one of the color channels in the image into a texture map that controls the brightness and darkness of different areas of the image.

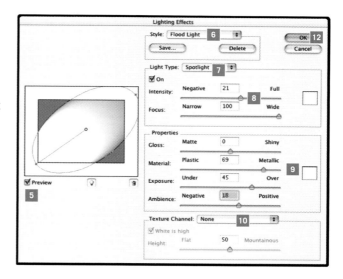

< T I P >

You can add multiple lights to an image by clicking the light bulb icon under the preview pane in the Lighting Effects dialog box.

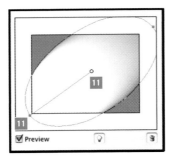

11. **Drag the small white circle in the preview pane to reposition the light, and the gray side handles on the ellipse to resize and rotate the light so that it looks like what's shown here.**

    Notice that the ellipse extends outside of the preview pane in this example.

12. **Click OK to apply the Lighting Effects filter with these settings to the Lighting layer.**

    The lighting effect should resemble the light shown here. Notice that the directional light adds dimension and life to the image.

< W A R N I N G >

Applying this filter is the only way to test the effect in your document because the Lighting Effects filter has no live image preview. If you aren't happy with the result, you can delete the Lighting layer and start over. The settings that you used will still be in place in the Lighting Effects dialog box. The Lighting Effects filter is tricky to work with. You may have to start over several times to make your document look like the final illustration in this tutorial.

13. **Click the New Snapshot button at the bottom of the History palette (Window→History).**

14. **Experiment with reducing the opacity of the Lighting layer, turning its visibility on and off, and even deleting the layer, just as you could with any layer.**

    Isolating the filter on a neutral layer gives you this editing flexibility that's otherwise lacking when you use a filter and preserves the original artwork.

15. **Click the Snapshot 1 state at the top of the History palette to return the image to the way that it looked before your experiments.**

16. **Choose File→Save and leave the document open for the next tutorial.**

Tutorial

» Creating a Layer Style

Layer styles are a more flexible method of applying special effects than filters. A layer style doesn't alter the actual pixels of the layer that it affects. You can edit, hide, or delete a layer style at any time. Also, layer styles come with many options, making them fully customizable. In this tutorial, you'll learn how to create and customize layer styles.

1. **Make sure that** 10_effects.psd **is still open from the last tutorial.**

2. **Click the triangle on the Screen Content layer set to collapse that layer set. Click in the empty Visibility field to the left of the Screening layer to display the text on that layer in the image. Select the Poster layer in the Layers palette.**

3. **Click the Add Layer Style button (the button with the *f* symbol) at the bottom of the Layers palette and choose Drop Shadow from the list of layer styles.**
   This adds a Drop Shadow layer style to the Poster layer and opens the Layer Style dialog box, in which you can customize that drop shadow.

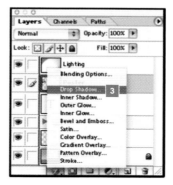

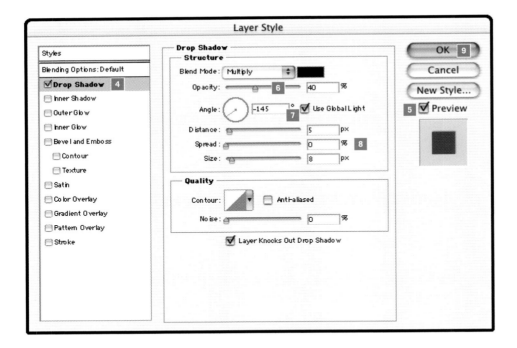

4. **Check that the Drop Shadow option in the Styles section displays a check mark and is highlighted.**
   The check mark indicates that the Drop Shadow layer style is active on the selected layer. The highlight is what makes the Drop Shadow settings appear on the right side of the Layer Style dialog box.

5. Make sure that there is a check mark in the Preview check box.
   This enables you to see a live preview in the document window of the layer style that you're creating. This preview updates as you change the settings in the Layer Style dialog box.

6. **Drag the Opacity slider to 40% in the Drop Shadow options section of the dialog box.**

Reducing the opacity of a shadow helps create a natural look.

7. **Set the angle to −145. Make sure that Use Global Light is checked.**
   Angle controls the direction of the shadow. The check mark next to Use Global Light ensures that this layer style shares the same lighting direction as other layer styles that you may add to this image. If you already had a shadow, bevel, or other directional layer style on another layer, changing the Angle to −145 here would change that layer style too. Keeping shadows and other effects at a consistent angle makes images look more realistic.

8. **Drag the Size slider to 8 and the Distance slider to 5.**
   Size and Distance determine how far the shadow extends beyond the edge of the artwork. Increasing the size of a shadow provides a softer effect.

9. **Click OK to accept the changes and return to the document.**
   Notice the drop shadow effect on the Poster layer in the

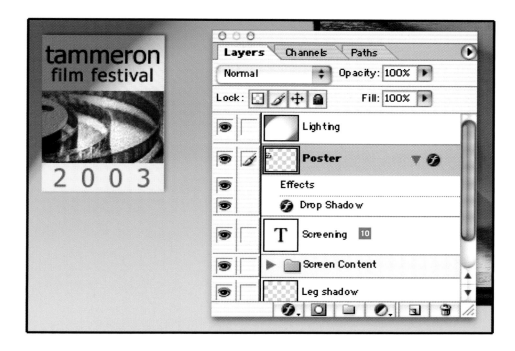

<**TIP**>
You can edit the settings that you've applied to this drop shadow layer style at any time by double-clicking its name in the Layers palette to reopen the Layer Styles dialog box.

<**TIP**>
Layer styles are very flexible. You can hide, delete, copy, or collapse an existing layer style straight from the Layers palette, as follows:

- To hide an individual layer style, click its eye icon in the Layers palette. To hide all the layer styles on a layer, click the eye icon next to the word *Effects* on that layer.

- To delete a layer style, click it and drag it to the Trash button at the bottom of the Layers palette. To delete all the layer styles on a layer, click the word *Effects* and drag it to the same Trash button.

- To copy a layer style from one layer to another, just click the layer style in the Layers palette and drag it just beneath the other layer until you see a black bar.

- To collapse your view of layer styles in order to tidy up the Layers palette, click the triangle next to the word *Effects*.

10. Double-click the Screening layer.
The Layer Style dialog box opens.

<**WARNING**>
Be careful not to click directly on the layer name, or you'll just highlight the layer name for renaming rather than open the Layer Style dialog box.

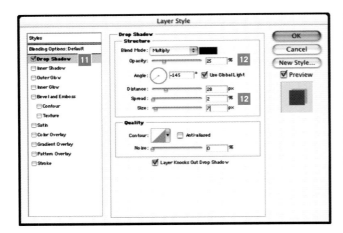

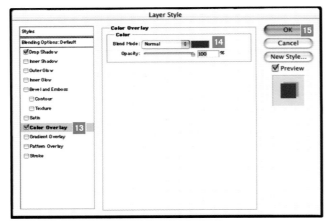

11. **Click the Drop Shadow item in the Styles section.**
    This applies a drop shadow to the selected layer (yet another way of creating a layer style) and opens the Drop Shadow settings on the right side of the dialog box.

12. **Set the opacity to 25%, the distance to 28 px, the spread to 2, and size to 7. View the preview of this shadow in the image, but do *not* click OK yet.**
    As the distance setting increases, a shadowed object appears to be farther away from the background. It is a good idea to create a light, soft shadow when using higher distance values, as you've done here.

13. **Click Color Overlay in the Styles section of the Layer Style dialog box.**
    This adds another layer style to the selected layer, and the Color Overlay options appear in the right pane. Note that the color of the screening text in your document changes to red, the default color for the color overlay.

14. **Click the Color field in the Layer Style dialog box to open the Color Picker. Type the following values in the RGB fields in the Color Picker: R:** 67, **G:** 109, **B:** 7. **Click OK.**
    The text in the image changes to purple.

15. **Click OK to accept the layer style settings and return to the document.**

16. **Choose File→Save and keep the document open for the next tutorial.**

Tutorial
» Saving a Layer Style to the Styles Palette

Photoshop takes much of the work out of creating special effects, but often you create a unique combination of layer styles that could be useful in the future. Photoshop provides the Styles palette to collect and save styles, an efficient way to reduce the time spent creating special effects and to guarantee consistency. It's easy to reapply these styles to a different layer or even to a different document. In this tutorial, you'll create a complex layer style, save it to the Styles palette, and then apply it to a different layer.

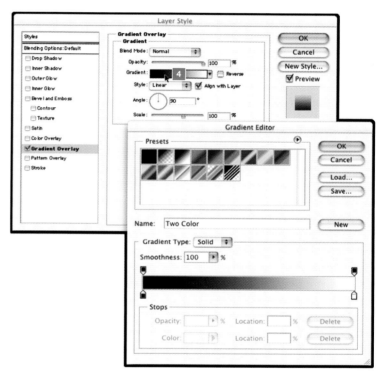

1. **Make sure that** 10_effects.psd **is still open from the last tutorial.**

2. **Expand the Screen Content layer set in the Layers palette and make all layers in the set visible.**

3. **Select the Film layer in the Layers palette. Click the New Layer Style button at the bottom of the palette and choose Gradient Overlay from the list of layer styles.**
   The Layer Style dialog box opens with the Gradient Overlay settings displayed.

<NOTE>
The Gradient Overlay layer style is another way to apply a gradient (in addition to the Gradient tool and Gradient Fill layer that you learned about in earlier sessions). The layer style method of applying a gradient has several advantages: This gradient applies only to one layer, is fully editable at any time, and doesn't affect the pixels of artwork in the image.

4. **Click the gradient sample in the Layer Style dialog box to open the Gradient Editor.**
   Be careful to click right on the gradient sample rather than on the arrow to the right of the gradient sample.

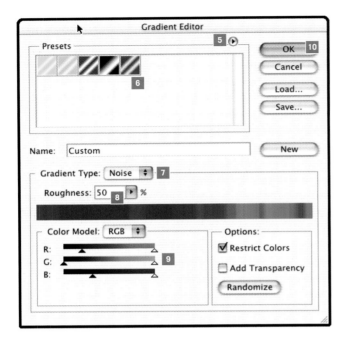

5. **Click the arrow at the top right of the Gradient Editor and choose Metals from the drop-down menu.**
   A set of prebuilt gradients appears in the Presets area of the Gradient Editor.

6. **Select the Steel Blue gradient in the Presets area of the Gradient Editor.**

7. **Select Noise from the Gradient Type drop-down list.**
   This produces a gradient with a banded appearance rather than a smooth one.

8. **Set Roughness to 50.**
   Roughness controls the intensity of the banding effect.

9. **Drag the red and blue color sliders to the right to match those shown here.**
   These sliders define the range of colors in the gradient.

<NOTE>
As you create your custom gradient, you can preview how it will look in the document (on the words "tentative hope with deb breener").

10. **Click OK in the Gradient Editor.**
    You are returned to the Layer Style dialog box in which you'll see your customized gradient.

11. **Choose Linear for the style, −90 for the angle, and 46% for the scale setting in the Gradient settings section of the Layer Style dialog box.**
    Linear is the type of gradient, Angle controls the direction of the gradient, and Scale defines the size of the gradient.

    Your custom gradient is complete. It's fine if yours looks a little different than the one shown here.

    Don't click OK in the Layer Style dialog box yet. You will add one more layer style to this layer before you close this dialog box.

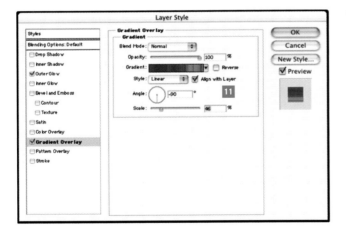

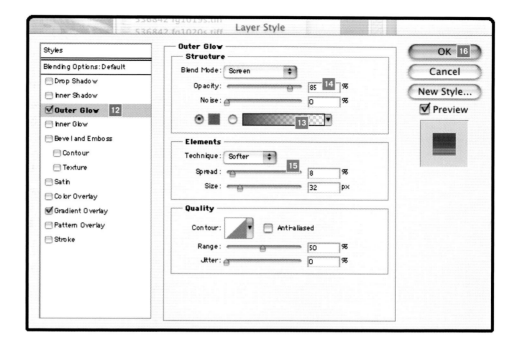

12. **Click Outer Glow in the Styles section of the Layer Style dialog box.**
An outer glow applies a gentle color around the outside of an object — in this case, text.

13. **Click the Color field in the Structure section of the Outer Glow settings to open the Color Picker. Select R: 158, G: 53, B: 120 from the Color Picker and click OK.**
This sets the color of the outer glow, which fades from this magenta color to transparent.

14. **Set the opacity to 85%.**
It's typical to have to increase the opacity of the default Outer Glow layer style to be able to see it against certain backgrounds.

15. **In the Elements section, set Technique to Softer, Spread to 8%, and Size to 32 px.**
These settings control the look and size of the glow.

16. **Click OK to close the Layer Style dialog box.**
Now that you have this combination of custom gradient and glow layer styles defined and applied, you can save them as a single style in the Styles palette for later use.

17. **Choose Window→Styles.**
The Styles palette opens. You will use the layer style to create a new style.

< W A R N I N G >
Don't be confused by the similarity of the terms *layer style* and *style*. A layer style can stand alone or be a component of a style. A style is made up of a combination of layer styles and is stored in the Styles palette.

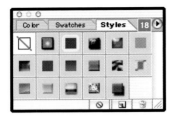

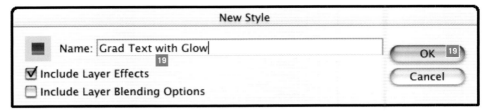

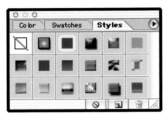

18. **Click the arrow on the right side of the Styles panel and select New Style.**
The New Style dialog box opens.

19. **Type** Grad Text with Glow **as the style name. Make sure that there's a check mark next to Include Layer Effects to ensure that the glow and gradient layer styles are included in the style. Click OK.**
The new style appears in the Styles palette.

< N O T E >

If you hover over any style in the Styles palette, its name will appear.

20. **Select the ST layer in the Layers palette.**
You will now apply the Grad Text with Glow style that you created to this layer of text.

21. **Click your new Grad Text with Glow style in the Styles palette.**
The layer style is now applied to the ST layer, and the words "subtitled english" in the image display the same style as the words on the Film layer. That's all there is to applying a style to the artwork on a layer.

22. **Choose File→Save and keep this document open for the next tutorial.**

Tutorial
» Creating a Shape Layer with a Style

You saw how easy it is to apply a style to a layer in the last tutorial. If you're creating a shape layer, you can kill two birds with one stone by creating the shape complete with a style, as you'll do in this tutorial.

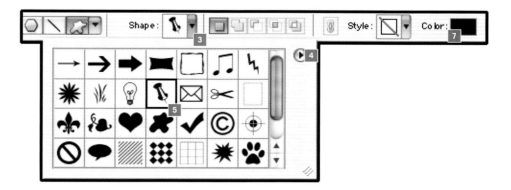

1. **Make sure that** 10_effects.psd **is still open from the last tutorial.**

2. **Click whichever Shape tool is showing in the toolbox and choose the Custom Shape tool from the hidden menu.**

<NOTE>

If you need to review how to use Shape tools and shape layers, turn back to Session 6.

3. **Click the Shape field down arrow on the Options bar to open the Shape Picker.**

4. **Click the arrow at the top right of the Shape Picker and choose Reset Shapes from the menu. Click OK at the prompt.**

5. **Select the Thumbtack shape from the Shape Picker.**

6. **Click anywhere on the Options bar to close the Shape Picker.**

7. **Click the Color field on the Options bar to open the Color Picker. Choose black (R: 0, G: 0, B: 0) in the Color Picker and click OK.**

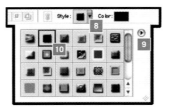

8. **Click the Style field down arrow on the Options bar to open the Style Picker.**

9. **Click the arrow at the top right of the Style Picker and choose Buttons from the menu. Click OK at the prompt.**
   The Style Picker now displays thumbnails that represent the contents of the Buttons set of style presets.

10. **Select the Basic Black style from the Style Picker. Click anywhere on the Options bar to close the Style Picker.**

   <TIP>
   Hold your cursor over any of the thumbnails in the Style Picker to see the name of that style.

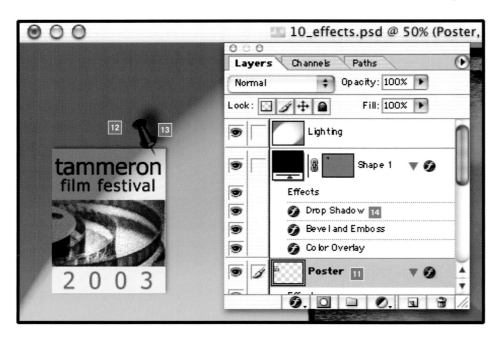

11. **Select the Poster layer in the Layers palette.**

12. **Hold the Shift key to constrain the height and width of the shape and drag in the image to create a small thumbtack shape complete with the Basic Black style.**
    Notice that there is a new shape layer in the Layers palette called Shape 1 that contains several layer styles (which make up the Basic Black style).

13. **Select the Move tool and drag the shape into place at the top-right edge of the poster in the image.**

14. **Double-click the Drop Shadow layer style on the Shape 1 layer.**
    This opens the Layer Style dialog box with the Drop Shadow settings displayed.

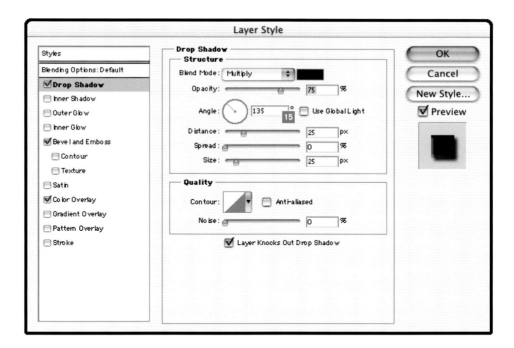

15. **Uncheck Use Global Light in the Layer Style dialog box and set the angle to 135.**
    This customizes one of the layer styles that is now attached to the Shape 1 layer.

16. **Drag the Shape 1 layer to the New Layer button at the bottom of the Layers palette to create a copy of the Shape 1 layer and its layer styles.**

17. **Make sure that the Move tool is still selected and the Shape 1 copy layer is selected. Hold the Shift key to constrain movement to a straight line and drag the duplicate shape to the left side of the poster in the image.**

<TIP>
Click a layer other than one of the shape layers to see the image without any vector outlines obscuring your view.

18. **Choose File→Save and leave the document open for the next tutorial.**

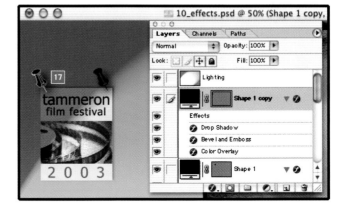

Tutorial

» Liquifying an Image

The Liquify feature, which has been moved to the Filter menu in Photoshop 7, at first appears to be a fun filter. As you explore the options the feature offers, the possibilities increase. The Liquify feature provides an invisible mesh framework for an image. You can use an impressive array of tools to distort the mesh, with the image details following the mesh. It's hard to imagine how the Liquify filter works without trying it. This tutorial gives you that chance, as you distort a preset pattern fill to make it your own.

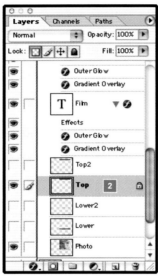

1. **Use** `10_effects.psd` **from the last tutorial.**

2. **Select the Top layer, which is located in the Screen Content layer set.**
   You will fill the area of artwork on this layer with a pattern fill.

3. **Choose Edit→Fill.**
   The Fill dialog box opens.

4. **Select Pattern from the Use list.**
   The Custom Pattern section becomes active.

5. **Click the Custom Pattern down arrow to open the Pattern Picker.**

6. **Click the arrow at the right of the Pattern Picker and choose Reset Patterns from the menu.**

7. **Select the Nebula pattern in the second row of the patterns.**

8. **Put a check mark in the Preserve Transparency box. Click OK.**
   The nontransparent pixels on the selected layer fill with the pattern. You'll use the Liquify filter to customize this fill.

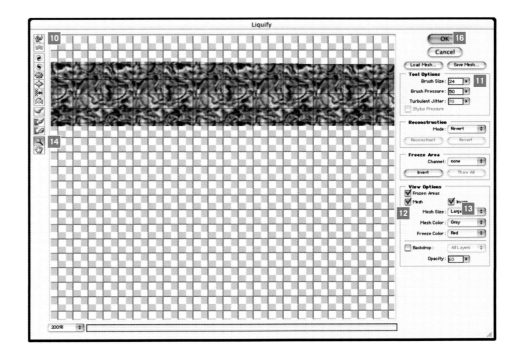

9. Choose Filter→Liquify.
The Liquify dialog box opens, displaying the artwork on the selected layer.

10. Select the Warp tool from the toolbox on the left side of the dialog box.
The tools determine the type of effect applied.

11. Set the brush size to 24 in the Tool Options section of the dialog box.

12. Click the Mesh check box in the View Options section of the dialog box to make the mesh visible.

13. Select Large from the Mesh Size drop-down list.

<TIP>
It isn't necessary to view the mesh as you use the brush to distort the image, but it is easier to understand what is happening when you can see the mesh moving.

14. Select the Zoom tool from the left side of the dialog box and click the artwork until the Zoom drop-down list in the bottom-left corner reads 200%.
It is easier to follow the distortion at a closer view. You are now ready to apply the Liquify effect to the pattern.

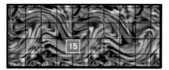

15. **Drag the brush shape in an alternating curve to distort the existing pattern.**
Work along the image, using the Hand tool to reveal a new section as needed. Don't be too perfect as you distort the pattern.

16. **Click OK to close the Liquify dialog box and return to your document.**
If you don't like the results, undo and try again.

17. **Choose File→Save and keep the document open for the next tutorial.**

Tutorial

» Restoring Content with the History Brush

The History Brush works by painting with the artwork from past or future states. In this tutorial, you'll use the History Brush to create a decorative effect. You'll apply filters and an adjustment over the fill that you created with the Liquify filter and then bring back selected areas of the original fill.

1. **Use** `10_effects.psd` **from the last tutorial.**

2. **Make sure that the Top layer is still selected in the Layers palette. Choose Image→Adjustments→Hue/Saturation.**
   The Hue/Saturation dialog box opens.

3. **Set the saturation to –60 and lightness to –30. Click OK.**
   This effect mutes the original fill.

4. **Choose Filter→Noise→Add Noise. Set the amount to 45 and click the Uniform option. Click OK to accept the changes.**
   Adding noise creates texture in the area of the fill. You'll now use the History Brush to bring back some of the original fill.

5. **Choose Window→History.**
   The History palette opens.

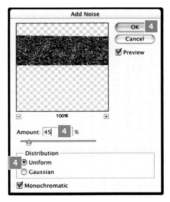
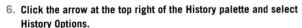

6. **Click the arrow at the top right of the History palette and select History Options.**
   The History Options dialog box opens.

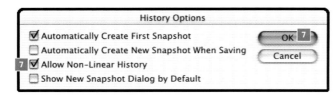

7. **Click the Allow Non-Linear History check box. Click OK.**

8. **Click in the empty box to the left of the Fill state in the History palette to set the layer that will show through when you paint with the History Brush in the following steps.**
   A History Brush icon appears beside the Fill state.

9. **Select the History Brush tool from the toolbox.**

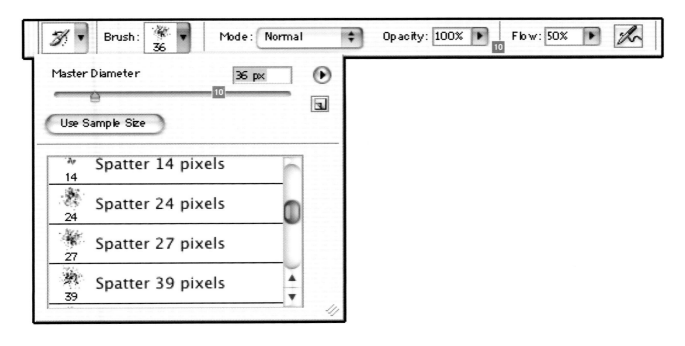

10. **Choose a spatter brush from the Brush pop-up palette on the Options bar and drag the Master Diameter slider to set the brush size to 36 px. Set the opacity to 100% and the flow to 50% on the Options bar.**
The spatter brush and reduced flow help to prevent obvious lines as you paint with the History Brush.

11. **Make sure that the Add Noise state is selected in the History palette. Paint along design lines in the pattern fill area with the History Brush.**
Work in random patterns for the best look. As the brush works along the fill, the original, bright layer appears through the darker filters. Continue until you are satisfied with the result.

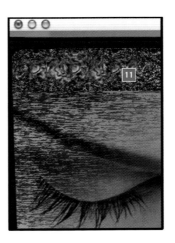

12. **As an extra exercise, click the Visibility field on the Jeny layer in the Layers palette. Try adding a purple color overlay and a white outer glow to the Jeny layer on your own. And make the other layers in the Screen Contents layer set visible.**
The final image for this session shows these effects added.

13. **Choose File→Save As, rename the file** 10_effects_end.psd, **navigate to your collages folder, and click Save.**

<NOTE>
If you desire a more artistic approach to revealing content from under subsequent effects, try the Art History Brush. It works similarly to the History Brush except that when you paint, the underlying content is revealed in a pattern, such as spirals or curls.

» Session Review

You've covered a lot of territory in the Photoshop special effects world. You now have the basics to do much more exploring. Special effects are best learned by wandering through the menus and experimenting with different combinations. Before you head off to discover your own style for special effects, check to see how much you remember from this session.

1. What is the keyboard command to repeat a filter? (See "Tutorial: Using Filters.")

2. Why would you feather a selection to use with a filter? (See "Tutorial: Filtering Selected Areas.")

3. How can you reduce the effect of a filter after it is applied? (See "Tutorial: Filtering Selected Areas.")

4. What is the name of the filter that creates sophisticated lighting effects? (See "Tutorial: Applying a Lighting Effect.")

5. How do you reposition or resize a lighting effect? (See "Tutorial: Applying a Lighting Effect.")

6. What is a layer style? (See "Tutorial: Creating a Layer Style.")

7. How do you preview a layer style? (See "Tutorial: Creating a Layer Style.")

8. What effect does a color overlay layer style apply? (See "Tutorial: Creating a Layer Style.")

9. How can you edit a gradient color for a gradient overlay? (See "Tutorial: Saving a Layer Style to the Styles Palette.")

10. What is the effect of an outer glow layer style? (See "Tutorial: Saving a Layer Style to the Styles Palette.")

11. How do you apply a saved style to a new layer? (See "Tutorial: Saving a Layer Style to the Styles Palette.")

12. How do you move the preview/working area in the Liquify dialog box to apply your effect to the complete image? (See "Tutorial: Liquifying an Image.")

13. What is the purpose of the mesh when creating a Liquify effect? (See "Tutorial: Liquifying an Image.")

14. What does painting with the History Brush do? (See "Tutorial: Restoring Content with the History Brush.")

15. What is the difference between the History Brush and the Art History Brush? (See "Tutorial: Restoring Content with the History Brush.")

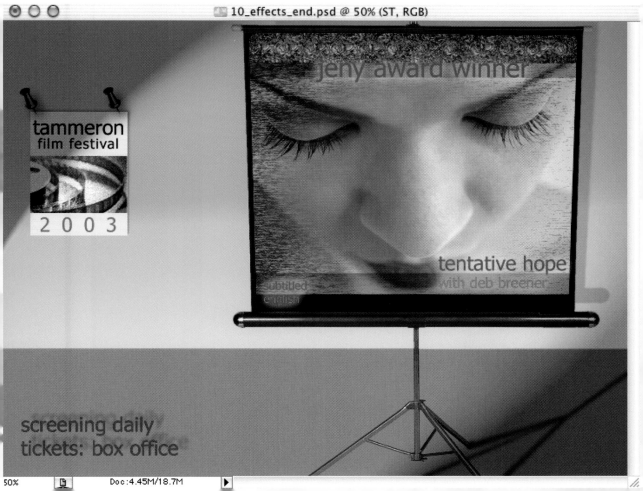

Part V
Text

tamme
03.02

27th

Creating and Formatting Text

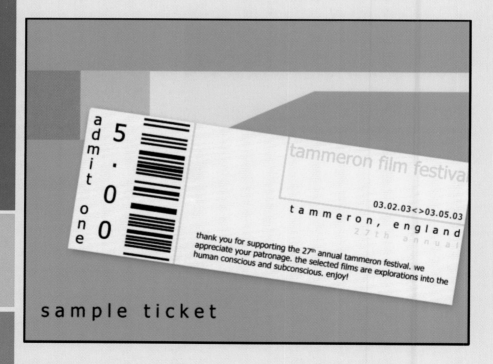

admit one

5.00
0

tammeron film festival

03.02.03<>03.05.03

tammeron, england
27th annual

thank you for supporting the 27th annual tammeron festival. we
appreciate your patronage. the selected films are explorations into the
human conscious and subconscious. enjoy!

sample ticket

Tutorial: **Using the Type Tools**

Tutorial: **Creating Paragraph Type**

Tutorial: **Formatting Type**

Tutorial: **Using Photoshop's Word-Processing Features**

Session Introduction

Photoshop offers powerful tools for working with text. In this session, you'll learn to use the Type tools as you add text and manipulate it with character and paragraph controls. You will also learn to work with Photoshop 7's new spell check and find and replace features to ensure accuracy in your text.

TOOLS YOU'LL USE
Horizontal Type tool, Vertical Type tool, Options bar, Character palette, spell check, and find and replace

CD-ROM FILES NEEDED
11_type.psd and 11_type_end.psd

TIME REQUIRED
60 minutes

Tutorial
» Using the Type Tools

When you select a Type tool and click in your document, Photoshop automatically creates a type layer. This special kind of layer can contain only text, which is vector-based and editable. In this tutorial, you'll learn the basics of creating text in Photoshop, including how to use the Horizontal and Vertical Type tools, how to set type options on the Options bar, and how to recolor existing text.

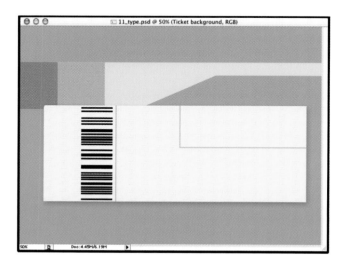

1. **Open** 11_type.psd **from the Session 11 Tutorial Files folder.**

2. **Make sure that the Ticket background layer is selected in the Layers palette. Click the New Set button at the bottom of the Layers palette to create a new layer set. Double-click Set 1 and name it** Ticket text. **Make sure that the Ticket text layer set is selected before moving to the next step.**

Photoshop's Vector-Based Type

Photoshop type has been completely vector-based since the last version of the program. This means that Photoshop type consists of resolution-independent mathematical font definitions rather than pixels. As a result, the text that you create in Photoshop has smooth outlines and can be scaled up or down without harming its appearance, as long as it is printed on a post-script printer or saved in Photoshop EPS or Photoshop PDF format (with the Include Vector Data option turned on in the save settings). Unfortunately, if you print on an inkjet printer, text becomes pixel-based, and no longer has these qualities. Text on a type layer is always editable with the Photoshop Type tools, unless you rasterize the layer (convert its contents from vector to pixel-based format) in order to add special effects, as you'll do in Session 12.

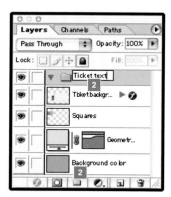

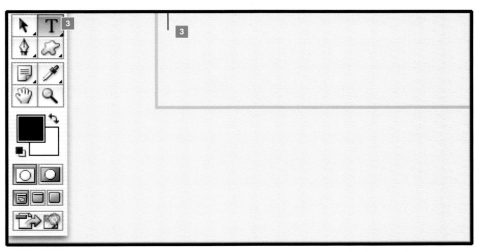

3. **Select the Horizontal Type tool in the toolbox and click in the box on the top right of the ticket in the document window.**
   The Horizontal Type tool is the default type tool. If it's not showing, click whichever type tool is displayed and choose the Horizontal Type tool from the hidden menu. When you click with this tool in the image, a new type layer, Layer 1, appears. Layer 1 is automatically included in the Ticket text layer set because that layer set was selected.

4. **Choose the following type settings in the Options bar — font family: Tahoma; font style: Regular; font size: 18 pt; anti-aliasing method: Sharp; and text alignment: left, as shown here.**

<NOTE>
Keep the following in mind when you're setting type options in the Options bar:

- Font family sets the typeface; font style sets the style of that typeface (such as regular, bold, italic, and bold italic). The font style drop-down list displays only those styles that are native to the selected typeface. If a typeface doesn't have a native bold or italic style, you can simulate that style using the Faux Bold or Faux Italic buttons that are located at the bottom of the Character palette (Window→Character).

- The font family and font style menus display fonts installed in your system, as well as fonts installed in the Adobe\Fonts folder (located in Program Files\Common Fonts in Windows, System Folder\Application Support in Macintosh OS 9, and Library\Application Support in Macintosh OS X). Fonts in the Adobe\Fonts folder appear only in Adobe applications.

- The default unit of measurement for font size in Photoshop is points, which is commonly used in print projects. To change this to pixels (for a Web project, for example) choose Preferences→Units & Rulers and set Type to Pixels. The only font size unit in ImageReady is pixels because that is the way type is measured on-screen.

- Anti-aliasing gradually blends the edges of text into the background for a smooth look, which you'll usually want in your print projects. You can choose from four anti-aliasing styles: Sharp (new to Photoshop 7) produces the sharpest anti-aliased text, Crisp the next sharpest, Strong the boldest, and Smooth the smoothest. None produces aliased text with jaggedy edges. None comes in handy when you are making small type for the Web, which might be hard to read if it were anti-aliased because the edges of individual characters might blur into one another.

- The Character and Paragraph palettes, which you'll practice using shortly, contain the same options that you'll find in the Type tool Options bar, as well as some additional options. You can set the duplicate options in the palettes or in the Options bar.

5. **Click the Color field on the Options bar to open the Color Picker. Enter R: 204, G: 204, B: 0 to set the color for all the text that you're about to enter on this type layer.**
   Another way to set the color of text that you're about to enter is to double-click the Foreground Color box in the toolbox and choose a color from the Color Picker.

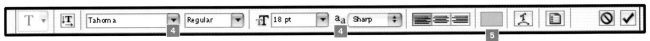

6. **Type** tammeron film festival.

7. **Click the Check Mark button on the Options bar to accept the text and exit text edit mode.**

   When you clicked inside the image with the Type tool back in step 3, you entered a special text edit mode. You are prevented from performing other actions in Photoshop until you exit text edit mode. One way to do this is to click the Check Mark button (officially the Commit button) on the Options bar to accept your text edits. You can accomplish the same thing by selecting another tool or by clicking any palette other than the Character and Paragraph palettes. Notice that there is also a Cancel button on the Options bar. Clicking this button cancels your text edits and takes you out of text edit mode.

   If Photoshop freezes up after you've made a text edit, it's probably because you haven't exited text edit mode. You'll know that you're still in text edit mode if you see Check Mark and Cancel buttons on the right side of the Options bar.

   <NOTE>
   Notice that the name of the type layer in the Layers palette automatically changes to the first few words of the text that you typed. This helps identify the layer. If you prefer, you can change the name of a type layer, just like any layer, by double-clicking the layer name.

8. **Select the Move tool and drag the text to the correct location in the image, as shown in the figure, if the text isn't already there.**

   Notice that selecting the Move tool while in edit mode automatically commits the type and selects the text layer.

   <NOTE>
   The kind of type that you just created is called point type. *Point type* consists of independent lines of type, as distinguished from type that wraps from line to line in paragraph style. You'll learn more about point type and paragraph type in the next tutorial.

9. **Select the Horizontal Type tool again. Change the font size in the Options bar to 8 pt. Click anywhere in the image away from the tammeron film festival text and type** 03.02.03<>03.05.03.

   You have to click far away from the existing text in order to create a separate type layer. If you click too close to existing text, Photoshop thinks that you want to edit that text and doesn't create a new layer for the text you're about to type.

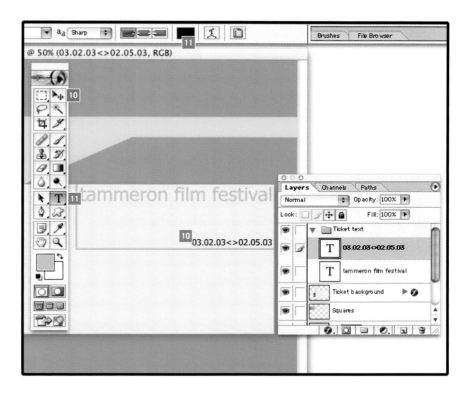

10. **Select the Move tool and move the date text into position just above the horizontal green line on the ticket. The right edge of the text should be close to the right edge of the ticket.**

11. **Select the Horizontal type tool again. Make sure that the 03.02.03 . . . type layer is selected in the Layers palette. Double-click the Color field on the Options bar and choose black (R: 0, G: 0, B: 0) from the Color Picker. Click OK.**
    This recolors all the text on the selected type layer to black. This is the quickest way to change the color of an existing type layer because you don't have to highlight any text.

<TIP>
To change the color of just part of the text on an existing type layer, select the Type tool and click and drag across that part of the text in the image. Then choose a new color from any of the color sources — the Color Picker (accessed by double-clicking the Color field on the Options bar or the Foreground Color box in the tool-box), the Color palette, or the Swatches palette. Click the Check Mark button on the Options bar. You'll notice a question mark in the Color field in the Options bar whenever you reselect this layer because the layer now contains more than one color of text.

<TIP>
There is another way to change the color of text on an existing type layer that enables you to preview colors in the image before you settle on a color. With the Type tool selected in the toolbox, click and drag across the text in the document window. This switches you to the appropriate type layer and highlights the text in the image. Press ⌘+H (Windows: Ctrl+H) on your keyboard to hide the highlighting so that you can see the color changes as they occur. Open the Color palette (Window➔Color) and move the sliders to try different colors, which you can see changing in the image. Or open the Swatches palette (Window➔Swatches) and click different swatches, which also causes changes to the text in the image. When you decide on a color, click the Check Mark button on the Options bar. If you try this method now, choose Edit➔Step Backward until your text appears as it did after step 11.

<NOTE>
So far, you have been using the default Horizontal Type tool, which enters text in a horizontal line. You can also enter text vertically in Photoshop, as you will see in the next few steps.

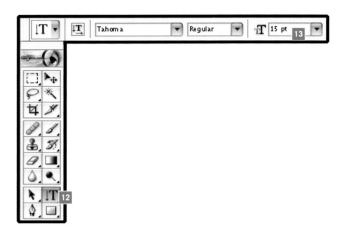

12. **Click and hold the Horizontal Type tool in the toolbox to display the hidden Type tool menu. Select the Vertical Type tool.**

13. **Position the cursor in the top-left corner of the ticket in the image. In the Options bar, make sure that the font is set to Tahoma, the font style is set to Regular, and the font color is set to black. Type** 15 pt **in the Font Size field and press Return or Enter on your keyboard.**

14. **Type** admit one**.**
    The text is positioned vertically in the image.

15. **Select the Move tool to adjust the position of the text if necessary. If not, click the Check Mark button on the Options bar to exit text edit mode.**

< T I P >
Vertical text is created with each letter in an upright position. You can change all the letters on a vertical type layer so that they are still in a vertical column but are lying on their sides by opening the Character palette (Window→Character), clicking the arrow at the top right of that palette, and choosing Rotate Character.

< T I P >
You can convert vertical text to horizontal text at any time (and vice versa) by selecting the type layer, selecting a Type tool, and clicking the Text Orientation button on the top left of the Options bar.

16. **Choose File→Save and leave this file open for the next tutorial.**

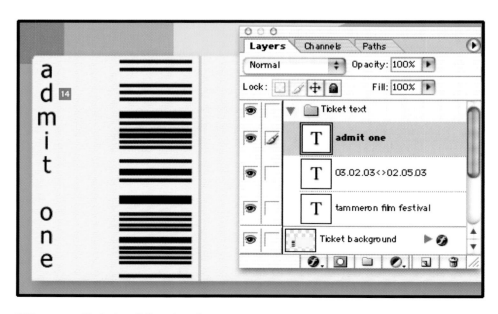

Tutorial
» Creating Paragraph Type

Photoshop offers two kinds of type, point and paragraph type. The type you created in the preceding tutorial was *point type*, text that continues across a line until you press the Return or Enter key on your keyboard. Clicking in the document with a Type tool selected creates point type. Point type is perfect for headlines, artistic typography, or short text passages. In this tutorial, you'll learn to create *paragraph type*, text that is created inside of a bounding box. Paragraph type wraps automatically to fit the area of the bounding box, and it can be reshaped, aligned, scaled, rotated, and distorted within the bounding box. Paragraph type is used for longer passages of text or when you require flexibility in the shape or alignment of a text area. With a Type tool selected, click and drag to define a bounding box and type in that box to create paragraph type, as you'll do in this tutorial.

1. **Make sure that** `11_type.psd` **is still open from the preceding tutorial.**

2. **Select the Horizontal Type tool from the hidden Type tool menu in the toolbox.**

3. **Click and drag in the lower portion of the ticket area to create a bounding box for paragraph type.**
   A new text layer is created, and dotted lines define a bounding box for text. Don't worry if your bounding box is a different size or shape than the one in the figure. You'll adjust the box shortly.

4. **Set the font size to 12 in the Options bar. Make sure that the other settings are as they were at the end of the last tutorial — font family: Tahoma; font style: Regular; anti-aliasing: Sharp; alignment: left; and color: black.**

5. **Type the following, without correcting the spelling errors. Note that two spaces follow the first and second period and the words *appericiate, concious,* and *subconcious* are misspelled. (You will remove the double spacing and fix the spelling in a later tutorial.)**
   thank you for supporting the 27th annual tammeron festival. we appericiate your patronage. the selected films are explorations into the human concious and subconcious. enjoy

<NOTE>
If you drew your bounding box to approximately the same size as the one in the figure, only part of the text appears in the bounding box, and you'll see a small cross in the handle at the bottom right corner of the bounding box. The cross indicates that the bounding box isn't big enough to accommodate the text. You'll fix that in the next step.

6. **Move your cursor over any handle of the bounding box. When the cursor changes to a double-pointed arrow, click and drag as necessary to accommodate the text.**
   The text reflows to fit in the expanded bounding box. The lines of text now end at different points than they did before.

7. **Click the Check Mark icon on the top right of the Options bar to accept the text edits.**
   The bounding box disappears as you exit text edit mode.

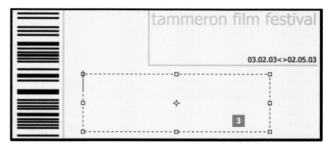

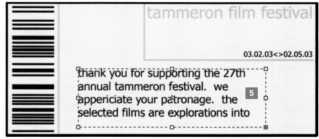

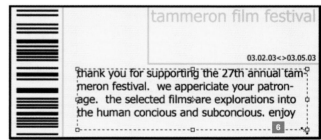

<TIP>
If you ever want to resize, rotate, or distort this text again, select a Type tool and click the text in the document to make the paragraph type bounding box reappear.

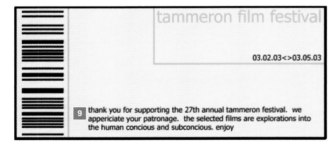

8. **With the thank you . . . type layer and the Type tool selected, change the font size in the Options bar to 8.**

   All the text in the layer changes size, and Photoshop automatically rewraps the resized text to fit the bounding box. This is all that you have to do to change the font size, font family, color, or other formatting attribute of all the text on a paragraph type layer at any time after text has been accepted. If you make a similar change before accepting the text, you have to click and drag to select the text first.

9. **Select the Move tool to move the text into position just above the bottom of the ticket area, as shown here.**

10. **Choose File→Save and leave this file open for the next tutorial.**

<TIP>
Another way to resize text in a paragraph type bounding box is to press Shift+⌘ (Windows: Shift+ Ctrl), click one of the corner handles, and drag. The text scales up or down as you change the size of the bounding box. Holding the Shift key keeps the text proportional.

<TIP>
You can change your mind about whether to use point or paragraph format after you enter your text by converting from one format to the other. Select your type layer in the Layers palette and choose Layer→Type→Convert to Point Text or Layer→Type→Convert to Paragraph Text, as appropriate. Make sure that all the paragraph text is visible before converting to point text because any text that falls outside the bounding box is deleted on conversion.

Tutorial

» Formatting Type

Creating words in a document is just the start if you want to produce attractive, legible text. In this tutorial, you'll get to know the Character and Paragraph palettes as you try out some of the powerful typographic features that they offer for formatting text.

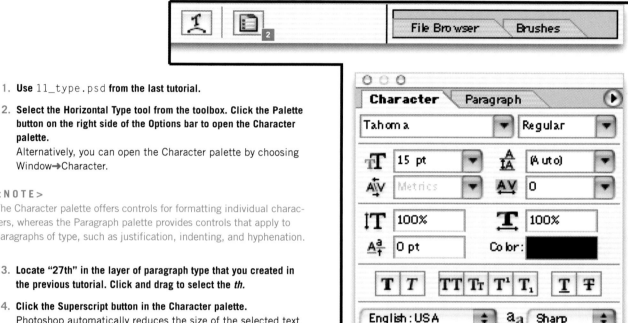

1. **Use** `11_type.psd` **from the last tutorial.**

2. **Select the Horizontal Type tool from the toolbox. Click the Palette button on the right side of the Options bar to open the Character palette.**
   Alternatively, you can open the Character palette by choosing Window→Character.

<NOTE>

The Character palette offers controls for formatting individual characters, whereas the Paragraph palette provides controls that apply to paragraphs of type, such as justification, indenting, and hyphenation.

3. **Locate "27th" in the layer of paragraph type that you created in the previous tutorial. Click and drag to select the** *th.*

4. **Click the Superscript button in the Character palette.**
   Photoshop automatically reduces the size of the selected text and raises its baseline above the other letters.

5. **Click the Check Mark button on the Options bar to accept the change.**

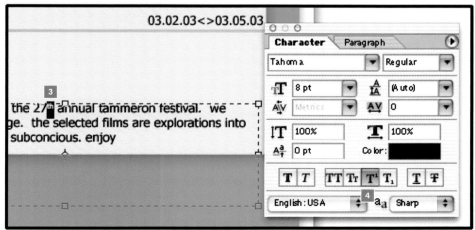

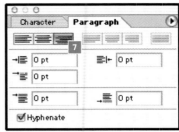

6. **Create a new layer of point text by clicking just below the green line and near the right edge of the ticket in the image.**

7. **Set the font size to 10 pt in the Character palette and make sure that the font color is still set to black and the font family and style to Tahoma Regular. Then click the Paragraph tab to switch to the Paragraph palette and click the right alignment button.**
   Alternatively, you can set all of these formatting options from the Options bar.

8. **Type the following on the same layer, pressing the Return or Enter key after *england* to create a line break:**
   tammeron, england
   27th annual

9. **Click and drag to select the first line of the text that you just typed.**

10. **Click the Character tab and type** 500 **in the Tracking field of the Character palette.**

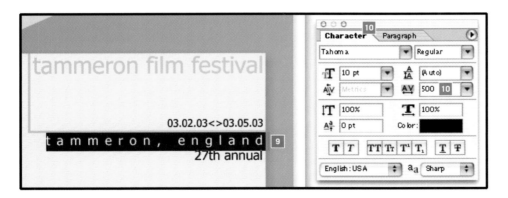

Tracking, Kerning, and Leading

Tracking and kerning are the two typography methods used to control spacing between characters in text. *Tracking* spaces all characters in a selection equally. *Kerning* is used to adjust the spacing between characters, often to correct awkward gaps or lack of space caused by individual character combinations.

Leading is the typography term for the spacing between lines. Tracking, kerning, and leading are controlled from the Character palette in Photoshop.

11. **Select the second line of text in the image. In the Character palette, type** 745 **for the Tracking value.**

12. **Click the Color field to open the Color Picker. Set the font color to R: 204, G: 204, B: 0 and click OK.**
    The Color field in the Character palette, like the one in the Options bar, will display a question mark because there are now two colors on the same layer.

13. **Set the font size to** 8.

14. **Select both lines of text in this layer in the document window. Click the leading field down arrow in the Character palette and choose 12 as the leading value.**
    The distance between the lines increases with this value. Note that many of the fields in the Character palette display no values. This is because those values are different in each line of text that is selected.

15. **Click the Check Mark button on the Options bar to accept the text changes.**

<TIP>
If you want to see the results of these changes without the high-lighting, press ⌘+H (Windows: Ctrl+H).

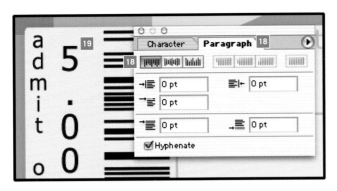

16. **Select the Vertical Type tool. Click beside the words "admit one" in the document to create a new point type layer.**

17. **Set the color to black and the font size to 24 in the Character palette.**

18. **Click the Paragraph tab to display the Paragraph palette. Click the Top Align button to align the top of the line of type that you're about to enter with your cursor.**

19. **Type 5.00 in the image.**

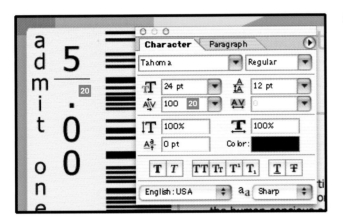

20. **Insert the cursor between the 5 and the . (period). Click the kerning field down arrow and choose 100.**
    The space between the 5 and the period increases.

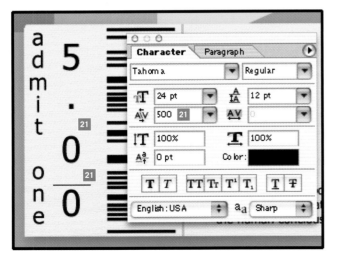

21. **Insert the cursor between the . (period) and the first 0. Type 500 in the kerning field for the kerning value. Repeat this for the space between the 0 and 0.**

22. **Select the Move tool if necessary to change the layer position or click the Check Mark button on the Options bar to accept the text changes.**

23. **Choose File→Save and keep this document open for the next tutorial.**

Tutorial

» Using Photoshop's Word-Processing Features

You may not add large areas of text to your Photoshop documents often, but when you do, you'll appreciate Photoshop 7's new spell checker and find and replace feature. It is easy to miss a spelling error in large text blocks. Also, sometimes you may decide to change one frequently occurring word to another. For these situations, Photoshop 7 has two new features that give you as much control over the content of type as you'd have in a word-processing program. In this tutorial, you'll first learn to use Photoshop's new spell checker with both paragraph and point type. Then you'll use the automated find and replace function.

1. **Check that** `11_type.psd` **is still open from the last tutorial.**

2. **Make sure that a Type tool is selected. Select your layer of paragraph text by clicking at the end of the first sentence.**
   The paragraph type bounding box appears.

3. **Choose Edit→Check Spelling.**
   The Check Spelling dialog box appears with the proper name *tammeron* highlighted in the text. The spell checker stops on the first misspelled word (or word that it doesn't recognize, such as *tammeron*) and highlights that word in the text. The suggested correct spelling appears in the Check Spelling dialog box.

4. **Click Ignore to leave the word *tammeron* unchanged.**
   The spell checker continues on to the next misspelled word — in this case, *appericiate*.

<NOTE>
If you are working often with a word that is identified as an error, such as *tammeron* for this project, you can add that word to Photoshop's dictionary. Simply choose Add when the word that you want to add is presented, and Photoshop won't see that word as an error in future checks.

5. **Click Change to accept *appreciate* as the correct spelling.**
   The corrected word now appears in the document, and the next misspelled word is highlighted.

6. **Click Change twice more when the spell checker stops on the misspelled words *concious* and *subconcious* to correct the spelling of those words (to *conscious* and *subconscious*).**

7. **Click OK at the Spell Checking Complete prompt to exit the spell checker.**

8. **Add an ! (exclamation point) at the end of the paragraph text and click the Check Mark button on the Options bar to accept the text edits.**

9. **Make sure that the Horizontal Type tool is selected and activate your layer of paragraph type by clicking before the words *thank you*.**

Check Spelling

Not in Dictionary:
tammeron

Change To:
timeworn

Suggestions:
timeworn
tangerine
tamarind
admiring
teamwork
itinerant

Language: English: USA
☐ Check All Layers

Done
④ Ignore
Ignore All
Change
Change All
Add

Check Spelling

Not in Dictionary:
appericiate

Change To:
appreciate

Suggestions:
appreciate

Done
Ignore
Ignore All
⑤ Change
Change All
Add

<NOTE>
Your document now has correct spelling, but you still have double spaces in the paragraph text block. You probably don't want double spaces in this document, so you can use the find and replace feature in Photoshop to quickly eliminate the double spaces.

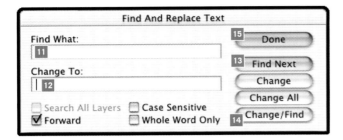

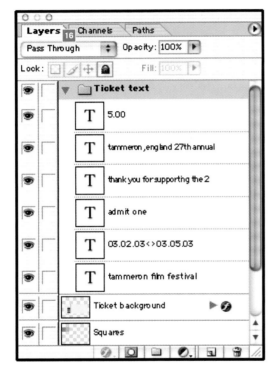

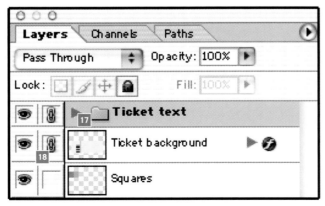

10. **Choose Edit→Find and Replace Text from the menu bar.**
The Find And Replace Text dialog box opens.

11. **Type two spaces with the space bar in the Find What field.**

12. **Type a single space with the space bar in the Change To field.**

13. **Click Find Next.**
Photoshop goes to the first occurrence of a double space and highlights the searched-for term.

14. **Click Change/Find.**
Photoshop makes the correction and proceeds to the next instance of double spacing that it finds.

<TIP>
You can also use the Change All setting in the Find And Replace Text dialog box. This setting replaces all search terms with the replacement with one click. However, it is a good idea to test a few replacements before you use the Change All setting. It is easy to replace a searched-for term with one that is missing a space or that has other tiny errors. These errors can be difficult to fix with a subsequent search.

15. **Click Done to exit the Find And Replace Text dialog box.**

<NOTE>
The text portion of this collage is complete, but the ticket area must be rotated to add more life and visual appeal to the page. In the following steps, you'll rotate all of your text layers with the ticket background.

16. **Open the Layers palette (Window→Layers) if it isn't open already.**
Your Layers palette should have all text layers residing in the Ticket text set. If this is not the case, move your layers as necessary. (See Session 8 if you require a refresher on working with layers.)

17. **Select the Ticket text layer set in the Layers palette. Click the arrow beside the layer set name to collapse the set.**

18. **Click the Link field beside the Ticket background layer.**
The Ticket background layer and the Ticket text layer set are now linked and will move as a unit.

19. **Choose Edit→Transform→Rotate.**
A bounding box appears around the ticket area of the document.

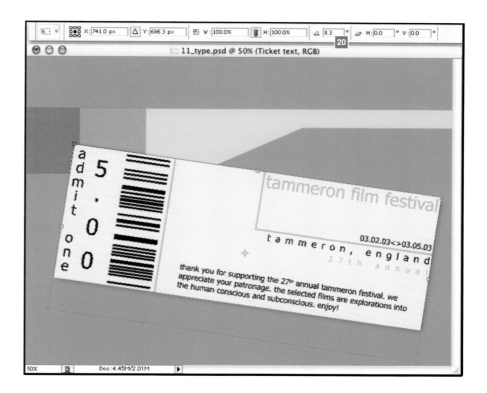

20. **Type** 8.3 **in the Rotation angle field on the Options bar.**

21. **Click the Check Mark button on the Options bar to commit the transformation.**

    Notice that the Options bar for the Transform commands has a Check Mark button for accepting changes just like the Options bar for the Type tool.

22. **Choose File→Save As, rename the document** 11_type_end.psd, **navigate to your collages folder, and click Save.**

    Congratulations! You've finished another collage for your final project.

Session Review

This session covers how to create point type and paragraph type, how to edit and format text, and how to check your text for accuracy with Photoshop's spell check and find and replace features. The following questions will help you review the materials in this session. You can find the answer to each question in the section noted.

1. How do you know when you're in text edit mode? (See "Tutorial: Using the Type Tools.")

2. Name three ways of exiting text edit mode. (See "Tutorial: Using the Type Tools.")

3. How do you create vertical text? (See "Tutorial: Using the Type Tools.")

4. What is the difference between point type and paragraph type? (See "Tutorial: Creating Paragraph Type.")

5. Name a situation to which point type is best suited and a situation to which paragraph type is best suited. (See "Tutorial: Creating Paragraph Type.")

6. How do you make paragraph type reflow? (See "Tutorial: Creating Paragraph Type.")

7. Can you convert point type to paragraph type, and vice versa? (See "Tutorial: Creating Paragraph Type.")

8. Name three places in Photoshop where you'll find controls for formatting text. (See "Tutorial: Formatting Type.")

9. What is the general purpose of the formatting controls in the Character palette? In the Paragraph palette? (See "Tutorial: Formatting Type.")

10. Define *tracking, kerning,* and *leading.* (See "Tutorial: Formatting Type.")

11. Name two new features in Photoshop 7 that you can use to make the content of text more accurate. (See "Tutorial: Using Photoshop's Word-Processing Features.")

admit one

5.00

tammeron film festival

03.02.03<>03.05.03

tammeron, england

27th annual

thank you for supporting the 27th annual tammeron festival. we appreciate your patronage. the selected films are explorations into the human conscious and subconscious. enjoy!

Special Text Effects

Tutorial: **Warping Text**

Tutorial: **Making Type Visible on Top of a Photograph**

Tutorial: **Rasterizing Type**

Tutorial: **Grouping Text and an Image**

Tutorial: **Converting Type to Shapes**

Session Introduction

In this session, you move beyond the basics of working with Photoshop type tools to apply special effects to your text. You'll learn to distort text using the Warp Text feature. You'll be introduced to curves and learn how to use a curves adjustment layer to create a backdrop that makes text legible against a photograph. You'll learn how to rasterize a type layer so that you can apply filters and other pixel-based features to text. You'll discover how to display an image inside text and convert text to a shape, with unlimited shape-editing possibilities. With these methods in hand, you'll have the power to create dynamic, artistic text effects.

TOOLS YOU'LL USE
Type tool, Warp Text feature, Curves dialog box, Rasterize command, filters, Grouping command, and Convert to Shape command

CD-ROM FILES NEEDED
12_texteffects.psd, 12_texteffects_curves.psd, 12_textimage.psd, and 12_texteffects_end.psd

TIME REQUIRED
60 minutes

Tutorial
» Warping Text

Adding motion and energy to a document by distorting the shape of text is easy with Photoshop's Warp Text feature. Warp Text is applied to a type layer, with both the type and the warp effect remaining editable. You have a lot of control over the parameters of the distortion effect, and you can remove the effect at any time to reinstate the original, undistorted text. In this tutorial, you will use the Warp Text feature to curve a line of text.

1. **Open** 12_texteffects.psd **from your folder of Session 12 tutorial files.**

2. **Select the Horizontal Type tool in the toolbox. If it's not showing, click whichever Type tool is displayed and choose the Horizontal Type tool from the hidden menu.**

3. **Select Tahoma font and set the font size to 24 and the color to black in the Character palette. Type** 175 **in the Tracking field.**

4. **Click near the bottom-left corner of the yellow square in the image. Type** tammeron the scene**.**
   A new text layer appears in the Layers palette.

5. **Click the Create Warp Text button on the Options bar.**
   The Warp Text dialog box opens.

<NOTE>
The text won't show clearly over some areas of the image, but you'll fix that in the next tutorial.

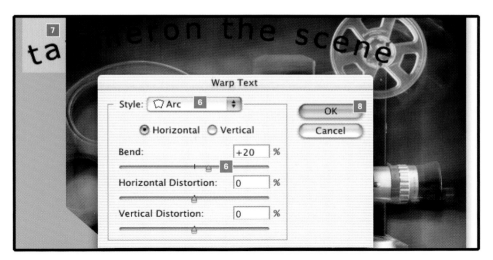

6. **Select Arc from the Style drop-down list. Move the Bend slider to +20.**
   Notice that the text in your document is now curved, as determined by the settings in the Warp Text dialog box. Experiment with some other settings if you'd like, but return to these settings before moving on to the next step.

7. **Click in the document and drag to move the warped text into place to match the figure.**
   Distorting the text moves it from its original starting point. This is all you have to do to reposition it while the Warp Text dialog box is open.

8. **Click OK to accept the Warp Text settings.**
   A new Warp Text icon appears in place of the Type icon in the Layers palette.

9. **Click the Check Mark button on the Options bar to accept your text edits.**

10. **Choose File→Save and keep this document open for the next tutorial.**

Tweaking Warped Text

Warped text remains editable in the same way as text on any type layer, which means that you can change its color, font, size, kerning, and so on in the Character palette, Paragraph palette, and Options bar, as you learned to do in the last session. The warp effect that you've applied also remains editable. To change or remove the distortion of warped text, select its layer in the Layers palette and click the Warp Text button on the Options bar to reopen the Warp Text dialog box. Change the settings as desired. Choosing None from the Style drop-down list removes the warp effect and returns the Warp Text icon to a Type icon in the Layers palette.

Tutorial

» Making Type Visible on Top of a Photograph

The text that you added in the previous exercise is not easily legible because there is too little contrast between the dark values in the photograph and the text. This is a common problem when placing text over a photographic-type image. In this tutorial, you'll learn how to solve this problem by adding a curves adjustment layer above the layer that contains the photograph. This lets the tones of the underlying image come through, while providing a background against which the text is legible.

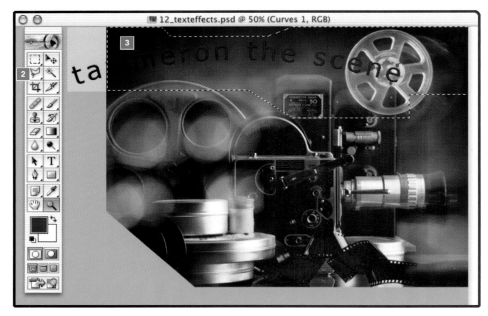

1. **Use** `12_texteffects.psd` **for this tutorial. That file should still be open from the preceding tutorial.**

2. **Click whichever Lasso tool is showing in the toolbox and select the Polygonal Lasso from the hidden tool menu.**

3. **Click from point to point to draw a polygonal selection similar to the one shown here.**

   The selection defines the area that you're about to lighten. Don't worry if your selection doesn't match this one exactly. Just make sure that it covers the text.

An Introduction to Curves

The Curves adjustment is a powerful tool that gives you precise control over the brightness and contrast of individual tones in an image. (This makes Curves superior to the general Brightness and Contrast adjustment that adjusts all tones in an image the same way.) The Curves dialog box may look intimidating at first, but it makes sense when you break it down. Here's a brief explanation of how it works.

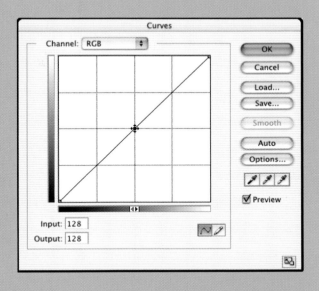

The horizontal bar at the bottom of the diagram is a scale that represents 256 grayscale tones (the maximum number of tones in an RGB image) from black on the left to white on the right. The horizontal scale is used to identify the original tones in an image. The vertical bar on the left side of the diagram is an identical tonal scale turned on its side, which is used to identify the tones to which you will remap the original tones. The diagonal curve line represents the tones in the open image. It always starts as a straight diagonal line. To adjust a particular tone in an image, you click that tone's representative spot on the curve line and drag up to lighten and down to darken. Nearby tones on the curve move with the selected tone.

For example, click near the middle of the diagonal curve line and look at the horizontal bar directly below that point on the horizontal bar for a visual representation of the middle gray tone that you've selected.

Drag the selected point up to the first intersection above it, as shown in the second figure. Look at the tonal bar directly to the left of the new location of that point, where you'll see a lighter shade than middle gray. You've mapped the original middle gray tone to this lighter tone wherever the original tone appeared in the image. You've also lightened neighboring tones because dragging the selected point upward changed other points on the curve, too. (You could have limited the effect on neighboring tones by clicking other places on the curve to add control points before dragging.)

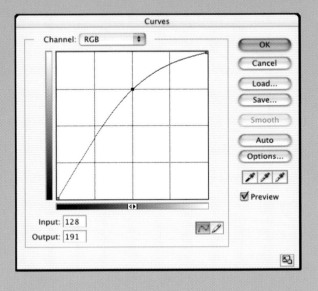

To cancel the adjustment and return the curve to its original state, press the Option (Windows: Alt) key to temporarily change the Cancel button to a Reset button and click the Reset button. In the following steps, you'll apply what you've learned here to lighten a selected area in the open image so that the text on top of that area is more legible. You'll learn more about curves in Session 14, in which you'll use curves to improve the look of a photograph.

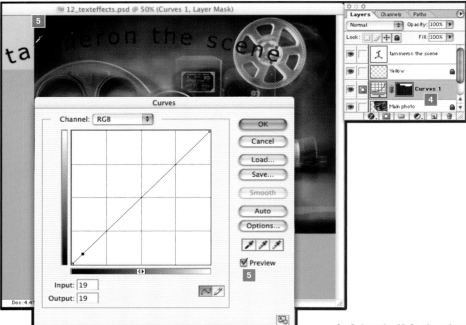

<NOTE>
Notice that the Curves 1 adjustment layer contains two thumbnails. The thumbnail on the left represents the adjustment. You can double-click that thumbnail at any time to reopen the Curves dialog box and edit the curve. The thumbnail on the right represents a layer mask that limits the effect of the adjustment to the area that you selected in step 3 (the white area of the mask).

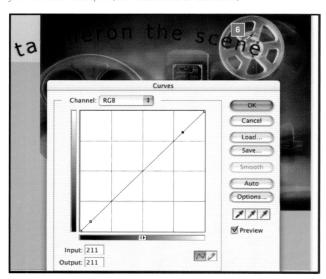

4. **Select the Main photo layer in the Layers palette. Choose Layer→New Adjustment Layer→Curves. Click OK in the New Layer dialog box.**
   This creates an adjustment layer called Curves 1 above the Main photo layer and opens the Curves dialog box.

<TIP>
Another way to create a curves adjustment layer is to click the New Fill or Adjustment Layer button (the black and white button) at the bottom of the Layers palette and choose Curves from the drop-down list.

5. **Make sure that the Preview check box is checked on the bottom right of the Curves dialog box. Move your cursor over the document window (where it changes to an eyedropper) and ⌘+click (Windows: Ctrl+click) the darkest part of the image that is under the text, as shown here.**
   This sets a point on the bottom left of the curve line representing the tone on which you clicked. You'll lighten this and neighboring tones shortly.

6. **⌘+click (Windows: Ctrl+click) a highlighted area in the middle of the reel on the right side of the image, as shown here.**
   This sets a point on the top right of the curve that will act as a control point, protecting highlighted areas that are brighter than this tone from becoming lighter when you lighten the dark areas. Making highlighted areas too bright would cause them to lose all detail.

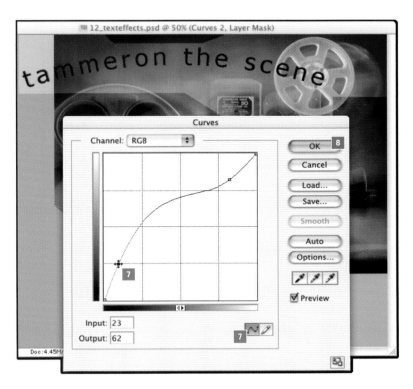

7. **Make sure that the default point tool is selected on the bottom right of the Curves dialog box. Click the solid point that you created on the bottom left of the curve line and drag up to the position shown here.**
   This lightens the darkest part of the selected area and neighboring tones. You can preview the change in the document as you drag to ensure that you lighten the selected area enough to make the text more legible.

<NOTE>
The active selection that you made in step 3 limits the effect of this adjustment to the selected area. If you didn't have an active selection, the adjustment layer would affect the entire image on the layers below it.

<TIP>
If you ever want to limit an adjustment layer to just the layer beneath it, Option+click on the line between the adjustment layer and the layer to be affected in the Layers palette. This groups the adjustment layer and the single affected layer.

8. **Click OK in the Curves dialog box.**

<NOTE>
You may be wondering why I didn't suggest the common solution to the text-on-photograph problem, which is to add a layer between the photograph and the text, draw a white rectangle on that layer, and lower the opacity of that layer to create a light area on which the text can be read. That isn't the best method because it treats the entire area the same way, flattening tone and losing detail in the image. Applying a curves adjustment layer instead lets the tonal variation in the underlying image show through. It also gives you more control over which tones to lighten.

9. **Choose File→Save. Leave** 12_texteffects.psd **open if you want to use it in the next tutorial. You'll have the option of starting the next tutorial with a fresh prebuilt file that's a copy of how** 12_texteffects.psd **should look at this point.**

Tutorial
» Rasterizing Type

All the type that you've worked with so far has been editable vector-based type. You can customize this kind of type with many of Photoshop's features, including layer styles, adjustment layers, warping, masks, and some transformations (such as scale, rotate, and skew). However, there are a few pixel-based features, most notably filter brush tools, that you can't apply to a type layer. You have to first rasterize the type layer, which changes the text on that layer from vector-based type to a bitmapped image of type. You'll learn how to rasterize a type layer in this tutorial.

1. **Make sure that** `12_texteffects.psd` **is open from the preceding tutorial, or if you prefer, use a prebuilt file,** `12_texteffects_curves.psd`, **from the Session 12 Tutorial Files folder on your hard drive.**

2. **Select the Yellow layer in the Layers palette.**

3. **Select the Type tool. In the Character palette, make sure that the font is set to Tahoma Regular. Set the font size to 30 and choose 100 for the tracking value.**

4. **Click the color well in the Character palette to open the Color Picker. Position the cursor over the yellow rectangle at the top of the image and click to sample the color under the eyedropper (R:246, G:210, B:10). Click OK.**
   The cursor changes to the Eyedropper tool when you move it over the document, enabling you to sample any color in the document.

5. **Click at the lower edge of the photo in the image and type** festival. **Select the Move tool and drag to position the text at the right edge of the document, as shown here.**

6. **Click the Check Mark button on the Options bar to accept your text edits.**

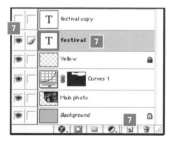

7. **Click the festival type layer and drag it on top of the New Layer button in the Layers palette to duplicate the type layer. Turn off the visibility of the festival copy layer by clicking its eye icon. Make sure that the festival layer is selected before the next step.**
   This step is just a precaution before you rasterize the festival layer in the next steps. Rasterizing converts editable type to a static bitmapped image. It's wise to keep a duplicate copy of the layer as editable type until you're satisfied with the rasterized layer.

8. **Choose Filter→Texture→Craquelure from the menu bar at the top of the screen.**

   This opens the dialog box shown here, telling you that the type layer must be rasterized before proceeding, warning that once rasterized, the text will no longer be editable, and asking whether you want Photoshop to rasterize the type.

9. **Click OK to rasterize the type.**

   The appearance of the text hasn't changed in the document, but the T icon marking the type layer has disappeared from the Layers palette. The festival layer is now a regular layer rather than an editable type layer. Clicking OK also opens the Craquelure filter dialog box.

10. **Leave the settings at their defaults in the Craquelure filter dialog box and click OK to apply the filter.**

    This filter adds texture to make the text stand out from the background image.

11. **Click the festival copy layer and drag it to the Trash icon at the bottom of the Layers palette when you're satisfied with the look of the rasterized festival layer.**

When to Rasterize Type

Here's a brief list of situations in which you'll want to rasterize a type layer:

» You must rasterize in order to apply a filter, as you've seen in this tutorial. Photoshop warns you of this and does the rasterizing for you when you try to invoke a filter.

» You must rasterize before you use any painting tool or fill feature on text. This means that you have to rasterize a type layer if you want to paint on text with the Brush tool, clone text with the Rubber Stamp tool, retouch text with the Healing Brush tool or Patch tool, erase text, use a History Brush on text, or use a darkroom tool on text. You must also rasterize before using the Gradient tool, Pattern tool, or gradient and pattern Fill options on text (although you can apply a Gradient Overlay or Pattern Overlay layer style to a type layer). You'll also have to rasterize before using the Stroke command, as you'll do in this tutorial. In most of these cases, you won't see a warning other than a small symbol. You'll have to figure out what the problem is and rasterize manually by choosing Layer→Rasterize→Type or Ctrl+clicking

(Windows: right-clicking) the type layer in the Layers palette and choosing Rasterize Layer from the contextual menu.

» You must rasterize type layers in order to combine them using the layer Merge commands.

» It's a good idea to rasterize type layers if your PSD file will be viewed on a computer on which the font you used isn't installed. Otherwise, the font will be converted to a different font on that computer, and the type won't look as you intended.

Keep in mind that when you rasterize a text layer, you lose all the editing power that Photoshop's vector text provides. A small change such as adjusting the tracking for a word becomes difficult — sometimes impossible — on a rasterized layer. Try to retain vector format at all times, unless you have a solid reason to rasterize text. Even if rasterizing is essential, delay the action as long as you can in case edits in other parts of your document demand edits in size, content, or color for your text.

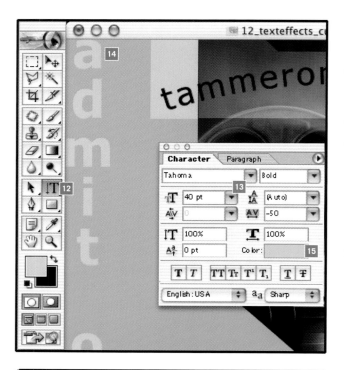

12. **Select the Yellow layer in the Layers palette. Click the Horizontal Type tool in the toolbox and choose the Vertical Type tool from the hidden Type tool menu.**

13. **Choose Tahoma Bold in the Character palette. Type** 40 **as the font size. Set the tracking to –50. It doesn't matter what text color you use because you will change it shortly.**

14. **Type** admit one **and position the text as shown here.**

15. **Click the color well in the Character palette to open the Color Picker. Move the cursor into the document window, where it turns to an eyedropper. Click the green background to change the admit one text to that color. Click OK.**

    You won't be able to see the admit one text in the document (although it's still there) because it is now the same color as the background.

16. **Choose Layer→Rasterize→Type from the menu bar at the top of the screen.**

    The T icon disappears from the admit one layer in the Layers palette. You have to rasterize this type layer in order to use the Stroke command in the next step.

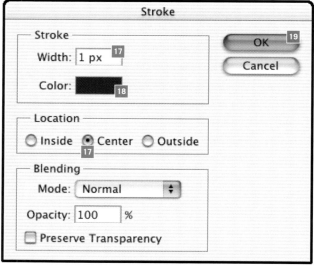

17. **Choose Edit→Stroke. In the Stroke dialog box, specify 1 px for the stroke width and Center for the location.**

18. **Click the Color field in the Stroke dialog box to open the Color Picker. Type the following values in the Color Picker to set the stroke color: R:** 76**, G:** 49**, B:** 30**. Click OK in the Color Picker.**

19. **Click OK in the Stroke dialog box.**

    You can see the text in the document again after the stroke is in place.

20. **Choose Filter→Blur→Gaussian Blur.**

21. **Set the Radius value to 1.0 in the Gaussian Blur dialog box and click OK.**
    The Gaussian Blur softens the stroke.

22. **Set the Opacity of the admit one layer to 50 in the Layers palette to soften the effect further.**

23. **Choose File→Save As and save the file as**
    12_texteffects_curves.psd **(whether you used your own file or the prebuilt file). Keep this document open for the next tutorial.**

<NOTE>
You may have wondered why I didn't suggest that you just apply a Stroke layer style to the type layer, which would have avoided having to rasterize the layer. That's because applying the Gaussian Blur filter to a Stroke layer style produces a hard edge, rather than the soft-edged blur that you see here.

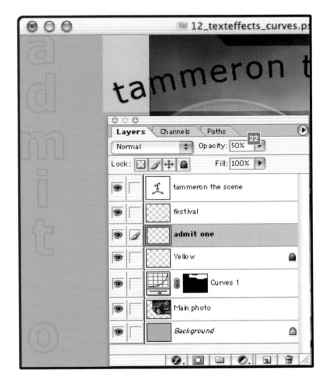

Tutorial

» Grouping Text and an Image

In this tutorial, you'll add another special skill to your text toolbox. You'll learn how to create text that looks like it's filled with a photograph. You'll be surprised at how simple it is to create this great-looking effect.

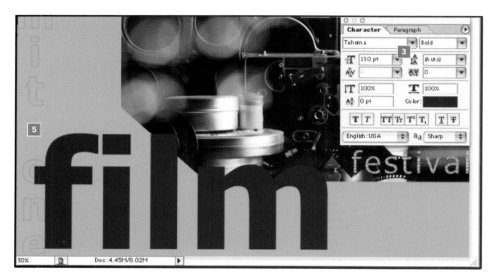

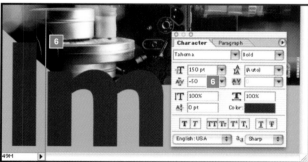

1. **Make sure that** 12_texteffects_curves.psd **is open from the last tutorial.**

2. **Select the Horizontal Type tool in the toolbox. If it's not showing, click the Vertical Type tool and choose the Horizontal Type tool from the hidden tool menu.**

3. **Set the font to Tahoma Bold in the Character palette. Type** 150 **in the font size field. Set the tracking to 0 for now.**
   The text color that you use doesn't matter because you will replace the fill with an image later in this tutorial.

4. **Select the festival layer in the Layers palette.**

5. **Click in the lower-left portion of the document and type** film.

6. **Click between the** f **and** i **in the word** film **and set the kerning to 25 in the Character palette. Click between the** i **and** l **and set the kerning to –50. Click between the** l **and** m **and set the kerning to –50.**
   Kerning is usually required to achieve balanced spacing between characters when you're working with very large fonts. That's because automatic spacing included with a font is generally set for smaller text.

7. **Click the Check Mark button on the Options bar to accept the text edits.**

8. **Open the file** 12_textimage.psd **from the Session 12 Tutorial Files folder on your hard drive.**
   This image is the fill for the text in the collage that you are building in your other open document, 12_texteffects_curves.psd.

9. **Position the two documents on your screen so that you can see them both.**

10. **Select the Move tool in the toolbox.**

11. **Click the title bar at the top of** 12_textimage.psd **to activate that document. Click the image layer and drag it to the document window of** 12_texteffects_curves.psd. **Release the mouse button.**
    This copies the image layer into your collage and creates a new image layer in that document.

12. **Click the title bar of** 12_textimage.psd **again and choose File→Close.**
    You'll be working in 12_texteffects_curves.psd for the rest of this tutorial.

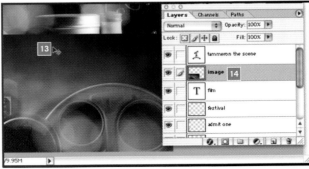

13. **Make sure that the image layer is selected in** 12_texteffects_curves.psd. **Click and drag in the document window to position the content of that layer over the word** *film.*
    You'll move this layer again later in the tutorial, so don't worry about exactly where it's positioned now.

14. **Drag the image layer immediately above the film layer in the Layers palette, if it isn't already there.**

15. **Press the Option (Windows: Alt) key and move the cursor over the line between the image layer and the film type layer until you see an icon with two circles. Click to group the two layers.**

    The word *film* now appears to be filled with the image, and the image layer in the Layers palette has a curved arrow indicating that it is part of a group. The portion of the image that is showing in your document may look different than this figure, depending on the relative position of your image and text when you grouped the layers.

16. **Make sure that the Move tool and the image layer are still selected and drag the image to a pleasing position within the text.**

    The grouped layers move independently of one another. You can move either one without the other, giving you control over which part of the image layer appears in the text. In the next step, you'll link the two layers so that they move together.

17. **Click in the Link field to the left of the film layer to link the two layers together. Click and drag to move the two layers together to the position shown here.**

    Leave a small area of space between the bottom of the characters in the word *film* and the bottom of the document. In the next tutorial, you'll convert the text to a shape and stretch the legs of the characters down to meet the bottom of the document.

18. **Choose File→Save and leave the document open for the next tutorial.**

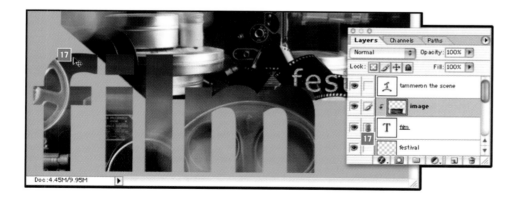

Tutorial
» Converting Type to Shapes

There may be times when you want to change the shape of individual characters in text. In order to do that, you have to first convert a type layer to a path, as you'll do in this tutorial. This tutorial comes in handy for creating unusual letters to introduce a text block or for creating typographic artwork.

1. **Make sure that** `12_texteffects_curves.psd` **is open from the last tutorial.**

2. **Select the film layer and choose Layer→Type→Convert to Shape.** The layer changes from a type layer to a shape layer in the Layers palette, and the text in the document now shows a thin vector outline. (Turn back to Session 6 if you need some review on shape layers.)

3. **Select the Black Arrow tool (officially the Path Selection tool) in the toolbox. With the film layer selected, click the letter *f* in the word *film* in the document to reveal the hollow anchor points on the vector outline.**

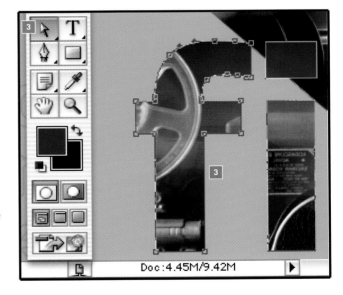

<N O T E>

You can also convert type to editable paths so that you can reshape individual characters. Follow the instructions for changing text to a shape, but choose Layer→Type→Convert to Work Path in step 2. You can edit paths created from type in the same way as any other paths (see Session 6).

Doc:4.45M/9.42M

Do ▶ 4.45M/9.42M

4. **Click the point at the lower-left edge of the letter *f* and drag that point down to touch the bottom of the document. Repeat this step with each of the points at the bottom of a letter in the word *film*.**
The end points of each letter should touch, or go slightly past, the lower edge of the document. Check that the image showing through the characters goes all the way to the bottom of the characters after this adjustment. If not, click in the Link field next to the Text image layer to unlink the layers and move the image within the text as you did in the last tutorial.

<TIP>
Although the text looks okay against the main image in the document, you can separate the characters from the main image, improving the legibility of the image-filled text, by adding a subtle drop shadow. Continue to the next step to add the shadow.

5. **Click the New Layer Style button at the bottom of the Layers palette and choose Drop Shadow.**
This adds a drop shadow to the word *film* and opens the Layer Style dialog box.

6. **Set the opacity to 36%, distance to 6 px, spread to 14%, and size to 16 px.**
See Session 10 for more on layer styles and their options.

7. **Click OK in the Layer Style dialog box to apply the drop shadow effect to the word *film*.**

<NOTE>
To finish this page, there's just one simple text block to add.

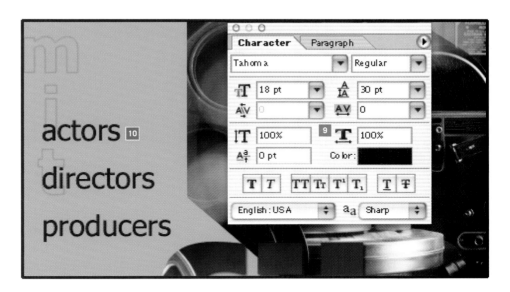

8. **Select the Horizontal Type tool in the toolbox and click in the blank space on the left side of the document.**

9. **Set the font to Tahoma Regular, font size to 18 pt, leading to 30 pt, kerning to 100, and font color to black in the Character palette.**

10. **Type the following, pressing Return or Enter on your keyboard after every line:**
    actors
    directors
    producers

11. **Select the Move tool and position the new text as shown in the final figure example.**

12. **Choose File→Save As, rename the file**
    12_texteffects_end.psd, **and save it in your collages folder for use in the final project.**
    The final figure in this chapter is the final text collage as it should look at this point and as it will appear in the film festival program guide that you'll put together at the end of the book. Keep this image in your collages folder until then. You'll find a copy of this finished file in the Session 12 Tutorial Files folder under the name 12_texteffects_end.psd.

» Session Review

This session covers Photoshop's more advanced capabilities for working with text. You distorted text with the Warp Text feature and manipulated a photograph with a curves layer so that your text would be easy to read. You rasterized text layers in order to apply filters and other effects to your type, and you filled text with an image. Finally, you converted text to shapes, which enabled you to manipulate individual text characters. Take a look at the following questions to remind you of how much you have learned.

1. How can you tell that a Warp Text effect is applied to text? (See "Tutorial: Warping Text.")

2. Does text with a Warp Text effect applied remain editable? (See "Tutorial: Warping Text.")

3. Why is it preferable to use curves, rather than layer opacity, to prepare an area on which to place type over a photograph? (See "Tutorial: Making Type Visible on Top of a Photograph.")

4. When you are preparing an area on which to place type over a photograph, how can you limit the area that will be affected by your curves adjustment layer? (See "Tutorial: Making Type Visible on Top of a Photograph.")

5. What does it mean to rasterize a text layer? (See "Tutorial: Rasterizing Type.")

6. How does the appearance of a type layer change in the Layers palette when that layer has been rasterized? (See "Tutorial: Rasterizing Type.")

7. What do you have to do before applying a filter to text in Photoshop? (See "Tutorial: Rasterizing Type.")

8. What are the reasons to delay or avoid rasterizing text layers? (See "Tutorial: Rasterizing Type.")

9. Name three situations in which you would have to rasterize a type layer to apply a feature. (See "Tutorial: Rasterizing Type.")

10. What text adjustment is usually necessary when working with large fonts? (See "Tutorial: Converting Type to Shapes.")

11. What command do you use to make text appear as if it is filled with a photograph? (See "Tutorial: Converting Type to Shapes.")

12. How do you manipulate the shape of text after converting from a type layer to a shape layer? (See "Tutorial: Converting Type to Shapes.")

Part VI
Working with Photographs in the Digital Darkroom

tamme
03.02
27th

Using Darkroom Tools

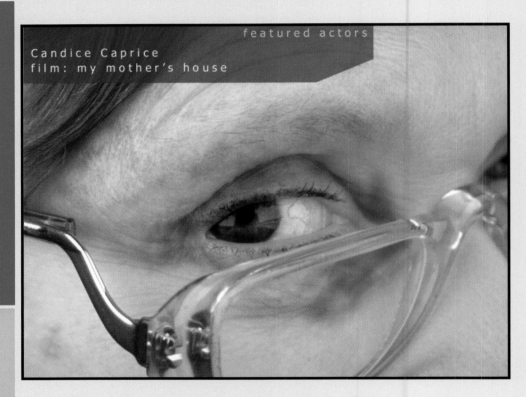

featured actors

Candice Caprice
film: my mother's house

Session Introduction

It's hard to think of Photoshop without thinking of photographs. Photoshop has always been an undisputed leader as a photo manipulation and correction tool. Nearly every image that is captured with a digital camera or scanned needs some adjustment, retouching, or repair.

In this session, you'll learn basic image correction skills using Photoshop's digital darkroom features. These features do the job of traditional darkroom tools and more. You'll correct imperfections in a photograph using the Clone Stamp tool and the new Healing Brush and Patch tools. You'll use the Dodge and Burn tools to adjust exposure and the Sponge tool to modify saturation. You'll use the Sharpen and Blur tools to adjust focus. You'll try out the Unsharp Mask and Gaussian Blur filters, and you'll create a shallow depth-of-field effect by blurring selected areas of a photograph.

TOOLS YOU'LL USE
Clone Stamp tool, Healing Brush tool, Patch tool, Dodge tool, Burn tool, Sponge tool, Blur tool, Sharpen tool, Unsharp Mask filter, and Gaussian Blur filter

CD-ROM FILES NEEDED
13_darkroom.psd and 13_darkroom.end.psd

TIME REQUIRED
90 minutes

Tutorial

» Removing Content with the Clone Stamp Tool

The Clone Stamp tool, sometimes called the Rubber Stamp tool, is useful for removing unwanted content from a photograph — scratches, dust spots, and even people or objects. It works by copying pixels from one part of an image and painting them into another. The Clone Stamp tool is ideal when the area that you want to repair has similar color, lighting, and texture to another part of the image. In this tutorial, you'll work with the Clone Stamp tool to remove some unsightly redness from the subject's eye in a photographic portrait.

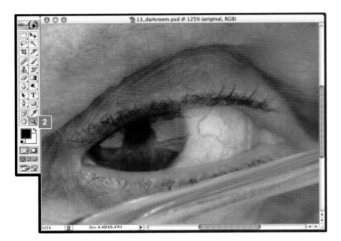

1. **Open** 13_darkroom.psd **from the Session 13 folder of tutorial files on your hard drive. Select the Portrait layer in the Layers palette.**

2. **Select the Zoom tool in the toolbox. Drag to zoom in on an area that includes the subject's eye.**
   The area that you defined when dragging the Zoom tool will fill your screen when you release the mouse button.

   < T I P >
   It is common practice to zoom to a high magnification for accuracy when working with darkroom tools. However, you must return to 100% view often to check how the changes that you make appear in the final view.

3. **Select the Clone Stamp tool in the toolbox.**

4. On the Options bar, choose the soft round, 17 px brush setting. Set Mode to Normal, Opacity to 100%, and Flow to 100%.

< T I P >

A soft brush often works best to blend the edges of the cloned pixels with the original. However, Photoshop's default soft brushes, which are set to 0% Hardness, sometimes make the cloned area look too blurry. If that's the case, undo your work and increase the hardness of the brush slightly by opening the Brushes palette, selecting Brush Tip Shape, and dragging the Hardness slider to the right.

< T I P >

Setting Opacity to 100% ensures that the original pixels will be completely covered by the cloned pixels. In some cases, you may find it best to lower opacity slightly to help blend cloned pixels with the original. Shoot for somewhere between 80% and 100% unless you want the original pixels to show through.

5. Make sure that there's a check mark in the Aligned box on the Options bar.

< N O T E >

The Aligned option has an important effect on the way the Clone Stamp tool works. When the Aligned option is checked, Photoshop takes a sample from a new location each time you click as you're painting with cloned pixels, and the sample and target locations always stay in the same relationship to one another. This is the option that you'll usually use because it avoids repeating the same pixels in different spots, making your cloning less obvious. When Aligned isn't checked, the original sample spot is always used as the source of cloned pixels. Uncheck Aligned only if you want to repeat an image several times in a document.

6. Leave Use All Layers unchecked.

When Use All Layers is checked, Photoshop samples pixels from all layers in a document and paints the merged sample on the active layer. Check Use All Layers if you want to copy content from more than one layer in a document or if you're cloning onto a separate layer as described in the following tip. There's no reason to check Use All Layers in this image because the main image is all on one layer.

< T I P >

Some retouchers prefer to create a new, empty layer on which to paint cloned pixels. This enables you to erase any mistakes and to compare a before and after view by varying the visibility of the new layer. If you want to try this, create a new layer above the Portrait layer. Add a check mark to the Use All Layers option on the Options bar. Make sure that the new layer is selected in the Layers palette and continue to clone as described in the following steps.

7. Option+click (Windows: Alt+click) to the right of the red vein to set the first sampling point.

This operation copies pixels from the area where you clicked. You will paint with these pixels in the next step.

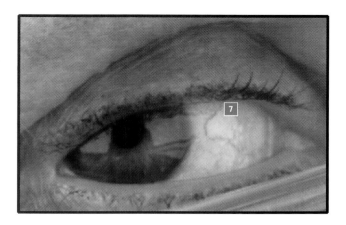

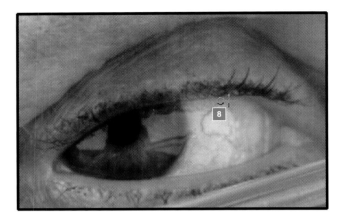

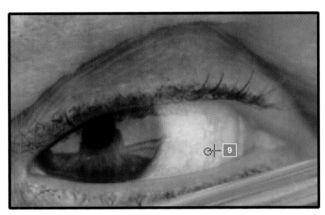

8. **Click the red line in the subject's eye immediately to the left of where you took the sample.**

   The Clone Stamp tool paints with the pixels that you sampled in step 7, and the red line disappears where you click.

9. **Move along the red line, clicking as you go to paint with the pixels that you're copying.**

   The Clone Stamp tool uses a new sampling point with each click because the Aligned option is activated. Each sampling point is marked by a cross and each target point by the round brush symbol. If a click creates a spot that doesn't blend well, choose Edit→Undo Clone Stamp and Option+click (Windows: Alt+click) in a different location to sample a new point.

<TIP>

Here are a few things that you can do to make your cloning more blended and less obvious:

- Avoid dragging the cursor when you paint with cloned pixels, which can result in a repetitive look. Instead click from point to point to dab the cloned pixels onto the image.

- Use a variety of sample points by Option(Alt)+clicking from time to time on different sides of the area that you're trying to cover.

- If you're cloning from a dark to a lighter area (for example, if you're trying to cover light dust spots), try setting Mode to Darken on the Options bar. And if you're cloning from a light to a darker area (for example, if you're trying to cover a dark blemish), try setting Mode to Lighten.

<TIP>

You can clone between images as well as within an image. Just Option+click (Windows: Alt+click) in the first image to set a sample point and click to paint in the other image. You can also clone from one layer to another in the same document by unchecking Use All Layers and switching active layers as you sample and paint.

10. **Choose File→Save. Leave this image open for the next tutorial.**

Tutorial
» Retouching with the Healing Brush Tool

The Healing Brush tool is one of the most important new features in Photoshop 7 for anyone who uses Photoshop to retouch photographs. The Healing Brush tool produces a similar effect to the Clone Stamp tool, but in a more subtle way. Instead of just painting pixels over an area, the Healing Brush automatically preserves the lighting, texture, and tones of the corrected area. In this tutorial, you'll use the Healing Brush tool to remove a large age spot from the subject's face.

1. **Make sure that** `13_darkroom.psd` **is still open from the last tutorial.**

2. **Click the eye icon on the Title layer in the Layer palette. Make sure that the Portrait layer is still selected.**
   This makes the Title layer invisible so that it's not a distraction.

3. **Make sure that you're still zoomed in to the eye area. Use the Hand tool to reposition the image, if necessary, so that the subject's eyebrow is showing.**

4. **Select the Healing Brush tool in the toolbox.**

5. **Click the Brush sample on the Options bar to open the Brush pop-up palette.**
   You have to use the Brush pop-up palette, rather than the Brushes palette, with the Healing Brush tool. The Brushes palette is grayed out.

6. **Set Diameter to 50 px, make sure that Hardness is set to 100%, and leave the other settings at their defaults in the Brush pop-up palette.**
   A hard-edged brush usually works better than a soft-edged brush with the Healing Brush tool.

<TIP>
There is one situation in which you may prefer using a soft-edged brush with the Healing Brush tool. If you're correcting an image that has a lot of noise, such as film grain, try using a soft-edged brush with the new Replace blending mode, which you'll find in the list of modes on the Options bar. The Replace mode helps eliminate the fuzzy edges that you may otherwise see on the correction.

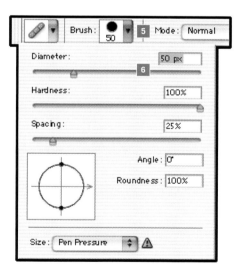

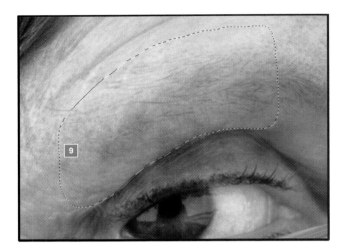

7. **Make sure that Sampled is selected as the source on the Options bar.**
   This is the default option, which you'll use most of the time. The alternative is to choose Pattern, which enables you to use one of Photoshop's prebuilt patterns as the source of healing pixels.

8. **Put a check mark in the Aligned box on the Options bar.**
   The Aligned option works the same way with the Healing Brush tool as it does with the Clone Stamp tool. See the last tutorial for a full explanation of the Aligned option.

9. **Select the Magnetic Lasso tool in the toolbox and drag a selection around the brown age spot on the left side of the subject's eyebrow, following the crease of the eyelid.**
   The selection restricts the area to be corrected. You can use any selection tool for this purpose. The Magnetic Lasso tool is efficient because it snaps to the change in contrast along the crease of the eyelid.

< N O T E >
Notice that the Healing Brush tool doesn't have a Use All Layers option like the Clone Stamp tool. This is because the Healing Brush tool can sample only from the active layer. There is also no Opacity option on the Healing Brush tool Options bar. Although you can't alter the opacity of the Healing Brush tool, you can get a similar effect by choosing Edit→Fade Healing Brush from the menu bar immediately after you use the Healing Brush tool. Lower the Opacity slider in the Fade dialog box and click OK. Remember that if you take any other action after applying the Healing Brush, the Fade option disappears.

< N O T E >
You can't make a Healing Brush correction on a separate empty layer, as you may be used to doing with the Clone Stamp tool. This makes sense because the Healing Brush tool relies on surrounding pixels in the target area to do the blending and there are no content pixels on an empty layer. If you're concerned about making permanent changes to an original layer, make a copy of that layer before you use the Healing Brush tool and turn off the visibility of the copy.

10. **Option+click (Windows: Alt+click) just below the age spot.**
    This samples the pixels that the Healing Brush tool will use to correct the area.

11. **Click and drag across the area to be corrected (the brown age spot).**
    Don't worry that the brush creates a dark area in the image as you drag. You won't see the true effect of the Healing Brush until you release the mouse button. At that point, the Healing Brush tool does its work, blending the texture, lighting, and tonality of the pixels surrounding the target area with the sampled pixels.

<NOTE>

The Healing Brush tool works well on blemishes and other imperfections such as the one that you repaired in this tutorial. It is sometimes less successful on areas of substantial damage, such as a tear or deep scratch in a photograph, because this tool attempts to repair, rather than cover up the damaged area. In that case, try the Clone Stamp tool, which covers the target area, or the Patch tool, which you'll find out about in the next tutorial.

<TIP>

You can use the Healing Brush tool to copy pixels from image to image and from layer to layer, just as you can with the Clone Stamp tool.

12. **Press ⌘+D (Windows: Ctrl+D) to cancel the selection. Choose File→Save and leave this document open for the next exercise.**

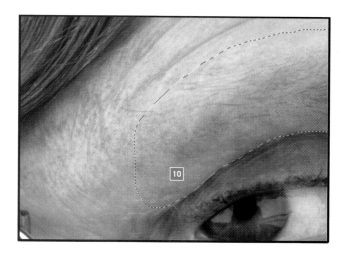

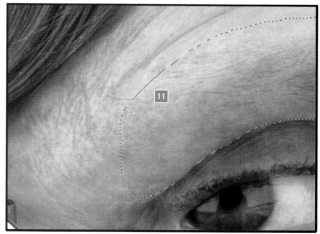

Tutorial
» Working with the Patch Tool

The Patch tool is another innovative tool that's new to Photoshop 7. It works in a similar way to the Healing Brush tool, in that it blends the sampled pixels with the pixels to be corrected. However, instead of sampling and painting with a brush, the Patch tool uses selections. In this tutorial, you'll use the Patch tool to remove blemishes from the subject's cheek.

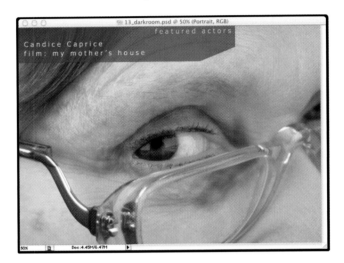

1. **Use** 13_darkroom.psd **from the last tutorial.**

2. **Select the Zoom tool in the toolbox and Option+click (Windows: Alt+ click) to zoom out to 50%.**
   When using the Patch tool, you are working with selections rather than brushes, so you don't need to work at a high magnification.

3. **Click the Healing Brush tool in the toolbox and select the Patch tool from the hidden menu.**

4. **Leave Source selected on the Options bar.**
   One of the only options for the Patch tool is whether the selection that you're about to make defines the source (the damaged area that needs repair) or the destination (the healthy pixels that you'll use to make the repair). I prefer to leave this option set to its default, Source, because then I can draw the selection to fit the damaged source area as closely as possible. A smaller selection usually produces a less noticeable patch.

<NOTE>
There are two ways to approach working with the Patch tool. You can use the tool to select the area that you want to replace, the damaged area. You then drag that area to the area of the document that you want to use as a correction, as you'll do in this tutorial. Alternatively, you can start by selecting the area that you want to use as the correction sample and drag it over the area that you want to correct.

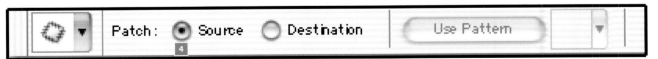

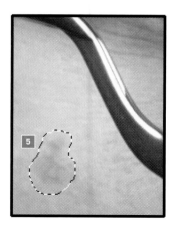
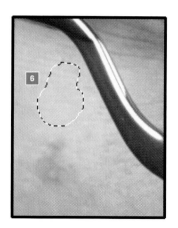
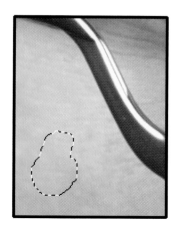

5. **Click and drag a selection with the Patch tool around the blemished skin on the subject's left cheek.**

Make sure to include all the damaged area in the selection, but don't make the selection any bigger than necessary. You want the selection to just fit the damaged area because the Patch tool will use the edges of the selected area to make its blending calculations.

<TIP>

There is no feathering option on the Patch tool Options bar. If you want to soften the edges of your selection, you have to first make the selection with the Patch tool and then choose Select→Feather from the menu bar at the top of the screen.

6. **Position your cursor in the middle of the selection. Click and drag the selection over an unblemished area of the cheek. Try the unblemished area directly above where you made the selection.**

7. **Release the mouse button.**

When you release the mouse button, the selection outline snaps back to the damaged area, and the Patch tool goes to work, blending the unblemished sample with the damaged area, taking into account the brightness, texture, and tonality of the pixels at the edges of the damaged area.

8. **Click outside the selection boundaries to cancel the selection.**

9. **Choose File→Save and leave this document open for the next tutorial.**

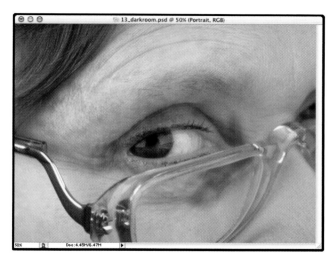

<TIP>

The Patch tool, like the Healing Brush tool, has no Opacity option. To reduce the opacity of the patch, you can choose Edit→Fade Patch Selection immediately after applying the Patch tool. Lower the Opacity slider in the Fade dialog box and click OK.

<NOTE>

The Patch tool, like the Healing Brush tool, acts only on the active layer, so you can't make repairs on a separate, empty layer. If you're concerned about modifying the original artwork, make a copy of the layer to be corrected before you use the Patch tool.

Tutorial
» Adjusting Exposure

Photoshop offers tools for selectively adjusting the exposure in an image, duplicating the effects known as *dodging* and *burning* in the traditional darkroom. The Dodge tool lightens areas of an image, simulating decreased exposure, and the Burn tool darkens, simulating increased exposure. In this tutorial, you'll lighten the subject's eye socket and darken the frame of her glasses.

1. **Check that** 13_darkroom.psd **is still open from the last tutorial.**

2. **Select the Zoom tool in the toolbox. Drag over the eye to magnify the view to 66.67%.**

3. **Select the Dodge tool in the toolbox.**
   You'll use the Dodge tool to lighten the dark area on the inside of the subject's eye socket.

4. **Click the Brush sample on the Options bar and select the 65 px soft round brush from the Brush pop-up palette. Set the range to Shadows and the exposure to 20%.**
   Setting Range to Shadows will make the Dodge tool affect dark areas of the image more intensely than lighter areas. Exposure controls the strength of the tool's lightening effect.

5. **Click your cursor in a random pattern over the inside eye socket area that needs to be lighter.**
   This step just starts the process. Don't try to accomplish the entire job of lightening the area at this point. Using a variety of shadows, midtones, and highlight settings to adjust the exposure of an area gives a more natural result.

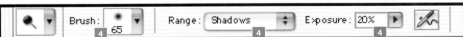

6. **Select Midtones from the Range field on the Options bar. Repeat step 5.**
   The Midtones range affects all pixels except very dark and very light pixels.

7. **Select Highlights from the Range field on the Options bar and lower the Exposure setting to 10%.**
   Setting the range to Highlights makes the Dodge tool have its greatest effect on light areas of the image. As you near the desired result, reduce your exposure. This gives you more control to blend the affected areas. Sometimes reducing brush size as you progress is a good idea as well.

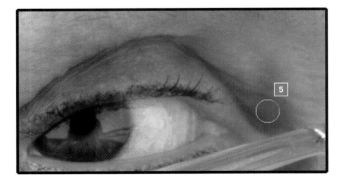

8. **Click in the lightest portions of the area that you are correcting.**

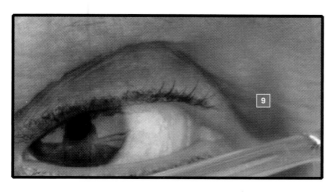

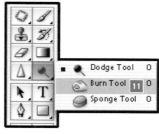

9. **Continue alternating between Shadow, Midtones, and Highlight settings on the Options bar as you click in the correction area until you are satisfied with the result.**
   Be prepared to use the Edit→Undo command at any time, especially as you near completion.

<NOTE>
The Burn tool works in the same way as the Dodge tool, except that it darkens pixels instead of making them lighter. You'll practice using the Burn tool as you darken the frame of the subject's glasses in the next steps.

10. **Select the Hand tool from the toolbox. Click and drag in the image until you can see the silver arm of the glasses frame.**

11. **Click the Dodge tool in the toolbox and select the Burn tool from the hidden menu.**

12. **Choose the 45 px soft round brush from the Brush pop-up palette. Set the range to Midtones and the exposure to 50% on the Options bar.**
    Because you are simply darkening an object rather than working with the subtleties of correcting flaws in human skin, you can apply the effect more aggressively.

13. **Click and drag along the arm of the glasses frame to darken the color.**
    Respect the original lighting pattern of the image and don't try to be too perfect. Leave small areas untouched, especially at the top of the frame where the light is strong.

14. **Choose File→Save. Leave the document open for the next tutorial.**

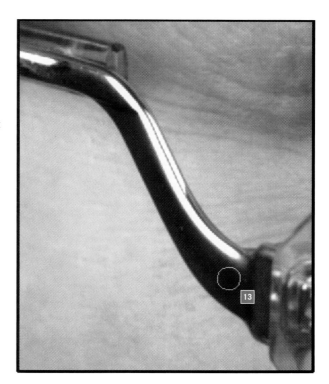

Tutorial
» Adjusting Saturation

In Photoshop, the Sponge tool adjusts color saturation to intensify or mute colors. In this tutorial, you'll increase the saturation, or *intensity,* of the color in the subject's eye to increase the reflection and add interest.

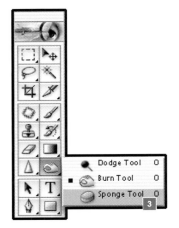

1. Make sure that 13_darkroom.psd **is still open from the last tutorial.**

2. **Select the Hand tool in the toolbox and move the image in the document window, if necessary, so that the eye fills the screen.**

3. **Click the Burn tool in the toolbox and select the Sponge tool from the hidden menu.**

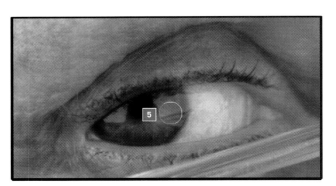

4. **Choose the soft round 65 px brush from the Brush pop-up palette. Make sure that Mode is set to Saturate on the Options bar and set the Flow option to 50%.**
   A soft brush prevents brush lines from forming as you apply the effect. The Flow setting controls how fast saturation changes as you use the Sponge tool.

5. **Click around the iris area, concentrating where the light is strongest at the right edge of the eye.**
   Be careful with the amount that you apply of this effect. When color saturation is increased too much, the color change can be startling.

6. **Choose File→Save. Leave the document open for the next tutorial.**

Tutorial

» Using the Sharpen and Blur Tools

Photoshop offers several ways to soften and sharpen images. You will start learning about these features with the Sharpen and Blur tools. When an image or a portion of an image is sharpened, the contrast between adjacent pixels is increased. Softening an image or area reduces the contrast between adjacent pixels. The Sharpen and Blur tools use brushes to increase and decrease the contrast, respectively. The Sharpen and Blur filters that you will work with later in this session affect the contrast across a selected area or the entire image. In this tutorial, you'll learn to work with the Sharpen and Blur tools by correcting imperfections caused by earlier operations.

1. **Make sure that** `13_darkroom.psd` **is still open from the preceding tutorial.**

2. **Select the Zoom tool and zoom in to 100%. Use the Hand tool to move the eye to the middle of the document window.**

3. **Select the Blur tool in the toolbox.**
   You'll use the Blur tool to soften the hard line of the crease in the eyelid.

4. **Choose the 45 px soft round brush from the Brush pop-up palette. Set the mode to Normal and the strength to 50% on the Options bar.**
   Choosing a large, soft brush helps the correction to blend into the surrounding pixels. Strength controls the intensity of the blur effect.

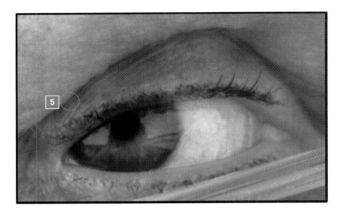

5. **Drag along the crease of the eyelid.**
   The pixels that are touched by the brush blend into each other, softening the line. Repeat this step until you are satisfied with the look.

6. **Choose File→Save, but keep the document open for the next step.**
   You are going to practice with the Sharpen tool, but won't keep the changes that you make. Saving now provides the opportunity to revert to the saved version as you experiment with the Sharpen tool.

7. **Select the Sharpen tool in the toolbox.**
   You'll use the Sharpen tool to increase the detail in the subject's eye.

8. **Choose the 27 px soft round brush from the Brush pop-up palette. Set the mode to Normal and the strength to 50%.**

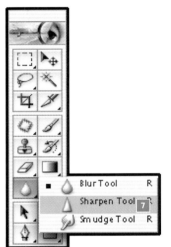

9. **Click and drag around the iris area.**
   As you drag the Sharpen tool, the contrast between pixels increases. If you move the tool too slowly as you drag or if you go over an area too many times, the contrast will continue to increase and will show up as artifacts in the image. Try a single click at times, rather than dragging.

10. **Choose Save→Revert as the last step to return to the previously saved version of the document.**

11. **Leave your document open for the next exercise.**

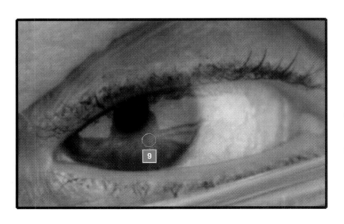

Tutorial
» Sharpening an Image with the Unsharp Mask Filter

The Unsharp Mask filter is one of Photoshop's most frequently used filters. It is rare to work with an image that doesn't need some level of sharpening with this filter. Images digitized by scanning or created with a digital camera always need sharpening, as do images that have been resized or transformed. The Unsharp Mask filter is usually the last operation in photo correction. In this tutorial, you'll apply it to the entire image that you corrected in this session.

1. **Make sure that** `13_darkroom.psd` **is still open from the last tutorial.**

2. **Select the Zoom tool and set the magnification for the image to 100%, if it isn't there already.**
   It is important to view your image at 100% as you apply the Unsharp Mask filter. Viewing at actual size provides an accurate view of how the filter is affecting the image.

The Unsharp effect looks more pronounced on-screen than it does in high-quality print output, due to the difference in resolution between screen display and print output. If you are sending files to a high-quality printer (above 133 lpi), you may want to provide a test file to the service bureau so that sharpening can be adjusted if necessary.

3. **Choose Filter→Sharpen→Unsharp Mask from the menu bar.**
   The Unsharp Mask dialog box opens, providing a preview of your image as well as the filter controls.

4. **Confirm that the Preview check box is checked.**
   The Preview option temporarily applies the Unsharp Mask controls to the image in the document window, where you can make a better overall assessment of how each setting affects the image than with the small preview pane in the dialog box.

5. **Move the Amount slider to 200.**
   Check the results in both the preview pane of the Unsharp Mask dialog box and the document. The amount of sharpening required normally goes up as file resolution increases.

6. **Click the Preview check box to uncheck it.**
   Toggling the preview in the document on and off is an excellent way to see the full extent of the effect. Note how the detail in the preview pane of the Unsharp Mask dialog box is much sharper than in the document. The document view isn't showing the effect of the Unsharp Mask filter, but the preview pane is.

Pay attention to all areas of the image. Applying a strong amount of the Unsharp Mask effect may provide excellent results for most of the image but produce unacceptable hard lines or artifacts in another.

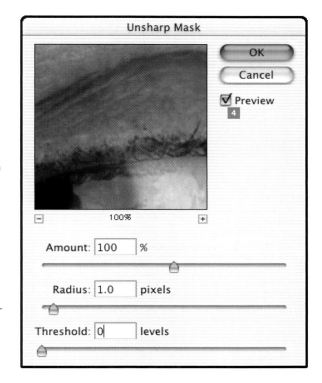

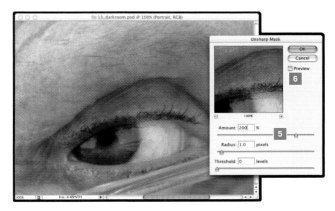

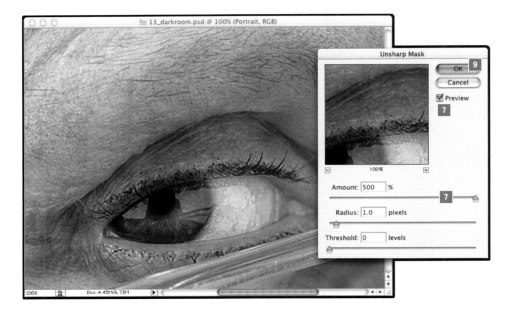

7. **Click the Preview check box to check it and move the Amount slider to 500.**

   You can now see the result of too much Unsharp Mask. Note how the skin above the eye has brown dots, and the frame of the glasses has an unattractive hard edge. Also, note the artifacts in the hair. Toggle the preview on and off a few times to observe all that is changing.

   <TIP>

   When you are new to the Unsharp Mask feature in Photoshop, it helps to preview at extreme levels to train your eye to watch for artifacts. Take the settings past where you think they look best and work your way back to the best combination of a sharp image without unwanted addtions.

8. **Move the Amount slider back to 200. Leave the other settings as they are for now.**

   Check your preview to make sure that this setting works for your image. The subtle differences in the application of the corrections in this session may mean that your image requires slightly more or less than this value.

9. **Click OK to return to the document and accept the Unsharp Mask settings.**

10. **Choose File→Save and leave the document open for the next, and final, tutorial in this session.**

Unsharp Mask Controls

The Unsharp Mask filter in Photoshop comes with three separate controls. The Amount setting controls the overall strength of the Unsharp Mask filter. Lower numbers have less effect. Values of 50 to 100% are common for low-resolution images, such as those for the Web. Images prepared for high-quality printing usually demand settings from 150 to 200% or more.

The Radius setting controls the number of pixels along an edge that are used for sharpening the image. Between 0.5 and 1 px is usually correct for low-resolution images. Higher-resolution images commonly require a setting between 1 and 2 px.

Threshold controls the amount of contrast that is required for Photoshop to determine what is an "edge." The default value of 0 levels sharpens every pixel and is often an acceptable setting. Increasing the value excludes some pixels and may help to prevent unwanted artifacts from appearing.

Tutorial

» Using the Gaussian Blur Filter for a Depth-of-Field Effect

The Gaussian Blur filter is the opposite of the Unsharp Mask filter. It softens the contrast between pixels in an image. The effect can range from a gentle softening, as you will create in this tutorial, to blending pixels so heavily that the original shape can't be found. In this tutorial, you'll use a feathered selection with the Gaussian Blur filter to make the subject's eye stand out clearly. This method creates an effect similar to a photographer manually decreasing the depth of field in portrait photography. Only the center of interest is in sharp focus, while the rest of the image is slightly out of focus.

1. **Check that** 13_darkroom.psd **is still open from the last tutorial.**

2. **Select the Zoom tool in the toolbox and set the magnification to 50% or less so that the entire image fits on your screen.**

3. **Select the Elliptical Marquee tool in the toolbox and draw an oval selection around the eye.**

4. **Choose Select→Feather from the menu bar.**
   The Feather Selection dialog box opens.

5. **Type** 30 **in the Feather Radius field. Click OK.**
   This setting feathers the selection gradually from the selected effect to the rest of the image over a 30 pixel wide radius.

6. **Choose Select→Inverse from the menu bar.**
   The area that was selected is now the only area on the document that isn't selected. The feather setting simply reverses.

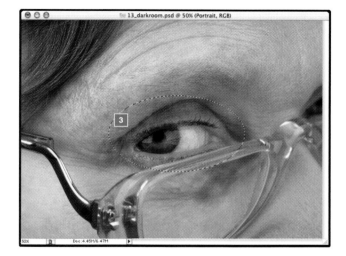

<TIP>

When you are working with feathered selections, you may find it helpful to use the Quick Mask mode for a visual definition of the selected area. The Quick Mask mode is invoked by clicking the Quick Mask Mode icon just below the color wells in the toolbox. The red area that appears when you switch to Quick Mask mode represents the area of the document that won't be affected. Anything that isn't covered by red will be affected by any changes that you make. Simply click the Edit in Standard Mode icon to cancel Quick Mask mode.

7. **Select the Zoom tool in the toolbox and increase magnification to 100%.**
   It is important to view at actual size when applying a Blur filter for the best preview accuracy.

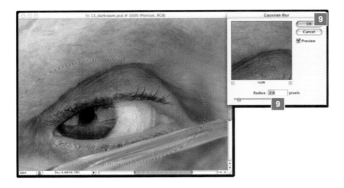

8. **Choose Filter→Blur→Gaussian Blur from the menu bar.**
   The Gaussian Blur dialog box opens.

9. **Set Radius to 2. Click OK to accept the Blur settings.**
   Note that the preview pane reflects the selected area. You want to soften the image, not produce a visible blur for this example. The eye, which is still in sharp focus, stands out well from the soft focus in the rest of the image, simulating a photographic shallow depth-of-field effect.

10. **Press ⌘+D (Windows: Ctrl+D) to deselect and use the Zoom tool to zoom out to 50% or less magnification so that you can see your image.**

11. **Click the eye icon beside the Title layer to return the layer visibility and complete this image.**

12. **Choose File→Save As, rename the image** 13_darkroom_end.psd, **and save it to your collages folder for use in the final project.**

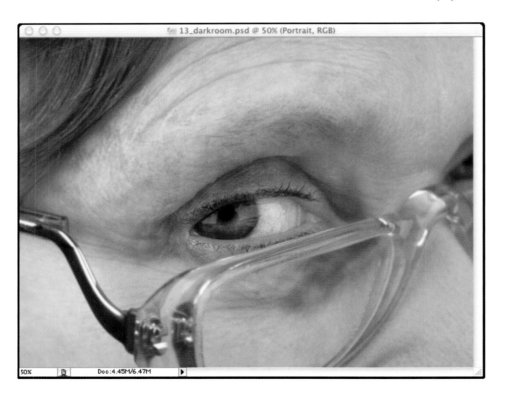

» Session Review

This session covers the many aspects of editing and adding effects to photos in Photoshop. It includes lessons on cloning, retouching images with the Healing Brush and Patch tools, adjusting exposure, adjusting saturation, sharpening, blurring and saturating an image, and creating depth of field. Here are some questions to help you review the information in this session. You'll find the answer to each question in the tutorial noted in parentheses.

1. When using the Clone Stamp tool, what happens when you sample pixels? (See "Tutorial: Removing Content with the Clone Stamp Tool.")

2. How does the Healing Brush tool differ from the Clone Stamp tool? (See "Tutorial: Retouching with the Healing Brush Tool.")

3. When you select an area using the Patch tool, what is the difference between specifying Source or Destination in the Options bar? (See "Tutorial: Working with the Patch Tool.")

4. What do the Dodge and Burn tools do? (See "Tutorial: Adjusting Exposure.")

5. Why change the range from Shadows to Midtones to Highlights when using the Dodge or Burn tools? (See "Tutorial: Adjusting Exposure.")

6. Which tool can be used to soften a hard line of pixels? (See "Tutorial: Using the Sharpen and Blur Tools.")

7. What undesired side effect can the Sharpen tool create? (See "Tutorial: Using the Sharpen and Blur Tools.")

8. At what point in the image correction workflow is it most common to apply the Unsharp Mask filter? (See "Tutorial: Sharpening an Image with the Unsharp Mask Filter.")

9. What is a sign that you have applied the Unsharp Mask filter too strongly ? (See "Tutorial: Sharpening an Image with the Unsharp Mask Filter.")

10. How can you preview the effect of an Unsharp Mask filter in the document window? (See "Tutorial: Sharpening an Image with the Unsharp Mask Filter.")

11. What do the Threshold and Radius settings for the Unsharp Mask filter control? (See "Tutorial: Sharpening an Image with the Unsharp Mask Filter.")

12. How does the Gaussian Blur filter create a softer appearance? (See "Tutorial: Using the Gaussian Blur Filter for a Depth-of-Field Effect.")

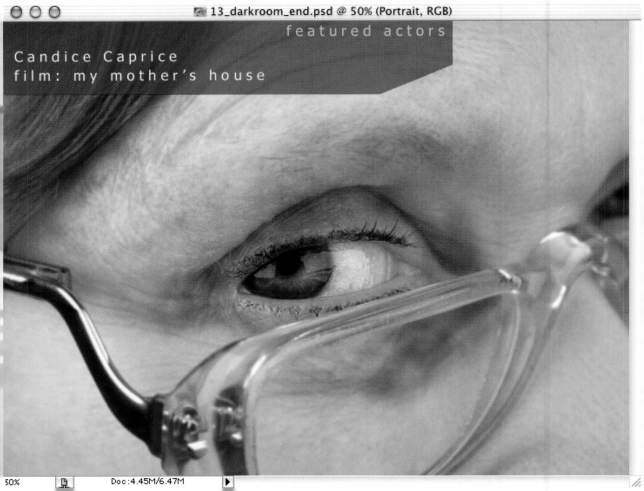

featured actors

Candice Caprice
film: my mother's house

Controlling Tone

○ ○ ○   14_tone.psd @ 50% (Portrait, RGB)

featured actors

Allison Reverent
film: finish line

50%   Doc:4.45M/5.78M

Tutorial: **Auto-adjusting Brightness and Contrast**

Tutorial: **Changing Auto-adjustment Defaults**

Tutorial: **Adjusting Brightness and Contrast with Levels**

Tutorial: **Adjusting Tonality with Curves**

Tutorial: **Saving and Loading Brightness Adjustment Settings**

Session Introduction

Almost every photo that you acquire, perhaps with the exception of an image that's profession-ally scanned at a service center, requires some tonal adjustment. Desktop flatbed scanners and digital cameras often produce images lacking optimal brightness and contrast. There is no one method or formula for tonal correction that's best for all images. Photoshop offers a number of tools for adjusting brightness and contrast. The trick is knowing how and when to use each, which is what you'll learn in this session. First you'll practice applying and customizing Photoshop's automatic tonal correction commands — Auto Levels and Auto Contrast. Then you'll move on to more sophisticated and effective correction methods using Levels and Curves adjustments.

TOOLS YOU'LL USE
Auto Levels command, Auto Contrast command, auto-correction options, Levels adjustment, Curves adjustment, Save Levels com-mand, and Save Curves command

CD-ROM FILES NEEDED
14_tone.psd, 14_tone_curves.psd, tone_levels.alv, tone_curves.acv, and 14_tone_end.psd

TIME REQUIRED
90 minutes

Tutorial

» Auto-adjusting Brightness and Contrast

When you need a quick tonal fix, you may be tempted to use either Auto Levels or Auto Contrast, which are commands that automatically adjust image brightness and contrast. These commands aren't recommended for professional tonal correction because they aren't as precise as the manual correction methods that you'll study in later tutorials. They give you little control over outcome, and they just don't work well on all images. However, they may be all you need to adjust an image like a snapshot or a photo that you're using for compositing. In this tutorial, you'll practice adjusting brightness and contrast with Auto Levels and Auto Contrast.

1. **Open** 14_tone.psd **from the Session 14 Tutorial Files folder on your hard drive. Make sure that there is no eye icon in the Visibility field on the Title layer in the Layers palette so that you can see the entire photograph on the Portrait layer.**
   14_tone.psd is a scanned image that appears to be too light and lacks contrast. The result is a dull, flat image that needs tonal correction.

<NOTE>
The first thing to do when you're correcting an image is to analyze what's wrong with it and evaluate what it needs. A photograph with good contrast typically has some areas of true white, some areas of true black, and a complete range of tones between white and black. This photo lacks a true black, resulting in an image that appears muddy and dull. To correct this, you need to make adjustments for darkening the image and creating a true black.

2. **Choose Image→Adjustments→Auto Levels from the menu bar at the top of the screen.**

   Applying Auto Levels adjusted brightness values and contrast to give the image a bolder, less washed-out appearance. However, the contrast is a little strong, and the printed result will display too much black, resulting in some loss of detail in the shadows on the left side of the photo, as you can see in this figure.

< N O T E >

Auto Levels adjusts brightness and contrast by remapping the lightest highlights in an image to white and the darkest shadows in the image to black. It also redistributes the gray values across the brightness scale between the black and white points. Although you want a true black and true white point in an image, you don't want important shadow areas to become so dark or important highlight areas to become so light that you lose detail in those areas. In this case, the Auto Levels command created a true white and true black in the image; however, the dark areas are a bit too black, causing the image to lose some shadow detail.

< N O T E >

Auto Levels works independently on each of the red, green, and blue channels in the image. This can sometimes change the color balance of an image, particularly if brightness and contrast vary among channels in the original image. In this case, applying Auto Levels has given the image a greenish cast. As you'll see in the next steps, Auto Contrast doesn't shift color balance.

3. **Choose Edit→Undo Auto Levels.**

   Undo the last adjustment to return to the original scan.

4. **Choose Image→Adjustments→Auto Contrast.**
   Auto Contrast, like Auto Levels, improves the contrast of the image, but also results in a slight loss of detail in the shadow areas, as you can see in this figure.

<NOTE>
Auto Contrast is similar to Auto Levels in that it shifts the darkest image values to black and the lightest to white. The difference between the two commands is that Auto Contrast doesn't treat each color channel independently. Instead, it works on a composite of all channels. As a result, you don't see a dramatic color shift when you apply Auto Contrast. Notice that the greenish cast is less noticeable in this image when you apply Auto Contrast than when you applied Auto Levels.

5. **Choose Edit→Undo Auto Contrast.**
   Undo the last adjustment to return to the original image. Keep the file open for the next tutorial.

<NOTE>
Because both Auto Levels and Auto Contrast produced less than satisfactory results (loss of detail in shadow areas), you'll try other correction methods on this image later in this session.

Tutorial
» Changing Auto-adjustment Defaults

When you use the auto-correction tools, the amount of correction is controlled by default settings established by Photoshop upon installation of the program. When adjustments made with auto-correction tools are too strong, you can override Photoshop's defaults with user-defined settings. In the preceding tutorial, the brightness and contrast adjustments made by Auto Levels and Auto Contrast were too extreme. To apply a more subtle correction, you can adjust the default auto-correction settings, as you'll do in this tutorial.

1. **Check that** 14_tone.psd **is still open from the last tutorial. If it's not, open the file of that name from the Session 14 Tutorial Files folder on your hard drive.**
   Be certain an image is open in the document window before attempting to change the auto-correction defaults. An image must be open in order to launch the Levels dialog box from which the auto-correction options are accessed.

2. **Make sure that the Portrait layer is still selected in the Layers palette. Choose Image→Adjustments→Levels.**
   This opens the Levels dialog box.

3. **Click the Options button in the Levels dialog box.**
   This opens the Auto Color Corrections Options dialog box, in which you can make changes that affect the behavior of the auto-correction commands and the Auto button in the Levels and Curves dialog boxes. This dialog box has been enhanced in Photoshop 7.

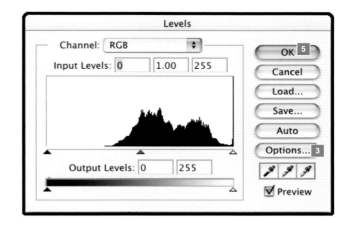

<NOTE>
If you attempt to open the Levels dialog box and the command is grayed out, you may have a layer selected to which levels can't be applied. Invisible layers, layers with vector objects, type layers, and other adjustment layers can't accept a levels adjustment.

<NOTE>
When you first open the Levels dialog box, take a moment to observe the bar chart, known as a *histogram*. This histogram shows you the entire range of possible grayscale values in an 8 bit image — from 0 (representing pure black) on the left to 255 (representing pure white) on the right. The black bell curve is actually a group of thin vertical bars symbolizing the data in this image. Each bar represents the frequency with which a particular tone is used in the image. Notice that no data appears on the far left side of the histogram. This means that there is an absence of black in this image, and the skew is in the direction of white, resulting in a light image. The sliders below the histogram can be adjusted to control brightness and contrast in the image, as you'll learn to do in the tutorial "Adjusting Brightness and Contrast with Levels" later in this session.

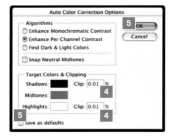

4. **Type** 0.01 **in the Shadows Clip box and** 0.01 **in the Highlights Clip box, replacing the original default values of 0.50.**
This reduces the amount of clipping that will be applied when you use the auto-correction tools.

< T I P >

To get a grasp on what the term *clipping* means, try doing the following: Move the black Input slider below the histogram to the right past the beginning of the data displayed in the bell-shaped curve. The data to the left of the black slider is cut off, or *clipped,* meaning that all values in the image that are darker than the value at which you've placed the black slider become pure black. (Return the black slider to the far left after you've observed this.) Moving the white slider to the left would have a parallel effect on the highlights. As a general rule, the more clipping that you apply to an image, the stronger the contrast appears. In the previous tutorial, you applied auto-corrections using Photoshop's default Clip values. The result was too much clipping, which produced an image with too much contrast. By adjusting the defaults and reducing the amount of clipping, you'll see less extreme brightness and contrast changes when you apply an auto-correction.

5. **Check the Save as Defaults check box. Click OK to close the Auto Color Correction Options dialog box, and OK again to close the Levels dialog box.**
This applies an automatic Levels correction, with your corrected Clip values, to the image, giving you the result that you see in the figure. Clicking Save as Defaults changes the Clip values that are used by all auto-correction tools, including Auto Levels, Auto Contrast, and Auto Color, and by the Auto buttons in the Levels and Curves dialog boxes.

6. **Choose File→Revert.**
This returns you to the original image so that you can compare changes made with the Auto Levels command and the corrected Clip values in the next step.

7. **Choose Image→Adjustments→Auto Levels.**
The new Clip values you set in step 4 are applied with the Auto Levels command.

8. **Choose Edit→Undo Auto Levels.**
This returns you to the original image again so that you can compare changes made with the Auto Contrast command in the next step.

9. **Choose Image→Adjustments→Auto Contrast.**
   Auto Contrast also uses the Clip values that you set in step 4.

10. **Choose Edit→Undo Auto Contrast.**

11. **Leave this file open for the next tutorial. Don't bother saving.**
    Table 14-1 summarizes each of the features Photoshop offers
    for correcting brightness and contrast. Study this chart and
    use it as a reference.

<NOTE>

In this figure, the Auto Levels and Auto Contrast adjustments
were made on the top two images, respectively, with the Photoshop
default auto-correction settings. The bottom two images were
adusted with Auto Levels and Auto Contrast, respectively, with the
Clip value in Auto Color Correction Options set to 0.01, as you did
in step 4.

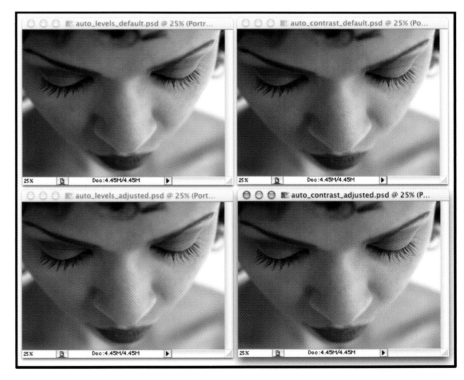

Table 14-1: Understanding Photoshop's Tonal Controls

Menu Command	Function
Auto Levels	When using Auto Levels, Photoshop analyzes the image and finds the lightest pixel and shifts it to white. That lightest pixel could be a 10% gray, 20% gray, or any other gray value. The point is that it's the lightest pixel in the document, and Photoshop makes it pure white. Then it finds the darkest pixel and makes it black. The remaining pixels are stretched out across a range of grays between the new white and new black. Depending on the amount of brightness in the original lightest and darkest pixels, Photoshop may make the overall image appear too dark or too light. In order to effectively use Auto Levels, start with a good scan with the lightest point close to white, the darkest point close to black, and an even range of tones in between. In most cases, your scans won't be evenly distributed between a white and black, and you'll need to use other methods for correcting the image brightness and contrast.
Auto Contrast	This command sets monochromatic contrast. In other words, it applies adjustment to a composite RGB channel as opposed to individual channels like the Auto Levels adjustment. The command works best on images with wide tonal ranges that are already in color balance.
Brightness/Contrast	Novice users are tempted to use the Brightness/Contrast command, which adjusts the entire image the same way, causing new problems even as it tries to fix an existing problem. You won't see any mention of this command beyond this point in the book. It will ruin the data in your file and should never be used. Forget it exists.
Curves	The Curves dialog box offers you even more control than the Levels dialog box for tonal corrections. You can adjust brightness values and reshape histograms for any of the 256 gray values. For correcting color, the Curves dialog box is the best tool in Photoshop.
Levels	The Levels command should always be your first stop when adjusting brightness and contrast or even just examining an image to determine where the gray values fall. By adjusting the input sliders, you can add snap and crispness to your images. Following the Levels adjustment, you can color correct or tweak grays in the Curves settings.

Tutorial
» Adjusting Brightness and Contrast with Levels

Whereas the auto-correction tools enable you to make only two adjustments at fixed values, the Levels dialog box offers you more control over midtones as well as highlights and shadows in an image. Although the auto-correction tools are quick and easy, you'll almost always get better results with the Levels command, which will frequently be your first stop when you're correcting an image. In this tutorial, you'll learn how to use the Levels dialog box to adjust brightness values and contrast in an image.

1. **Use the file that you left open from the last tutorial.**

2. **Choose Image→Adjustments→Levels.**
   The Levels dialog box opens. The histogram displays a range of 256 gray levels beginning with the black point on the left of the histogram to the white point on the right side of the histogram. The data between these two points displays the frequency with which each of the 256 levels of gray are found in this image. For example, the tall spike at the left of the histogram indicates that there is a lot of the corresponding dark gray color in this image, and the short vertical lines on the right side of the histogram indicate that there is very little of those particular shades of light gray in this image. In the following steps, you'll learn how to adjust the range of tones in this image by moving the input sliders located directly below the histogram.

<NOTE>
The Input Levels fields tell you the numerical value of the tone just above each slider. You'll notice that the value at the far left of the histogram (above the black slider) is 0 (zero) and the value at the far right (above the white slider) is 255. Zero is counted as one value; hence the total number of grays in this 8-bit image equals 256.

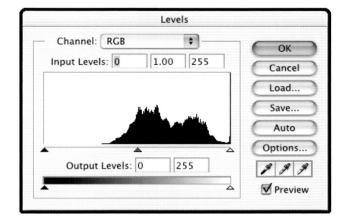

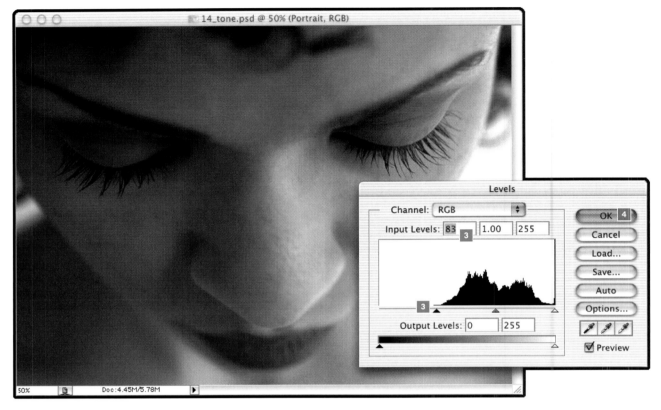

3. **Click the left slider below the histogram and move it to where the data first appears on the left side of the histogram. Make sure that the left Input Levels box reads 83 after you move the slider.**
Before you moved the slider, the histogram revealed no data above the left input slider. The histogram was skewed to the right, indicating that there was no true black in the original image and that the image contained more light than dark tones. By moving the left input slider to the right, you turned lighter pixels into darker pixels resulting in an overall improved contrast. The right side of the histogram contains sufficient data; therefore, there is no need to move the white slider to the left.

4. **Click OK in the Levels dialog box.**
This applies your levels adjustments to the image. Windows users: This method for adjusting levels is one that you'll always use. Macintosh users: You have another, alternative method available to you as explained in the following steps.

5. **Macintosh users only: Choose Edit→Undo Levels.**
Moving sliders in the Levels dialog box is a bit of guesswork. Although Photoshop provides you with dynamic feedback, you may be confused as to where exactly the slider belongs and how much clipping will occur in the image. Macintosh users have more help from Photoshop than Windows users, as you'll see in the next steps.

6. **Macintosh users only: Choose Image→Adjustments→Levels to open the Levels dialog box.**

7. **Macintosh users only: Press the Option key on your keyboard and drag the left Input slider to the right. Stop the slider when you first begin to see pixels appear in the document window (which should correspond with an input level of about 83).**

   Photoshop dynamically shows you which pixels will be clipped (turned to pure black) as the Input slider is moved. You don't want to shift too many pixels to black because you'll lose detail in the shadow areas. As long as the pixels that you see are separated by some white space (rather than appearing as a solid clump), the area that includes these black pixels will retain detail.

8. **Macintosh users only: Click OK to apply the Levels adjustment to the image with your manually adjusted settings.**

9. **Choose File→Save. Keep the file open and move immediately on to the next tutorial. Don't take a break yet, if you can help it, because the next two tutorials depend on leaving this file open and working on it further without closing.**

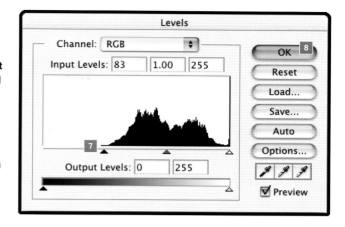

< N O T E >

RGB files contain three separate channels of color information, which contain gray levels for the red, green, and blue colors in an image. You can apply levels corrections for each individual channel in order to adjust color balance. At the top of the Levels dialog box, the Channel button shows the composite RGB channel selection. Click that button to open a drop-down list from which you can select the red, green, or blue channel. Then move the sliders to adjust levels for the selected color channel. For more information regarding channels, see Session 15.

< N O T E >

After you set the black and white points in the Levels dialog box, you may still find that an image is too dark or too light overall. In that case, click and drag the gray Input slider in the Levels dialog box to adjust the gray midtone without further affecting the very white highlights or the very black shadows. If a simple adjustment of the gray slider doesn't get you the look that you want, move on to adjust gray tones with the Curves dialog box, as you'll learn to do in the next tutorial.

Adjusting High Bit Depth Images

Most of the new desktop scanners that you can purchase today enable you to capture 30 to 36 bits of information per pixel. Photoshop images normally contain only 8 bits per pixel. Your scanner is capturing more data when you scan at the higher bit depths. If you have a scanner capable of scanning at these higher bit depths, always scan your images at these values because you'll capture more data and you'll ultimately get a better scan. When the scan opens in Photoshop, choose Image→Mode→16 Bits/Channel to edit the file with 16 bits of information per channel. You can't use all of Photoshop's tools on 16 bit per channel images, but you can adjust tonality with all the tools used for brightness and contrast adjustments.

There is a big difference between 8 bit/channel images and 16 bit/channel images with regard to the amount of data that you work with when making your brightness and contrast adjustments. When you adjust an 8 bit/channel image with the black point and white point sliders, the gray values in the image are stretched across the tonal range, and you often find gaps between the gray levels when you return to the histogram in the Levels dialog box. These gaps represent an absence of grays. In severe cases, the result can lead to *posterization* — an undesirable effect that appears mottled and banded.

When a scan is adjusted in 16 bit/channel mode, the image contains thousands of grays (just how many can vary because Photoshop treats any image that's greater than 8 bit as a 16 bit per channel image). As you move the sliders in the Levels dialog box, there is plenty of information to result in a smooth transition of grays without gaps between individual tones.

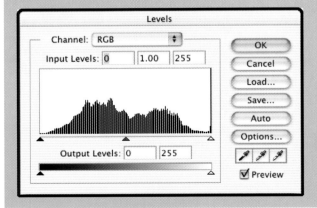

In the preceding figure, adjustments were made on an 8 bit per channel image in the Levels dialog box, and the Levels dialog box was reopened to view the histogram after adjustment. Notice the gaps between each frequency along the histogram.

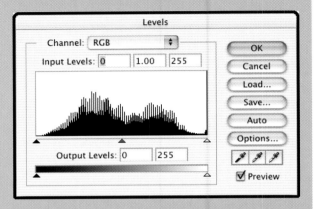

This figure shows the same image at 16 bits/per channel when the sliders were moved to make the brightness adjustments. When the Levels dialog box was reopened, the transition of grays yields more data along the histogram.

If you adjust levels or make other tonal corrections on an image set to 16 bit/channel, as a last step, choose Image→Mode→8 bits/channel to downsample to 8 bits per channel. You have to do this in order to use other Photoshop features, such as filters and layers, that aren't available for 16 bit/channel images. Another reason to convert back to 8 bit/channel is if you plan to export the image to other image applications, many of which don't support 16 bit/channel images.

Tutorial
» Adjusting Tonality with Curves

In this tutorial, you'll learn how to use the Curves dialog box for adjusting tonal range in an image. The Levels dialog box that you worked with earlier is a good tool for making brightness and contrast changes, as well as some minor midtone adjustments. As a common practice, you'll find using Levels to adjust brightness and contrast is a good first step because the Levels histogram shows you where all the image pixels fall and gives you a clue as to where to move the sliders for making brightness and contrast adjustments. However, Levels only enables you to address a single midtone point by moving the center Input Level slider. With the Curves dialog box, you can change any gray level among the 256 grays and make any one of those grays darker or lighter, resulting in a change to the midtones between the black and white points. In a typical workflow, you first adjust the brightness and contrast in the Levels dialog box and then move to the Curves dialog box to adjust midtones.

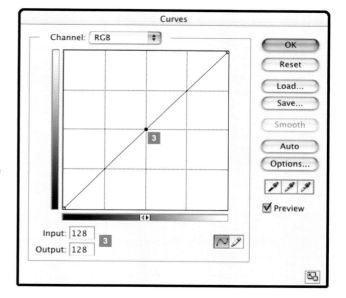

1. **Use** 14_tone.psd, **which should be open from the last tutorial.**

2. **Choose Image→Adjustments→Curves.**
   The Curves dialog box opens. The diagonal line beginning in the lower-left corner and extending to the upper-right corner represents the linear progression of grays from 0 (black) to 256 (white). At any one of the gray levels in the Curves dialog box, you can make tonal adjustments.

3. **Click the middle of the curves line in the dialog box.**
   The Input and Output fields at the lower left of the Curves dialog box give you a numerical readout of the location of the selected point. If you didn't get the point exactly at the middle point, use these fields to center it by making sure that the point is selected (it should be solid instead of hollow) and typing **128** in the Input field and **128** in the Output field.

<NOTE>
To make tonal corrections to an image, you first click the line to add one or more points to the line. You drag a point up and to the left on the diagram to bend the line in that direction and lighten the image; you drag a point down and to the right to bend the line the other way and darken the image. The resulting shape of the curved line determines how tones are remapped in the image.

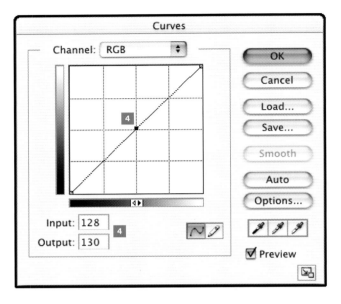

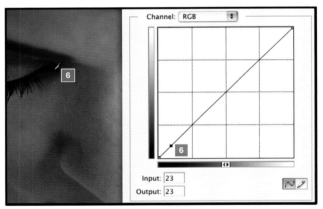

4. **Move the plotted point to a position to slightly above the center so that the Input box in the lower-left corner of the Curves dialog box reads 128 and the Output box reads 130.**

It may be easier to type **130** in the Output box with the point selected rather than try to move it this slightly. The image is a little dark in the midtones. This slight adjustment lightens it up just a bit by moving the midpoint.

< N O T E >
Curves adjustments should be slight if you begin with a good tonal range (as is true of this image following your Levels adjustments in the last tutorial).

< N O T E >
Here's a technique that will help you visualize what any point on the curves line represents and what you'll accomplish when you adjust that point. Create a point anywhere on the line and move your eye down to the black-to-white horizontal bar directly beneath that point to see a visual representation of the tone of gray that that point represents. Move the point slightly up or down. Now move your eye to the vertical bar on the left of the diagram to see the tone of gray to which you've remapped the original tone. The numbers in the Input and Output boxes are numerical representations of the same thing. Numerical values in the Input box correspond to shades on the horizontal bar, and values in the Output box correspond to shades on the vertical bar.

5. **Option+click (Windows: Alt+click) in several of the darkest areas of the image. Notice that each time you click, a hollow circle appears temporarily on the line in the Curves dialog box, telling you that this is the part of the line that controls the dark parts of the image.**

In the next step, you'll set a point in this part of the line so that you can adjust that area of the image to restore it to true black (because the whole image was lightened slightly by your last adjustment). You could set the point manually by clicking on the line in the general area in which you saw the hollow circles, but the next step teaches a more precise way of setting that point.

6. **⌘+click (Windows: Ctrl+click) in the part of the image that you think should be pure black, such as the subject's left tear duct. You'll see a solid circle appear on the bottom left of the line in the Curves dialog box, in approximately the location that you see in the figure.**

Don't worry if your point isn't at the exact same location or your Input and Output numbers aren't exactly the same as those shown here.

7. Click and drag the point that you created in step 6 down slightly toward the bottom of the diagram.

This restored the darker shadow areas, keeping a true black in the image, but didn't affect the highlight areas. They are protected from moving by the point that you set at the center of the curve line. In the next step, you'll darken the highlights slightly to make up for whatever lightening occurred in that area when you adjusted the center point back in step 4.

8. ⌘+click (Windows: Ctrl+click) in an area of the image that has the brightest highlight of which you'd like to retain the detail (such as the area to the right of the subject's right eyebrow). You'll see a solid circle appear on the top right of the line in the Curves dialog box, in approximately the location that you see in the figure.

Again, don't worry if your point isn't at the exact same location or your Input and Output numbers aren't exactly the same as those shown here.

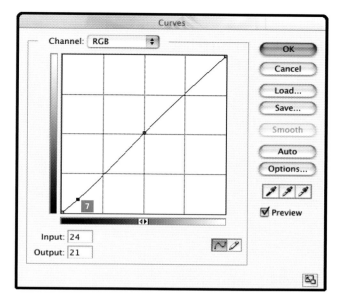

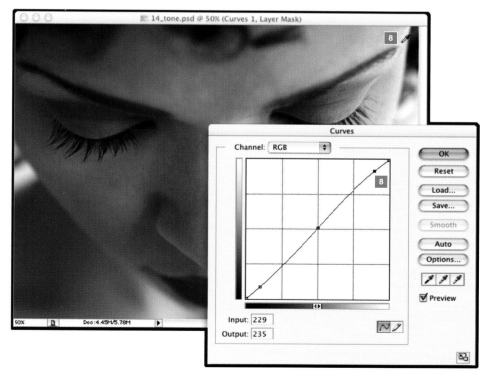

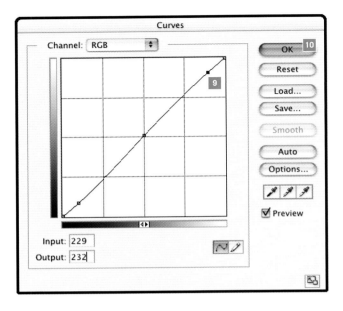

9. **Click the point that you created in step 8 and drag down to move it toward the bottom of the diagram very slightly.**
   This adjustment restores a little highlight detail.

10. **Click OK in the Curves dialog box.**

11. **Keep the file open and move immediately on to the next tutorial. Again, don't take a break just yet because the next tutorial depends on this one.**

< N O T E >

Notice that the Curves adjustments were slight. When you're adjusting in the Curves dialog box, don't make severe adjustments, or the image can become posterized or appear to have dull flat tones instead of crisp contrast. The Levels adjustment that you made in the preceding tutorial was almost adequate to correct the brightness and contrast in the document. The slight Curves adjustments for midtones, shadows, and highlights preserve the highlight and shadow details. The color of the image also needs some adjustment. At this point, try to understand the tonal adjustments, and you'll handle color correction in the next session.

Tutorial

» Saving and Loading Brightness Adjustment Settings

In the last two tutorials, you made Levels and Curves adjustments. In some workflows, you may have a number of images that need the same brightness adjustments. Rather than individually apply new settings to each image, you can save the adjustments made to an image and load the same adjustments into other images. In this tutorial, you'll learn how to save and load Levels and Curves settings.

1. **Use the file with the Levels and Curves adjustments from the last tutorial. If you don't have the file open, repeat the Levels and Curves adjustments made in the two preceding tutorials before continuing on with this tutorial.**

2. **Press ⌘+Option+L (Windows: Ctrl+Alt+L).**
   When you use these modifier keys to reopen the Levels dialog box, you'll see the last settings applied in the dialog box. If your file has remained open since the tutorial in which levels were discussed, you should see the Input slider for the black point resting at 83 in the Input Levels box. If you didn't keep your file open, you need to open the original 14_tone.psd file and make the Levels adjustment again.

3. **Click the Save button in the Levels dialog box.**
   The Save dialog box opens.

4. **Name the file tone_levels.alv. Click the Save button.**
   The .alv extension is Photoshop's default file extension for Levels settings. Be sure to save the file in a folder that you can easily find on your hard drive.

5. **Click Cancel in the Levels dialog box.**

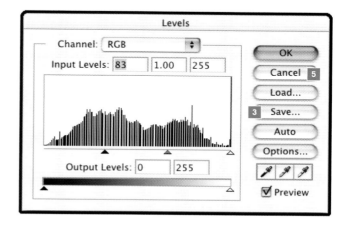

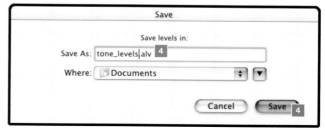

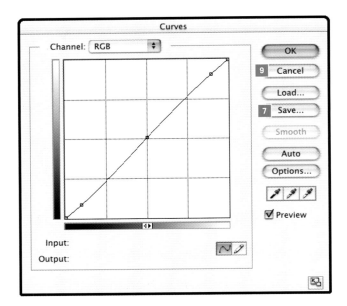

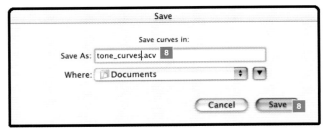

6. **Press ⌘+Option+M (Windows: Ctrl+Alt+M).**
   The Curves dialog box opens, and the last adjustments made are shown.

7. **Click the Save button.**
   The Save dialog box opens.

8. **Type** tone_curves.acv **and click the Save button.**
   The .acv extension is Photoshop's default file extension for Curves settings. Be certain to save the file in the same folder as the Levels settings.

9. **Click Cancel in the Curves dialog box.**

10. **Save the file as** 14_tone_curves.psd. **Close the file after saving.**
    The Levels and Curves adjustments have been made to this image. Saving the file preserves the brightness, contrast, and tonal corrections that you made. The settings have all been saved in two separate files.

11. **Open the original uncorrected file** 14_tone.psd **from the Session 14 Tutorial Files folder on your hard drive.**
    The file needs the same tonal corrections made in the previous tutorials. Rather than revisit the dialog boxes, you'll load the settings saved from steps in this tutorial.

12. **Choose Image→Adjustments→Levels.**
    The Levels dialog box opens.

13. **Click Load.**

    The Load dialog box opens and displays all files with an .alv extension.

14. **Select** tone_levels.alv **and click the Load button.**

    Photoshop returns you to the Levels dialog box, and the adjusted Input Levels setting appears and is applied to the image. Note that a copy of this levels file is in the Session 14 Tutorial Files folder if you need it.

15. **Click OK in the Levels dialog box to accept the settings.**

16. **Choose Image→Adjustments→Curves.**

    The Curves dialog box opens.

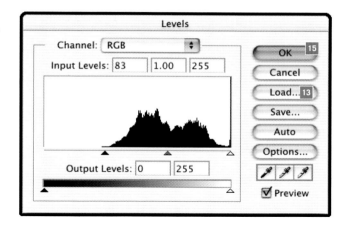

17. **Click Load.**

    The Load dialog box opens and displays all files with an .acv extension.

18. **Select** tone_curves.acv **and click the Load button.**

    Photoshop returns you to the Curves dialog box, and the settings are applied to the Curves adjustment. Note that a copy of this curves file is in the Session 14 Tutorial Files folder if you need it.

19. **Click OK to accept the settings.**

20. **Choose File→Save As, name the image** 14_tone_end.psd, **and save it to your desktop. You'll use this file again in the next session.**

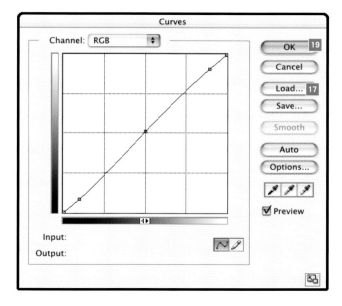

» Session Review

This session covers how to adjust tonal values (brightness and contrast) in images. You first learned how to adjust brightness and contrast automatically using the Auto Levels and Auto Contrast commands, and then you worked in the Levels dialog box where you applied adjustments manually for brightness and contrast changes. Later, you made adjustments for tonal corrections in the Curves dialog box and learned how to save and load settings.

1. How do you use auto-correction tools? (See "Tutorial: Auto-adjusting Brightness and Contrast.")

2. When would you use Auto Levels and Auto Contrast? (See "Tutorial: Auto-adjusting Brightness and Contrast.")

3. How do you control the amount of adjustment with auto-correction tools? (See "Tutorial: Auto-adjusting Brightness and Contrast.")

4. What is a histogram? (See "Tutorial: Adjusting Brightness and Contrast with Levels.")

5. If there are 256 levels of gray in an 8 bit image, why does the largest number in the Levels dialog box appear as 255? (See "Tutorial: Adjusting Brightness and Contrast with Levels.")

6. What's bit depth? (See "Tutorial: Adjusting Brightness and Contrast with Levels.")

7. What's the difference between 8 bit and 16 bit images? (See "Tutorial: Adjusting Brightness and Contrast with Levels.")

8. When are curves used? (See "Tutorial: Adjusting Tonality with Curves.")

9. What are curves input and output levels? (See "Tutorial: Adjusting Tonality with Curves.")

10. How can you apply the same brightness, contrast, and tonal adjustments to several images? (See "Tutorial: Saving and Loading Brightness Adjustment Settings.")

Session 15

Adjusting Color

15_tone.psd @ 50% (Portrait, RGB)

featured actors

Allison Reverent
film: finish line

50%   Doc:4.45M/5.78M

Tutorial: **Adjusting Color Balance**

Tutorial: **Adjusting Hue/Saturation**

Tutorial: **Adjusting Color with Curves**

Tutorial: **Adjusting Color with Variations**

Session Introduction

After you address brightness and contrast corrections in images, the next step involves correcting color. Even with some of the best desktop scanners and digital cameras, you'll typically find a need for making some kind of color correction. In this session, you'll look at methods used in Photoshop for correcting color, including adjustments using the Color Balance, Hue/Saturation, Curves, and Variations features.

TOOLS YOU'LL USE
Color Balance command, Hue/Saturation command, Curves command, Channels command, and Variations command

CD-ROM FILES NEEDED
15_tone.psd, 15_tone_clean.psd, and 15_tone_end.psd

TIME REQUIRED
90 minutes

Tutorial
» Adjusting Color Balance

Photoshop offers a number of color correction tools. The Color Balance adjustment is one of the easiest to use, but it also offers you less control than more sophisticated color correction methods such as curves. You'll probably prefer other methods if you're doing professional color correction, but Color Balance may be sufficient when you need a quick color correction fix for a snapshot or personal project. You'll practice applying a Color Balance adjustment in this tutorial.

1. **Open the file** 15_tone.psd **from the Session 15 Tutorial Files folder. This is a copy of the file** 14_tone_end.psd **that you completed in Session 14, so you can use that file if you prefer.**
   The file has already been corrected for brightness and contrast in Session 14.

2. **Make sure that the Portrait layer is selected in the Layers palette. Choose Layer→New Adjustment Layer Image→Color Balance and click OK in the New Layer dialog box.**
   This creates a new Color Balance adjustment layer above the Portrait layer and opens the Color Balance dialog box.

<N O T E>
You could color correct directly on the Portrait layer by choosing Layer→Adjustments→Color Balance, but it makes sense to perform color corrections on separate adjustment layers because adjustment layers don't affect the original pixels of artwork, they can be reopened and edited at any time, and they can be deleted at will. Remember that an adjustment layer affects all the layers beneath it in the Layers palette unless you group it with one layer (although this isn't an issue in this image).

<N O T E>
The first thing to do when you're color correcting is to analyze the image to determine whether it has an unacceptable color cast and determine how you're going to correct that color cast or other color problem. Keep in mind that each of the primary colors in an RGB image has a complementary color. The color complements are red/cyan, green/magenta, and blue/yellow. Adjusting the problem color or its complement will often be all the color correction that you need to do. In this case, the image needs a slight bit of red to bring the flesh tones to a more neutral appearance. In the Color Balance settings, you'll add a little red and make some slight adjustments to the Green and Blue channels.

3. **Make sure that Preview is enabled in the Color Balance dialog box so that you can see a live preview of your adjustments in the document window. Select Midtones to work on the color of the midtones first. And make sure that Preserve Luminosity is checked in order to protect the tonal balance that you worked so hard to correct in the last session.**

   Preserve Luminosity keeps the overall image brightness fixed while you make adjustments to color balance. You can adjust colors in the shadows, midtones, and highlights separately using the radio buttons in this dialog box.

4. **Move the Cyan/Red slider away from Cyan and toward Red, until 15 appears in the first Color Levels box.**

   You may be wondering how to know exactly where to set any of the color sliders. One way to work is to move the slider to an exaggerated position to see the results of the adjustment and back it off by moving slowly back toward the middle. With Preview enabled, Photoshop offers you dynamic viewing as the sliders are moved.

5. **Click the Magenta/Green slider and move it away from Magenta toward Green, until the second Color Levels box at the top of the dialog box reads 3.**

   Moving the slider away from magenta reduces the magenta in the image.

6. **Click the Yellow/Blue slider and move it toward Blue to 9.**

   This adjustment adds a little blue and reduces the yellow slightly.

7. **Uncheck and then recheck the Preview box to compare the way that the image looked before and after this adjustment.**

   Notice that the color adjustment is slight.

8. **Click OK to accept the changes.**

9. **Choose File➔Save and keep** 15_tone.psd **open for the next tutorial.**

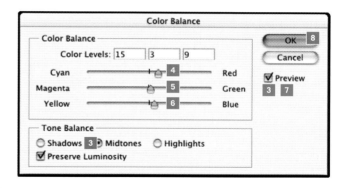

<NOTE>

Adjusting the color balance changes the mix of colors in the image. However, changes in color or the intensity of the color aren't handled in the Color Balance dialog box. For these changes, you need to use Hue/Saturation corrections. Therefore, this tutorial is one half of the equation that may be needed for some images. To continue your color correction, move on to the Hue/Saturation dialog box, as explained in the next tutorial.

Tutorial
» Adjusting Hue/Saturation

In the previous tutorial, you adjusted color balance and made corrections for any color cast that may appear in an image. The color value and intensity of a color are handled in the Hue/Saturation dialog box. In this tutorial, you'll learn how to apply a Hue/Saturation adjustment.

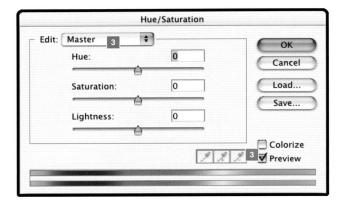

<NOTE>

The Hue/Saturation dialog box enables you to adjust three different parameters of color: Hue, Saturation, and Lightness. *Hue* means the color value. Moving the Hue slider applies colors as if you were moving 360° around a color wheel. *Saturation* means the intensity of color. *Lightness* means the brightness of color. The Lightness slider affects all tones in an image equally, so it's best to avoid using this slider and adjust brightness in the Levels or Curves dialog box instead.

1. **Make sure that** 15_tone.psd **is still open from the last tutorial.**

2. **Choose Layer→New Adjustment Layer→Hue/Saturation and click OK in the New Layer dialog box.**
   This adds a Hue/Saturation adjustment layer above the Color Balance adjustment layer in the Layers palette and opens the Hue/Saturation dialog box.

3. **Make sure that Colorize is disabled in the Hue/Saturation dialog box, Master is selected in the Edit drop-down list, and there's a check mark next to Preview.**

<NOTE>

If Colorize is selected, the entire image is shifted to the same Hue and Saturation, with only brightness varying from pixel to pixel. When you're adjusting color, you'll want Colorize to be disabled. Master applies the adjustments that you're about to make to all the colors in the image equally, rather than to just a particular range of colors (such as reds, yellows, and so on).

4. **Drag the Saturation slider to +3. Click OK in the Hue/Saturation dialog box.**

   This adjustment makes all the colors in the image slightly more vibrant. There's no reason to change the Hue or Lightness setting of this image in the Hue/Saturation dialog box because the brightness of this image was already adjusted in the last session, and the Hue was addressed in the last tutorial when you adjusted color balance.

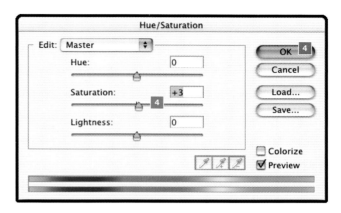

<NOTE>

The combination of the Color Balance and the Hue/Saturation adjustments brings the sample image into a better color balance, resulting in more neutral skin tones. These adjustments were minor because this image didn't have much of a color cast or saturation problem at this point.

5. **Choose File→Save and keep this image open for the next steps.**

   To gain a little more understanding about how Hue/Saturation adjustments affect an image, you'll learn how to use this feature to apply a special effect in the following steps.

6. **Choose Image→Mode→Grayscale. You'll see a warning that changing modes will discard adjustment layers (because grayscale mode doesn't support adjustment layers). Click Merge.**

   This eliminates all color from the image in preparation for adding a sepia tone to the image using Hue/Saturation adjustments. Sepia toning is often applied to old photos for photo restoration. Before you begin to colorize an image with a sepia effect, you must first strip all color from the image, as you did in this step.

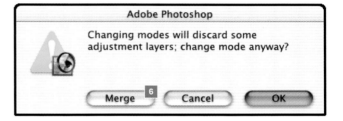

7. **Choose Image→Mode→RGB Color.**

   In order to colorize an image, you must convert it back to RGB mode because the file needs to be in a mode that can accept the application of color.

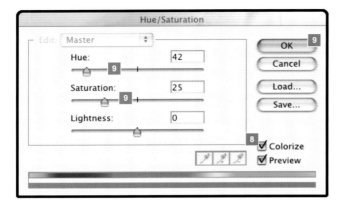

8. **Choose Layer→New Adjustment Layer→Hue/Saturation and click OK in the New Layer dialog box. In the Hue/Saturation dialog box, click the Colorize check box.**
   Colorize is the secret to this effect. It enables you to add a monochrome hue to the entire image.

9. **Move the Hue slider to the left to 42 to change the color. Move the Saturation slider to the left to 25 to tone down the effect. Click OK in the Hue/Saturation dialog box.**
   The image appears with a sepia effect.

10. **Close the file without saving.**

<NOTE>
Photoshop provides you with another, automatic method for sepia toning in the Actions palette. Actions are a series of Photoshop commands that can be applied to multiple images in batch mode or individually to separate images. To use the Sepia toning action, eliminate all color from your photos by choosing Image→Mode→Grayscale and then convert them back to RGB by choosing Image→Mode→RGB Color. Open the Actions palette and select Sepia toning (layer) in the palette and click the right pointing arrow at the bottom of the dialog box. Photoshop runs through a series of steps and converts the image to a sepia tone.

Tutorial
» Adjusting Color with Curves

The best tonal and color control feature in Photoshop is the Curves adjustment. In Session 14, you used Curves to correct the tonal range of an image, making adjustments to brightness in the midtones, highlights, and shadows. The Curves command can also be used for color balance. In this tutorial, you'll learn how to use the Curves dialog box to correct color.

1. **Open** 15_tone_clean.psd **from the Session 15 Tutorial Files folder.**
   This file is another copy of the file that you completed at the end of the last session, 14_tone_end.psd. The image has been corrected for brightness and contrast only. Make sure that you don't use a file in which you have already made color adjustments.

2. **Choose Layer→New Adjustment Layer→Curves and click OK in the New Layer dialog box.**
   The Curves dialog box opens.

3. **Select Red from the Channel drop-down list.**
   A little red needs to be added to the image to warm it up. You can make adjustments to individual channels in the Curves dialog box.

4. **Click in the center of the Curves line to create a point there. Type** 128 **in the Input box and** 138 **in the Output box.**
   Notice that the point moves up slightly. This moves the red channel towards white, allowing more red light to show through the Red channel and increasing the red tint of the image.

5. **Click OK and observe the results.**
   The image could use a little more warmth and a little bit of saturation. To saturate the entire image, you'll use the Hue/Saturation tool.

6. **Choose Layer→New Adjustment Layer→Hue/Saturation and click OK in the New Layer dialog box. Move the Saturation slider to the right to +5.**

7. **Click the Preview check mark off and on for a comparative view of the effect of increasing the saturation. When you're done, click OK to accept the adjustment.**
   You'll notice that the flesh tones appear more neutral after making this adjustment in the Hue/Saturation dialog box.

8. **Close this file without saving. It's important that you don't save over** 15_tone_clean.psd **in the Session 15 Tutorial Files folder because you'll be using that file again in the next tutorial.**

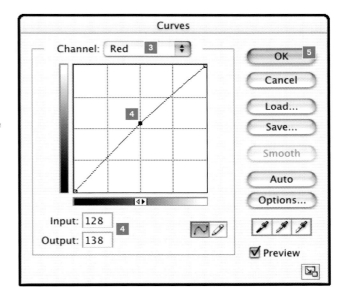

<NOTE>
As you become more experienced in Photoshop, you'll find the Curves adjustment a more sophisticated approach for adjusting color. The ability to access each individual channel and adjust any one of the 256 gray levels in the channels provides you with many more options than those found in the Color Balance and Hue/Saturation dialog boxes.

Using Curves for Color Correction

When you shoot your own images for Web hosting or printing, it will often be advantageous to use a gray card. You can obtain a 10% gray card at a photo finishing laboratory or a photo supplier. When you shoot your own images, place the gray card in a visible area of the image.

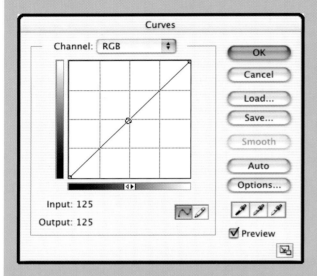

After scanning a photo or acquiring a digital camera image, open the Info palette in Photoshop and then open the Curves dialog box. Move the cursor to the image of the gray card in the photo. Click the mouse button and move the cursor around the photo until the bubble appearing on the Curve line is positioned close to the midpoint.

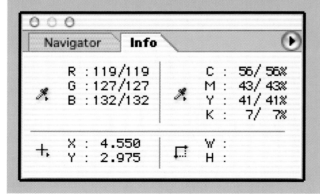

Observe the readout in the Info palette for the RGB values. A true neutral gray results in all three RGB values at 128. Write the values from the Info palette on a piece of paper. If, for example, your readout is R: 119, G: 127, B: 132, these values should all be brought to the same value if the sampled pixel is a neutral gray. To bring each channel to the same value as the other two respective channels, identify the value between the extremes. In this example, the mid value is the Green channel at 127. Thus, the Red channel at 119 and the Blue channel at 132 need to be moved to the Green value of 127.

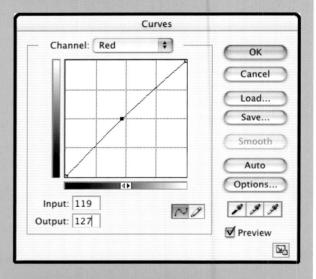

From the drop-down list at the top of the Curves dialog box, select the Red channel. Click along the curve line at any point. Enter the Red point value from the readout made in the Info palette into the Input box (in this example, 119). For the Output value, enter the midpoint value (in this example, the Green value of 127).

Perform the same steps for the Blue adjustment: Select Blue from the Channel drop-down list. Click a point on the Curve line and enter an Input value of 132 and an Output value of 127. The result of these adjustments is remapping the two channels to the third channel at the midtone range. This method provides a way to do quick color adjustments without having to do a lot of guesswork.

Tutorial

» Adjusting Color with Variations

The easiest method was saved for last. If you've been struggling with color correction up to this point, fear not. The Variations tool can help the most novice user correct color in Photoshop documents. You still need to work with an image where the brightness and contrast corrections have been made, but when image brightness is correct, you can apply color correction in a more intuitive manner with Variations. This tutorial teaches you how to use the Variations tool.

1. **Open** 15_tone_clean.psd **again from the Session 15 Tutorial Files folder.**
   Once again, you'll use the image that's been corrected for brightness and contrast.

2. **Choose Image→Adjustments→Variations. Click the radio button for Midtones at the top of the dialog box, if it isn't currently selected.**
   In the Variations dialog box, you'll see thumbnail views of the current image and the image as it would look after various adjustments to color and brightness.

3. **Select the slider in the top-right corner of the Variations dialog box and move it to the left toward Fine. Rest the slider at the second hash mark from the left.**

<NOTE>
When you apply Variations, you can control the amount of adjustment applied to your image by moving the slider toward Coarse for a stronger change in color or toward Fine for less application. This image needs only a slight adjustment. Therefore, you move the slider to a finer setting.

4. **Click the More Red thumbnail.**
   Notice that when you click, the center thumbnail shows you the result of your adjustment, and all the other thumbnail views are updated to show you what the image will look like if you click another thumbnail.

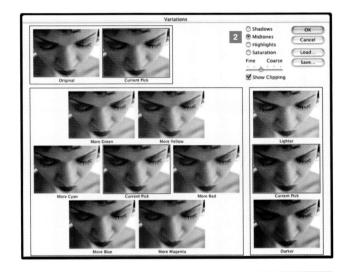

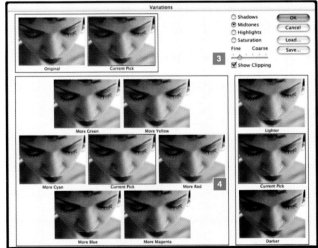

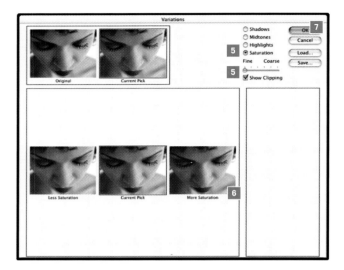

<NOTE>
There's another automatic color correction tool that's new to Photoshop 7, called Auto Color. It is designed to eliminate color casts from photos. However, like the other automatic correction tools (Auto Levels and Auto Contrast), it doesn't work on all images (including the image that you've been using in this session). Auto Color works by finding the average lightest and darkest pixels in an image and using them as the black and white points. It also attempts to adjust midtones to neutral. If you're interested in trying this new feature, choose Image→Adjustments→Auto Color.

5. **Click the radio button for Saturation. Move the slider one more position to the left for the least amount of correction to be applied.**
Notice that the Variations dialog box enables you to combine adjustments for color balance, brightness, and saturation. Unlike the tools used in previous tutorials, you can make all your color corrections in a single dialog box.

6. **Click once on the More Saturation thumbnail.**
Once again, the adjustment is slight. You add a little saturation, much like the saturation adjustment made in the Hue/Saturation dialog box explained in an earlier tutorial.

7. **Click OK in the Variations dialog box. Press ⌘+Z (Windows: Ctrl+Z) twice to toggle back and forth between the changes made and the original image as it was opened in Photoshop.**
Note that Variations is an intuitive, visual approach for making color corrections. The use of the thumbnail views and the ability to address all the color correction parameters in a single dialog box afford you a much easier approach for adjusting color.

8. **Make sure that you redo the last correction that was applied to the document. Click in the Visibility field on the Title layer in the Layers palette to add an eye icon and make the title visible in the document.**

9. **Choose File→Save As. Name the file** 15_tone_end.psd **and save it to the collages folder as an image for your final project.**

» Session Review

This session covers how to correct color in images scanned from desktop scanners or acquired from digital cameras. You experimented with different color adjustment tools, including Color Balance, Hue Saturation, Curves, and Variations.

1. How is a color cast removed from an image with the Color Balance feature? (See "Tutorial: Adjusting Color Balance.")

2. What are hue and saturation? (See "Tutorial: Adjusting Hue/Saturation.")

3. How do you colorize an image? (See "Tutorial: Adjusting Hue/Saturation.")

4. How do you adjust color with the Curves dialog box? (See "Tutorial: Adjusting Color with Curves.")

5. How do you adjust color in only one channel? (See "Tutorial: Adjusting Color with Curves.")

6. How do you increase or decrease the amount of color in an image using Photoshop's Variations feature? (See "Tutorial: Adjusting Color with Variations.")

7. How can you adjust for color cast and saturation in a single dialog box? (See "Tutorial: Adjusting Color with Curves.")

Allison Reverent
film: finish line

Part VII
Preparing Art for Print and Web

Session 16

Creating Graphics, Pages, and Gallery Sites for the Web

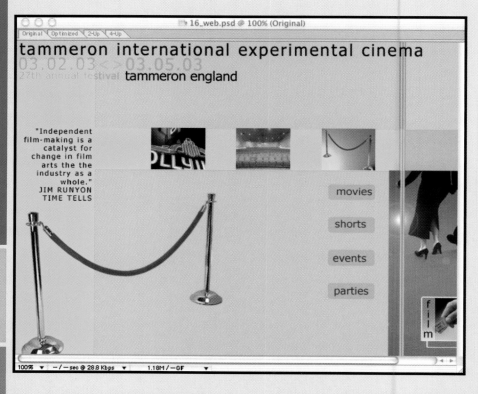

Tutorial: **Laying Out a Web Page in Photoshop**

Tutorial: **Switching to ImageReady**

Tutorial: **Slicing**

Tutorial: **Creating Rollovers**

Tutorial: **Creating and Applying Rollover Styles**

Tutorial: **Making Secondary Rollovers**

Tutorial: **Creating a Rollover Animation from Layered Artwork**

Tutorial: **Fine-Tuning a Sliced Layout**

Tutorial: **Optimizing Slices**

Tutorial: **Outputting Web-Ready Images and HTML**

Tutorial: **Making a Web Photo Gallery in Photoshop**

Session Introduction

It's common to design a Web site to complement print collateral for an event. In this session, you'll create the opening page of a Web site that complements the film festival program guide you've made in the other sessions of this book. You can do much of the design and development work for a Web site in Photoshop and ImageReady, even if you don't know the first thing about programming. You'll set up a page layout in Photoshop. Then you'll move to ImageReady to slice the page, create rollovers, and make an animation. You'll optimize the slices for fast Internet download and save images and HTML code from ImageReady. Along the way, you'll learn tips and tricks for designing for the Web. Finally, you'll use Photoshop's Web Photo Gallery feature to automatically create an entire Web site from a folder of images.

TOOLS YOU'LL USE
Photoshop's Rounded Rectangle tool, layer sets, link icons, Move tool, Distribute Edges button, Jump To button, Save for Web dialog box, and Web Photo Gallery feature

ImageReady's Slice tool, Slice Select tool, Slice palette, Hide Auto Slices button, New Layer Based Slice command, Layers palette, Rollovers palette, Create Rollover State button, Create Layer Based Rollover button, Add Layer Style button, Hide Slices button, Preview button, Copy and Paste Layer Styles commands, Styles palette, New Style command, Animation palette, Optimize palette, Optimized tab, Color Table palette, and Map to Transparency button

CD-ROM FILES NEEDED

16_web.psd, 16_web_buttons.psd, 16_web_rolls.psd, 16_web_rollstyle.psd, 16_web_secondroll.psd, 16_web_animroll.psd, 16_web_optimized.psd, 16_web_end.psd, pinkstroke.gif, and the images folder

TIME REQUIRED
90 minutes

Tutorial
» Laying Out a Web Page in Photoshop

Photoshop is the ideal program for making graphics for the Web because it has the tools to create graphics that are as simple or as visually rich as a particular site requires. You can make each graphic for a Web page individually in Photoshop and then piece them all together in a Web-authoring program. Or you can lay out an integrated design for a whole Web page in Photoshop, slice up portions of the page layout, and save those slices as individual GIFs and JPEGs. You even have the option of saving HTML code containing JavaScript and cascading style sheets to make the page functional. In this tutorial, you'll begin this process by completing a page layout that's been started for you and adding a column of buttons. You'll use some skills that you learned in preceding sessions, such as using shape tools, type, and layers, and you'll learn some new skills, such as how to align graphics on separate layers.

1. **Open** 16_web.psd **from the Session 16 Tutorial Files folder on your hard drive in Photoshop. If you see a Missing Profile warning, choose Leave As Is (Don't Color Manage) and click OK.**
There is no reason to add color profiles to images for the Web because Web browsers can't read them. This file was made with no color profile embedded for that reason. If your Photoshop color settings are still set to U.S. Prepress Defaults, Photoshop is following the instruction in those settings to ask what to do when opening a document that is missing a profile.

< N O T E >
This is a page layout in progress. It has several individual layers to accommodate the separate pieces of artwork for the features that you'll be including in the Web page: rollovers, animation, and background art. Layer sets come in handy to manage all these layers. Click the arrow on each layer set in the Layers palette to expand that layer set so that you can see which layers are in the set. Click the same arrows again to collapse the layer sets.

< W A R N I N G >
Check that you've opened this file in Photoshop, not ImageReady, for the purposes of this tutorial. I recommend that you work in Photoshop at this stage because Photoshop has greater image-editing capabilities than ImageReady.

< T I P >
If you're creating a Web page layout from scratch in Photoshop, in the File→New dialog box set the width and height to the screen size in pixels that you think matches the screen resolution used by your target audience (for example, 800 x 600 pixels minus some pixels to account for browser interface elements). Ignore the resolution field, which is irrelevant when you're measuring in pixels rather than inches. Set Mode to RGB because that's the only color mode supported by the Web.

2. **Select the secondary rollovers layer set at the top of the Layers palette. Click the New Layer Set button at the bottom of the palette to create Set 1. Double-click Set 1 and rename it** movies.

3. **Select the Eyedropper tool in the toolbox and click in the olive green box at the top right of the image to set olive green as the foreground color.**

4. **Click the Shape tool in the toolbox and choose the Rounded Rectangle tool from the hidden menu. Set the Radius field in the Options bar to 5 px.**
   This will create a rectangle with slightly rounded corners.

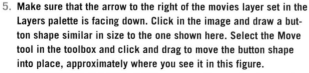
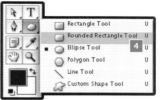

5. **Make sure that the arrow to the right of the movies layer set in the Layers palette is facing down. Click in the image and draw a button shape similar in size to the one shown here. Select the Move tool in the toolbox and click and drag to move the button shape into place, approximately where you see it in this figure.**
   The downward direction of the arrow on the movies layer set ensures that the new layer will be located inside that layer set.

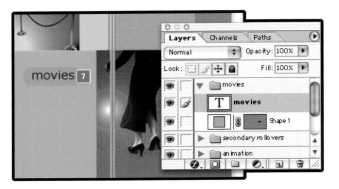

6. **Select the Type tool in the toolbox. Click the Color box in the Options bar and choose a dark turquoise (try R: 0, G: 51, B: 51) in the Color Picker. Set the other fields in the Options bar to match the values shown here (Verdana, Regular, 4 pt, Smooth).**

7. **Type the word** movies **in the image.**
   The word *movies* appears in the document, and a new type layer appears inside the movies layer set in the Layers palette.

8. **Select the Move tool in the toolbox and position the text** *movies* **on top of the button in the image.**

9. **Drag the movies layer set (not the movies type layer) to the New Layer Set button at the bottom of the Layers palette.**
   This creates a copy of the movies layer set and its contents. You'll still see only one movies button in your image because the duplicate button is located directly on top of the original.

10. **Double-click the movies copy layer set in the Layers palette and rename it** shorts**.**

11. **Select the Type tool in the toolbox. Click and drag across the word** *movies* **in the image and type** shorts**.**
   This changes the text on the duplicate button.

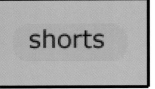

12. **Click the arrow at the top right of the Layers palette and choose Merge Layer Set.**

    This merges the shorts layer set and its contents into a layer that takes the name of the layer set — the shorts layer. The button is no longer an editable shape layer, and the type is no longer editable separately from the button.

13. **Select the Move tool in the toolbox. Press and hold the Shift key, click in the image, and drag the shorts button to the bottom of the column of buttons that you're creating.**

    Holding the Shift key constrains movement to a straight vertical line so that the buttons will be aligned vertically in the image. It doesn't matter how far down you drag the shorts button for now. You'll set the spacing between the buttons at the end of this tutorial.

14. **Repeat steps 9 through 13, except that in step 10 rename the new layer set** events **and in step 11 type the word** events **in the image. Repeat steps 9 through 13 again, except this time in step 10 rename the new layer set** parties **and in step 11 type the word** parties **in the image.**

15. **Select the original movies layer set in the Layers palette. Click the arrow on the top right of the Layers palette and choose Merge Layer Set.**

    You should now have four layers — shorts, events, parties, and movies — each containing a button with different text. In the next steps, you'll put equal space between the buttons.

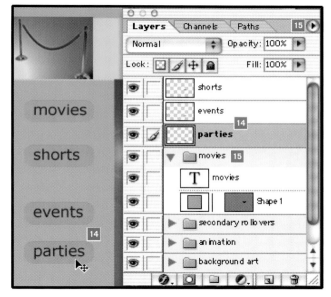

16. **Click the movies layer and move it to the top of the stack in the Layers palette.**

17. **Make sure that the movies layer is selected in the Layers palette. Click in the link field to the left of the shorts, events, and parties layers to link those three layers to the movies layer.**

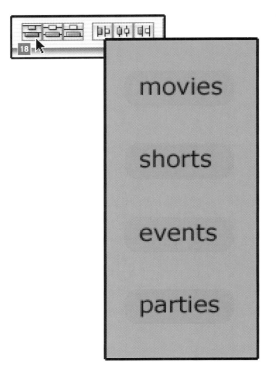

18. **Select the Move tool in the toolbox. On the Options bar, click the Distribute Top Edges button.**

    This puts equal spaces between the buttons, measuring from their top edges. This method is quicker and more precise than trying to space items on separate layers manually using the Move tool.

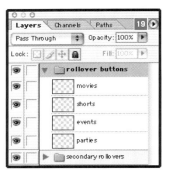

19. **Click the arrow on the top right of the Layers palette and choose New Set from Linked. Type** rollover buttons **as the name of your new layer set and click OK.**

    This creates a new layer set that contains the four button layers movies, shorts, events, and parties.

20. **Choose File→Save As, name the image** 16_web_ buttons.psd**, and leave it open for the next tutorial.**

Tutorial
» Switching to ImageReady

In this short tutorial, you'll find out how to switch between Photoshop and ImageReady to edit the same document in either application.

1. **Make sure that** `16_web_buttons.psd` **is still open in Photoshop from the last tutorial. If it's not, open it in Photoshop now. If you didn't save your own version, you can open a fresh file of that name from the Session 16 Tutorial Files folder.**

2. **Click the Jump To button at the bottom of the Photoshop toolbox.**
   This opens `16_web_buttons.psd` in ImageReady.

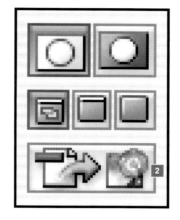

<**NOTE**>
ImageReady also has a Jump To button in its toolbox, which switches an open document back to Photoshop for further editing there. The advantage of using these Jump To buttons, rather than closing a file in one program and opening it in the other, is that the file automatically updates in one of the programs with the changes that you've made to it in the other. With both Photoshop and ImageReady open, you can easily use the exclusive features offered in each program when you're editing a document. For example, you can add an adjustment layer to a thumbnail graphic in Photoshop and jump to ImageReady to make that thumbnail into a working rollover button.

3. **Leave** `16_web_buttons.psd` **open for the next tutorial.**

<**WARNING**>
It's easy to get confused about whether you're working in Photoshop or ImageReady because the two interfaces do look so much alike. Here's a clue that you can rely on. The ImageReady document window has a series of tabs at the top, which are used when you're optimizing slices for output to the Web. Photoshop doesn't have these tabs. So if you're ever not sure where you are, look for these telltale tabs.

What's the Difference between Photoshop and ImageReady?

You'll notice that Photoshop 7 and ImageReady 7, which ship together, seem to be a lot alike. The interfaces look very similar. In addition, the two programs have several tools and features in common. So what is the difference? The short answer is that Photoshop is oriented toward traditional image editing, whereas ImageReady was created specifically for the purpose of making Web graphics. ImageReady doesn't have all the sophisticated image-editing features that you'll find in Photoshop. On the other hand, ImageReady can do Web-oriented tasks, such as creating functioning rollovers and animations, that Photoshop can't.

Therefore, it makes sense to create content and lay out a page in Photoshop and jump to ImageReady to program rollovers, create animations, and otherwise prepare the page for the Web. You can always jump back to Photoshop temporarily if you need a specific editing tool that you can't find in ImageReady.

What makes the choice of program a little more complicated is that there are some Web-oriented tasks — such as slicing and optimizing — that you can do in either Photoshop 7 or ImageReady 7. When you get to those tasks in the following tutorials, I'll offer my recommendations about which program to use and why.

Tutorial
» Slicing

In this tutorial, you'll learn how to slice a large image into smaller images in ImageReady. You'll learn how to slice manually with the Slice tool and how to slice automatically using layer-based slicing. You'll also get an understanding of what a slice is and when and why to slice an image.

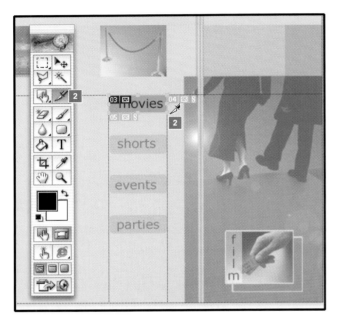

<NOTE>

You can do slicing in either Photoshop or ImageReady, but make sure that you're working in ImageReady, not Photoshop, for the purposes of this tutorial. You'll probably slice most often for the purpose of creating rollovers, which you can only perform in ImageReady, not in Photoshop. If you're slicing for other purposes (see the "What Is a Slice?" sidebar later in this tutorial) and you're more comfortable with Photoshop, go ahead and slice there. Although some controls are in slightly different places, the process of slicing in Photoshop is very similar to slicing in ImageReady.

1. **Check that** 16_web_buttons.psd **is open from the last tutorial. If it's not, choose File→Open from ImageReady's menu bar and open** 16_web_buttons.psd **from the Session 16 Tutorial Files folder on your hard drive.**

2. **Select the Slice tool in the toolbox. Click and drag around the outside of the movies button in the image to create a slice manually.**

<NOTE>

Notice that there are now a number of slices — the slice that you drew (called a *user slice*) and slices that ImageReady drew to fill in the gaps (called *auto slices*). Each time that you create a slice, ImageReady regenerates auto slices to accommodate the new slice. The nature of each slice is described by its slice boundaries, numbers, and icons. User slices are surrounded by a solid yellow boundary. Auto slices are surrounded by dotted blue lines. A selected user slice is clear. The auto slices are partially opaque. Each slice has a number, which ImageReady assigns as an identifier. The user slice number is blue. The auto slice numbers are gray. Each slice has an icon, which identifies the nature of the slice — such as user slice, auto slice, or layer-based slice. You can vary the appearance of slice lines, numbers, icons, and opacity in ImageReady's preferences (Macintosh OS X: ImageReady→Preferences→Slices) (Windows and Macintosh OS 9: Edit→Preferences→Slices).

<TIP>

It doesn't matter which layer is selected in the Layers palette when you draw a slice manually because a slice affects all the underlying artwork, regardless of the layer on which the artwork is located.

3. **Select the Slice Select tool from the toolbox. It's located behind the Slice tool in a hidden menu.**

4. **Click the anchor points on the slice boundaries and pull the slice boundaries in close to the movies button.**

This ensures that the image that will be created from this slice won't be bigger than necessary. Bigger images take longer to download on the Web.

<NOTE>

Slices can be modified in numerous other ways. Click the Slices menu at the top of the screen to see a list of commands that you can apply to slices (including duplicate, combine, divide, delete, link, arrange, align, and distribute). Some of these choices are grayed out because you don't have multiple slices selected.

5. **Select the shorts layer in the Layers palette and choose Layer→New Layer Based Slice from the menu bar at the top of the screen.**

This automatically creates another kind of slice called a *layer-based slice,* which hugs the artwork on the shorts layer. Notice that there is now a special icon on the shorts layer in the Layers palette, indicating that this layer has a layer-based slice.

<NOTE>

Notice that ImageReady generated new auto slices when you added this layer-based slice.

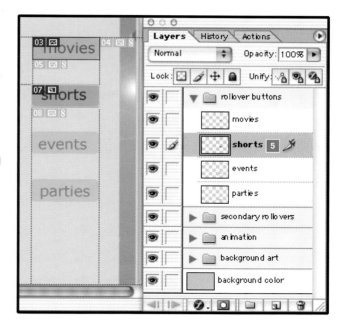

6. **Make sure that the Slice Select tool is still selected. Click the Hide Auto Slices button on the Options bar.**

This hides, but doesn't delete, the auto slices that ImageReady made so that it's easier to see the slices that you created. This button is a welcome addition to ImageReady 7.

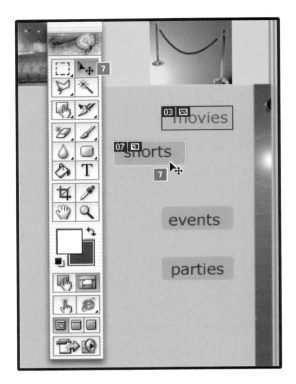

7. **Select the Move tool from the toolbox and click and drag in the image to move the shorts button. When you're done, press ⌘+Z (Windows: Ctrl+Z) to return the shorts button to its original position.**
   Notice that moving the artwork encompassed by a layer-based slice causes the slice to move with the artwork. This means that you can change your mind about the location of artwork without having to redo all your slicing. This is a significant advantage over manually drawn user slices, which don't move with the underlying artwork.

   < N O T E >
   Layer-based slices come in most handy when you're slicing rollovers. That's because they expand to cover the artwork on all states of a rollover, which is another quality user slices don't have. This means that you could use bigger artwork on the Over state than on the Normal state of a rollover. For example, you could have a glow, a stroke, or even an animated highlight appear outside of the normal edges of a graphic on the Over state, and the slice would expand to include that extra artwork.

8. **Make sure that the slice encompassing the shorts button is still selected in the image and that the Slice Select tool is selected in the toolbox. Click the Slice Palette button on the Options bar.**
   This opens the Slice palette.

What Is a Slice?

Slices represent individual images that you can cut out of a larger image, such as the buttons that you'll slice from this page layout. There are several reasons for you to slice an image:

» An image may have parts that compress better (for faster Web download) in one file format and parts that compress better in another file format. For example, as you'll learn later in this session, JPEG is the best file format for compressing a photograph for the Web, while GIF is the best file format for compressing graphic artwork.

» You may want to create a rollover in part of a larger image, like a rollover button in a page layout. A *rollover* consists of two or more smaller images that alternate when the user moves her cursor over and away from the item. So unless you want your entire page layout to act as a rollover, you

have to slice to isolate a section of the page layout from which to make rollovers.

» You may want to create an animation in part of a larger image. Unless you want the entire image to be animated, you have to isolate that area.

» You may be concerned about the apparent speed with which a Web page downloads. In some cases, a collection of small images appears to download faster than one large image because some pieces come up in a Web browser before others. It's difficult to predict whether total download time will actually be faster in a given case if a large image is cut into smaller images because that can depend on situational factors such as Internet traffic and routing.

9. **Click the double-pointed arrow on the Slice tab, until the Slice palette is expanded so that you can see all its options, as shown here.**

10. **Type** -55 **in the T (Top) field and** 55 **in the B (Bottom) field in the Layer Apron section of the Slice palette. This moves the shorts slice down in the image until it is over the events button, rather than the shorts button. Press ⌘+Z twice to undo this change.**
This new positioning feature in ImageReady 7 gives you some ability to move and resize a layer-based slice, but it isn't as user-friendly as the click-and-drag method of modifying a user slice that you tried earlier.

11. **Click in the Name field of the Slice palette and type in** shorts.
The slice name will become part of the name of the image file that will be created from this slice (shorts.gif). Therefore, follow Web filenaming conventions when you name a slice (no spaces, no uppercase, and no odd characters).

12. **Make sure that the Type field is set to Image.**
This ensures that ImageReady will create an image from the artwork under the selected slice when you save. You'll learn when to change this option to No Image in the "Fine-Tuning a Sliced Layout" tutorial later in this session.

13. **Check that the Slice Select tool is still selected in the toolbox. Click the slice encompassing the movies button in the image and type** movies **in the Name field of the Slice palette.**
This names the movies slice.

14. **Choose File→Save and keep this file open for the next exercise.**

< N O T E >

If you wanted to create a link from your sliced button to a Web page, you would type the URL of that page in the URL field of the Slice palette. To link to a page in another Web site, you'd type the full URL of that site (for example, **http://www.shortfilms.net**). It's more difficult to create a link to a page inside of the Web site you're creating, unless you're sure of what the internal path to that page will be. Many designers do not set their links in ImageReady. Instead they bring files saved from ImageReady into an HTML editor to create links.

Tutorial
» Creating Rollovers

Now that you know the basics of slicing, you're primed to make rollovers in those slices. Making rollovers is easier than ever using ImageReady 7's new Rollovers palette, which displays each slice and each state of all your rollovers. (The Rollovers palette will also display animation frames and image maps if you tell it to.) In this tutorial, you'll turn the static buttons that you made earlier in this session into interactive rollover buttons that change appearance when a viewer clicks them in a Web browser. You'll learn how to use the Rollovers palette and how to create a Rollover state, edit the Rollover state, and copy and paste rollover effects from one button to another.

1. **Make sure that** `16_web_buttons.psd` **is open from the last exercise.**

<WARNING>
Your file should be open in ImageReady, rather than Photoshop, for this and the following tutorials. ImageReady is the only one of the two programs in which you can make working rollovers.

2. **Choose Window→Show Rollovers to display the Rollovers palette.**
   The Rollovers palette displays the Normal state of your page layout, which is the way the page looks when it first opens in a Web browser. This palette also displays both of the slices that you made in the last tutorial: the movies slice, which you created manually with the Slice tool, and the shorts slice, which you created with the layer-based slicing command.

3. **Select the movies slice in the Rollovers palette to begin creating a rollover in this slice.**
   This causes the movies slice to appear selected in the image, as well as in the Rollovers palette.

4. **Click the Create Rollover State button at the bottom of the Rollovers palette.**
   This creates an Over state for this rollover. The Over state is the way the artwork (the movies button) in this slice looks when a viewer rolls his cursor over the slice. You'll create the look of the movies button in its Over state in the next step.

<NOTE>
If you can't see all the states in your Rollovers palette that you see in this figure, click the diagonal lines on the bottom-right corner of the Rollovers palette and drag to expand the palette.

<NOTE>
If you've skipped ahead to this tutorial because you can't wait to learn about rollovers, I suggest that you back up a little and work through the preceding tutorial on slicing. Slicing and rollovers are closely related subjects. For example, every rollover must be located in a slice (or in an image map hotspot), and the design of a rollover depends in part on whether it's located in a layer-based slice (which is the only kind of slice that expands to accomodate all rollover artwork, that moves along with underlying artwork, and that supports rollover styles).

5. **Make sure that the Over state of the movies slice is selected in the Rollovers palette. Select the movies layer in the Layers palette. Click the Add Layer Style button (the button with the *f* icon) at the bottom of the Layers palette and choose Inner Shadow from the pop-up menu of layer styles.**

   This adds an inner shadow layer style to the movies layer — but only for the Over state of the movies button. In other words, the inner shadow will appear only when a viewer moves her cursor over the movies button in a Web browser.

<NOTE>
Adding a layer style activates the Inner Shadow Layer Options palette, in which you can customize that layer style, as you'll do next.

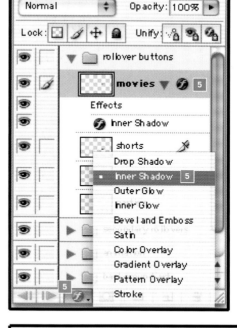

6. **Click the color field in the Inner Shadow Layer Options palette and select a dark green color (try R:51, G:51, B:0) to customize the inner shadow.**

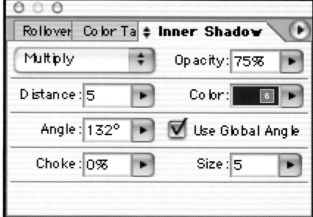

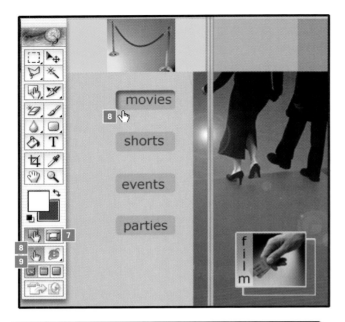

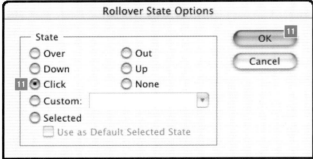

7. **Click the Hide Slices button in the toolbox to hide the slice boundaries so that you can get a better view of this rollover effect in the document window.**

8. **Click the Preview button in the toolbox and move your cursor over the movies button in the image to preview the inner shadow rollover effect.**
   Congratulations! You've made your first rollover.

9. **Click the Preview button again to turn off the preview mode.**

10. **Double-click the Over state of the movies slice in the Rollovers palette.**
   This opens the Rollover State Options dialog box.

11. **Choose the Click state and click OK in the Rollover State Options dialog box.**
   This changes the event that triggers the movies button rollover from a mouse over to a mouse click. To see how this works, click the Preview button and try moving your cursor over the movies button (nothing happens) and then clicking the movies button (success!).

<NOTE>
The Click state causes some browsers to create a sticky blue line around the rollover button. This is an idiosyncrasy of the browser and not something that you can control from ImageReady. There's no great solution for this problem other than to use another browser for previewing or have a knowledgeable coder tweak the saved rollover code in a text editor.

<NOTE>
There are a number of states available in the Rollover State Options dialog box. The ones that you'll use most are the Over, Down, and Click states. The Selected state, which is new to ImageReady 7, comes in handy for making drop-down menus or for keeping an active button state selected on a page to act as a navigation clue to the viewer. The Over state occurs when a viewer passes a cursor over an area. The Down state occurs when a viewer presses and holds the mouse button down. It ends when the viewer releases the mouse button. The Click state occurs when a viewer presses and releases the mouse button. It ends when the viewer releases the mouse button. The Selected state is similar to the Click state (in that it is activated by a click), but it remains in effect until the viewer clicks another item that has a Selected state.

It's easy to forget to turn off preview mode, which you have to do in order to perform other tasks in ImageReady. Fortunately, ImageReady will remind you.

<NOTE>
If you prefer to preview your rollover in a Web browser, rather than inside ImageReady, click the Preview in Default Browser button (which has an *e* icon if your default browser is Internet Explorer). A Web browser opens, displaying the page with a working rollover and a white box with information about the page.

12. **Make sure that the Click state of the movies slice is selected in the Rollovers palette. Choose Layer→Layer Style→Copy Layer Style from the menu bar at the top of the screen.**

This copies the customized inner shadow layer style that's on the Click state of the movies slice, so you can apply the same layer style to a state of another button. This is a quick way to produce buttons that have different content but the same look.

<NOTE>

If you've read ahead to the next tutorial, you may be wondering why you can't create a reusable rollover style from the Over state of the movies slice, rather than copy and paste the layer style as you did in the preceding steps. The answer is that rollover styles are only available if you use layer-based slicing. You sliced this movies button manually, so you don't have the option of creating a rollover style.

13. **Select the shorts slice in the Rollovers palette. Click the Create Rollover State button at the bottom of the Rollovers palette.**

This creates an Over state for the shorts slice.

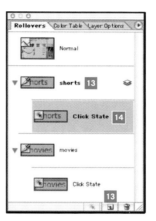

14. **Double-click the Over state of the shorts slice in the Rollovers palette. Choose Click from the Rollover State Options dialog box and click OK.**

This changes the event that triggers the shorts button rollover from a mouse over to a click.

15. **Choose Layer→Layer Style→Paste Layer Style from the menu bar at the top of the screen.**

This pastes your customized inner shadow layer style to the Click state of the shorts slice.

16. **Click the Preview button in the toolbox and click the shorts button and the movies button in the document window.**

Both buttons now display an inner shadow when you click them.

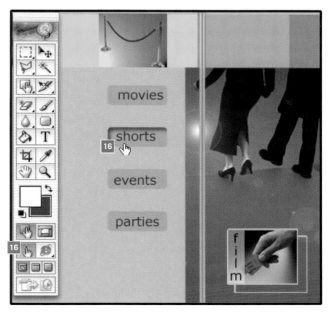

17. **Choose File→Save As, name this file** 16_web_rolls.psd, **and move right on to the next tutorial with this file open.**

Tutorial
» Creating and Applying Rollover Styles

In this tutorial, you'll learn how to create a layer-based slice and a rollover all at once, using a button on ImageReady's new Rollovers palette. Then you'll capture the style and functionality of that rollover as a rollover style in the Styles palette. You'll see how easy it is to create another rollover button by applying that rollover style.

1. **Use** `16_web_rolls.psd` **as you saved it from the last tutorial. Or open a fresh file of the same name from the Session 16 tutorial files on your hard drive.**

2. **Click the Create Layer Based Rollover button at the bottom of the Rollovers palette.**
   This is a shortcut that you can use to create a layer-based slice and a new rollover state all at once! Notice that you now have a new slice, 16_web_rolls_events, and an Over state for that slice displayed in the Rollovers palette. You can tell this is a layer-based slice from the layer-based slice symbol on the events layer in the Layers palette. This new feature is a real time-saver when you're making rollover buttons from layered artwork.

3. **Double-click the new 16_web_rolls_events slice in the Rollovers palette. Type** events **to give the slice a more manageable name.**

4. **Double-click the Over state on the events slice in the Rollovers palette and change the trigger event to Click in the Rollover States Options dialog box, just as you did in the preceding tutorial.**

5. **Click the movies layer in the Layers palette. Select the Click state of the movies slice in the Rollovers palette. Choose Layer→Layer Style→Copy Layer Style. Select the Click state of the events slice in the Rollovers palette and choose Layer→Layer Style→Paste Layer Style — as you learned to do in the preceding tutorial.**

6. **Choose Window→Styles to display the Styles palette. Click the Create New Style button at the bottom right of the palette.**

<NOTE>
The Styles palette displays thumbnails representing a collection of prebuilt combinations of layer styles that you can apply to artwork. The style thumbnails with a black triangle in the upper-left corner are rollover styles. They contain not only style information, but also functional information that makes a rollover work. In the next steps, you'll create a custom rollover style from your events button and apply it to the parties button in your page layout.

You should be working in ImageReady, not Photoshop, for this tutorial.

<NOTE>
The Create Layer Based Rollover button won't help you unless your rollover artwork is on its own layer. This is another reason to put each piece of art on a separate layer when you're creating the content of an image like this page layout, as long as you have enough RAM and storage space to handle the large file that can result from lots of layers.

7. **In the Style Options dialog box, type** web roll **in the Name field. Leave the default check marks in the three check boxes and click OK.**

   This creates a new style in the Styles palette called web roll. The check mark next to Include Rollover States ensures that your new style will be a rollover style. (You can leave the default check mark next to Include Blending Options even though you haven't set any special layer blending options in this particular style.)

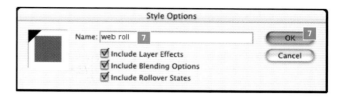

8. **Place your cursor over the gray style thumbnail with the black arrow in the corner at the bottom of the Styles palette.**

   This is your new rollover style, as you can tell from the name web roll that pops up. In the next step, you'll see how incredibly easy it is to apply this style to a graphic.

9. **Click the web roll rollover style in the Styles palette and drag it on top of the parties button in the image.**

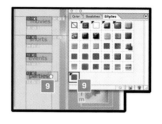

<NOTE>

That's all there is to applying a rollover style. You don't have to select a particular layer in the Layers palette first or create a slice around your target graphic (the parties button in this case). A rollover style creates a new layer-based slice around the target graphic, applies style information, and adds JavaScript to the target graphic to make it a functioning rollover.

10. **Click the Preview button in the toolbox and click the parties button in the image to see the rollover behavior that the parties button acquired from the rollover style.**

<TIP>

Click the Hide Slices button in the toolbox to get a better look at the preview.

11. **Choose File➔Save As, name the file** 16_web_rollstyle.psd, **and leave it open for the next tutorial.**

Tutorial
» Making Secondary Rollovers

Secondary rollover is a fancy name for a rollover event taking place in a different place in an image than the spot that triggers that rollover. In this tutorial, you'll learn how to create a secondary rollover using ImageReady's Rollovers palette. Keep in mind as you work through this tutorial that there are many steps. The secret to not getting lost is to follow carefully and methodically through the steps. If you get confused, I recommend that you just start again rather than try to fix things.

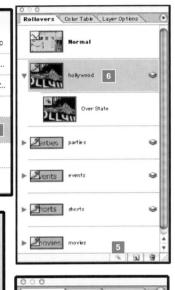

1. **Use** 16_web_rollstyle.psd, **which you saved from the last tutorial, or open a fresh file of the same name from the Session 16 tutorial files on your hard drive.**

You still should be working in ImageReady, not Photoshop, for this tutorial.

2. **Click the arrow next to each of the slices in the Rollovers palette to collapse those slices and make more room available in the palette.**

3. **Click the arrow next to the rollover buttons layer set in the Layers palette to collapse that layer set. Click the arrow next to the secondary rollovers layer set to expand that layer set.**

4. **Select the hollywood roll layer in the Layers palette.**

5. **Click the Create Layer Based Rollover button at the bottom of the Rollovers palette.**
   This creates a layer-based slice around the Hollywood thumbnail in the image and an Over state for that slice in the Rollovers palette.

6. **Double-click the name of the new slice in the Rollovers palette and rename it** hollywood.

7. **Select the Slice tool in the toolbox and draw a slice around the quotation on the left side of the document window. Make the slice a little taller than the quotation.**
   The quotation that appears in this slice will change as the viewer rolls over different thumbnails. You can test whether the slice is tall enough to accommodate each of the quotations that will appear in this location by turning the eye icons of the four quotation layers on and off in the Layers palette.

8. **Double-click the name of the new slice in the Rollovers palette and rename it** quote.

9. **Select the Over state of the hollywood slice in the Rollovers palette.**
   This causes the hollywood roll layer to be selected in the Layers palette.

10. **Click the Add Layer Style button at the bottom of the Layers palette and choose Stroke from the pop-up menu of layer styles.**

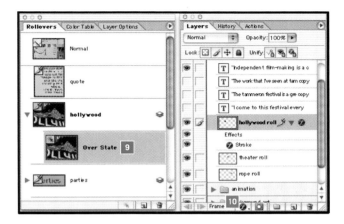

11. **Choose Window→Layer Options/Style if the Stroke palette is not showing on your screen. Click the Color box in the Stroke palette and choose a magenta (try R:204, G:0, B:51). Change the middle button on the left to Inside and leave the rest of the settings as they are.**
    When a viewer moves a cursor over the Hollywood thumbnail in a Web browser, a red line will appear inside the border of the thumbnail.

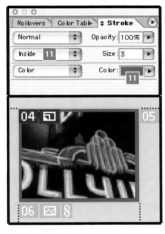

If you forget to change the middle button on the left of the Stroke palette to Inside, the stroke will appear on the outside of the thumbnail and will distort the size of your slices. This is because layer-based slices like this one expand to accommodate the size of any underlying artwork. Although this flexibility of layer-based slices is a good thing, it can trip you up if you don't watch out.

<NOTE>
The last step, in which you added a stroke layer style, creates the first of two rollover effects for the hollywood slice. This is a local effect, just like the local rollover effects that you created for the green navigation buttons in the previous tutorials. Up to this point, there's nothing in this tutorial that's new to you. The next steps introduce three new concepts:

- You can have more than one rollover effect triggered by the same action.

- A rollover effect can occur somewhere other than the spot where the viewer triggers the effect. This is called a *secondary rollover effect*.

- Applying layer styles isn't the only way to create a rollover effect. In this tutorial, you'll create a different look for each rollover state by turning the visibility of various layers on or off. You'll see what I mean as you work through the following steps.

12. **Make sure that the Over state of the hollywood slice is still selected in the Rollovers palette. Click the eye icon next to the "Independent film-making . . ." type layer in the Layers palette so that the eye icon disappears.**

This will hide the "Independent film-making . . ." quotation in the image when a viewer rolls a cursor over the Hollywood thumbnail.

13. **Click the empty Visibility box next to the "The work that I've seen . . ." type layer in the Layers palette.**

This will reveal the "The work that I've seen. . ." quotation in the image when a viewer rolls a cursor over the Hollywood thumbnail. In other words, when the hollywood rollover is triggered by moving a cursor over the thumbnail, the graphic on the far right will change so that one quotation appears in place of the other.

14. **Click the Hide Slices button in the toolbox. Then click the Preview button in the toolbox and move your cursor over and away from the Hollywood thumbnail to preview the dual local and secondary rollover effects.**

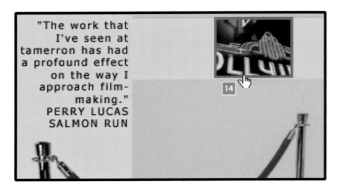

15. **Repeat steps 9 through 14, except use the theater thumbnail as the rollover trigger, make the "The work that I've seen . . ." type layer invisible, and make the "The tamerron festival is . . ." type layer visible on the Over state of the theater slice.**
If you get lost, see the following note.

<**N O T E**>
Here's a quick review of the steps outlined above as they apply to the theater rollover:

- Select the theater roll layer in the Layers palette.
- Click the Create Layer Based Rollover button at the bottom of the Rollovers palette.
- Double-click the name of the new slice in the Rollovers palette and rename it **theater**.
- Select the Over state of the theater slice in the Rollovers palette.
- Click the Add Layer Style button at the bottom of the Layers palette and choose Stroke.
- Set the fields in the Stroke palette just as you did in step 11.
- Hide the eye icon on the "The work that I've seen . . ." layer.
- Add an eye icon to the "The tamerron festival is . . ." layer.
- Click the Preview button and try out your rollovers.

16. **Repeat steps 9 through 14, except use the rope thumbnail as the rollover trigger, make the "The tamerron festival is . . ." type layer invisible, and make the "I come to this festival . . ." type layer visible on the Over state of the rope slice.**
I'll leave you on your own to work through this one. It's good practice. Don't worry if you can't make it work. If that happens, chalk it up to the learning curve and move on to the next tutorial.

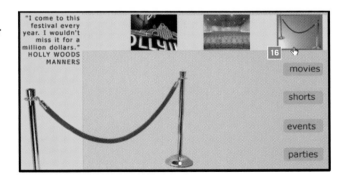

17. **Choose File→Save As, name this file** 16_web_secondroll. psd, **and leave the file open for the next tutorial. Be careful not to save over the file of the same name in the Session 16 Tutorial Files folder.**

Tutorial
» Creating a Rollover Animation from Layered Artwork

This tutorial covers GIF animation. It builds on what you've learned so far in this session about making interactive Web graphics, adding another important element — motion. In this tutorial, you'll learn how to create a GIF animation in ImageReady by making different artwork visible on different frames in the animation. You'll also learn how to trigger an animation with a rollover. The trick here is to follow the instructions in exactly the order they're given, or your animation may not work as planned.

1. **Use** `16_web_secondroll.psd` **which you saved from the last tutorial. Or open a fresh file of the same name from the Session 16 tutorial files on your hard drive.**

You should be working in ImageReady, not Photoshop, for this tutorial. That's because you can't program animations in Photoshop. ImageReady has exclusive claim to this area.

2. **Click the arrows next to each of the slices in the Rollovers palette to collapse those slices and rollovers and make more room available in that palette.**

3. **Click the arrow next to the secondary rollovers layer set in the Layers palette to collapse that layer set. Click the arrow next to the animation layer set to expand that layer set.**

4. **Select the ticket image layer in the Layers palette.**

5. **Click the Create Layer Based Rollover button at the bottom of the Rollovers palette.**
   This creates a layer-based slice around the ticket thumbnail at the bottom right of the image and an Over state for that slice in the Rollovers palette. This slice will become the trigger for the rollover.

6. **Click the new slice in the Rollovers palette and rename it** ticket **in the Name field of the Slice palette.**

7. **Select the film layer in the Layers palette. Choose Layer→New Layer Based Slice from the menu bar at the top of the screen.**
   This creates a slice around the small area of opaque white and text that will be animated. You're isolating the animation so that the images that it contains are as small as possible.

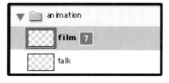

8. **Double-click the name of the new slice in the Rollovers palette and rename it** animate**.**

<NOTE>
Notice that the animate slice and the ticket slice physically overlap in the image. The stacking order of overlapping slices determines which image displays on top of which in a Web browser. Stacking order can be hard to see in the document window. Take a look at the order of slices from top to bottom in the Rollovers palette if you need to know the stacking order of a particular slice. (In this case, the animate slice is at the top of the stack because it was created last.) The easiest way of rearranging slice stacking order is by clicking on a slice in the Rollovers palette and dragging it to a different position in that palette.

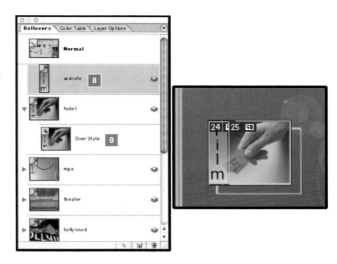

9. **Select the Over state of the ticket slice in the Rollovers palette.**

<NOTE>
In the next steps, you'll be creating an animation. Selecting the Over state of the ticket slice before you begin making this animation is a crucial step. It is what will cause the animation to be triggered by a rollover, so when a viewer moves a cursor over the ticket thumbnail, the animation will begin playing. If you wanted the animation to begin playing immediately upon the page loading in a Web browser, you would select the Normal state at the top of the Rollovers palette before programming the animation.

10. **Choose Window→Animation to display the Animation palette.**
Notice that there is one default frame in the Animation palette, which represents the image before the animation starts. In that frame, the word *film* is showing because it is at the top of the stack of layers in that position in the image.

<TIP>
Click the Hide Slices button in the toolbox to make it easier to see the changes that you're making in the document window.

11. **Click the Duplicate Current Frame button at the bottom of the Animation palette.**
This copies Frame 1 and displays it in the Animation palette as Frame 2. In the next step, you'll make a change in Frame 2.

12. **Make sure that Frame 2 is selected in the Animation palette. (Notice the gray shading and black border around Frame 2 in the figure, indicating that it is the selected frame.) Click the eye icon on the film layer in the Layers palette to remove that eye icon and hide the film layer on Frame 2.**
This leaves the talk layer showing on Frame 2.

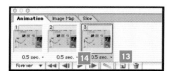

13. **Click the Duplicate Current Frame button at the bottom of the Animation palette.**

    This copies Frame 2 and displays it in the Animation palette as Frame 3. In the next step, you'll make a change in Frame 3.

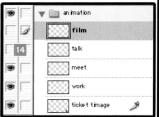

14. **Make sure that Frame 3 is selected in the Animation palette. Click the eye icon on the talk layer in the Layers palette to remove that eye icon and hide the talk layer on Frame 3.**

    This leaves the meet layer showing on Frame 3.

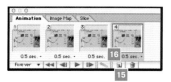

15. **Click the Duplicate Current Frame button at the bottom of the Animation palette.**

    This copies Frame 3 and displays it in the Animation palette as Frame 4. In the next step, you'll make a change in Frame 4.

16. **Make sure that Frame 4 is selected in the Animation palette. Click the eye icon on the meet layer in the Layers palette to remove that eye icon and hide the meet layer on Frame 4.**

    This leaves the work layer showing on Frame 4.

17. **Click the Play button at the bottom of the Animation palette to preview the animation so far. You can watch it play in the document window.**

18. **Shift+click the frames of the animation to select them all. Click the tiny arrow underneath any one of the frames and choose 1.0 sec.**
    This delays the timing of each of the frames in the animation.

19. **Click anywhere in the Animation palette to deselect all the frames. Then click the tiny arrow under the last frame and choose 2.0 sec.**
    Now the animation will pause on the last frame. Now that you've tested your animation, in the next step you'll test its rollover trigger.

20. **Click the Preview button in the toolbox and move your cursor over the ticket thumbnail in the document window. In just a second, the animation will begin playing.**
    That's all there is to creating an animation triggered by a rollover.

21. **Choose File→Save As. Name the file** 16_web_animroll. psd **and keep it open for the next tutorial, in which you'll fine-tune the slices in your page layout prior to optimizing and saving.**

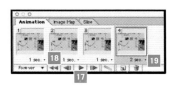

<NOTE>

The animation that you've created in this tutorial is based on hiding and revealing layers containing different artwork. This is called frame-by-frame animation. ImageReady offers another animation method as well, called *tweening*. If you'd like to try tweening, select Frame 2 in the Animation palette. Click the Tween button (the button with a series of small circles) at the bottom of the Animation palette. In the Tween dialog box, leave the settings at their defaults for now and click OK. ImageReady creates a fade effect by tweening the opacity of the artwork on Frames 1 and 2. You could do the same thing between each pair of adjacent frames to create a slide show of all four pieces of artwork with fade-ins. There are lots of other effects that you can achieve using combinations of tweening and frame-by-frame animation. Keep in mind that you're limited to tweening layer opacity, position, and layer effects. Now that you know the basics of animation in ImageReady, go ahead and experiment. You can save any animation that you create as an animated GIF or as a QuickTime movie.

Tutorial
» Fine-Tuning a Sliced Layout

In this tutorial, you'll slice areas to be optimized separately as GIFs and JPEGs, arrange the stacking order of slices, and designate some slices as no-image slices in preparation for optimizing in the following tutorial.

1. **You can use** 16_web_animroll.psd, **which you saved from the last tutorial, although you may be better off starting with a fresh file because the recent exercises have been relatively complex. You'll find a prebuilt version of** 16_web_animroll.psd **with the Session 16 tutorial files on your hard drive.**

This tutorial takes place in ImageReady.

2. **Click the arrow on the background art layer set in the Layers palette to expand that layer set. Select the walk photo layer. Choose Layer→New Layer Based Slice to put a slice boundary around that photo.**
Notice that the small ticket and animate slices you worked with in an earlier tutorial have disappeared behind this big new slice. You'll fix that in the next step.

Slicing Review

In the preceding tutorials, you sliced the components of your rollovers and your animation in order for them to be functional inside of the larger page layout. There are some other areas in this image that call for slicing before you optimize and save the pieces of this Web page design.

First, you'll slice the remaining photographic elements separately from the graphic artwork so that you can optimize the photographs as JPEGs and the graphics as GIFs. JPEG (which stands for Joint Photographic Experts Group) is the format that almost always results in smaller and better-looking photographs. GIF (Graphics

Interchange Format) is the format that usually results in smaller and better-looking graphics (unless a graphic has a substantial area of continuous tone, such as a big glow or bevel).

Second, you'll use slicing to isolate no-image areas — areas that have no content except for the solid blue background. If you save those areas as GIFs, they will look fine, but they will contribute needlessly to the overall file size of the page. It's more economical to use HTML code to fill in a solid color background with virtual color.

3. **Select the new slice in the Rollovers palette. Double-click the slice name in the Rollovers palette and rename it** walk. **Rearrange slices in the Rollovers palette so that the film layer is above the ticket layer, which is above the walk layer.**

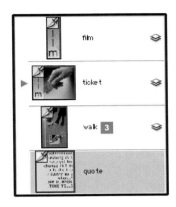

<NOTE>
You can name slices in the Rollovers palette as you just did or by typing into the Name field in the Slice palette. It's worth taking an extra minute to name your important slices in either location to avoid ending up with GIFs and JPEGs made from slices that are difficult to identify.

4. **Select the Slice tool and click and drag around the rope photo on the left of the page layout. Double-click the slice name and rename it** big_rope.
This is a mixed slice, with some photographic and some graphic content. You won't know until you optimize whether this slice compresses best as a JPEG or a GIF. But there's little doubt that it deserves customized treatment in the optimization process.

5. **Click the big_rope slice in the Slice palette and drag it below the quote slice.**

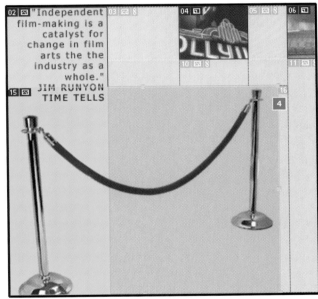

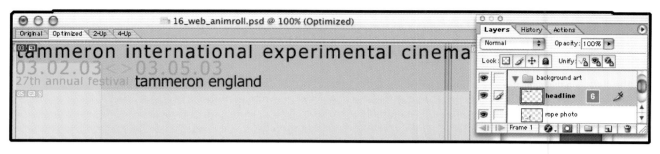

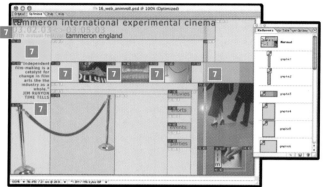

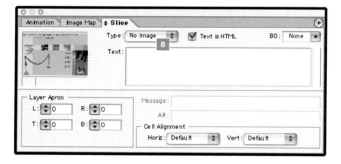

6. **Click the headline layer in the Layers palette and choose Layer→New Layer Based Slice. Name this slice** headline **in the Rollovers palette.**

   I've suggested that you slice the headline to optimize it separately as a GIF with just the right number of colors. Solid color text usually compresses best as a GIF.

7. **Select the Slice tool and drag slices around all the remaining graphic areas in the page layout, except the plain blue background areas. If you're really organized, name each of these slices** graphic1, graphic2, **or something similar.**

   Consult this figure if you have any questions about what to slice. To refresh your memory, the slices with blue numbers are the important slices, which were created manually or with layer-based slicing in the course of these tutorials. The slices with gray icons are auto slices generated by ImageReady.

8. **Shift+click all the empty blue slices to select them all. Click the Type button in the Slice palette and choose No Image.**

   This instructs ImageReady not to make images from these slices, allowing a savings in the overall file size of the page. If you're wondering why these slices now have blue numbers and icons, it's because changing them to no-image slices also promoted them to user slices, allowing them to be moved around and resized just like slices that you made yourself.

9. **Choose File→Save and keep this file open for the next tutorial.**

Tutorial
» Optimizing Slices

In this tutorial, you'll optimize the slices in your Web page layout in Web-compatible image formats — JPEG or GIF. Your goal when optimizing is to create files for the Web that strike the best compromise between size and appearance.

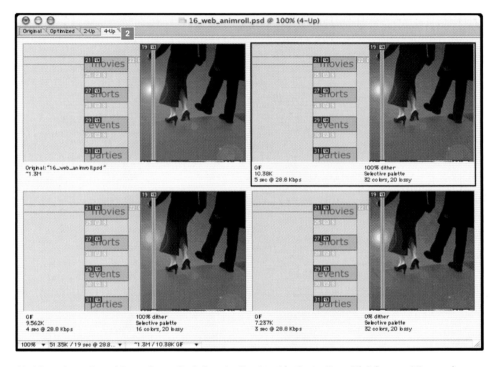

1. **Continue to work in ImageReady, with** `16_web_animroll.psd` **open from the last tutorial.**

2. **Click the 4-Up tab in the document window.**
   This tab has four panels. The top-left panel displays the original PSD file. The other three are previews of how the image would look optimized at different combinations of optimization settings. You can use these panels to compare the results of different settings that you choose in the Optimize palette.

3. **Select the Hand tool in the toolbox. Click in any of the previews and drag until you see the photo shown here.**
   The preview in which you click is the active preview, identifiable by its black border.

4. **Select the Slice Select tool in the toolbox and click the large slice that encompasses the walk photo in the active preview pane.**
   The optimization settings that you choose apply only to this selected slice.

You may be wondering about the small icon to the right of the Quality field. Clicking this icon displays a dialog box in which you can set parts of an image or a slice to be optimized at a lower quality than other parts of that same image or slice, based on areas that you've isolated with a mask. In some cases, this reduces the overall file size, but it doesn't work for every image. If you want to experiment with it, go back to the original image, add a channel in the Channels palette, and paint with black to create a mask in that channel. Then return to this dialog box and use the black and white sliders to separately optimize the image under the corresponding parts of the mask. Frankly, I don't usually take the extra time to do this unless I'm absolutely required to reduce a JPEG below a particular file size.

5. **Choose Window→Optimize to display the Optimize palette. Set the format of the selected preview to JPEG because this is a photograph. Click the arrow at the top right of the Optimize palette and choose Repopulate Views.**
This sets all three of the previews to JPEG format, with different JPEG quality settings. Notice that there are degraded areas, called *artifacts,* in the previews with the lower JPEG quality setting.

6. **Move the Quality setting in the Optimize palette until it's as low as it can go without the selected preview displaying unacceptable artifacts. Check the file size at the bottom left of the selected preview as you adjust the quality.**
Quality is the primary control for optimizing a JPEG.

7. **Add a small amount of blur with the Blur setting in the Optimize palette.**
Blurring a photograph, or otherwise reducing its contrast, can help reduce file size. I was satisfied with this photograph at the settings that you see in this figure (File Size: around 7KB, Quality: 50, Blur: 0.12), but there is no right answer. Optimizing always involves some subjective judgment.

8. **Select the Hand tool and move the image until you see the green rollover buttons in the preview pane. Select the Slice Select tool.**

What Is Optimizing?

Optimizing means choosing settings by which each slice will be compressed in a format that's supported by the Web — GIF or JPEG. (GIF and JPEG are currently the only commonly used file formats for static Web graphics.) Optimizing is always a balancing act between objective measures of file size and subjective evaluations of image quality. In general, the higher the image quality, the greater the file size, and vice versa. Your job is to find the best compromise for each slice.

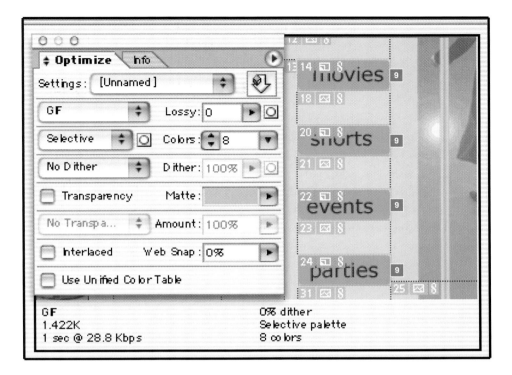

9. **Hold the Shift key down while clicking in all four of the buttons to select them all at once. Choose Slices→Link Slices from the menu bar at the top of the screen.**

   Notice that the slice icons and numbers in the four selected slices are all the same color. This means that you only have to optimize once to compress all four of the linked slices the same way.

10. **Click the arrow next to the movies slice in the Rollovers palette and select the Click state of the movies slice.**

    This causes the movies button in the image to display the inner shadow that you applied to the Over state of this button. You should judge the appearance of these rollover buttons in the Click state, as well as in the Normal state, when you're choosing optimization settings for these linked slices.

< N O T E >

It's important to realize that when you optimize a rollover, the optimization settings that you choose for a slice affect the artwork on all states of a rollover. For example, if you optimize these rollover buttons while judging their appearance only in the Normal state (in which the buttons have no shadow), you may be surprised to find that when you click one of the buttons in a Web browser, its inner shadow looks terrible. That's because shadows contain a variety of colors that you may not have accounted for when you optimized the button looking only at its Normal state. The solution is to check optimization settings on all states of a rollover graphic, as you're doing here.

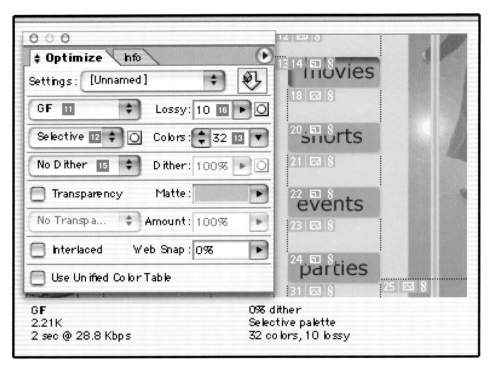

11. **Change the File Format to GIF in the Optimize palette.**
    Graphics with areas of solid color usually compress better as
    GIFs than JPEGs.

12. **Choose Selective, Adaptive, or Perceptual as the color palette.**
    GIFs, unlike JPEGS, can contain no more than 256 colors.
    The color palette determines which 256 colors you'll choose
    from when you optimize this image. These three color palettes
    are all based on the actual colors in the original image, so
    they are preferable to the other palette choices. (It doesn't
    much matter which of the three you choose. They're very simi-
    lar to one another.)

<N O T E>
There's no compelling reason to limit your colors to the Web
palette because today almost all computers can display more than
256 colors. So don't bother with the Web palette unless you're
designing a site for an audience with outmoded computers or
you're designing for a device other than a computer, such as a PDA
or a wireless phone.

13. **Use the Colors slider in the Colors field to reduce the number of
    colors in the selected slices as low as you can go without degrad-
    ing the image (try 32 colors). Remember to look at the button with
    the shadow as well as the buttons in the Normal state.**
    Reducing the number of colors in an image is the main way to
    reduce the file size of a GIF.

14. Look at the Color Table palette (Window→Color Table) to see a catalog of all the colors that will be left in the selected slices after optimizing.

If you increase the number in the Colors field of the GIF Optimize palette, you'll see more colors here. The more colors, the higher the file size of the image.

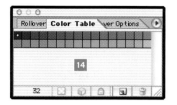

<NOTE>

The Color Table palette has a number of interesting features. You can make any color in an image transparent by selecting it in the Color Table palette and clicking the Map to Transparency icon at the bottom of the palette, as explained in the upcoming sidebar. You can also shift a color to the nearest Web-safe color by clicking the cube at the bottom of the Color Table palette. A diamond in a color identifies a Web-safe color. A square in a color (created by clicking the lock icon at the bottom of the Color Table palette) means that the color cannot be eliminated from the image, even if the number of colors in the palette is reduced.

15. Change the dither control in the Optimize palette to No Dither to decrease file size.

16. Increase the Lossy field a little (try around 10) to reduce the file size further.

Use a light touch with this setting. Too much lossy compression can degrade the appearance of an image.

<NOTE>

Dither is a method used to simulate a color that isn't available in the Color Table palette by placing tiny dots of colors next to one another (kind of like pointillist painting). Dither can be helpful in some circumstances — for example, to optimize a photograph as a GIF for purposes of including it in a GIF animation. However, dither increases file size; so turn it off if it's not necessary.

<NOTE>

Notice that the Dither field, as well as the Lossy and Palette fields, has an icon that allows you to vary the settings within a GIF, much like the icon next to the JPEG Quality setting covered earlier in this tutorial. These all work on the basis of channel masks and only sometimes result in significant file savings, as explained earlier with regard to the JPEG setting.

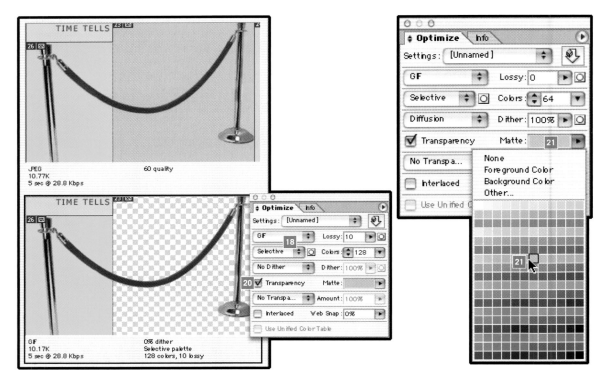

17. **Select the Hand tool and move the image until you see the red rope in the preview panes. Make sure that the Slice Select tool is still selected and click the slice that contains the red rope against a blue background.**

18. **Choose settings in the Optimize palette to match those shown here (GIF, Selective palette, 128 Colors, No Dither).**

    Notice that this slice also looks acceptable and comes to approximately the same file size optimized as a JPEG of 60 quality, as shown in the top preview pane in this figure. The reason to optimize this slice as a GIF rather than a JPEG is that, of the two file formats, only GIF honors the transparent pixels in this artwork, as you'll see in the next steps.

19. **Click the eye icon on the background color layer in the Layers palette to make that layer invisible.**

20. **Click the Transparency check box in the Optimize palette to add a check mark. You can now see through to the gray-and-white pixels that represent transparency in the preview pane that's set to GIF.**

    By contrast, you see no transparent pixels in the preview pane set to JPEG. There is no transparency check box in the JPEG Optimize palette because the JPEG file format doesn't honor transparency. Instead, you'll see a solid color behind the rope in the JPEG preview pane.

21. **Click the Matte box to open the Color Picker and choose a color similar to the light blue background color (try R:163, G:204, B:204).**

    Adding a matte color that's similar to the color that you expect to predominate in the Web page background eases the transition between that background and the semitransparent edges of a foreground image. The reason to add a matte is to avoid the unattractive light halo that you may have seen around some images on the Web.

<NOTE>

Steps 18–20 illustrate an important point. If you ever want to retain transparent pixels while optimizing an image for the Web, you must optimize that image as a GIF, not a JPEG. This holds true even if you're dealing with the kind of image that you'd normally optimize as a JPEG, such as a photograph. When would you want to retain transparency in an optimized image? One example is if you plan to put a patterned background behind an image, as you'll practice doing in the next tutorial.

22. **Continue moving around the image, selecting each image slice with the Slice Select tool and choosing optimization settings for that slice in the Optimize palette. When you've finished, choose File→Save As and name the image** 16_web_optimized.psd. **Leave the file open and move right on to the next tutorial, in which you'll learn how to save these multiple slices as optimized GIFs and JPEGs.**

<NOTE>

You can check the total file size of all the optimized images in your page layout from the information menus at the bottom of the document window. Mine added up to around 47KB, which is a respectable size for an entire Web page.

Creating Transparency

If you want transparency in a GIF, it's best to create the transparency in the original PSD file (for example, by using the Magic Eraser or by turning off a solid color layer as you did here).

New to ImageReady 7 is the ability to map or convert a nontransparent color to transparency while you're optimizing an image as a GIF. Select a color in the Color Table palette and click the Map to Transparency icon at the bottom of the palette to convert all pixels of that color in the image to transparent pixels. You could repeat this with more colors. However, you'll find that the transition between transparent pixels and colored pixels in an image is

not smooth when you rely on the Map to Transparency method because the GIF format supports a lower level of transparency than the PSD format. This allows for fewer levels of semitransparent pixels along the edges of an image to ease the transition to a fully transparent area.

Optimizing in Photoshop

In this tutorial, you've learned how to optimize using ImageReady's Optimize palette, Color Table palette, and document window tabs. The process is very similar in Photoshop, although it takes place there in a separate interface called the Photoshop Save For Web dialog box (accessed by choosing File→Save for Web). If you are working in Photoshop and find it more convenient to optimize there, go ahead and do so.

You should have no trouble understanding the controls that you'll see in Photoshop after learning how to optimize in ImageReady. Notice in this figure of Photoshop's Save For Web dialog box that there are optimization controls on the right that are just like those in ImageReady's Optimize and Color Table palettes, and the tabs in the middle portion of Photoshop's Save For Web dialog box are like the tabs in ImageReady's document window.

I've chosen to teach optimizing in ImageReady because that is the place that you'll find yourself most frequently when you're making images for the Web, especially if your site includes rollovers, animations, or image maps. I also find that ImageReady's palette system is a little more user-friendly than Photoshop's Save For Web dialog box. For example, you have to exit Photoshop's Save For Web dialog box if you want to make changes to the original image, but in ImageReady, you can click back and forth between the Original and Optimized tabs to modify the original while you're in the middle of optimizing. It's also relatively hard to find and access some frequently used commands in Photoshop's Save For Web dialog box. For example, the Output settings, which are covered in the next tutorial, are buried in a menu accessible from the arrow on the top right of the Save For Web dialog box. ImageReady's Output settings are more easily accessible from the top level of the File menu. Otherwise, the two programs have very similar optimization controls and engines.

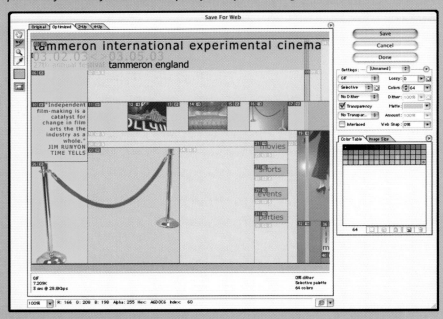

Tutorial

» Outputting Web-Ready Images and HTML

In this tutorial, you'll have ImageReady convert your optimized slices to GIFs and JPEGs and save them. ImageReady will also generate HTML code, which includes instructions for a background, a table to reassemble your images and hold them in place, and JavaScript to make your rollovers functional.

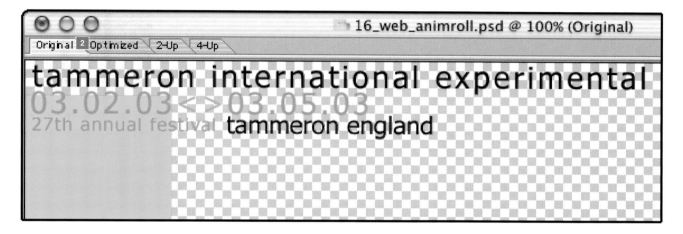

1. Use the file `16_web_optimized.psd`, which should be open from the last tutorial. Alternatively, open the file of that same name provided for you in the Session 16 Tutorial Files folder.

2. Click the Original tab in the document window. You'll see a gray-and-white checkerboard pattern, like the one shown here. If you don't, click the eye icon on the background color layer in the Layers palette to hide the blue background.

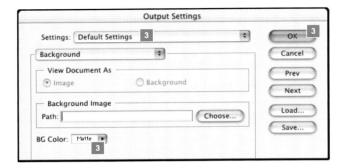

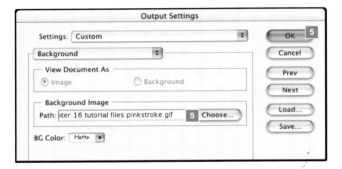

3. **Choose File→Output Settings→Background. Select Default Settings from the Settings menu to clear any settings that may be there from the last time that you used this dialog box. Click the BG Color field and choose Matte. Click OK.**
   This sets the background color of the entire Web page to the light blue color that you chose in the Matte field of the Optimize palette in the last exercise. If you didn't choose a matte color then, click the arrow next to the BG Color field and choose a light blue. A code for this color will be embedded in the HTML code that ImageReady writes for you. Using HTML, rather than a graphic, to create a solid color background is a smart move because it will result in a Web page with a lower overall file size.

4. **Click the Preview in Browser icon in the toolbox to preview the optimized page layout in a Web browser.**
   Notice the blue background, which is the result of HTML code, rather than a blue graphic.

5. **Return to ImageReady and choose File→Output Settings→Background again. This time, click the Choose button and navigate to** pinkstroke.gif **in the Session 16 tutorial files on your hard drive. Click OK.**

6. **Click the Preview in Default Browser button on your toolbox.**
   You'll see a patterned background showing in the transparent areas of the foreground images.

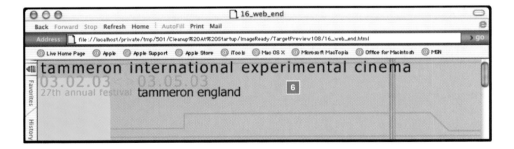

<NOTE>
The background image used in this tutorial is a small GIF that's only 1.2KB in file size because it uses only two colors. ImageReady will include code in the HTML that will cause this small image to repeat itself over and over in a Web browser to give the illusion of a large patterned background. This can result in significant file savings over using a large graphic background. You can make your own small images to use as patterned backgrounds. Give it a try in your spare time.

7. **Choose File→Save As, name this final image** 16_web_end.psd, **and click Save.**

This saves your PSD source file with all its layer and slicing information. It's a good idea to keep the source files for your Web images in a safe place so that you can come back to them to make changes later if necessary. This is preferable to trying to change the individual GIFs or JPEGs saved from the PSD file because neither GIFs nor JPEGs have layers and JPEGs degrade in quality each time you resave them.

8. **Choose File→Save Optimized. Make sure that Format (Windows: Save as Type) is set to HTML and Images and that Slices is set to All Slices. Click Save.**

It may take a moment for ImageReady to create all the individual GIFs and JPEGs that result from your slices and rollovers.

< N O T E >

Be sure to choose HTML and Images rather than just Images in the Format (Windows: Save as Type) field of the Save Optimized dialog box, if you want to save the code that will make your rollovers functional and reassemble all the GIFs and JPEGs into your Web page layout. If you choose just Images, you can take all the GIFs and JPEGs generated by ImageReady and code them in an HTML editor or by hand.

9. **Take a look at the folder on your hard drive to see the HTML file** (16_web_end.html) **and images folder full of GIFs and JPEGs that ImageReady saved for you.**

Notice that your hard work in naming slices paid off. In the images folder, you'll find that the important GIFs and JPEGs in your page layout can be identified by their meaningful names.

That's the last step in this long journey to creating a Web page in Photoshop and ImageReady. Go on to the last tutorial in this session if you want to know how to get Photoshop to create an entire Web site for you automatically, without all this hard work!

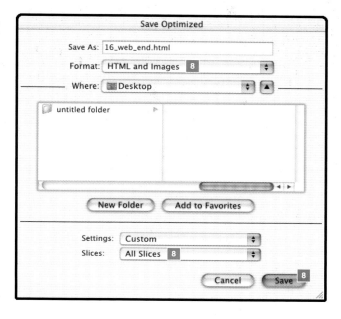

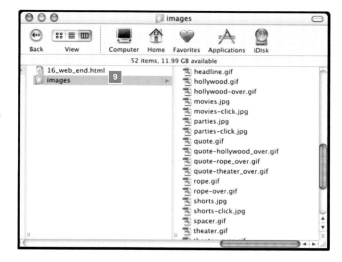

Tutorial

» Making a Web Photo Gallery in Photoshop

In this short tutorial, you'll learn how to have Photoshop make an entire Web site for you automatically from a folder of images. All you have to do is put the images in a folder and click a button.

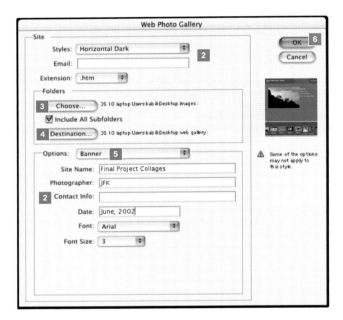

1. **Launch Photoshop if it's not already open. Choose File→Automate→Web Photo Gallery from the menu bar at the top of the screen.**

2. **Fill in the settings in the Web Photo Gallery dialog box. You can match the settings here or try your own.**
   You don't have to fill in all the fields if there is certain information that you don't want on the site.

3. **Click the Choose button in the Folders section and navigate to the folder of source images for your Web photo gallery site — in this case, the images folder in the Session 16 Tutorial Files folder on your hard drive.**

4. **Click the Destination button and navigate to the folder in which you want to save your Web gallery site. I suggest that you make a new folder to keep all of the files Photoshop produces.**

5. **Click the Options button and cycle through other screens in which you can choose options for how your images and text will appear on the pages of the Web photo gallery. If you prefer, you can leave them all at their defaults for now.**

6. **Click OK and wait while Photoshop resizes all your images to thumbnails and to gallery size, writes the HTML for each page of the site, organizes the files into folders, and even opens a Web browser in which you can view the site that it created for you.**

<NOTE>
The Styles field contains a number of prebuilt styles for the Web site Photoshop will build for you. Frankly, most of these are pretty plain. You can spruce up the final product by taking all the files Photoshop produces into an HTML editor and making style changes to the Web pages there. Alternatively, you can customize a Web photo gallery style right in Photoshop using a relatively complicated system of HTML tokens. Or you can just accept the default styles for what they are — a quick and easy way of preparing a folder of images to be displayed on the Web.

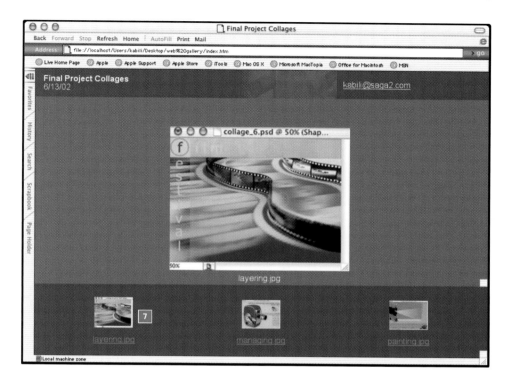

7. **Click the thumbnails and navigation arrows in your Web browser to enjoy your new Web photo gallery site.**

<NOTE>
When you're making your own Web photo gallery, all you have to do to prepare is put your source images into a folder and name them the way that you want their captions to appear on the Web site. You may want to resize them first so that they're not huge. You could make them all the same size in one dimension so that they line up nicely on the thumbnails page, but that isn't crucial.

<NOTE>
For now, your Web photo gallery site exists only on your hard drive. Consult your Internet service provider about how to upload Web site files to the provider's Web server. The provider should tell you the directory path, your username, and usually a password. You can use an FTP program such as Fetch on a Macintosh or WS-FTP in Windows to upload. Some ISPs provide a user-friendly interface on the Web that you can use to upload files. One thing to remember is that you have to upload all the files and folders that Photoshop made for you and keep them in the same relationship to one another on the server that they were in on your hard drive. Don't move files from one folder to another or rename any of the files or folders, or you'll have broken links on your Web photo gallery site.

» Session Review

This session covers how to create Web graphics in Photoshop and ImageReady. You added buttons to a page layout and then switched to ImageReady to create rollovers and animation, slice the page layout, and create individual GIFs and JPEGs. You also created a Web photo gallery site.

1. How do you create equal spaces between buttons that are on separate layers in Photoshop? (See "Tutorial: Laying Out a Web Page in Photoshop.")

2. What do the Jump To buttons in Photoshop and ImageReady do? (See "Tutorial: Switching to ImageReady.")

3. Name three reasons that you may want to slice an image. (See "Tutorial: Slicing.")

4. Can you have more than one rollover effect triggered by the same rollover button? (See "Tutorial: Making Secondary Rollovers.")

5. What is a secondary rollover? (See "Tutorial: Making Secondary Rollovers.")

6. Can you program a rollover in either Photoshop or ImageReady? (See "Tutorial: Creating Rollovers.")

7. Name two ways to create a slice. (See "Tutorial: Slicing.")

8. How do you create a layer-based slice? (See "Tutorial: Slicing.")

9. Name one advantage layer-based slices have over slices drawn manually with the Slice tool. (See "Tutorial: Slicing.")

10. What is an auto slice? (See "Tutorial: Slicing.")

11. Is there a way to hide slices in ImageReady so that you can see your image more clearly while you're working on it? (See "Tutorial: Creating Rollovers.")

12. What kind of slice do you have to use if you plan to create a rollover style from the contents of the slice? (See "Tutorial: Creating and Applying Rollover Styles.")

13. How do you apply a rollover style to artwork? (See "Tutorial: Creating and Applying Rollover Styles.")

14. What is the crucial step to ensure that an animation will be triggered by a rollover? (See "Tutorial: Creating a Rollover Animation from Layered Artwork.")

15. What Photoshop feature creates an entire working Web site for you automatically? (See "Tutorial: Making a Web Photo Gallery in Photoshop.")

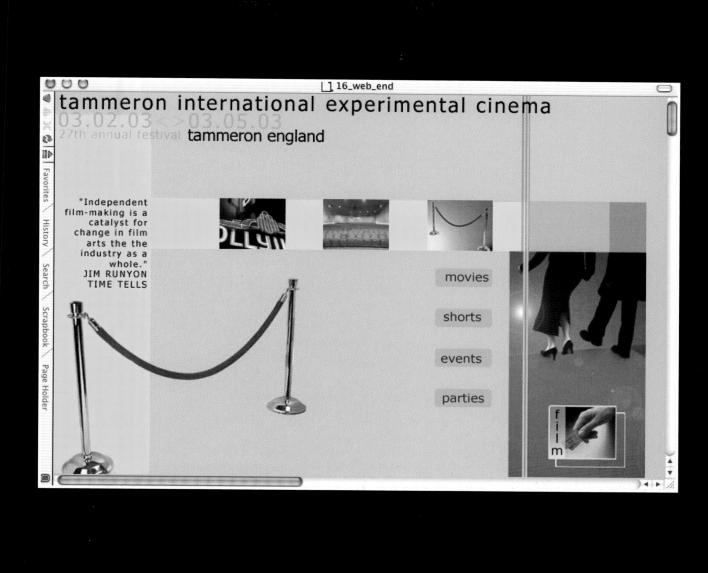

Session 17

Printing

08_fest_end.psd @ 50% (background set, RGB)

film
festival

tammeron england
03.02.03<>03.05.03

27th annual festival
2003

50%   Doc:4.45M/31.5M

Tutorial: **Adding File Information**

Tutorial: **Setting Up the Document for Printing**

Tutorial: **Using Page Setup**

Tutorial: **Printing to a Desktop Printer**

Tutorial: **Creating a Contact Sheet**

Session Introduction

In this session, you'll learn how to prepare image files for print in Photoshop, print to a desktop printer, and set up files for professional printing at a service bureau. You'll use the project files that you created as you worked through this book, printing composites of the final pages of the film festival program guide on your desktop printer and preparing the final files for professional printing.

TOOLS YOU'LL USE
File Info command, Proof Setup command, Proof Colors command, Mode command, Page Setup, Print command, Contact Sheet II command, and desktop color printer

CD-ROM FILES NEEDED
04_films_end.psd, 06_sponsors_end.psd, 07_tix_end.psd,
08_fest_end.psd, 09_screening_end.psd, 10_effects_end.psd,
11_type_end.psd, 12_texteffects_end.psd, 13_darkroom_end.psd,
15_tone_end.psd, 17_contactsheet-1.psd, and 17_contactsheet-2.psd

TIME REQUIRED
90 minutes

Tutorial
» Adding File Information

When you're preparing a document for print, you may want to add some file information (sometimes called *metadata*) to the document. This information can help you keep documentation associated with an image stored directly in the file for later reference. You can also print file information onto a proof or final print.

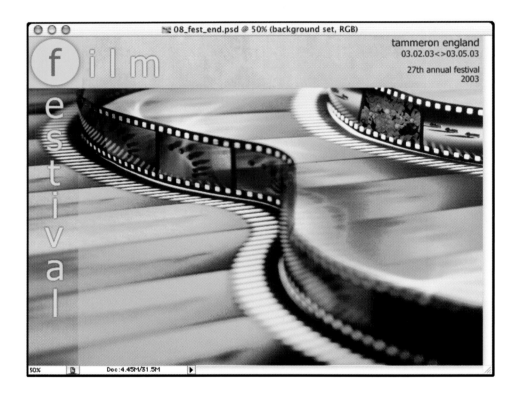

1. **Open the file** 08_fest_end.psd **from your collages folder.**

<NOTE>
Throughout this session, you'll use the final files that you created and saved to the collages folder. You'll start with the file for the cover of your film festival program guide — 08_fest_end.psd. Begin each tutorial with that image. Then apply the same steps to each of the final files created in other sessions. There are ten final files all together. (Not all the sessions resulted in a final file for print.) They are listed at the beginning of this session, and a copy of each has been put inside the collages folder in the Session 17 Tutorial Files folder.

2. **Choose File→File Info.**
   This opens the File Info dialog box to its General section. Here you can add general information about the file, copyright information, and a printable caption.

<NOTE>
In a real-world environment, the information that you add in the File Info dialog box is typically for your own use. Print centers and service bureaus rarely look for file information specific to printing a job. They frankly don't have time to examine each image for information before printing it. Therefore, think about the kind of information that you want to add for your own records or within your own workgroup and supply that information.

3. **Add file information and a caption.**
   You can fill in any or all of the fields as you like. Be certain to add some descriptive information in the Caption field. The information that you supply for the caption will be visible on the print that you make on your desktop color printer.

4. **Enter copyright information.**
   If you choose Copyrighted Work from the Copyright Status drop-down list, a copyright symbol (©) appears in the title bar of the file's document window to inform viewers that the image is copyrighted. You can also add a direct link to the copyright owner's Web site by typing a full URL in the Owner URL field. The information that you enter in the Copyright Notice field is only viewable if someone opens this File Info dialog box, so if you're serious about recording a copyright, you may want to embed a digital watermark. (See the Photoshop Help files for information on how to register and use the Digimarc plug-in that comes with Photoshop.)

5. **Click the Section down arrow and take a look at the other panes of potential file information.**
   The Keywords pane is a place to add descriptive words that are searchable with some server and browser utilities. The Categories and Origin panes are designed for cataloging systems used by news services, but you may be able to adapt these fields to your own purposes. The EXIF pane shows you information about the image that is usually created by a digital camera (although in this case the image comes from Photoshop because that's where the image was created). EXIF data can include information ranging from the date a photo was made to all kinds of exposure information, and is quite useful for a digital photographer.

6. **Click OK.**
   This appends the file information to the file. It can be accessed at any time by reopening the File Info dialog box.

7. **Choose File→Save.**
   You can save over the file in the collages folder.

8. **Open each of the other files from your collages folder**
   (04_films_end.psd, 06_sponsors_end.psd, 07_tix_end.psd, 09_screening_end.psd, 10_effects_end.psd, 11_type_end.psd, 12_texteffects_end.psd, 13_darkroom_end.psd, 15_tone_end.psd) **and add a caption to be printed with each file. Choose File→Save to resave each file.**
   You can use either the files that you saved into your collages folder as you worked through this course or the prebuilt copies of those files, which you'll find in the Session 17 Tutorial Files collages folder.

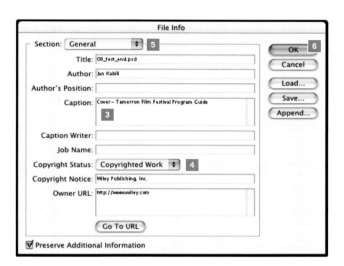

<NOTE>
To print the information on your output that's contained in the Caption field, choose File→Print with Preview and check Caption when you're ready to print.

<NOTE>
All the steps in this session's tutorials assume that you have a desktop color printer. If you have a grayscale laser printer, you can follow the same steps to produce a composite grayscale proof. If you don't have a printer attached to your computer, you can prepare the file for printing and take it to a service center where a composite color proof can be obtained.

Tutorial
» Setting Up the Document for Printing

When preparing files for commercial printing, you need to ensure that the images that you create in Photoshop are properly set up for high-end output. In this tutorial, you'll learn some steps that should be routinely followed when preparing files for commercial printing.

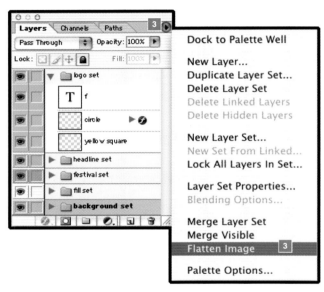

1. **Open the file** 08_fest_end.psd **that you saved at the end of the preceding tutorial, if it isn't already open.**

2. **Click the arrow on each layer set and check that each layer has an eye icon. If you find a hidden layer that doesn't display an eye icon, click in that layer's Visibility field to add an eye icon.**
   Be sure to do this before flattening a file (as you'll do in the next step), or you'll lose the hidden layers when you flatten.

3. **Click the arrow at the top right of the Layers palette and choose Flatten Image.**
   If you inadvertently hid a layer, Photoshop prompts you as to whether you want to delete hidden layers. If you see that prompt, double-check your Layers palette to be certain hidden layers don't contain content needed in the final image.

4. **Choose View→Proof Setup from the menu bar at the top of the screen and make sure that there's a check mark next to Working CMYK in the drop-down list. If there isn't, click Working CMYK.**
   This ensures that the Proof Colors command you'll invoke in the next step will display a preview of your image in the CMYK working space that is defined in your color management settings. If you followed the instruction back in Session 4 to set your color management settings to U.S. Prepress Defaults, your CMYK working space will have been automatically set to the commonly used U.S. Web Coated (SWOP) v2. If you'd like to check this, choose Photoshop→Color Settings (Windows and Macintosh OS 9: Edit→Color Settings) and look under Working Spaces→ CMYK. (You can change this setting now if necessary.) If your service bureau uses a different CMYK working space, you can change this setting to match their specifications.

5. **Choose View→Proof Colors and observe the image in the document window.**
   This shows you how this RGB image will look when converted to CMYK for commercial printing. Notice the RGB/CMYK designation in the title bar of the document window, which indicates that you're looking at a preview of the image conversion.

< W A R N I N G >
Always keep a copy of a flattened file in Photoshop format with layers intact. Otherwise, you'll lose the layers for good when you flatten.

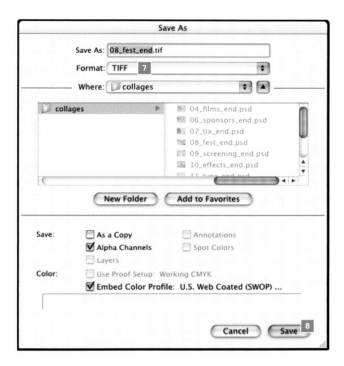

<NOTE>

Part of file preparation for commercial printing is to convert your Photoshop documents to the proper color mode. For offset printing that uses a four-color process, the files need to be converted from RGB to CMYK (cyan, magenta, yellow, and black) process inks. Before converting the file to CMYK, you can soft proof your Photoshop files on-screen. If colors in your document shift when viewing them as CMYK, you may need to edit your images. The colors used in the tutorial files don't show a color shift as you'll notice when you view them as CMYK. Therefore, you won't need to edit color in the final files saved to the collages folder.

6. **Choose Image→Mode→CMYK Color.**
   This converts the image from RGB color mode to CMYK color mode. You can usually expect to see some color shift when you convert an image because the CMYK color mode supports a narrower gamut of colors than the RGB color mode. However, the shift is negligible in this file.

7. **Choose File→Save As. Select TIFF for the file format.**
   This automatically changes the name of this copy of the file to 08_fest_end.tif. Note that this is a copy of the original file; it won't write over your PSD format file that retains all the layers.

8. **Click Save.**
   After you click Save, the TIFF Options dialog box opens.

9. **Set Image Compression to None and set Byte Order to the platform that you are working on (IBM PC or Macintosh). Click OK to save the file.**
   If all your layers have been flattened, you won't have any other options in the TIFF Options dialog box.

10. **Repeat steps 1 through 9 for soft proofing and saving files as TIFFs on all the other PSD files in the collages folder** (04_films_end.psd, 06_sponsors_end.psd, 07_tix_end.psd, 09_screening_end.psd, 10_effects_end.psd, 11_type_end.psd, 12_texteffects_end.psd, 13_darkroom_end.psd, 15_tone_end.psd).

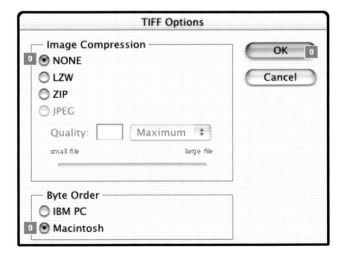

Using the TIFF format

Photoshop files usually wind up in other programs when printed at commercial print shops. Rarely will you find a commercial service center using Photoshop to ultimately print a file. If you import Photoshop files into other applications, you need to use a format acceptable to the authoring application. TIFF (Tagged Image File Format) is the most popular of all of Photoshop's formats for getting files into other applications and printing by commercial printers. Virtually any professional authoring program will accept TIFF as an import format.

In Photoshop 7, the TIFF options have been expanded over previous versions of the program, and more attributes can be assigned to the format before saving. These attributes are set in the TIFF Options dialog box after you name a file and click the Save button. They include the following:

» Image Compression: Image compression reduces file sizes according to the compression scheme used when saving the file. For your own use, choose LZW or Zip compression to save and print your files to your desktop printer. LZW and Zip are *lossless* compression schemes, which means that no image degradation occurs when compressing the file. If you choose JPEG compression, pixels will be discarded by Photoshop during compression. The result may visibly degrade the image. For files that will be sent to commercial print shops, use None as your choice and save files without compression. Even though all popular layout and illustration programs can accept compressed TIFFs as imports, compressing a TIFF can lead to problems when the print shop tries to color separate your file. As a rule, most print shops will ask you to not compress your TIFFs.

» Byte Order: If you're working in Photoshop running under Windows, select IBM PC as the byte order. If working on a Macintosh, use Macintosh as your choice.

» Save Image Pyramid: This option permits you to save multiple image resolutions. Try to visualize a pyramid. The top of the pyramid is the lowest resolution, and the bottom of the pyramid represents the highest resolution. When a file is imported into a program that supports TIFF pyramids, a dialog box opens that enables you to choose which resolution you want to use. Unfortunately, other than Adobe InDesign, no programs currently support pyramids — including the current version of Photoshop. Until more support is offered by other programs, you may want to leave this item unchecked.

» Save Transparency: For Photoshop images containing transparency, check this box, and other applications will honor the transparency.

» Layer Compression: TIFF files can be saved with layers preserved. Photoshop saves a flattened version along with a layered version when saving in layered TIFF format. If layers are present, you can decide what compression to apply to the individual layers. If sending files off to service centers, you're better off flattening images and saving without layers. The image overhead in terms of file size will be reduced when saving flattened images. If you must save a file with layers preserved for a service center, use the RLE layer compression.

Tutorial
» Using Page Setup

The first stop to make when printing to a desktop printer is the Page Setup dialog box. As with many other Photoshop features, there is more than one way to invoke Page Setup. You can choose to open the Page Setup dialog box from a menu command or from within the Print dialog box. In this tutorial, you'll learn how to open Page Setup from a menu command and then to assign page attributes for the document to be printed.

1. **Open the file** 08_fest_end.tif **that you saved in the preceding tutorial.**

Macintosh OS 9 users only need to open the Chooser and select a printer at this point.

2. **Choose File→Page Setup and make sure that the Settings field is set to Page Attributes.**
   Your Page Setup dialog box may look different than the one shown here, depending on your operating system and the printer that you have attached to your computer.

3. **Set Format for: to the printer that you want to use.**
   If you have only one printer attached to your computer, you can skip this step. If you work in an office environment or have multiple printers attached to your computer, you need to choose one of them from this list.

4. **Set Paper Size to US Letter and Orientation to Landscape. Leave Scale set to 100%.**

5. **Click OK.**

6. **Keep the file open and move immediately to the next tutorial.**

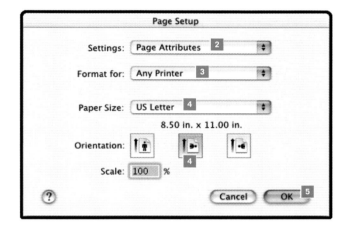

<TIP>
Never scale an image in the Page Setup dialog box. Use the Image→Image Size command if you have to change the size of an image.

<NOTE>
Alternatively, the Page Setup dialog box can be selected from the Print dialog box when you choose File→Print.

Tutorial
» Printing to a Desktop Printer

After you make choices in the Page Setup dialog box for printer type, page size, and orientation, you're ready to print your Photoshop document. In this tutorial, you'll learn how to send your file to your desktop printer.

1. **Make sure that** `08_fest_end.tif` **is still open from the previous tutorial.**

2. **Choose File→Print with Preview.**
   The Print dialog box opens with a preview of the image to be printed. In this dialog box, you define attributes for the print, and you can further establish the position on the page where the image will be printed.

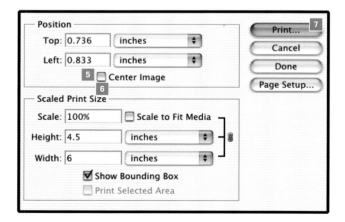

< N O T E >
Your printer software may present other dialog boxes after step 7. Consult your printer manual for instructions.

3. **Check the Calibration Bars, Registration Marks, Corner Crop Marks, Center Crop Marks, and Labels check boxes. Notice that these items are now represented in the print preview in this dialog box.**
   The items checked in the Print dialog box will be included on the printed piece. When a document is printed at a commercial print center, crop and trim marks are usually printed with the piece. The document is printed on oversized paper and cut on the trim lines. The calibration bars and registration marks are used by commercial printers to calibrate inks and register the four individual separations into the composite print. Although you don't need these marks on the copies you print on your desktop printer, it may be helpful to print them on your hard proofs before sending your files to the printer.

4. **Check Caption in the Print dialog box.**
   When Caption is checked, the caption information that you added in the File Info dialog box will appear on your final print (although you won't see it in the preview of the image in the Print dialog box).

5. **Click the Center Image check box to remove the check mark. Position the mouse cursor on the image preview and move the image to a new location on the page.**
   Photoshop offers you control over where the image will appear on the printed page. This option can be helpful in case you want to handwrite annotations or notes on the printed pieces to provide instructions to your printer.

6. **Click the Center Image check box to re-enable it.**
   To create your own printed proofs, you won't need to relocate the image. Return to centering the image before printing the file.

7. **Click Print.**
   The file will be printed to your desktop printer.

8. **Open each additional TIFF file that you saved to your collages folder back in the tutorial "Setting Up the Document for Printing"** (`04_films_end.tif`, `06_sponsors_end.tif`, `07_tix_end.tif`, `09_screening_end.tif`, `10_effects_end.tif`, `11_type_end.tif`, `12_texteffects_end.tif`, `13_darkroom_end.tif`, **and** `15_tone_end.tif`) **and print each to your desktop printer following the steps in the previous tutorial and this tutorial.**

Tutorial
» Creating a Contact Sheet

Photoshop gives you the option of organizing your images as thumbnails on individual pages — much like photo labs print film frames on contact sheets. With a simple menu command, you can have Photoshop create a contact sheet of your images, print the contact sheet, and store the images in a folder for reference. In this tutorial, you'll learn how to create a contact sheet.

1. **Choose File→Automate→Contact Sheet II.**
   You should have no documents currently open in Photoshop. The command can be exercised without a document in view.

2. **In the Contact Sheet II dialog box, click Choose.**
   The Select Image Directory dialog box opens.

3. **Select the collages folder on your hard drive and click the Choose button.**
   You are returned to the Contact Sheet II dialog box.

4. **Leave the page size at the default size, 8 x 10. Type 3 in the Columns box and 3 in the Rows box. Select Arial for the font type from the drop-down list at the bottom of the dialog box.**
   Leave the other defaults as they are.

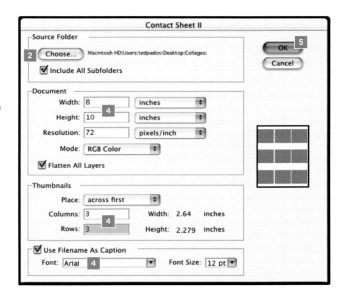

< N O T E >

If you want to print your contact sheet to your desktop color printer, change the resolution from 72 ppi to the resolution recommended by your printer manufacturer (between 240 and 300 ppi for most inkjet printers). After Photoshop creates the contact sheet, follow the steps in the previous tutorials to print the document.

5. **Click OK.**
   Photoshop opens each image contained in the collages folder, flattens the image, down-samples the image to 72 ppi, applies the filenames as captions, and locates the image in position on the canvas. After a few moments, the completed contact sheet is generated with each image appearing on a separate layer.

<NOTE>
If you have more than nine images, Photoshop creates more than one contact sheet, placing nine images on each contact sheet.

6. **Choose File→Save and save the two contact sheets to your desktop as** `17_contactsheet-1.psd` **and** `17_contactsheet-2.psd`.

   The contact sheets are ready for storage and can be kept handy for future reference. You can print the file, but the resolution will be low, and the images will appear pixelated. If you want to keep a permanent record with a printed file, repeat the steps and set the image resolution for your printer in step 4.

» Session Review

This session covers how to print files to desktop printers, set up files for commercial printing, and create a contact sheet for storing thumbnail images of your projects. This session hopefully started you in the right direction with printing. There's more to be learned, so be certain to study, practice, and run your own tests with your equipment and professional print centers.

1. How do you add a caption? (See "Tutorial: Adding File Information.")

2. How do you print a caption? (See "Tutorial: Printing to a Desktop Printer.")

3. How do you view how an RGB file will look converted to CMYK colors? (See "Tutorial: Setting Up the Document for Printing.")

4. How do you convert an RGB file to CMYK color mode? (See "Tutorial: Setting Up the Document for Printing.")

5. In which format should you save files for output on commercial printers? (See "Tutorial: Setting Up the Document for Printing.")

6. How do you control where an image prints on a page? (See "Tutorial: Printing to a Desktop Printer.")

7. How do you create a contact sheet in Photoshop? (See "Tutorial: Creating a Contact Sheet.")

Congratulations on completing this course! The prints that you hold in your hand are testimony to all that you've learned. Now it's time to apply these lessons to your own work. And don't forget to keep this book handy for review, consultation, and practice.

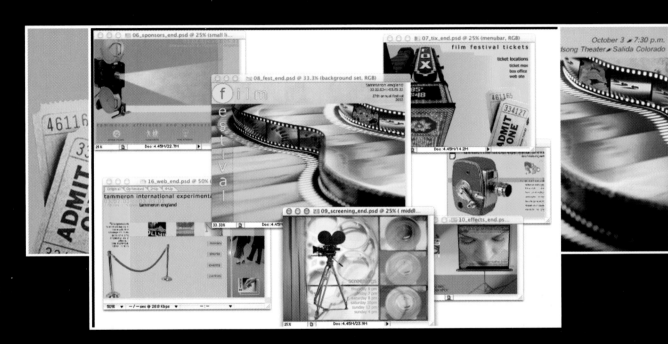

Appendix A

What's on the CD-ROM

This appendix provides you with information on the contents of the CD-ROM that accompanies this book. For the latest and greatest information, please refer to the ReadMe file located at the root of the CD-ROM. Here is what you will find:

» System Requirements

» Using the CD-ROM with Windows and Macintosh

» What's on the CD-ROM

» Troubleshooting

System Requirements

Make sure that your computer meets the minimum system requirements listed in this section. If your computer doesn't match up to most of these requirements, you may have a problem using the contents of the CD-ROM.

For Windows 98, Windows 2000, Windows NT, Windows Me, or Windows XP:

» PC with a Pentium class III or 4 processor

» At least 128MB of total RAM installed on your computer

» At least 280MB of free hard drive space

» A color monitor with at least 800 x 600 resolution and a 16-bit video card

» A CD-ROM drive

For Macintosh:

» Macintosh OS computer with a G3 or G4 PowerPC processor running OS 9.1, OS 9.2, or OS X

» At least 128MB of total RAM installed on your computer

» At least 320MB of free hard drive space

» A color monitor with at least 800 x 600 resolution and a 16-bit video card

» A CD-ROM drive

Using the CD-ROM with Windows

To install the items from the CD-ROM to your hard drive, follow these steps:

1. Insert the CD-ROM into your computer's CD-ROM drive.

2. The interface will launch. If you have autorun disabled, choose Start→Run. In the dialog box that appears, type **D:\setup.exe**. Replace D with the proper letter if your CD-ROM drive uses a different letter. (If you don't know the letter, see how your CD-ROM drive is listed under My Computer.) Click OK.

3. A license agreement appears. Read through the license agreement and then click the Accept button if you want to use the CD-ROM. (After you click Accept, you'll never be bothered by the License Agreement window again.)

   The CD-ROM interface Welcome screen appears. The interface coordinates installing the programs and running the demos. The interface basically enables you to click a button or two to make things happen.

4. Click anywhere on the Welcome screen to enter the interface. This next screen lists categories for the software on the CD-ROM.

5. For more information about a program, click the program's name. Be sure to read the information that appears. Sometimes a program has its own system requirements or requires you to do a few tricks on your computer before you can install or run the program, and this screen tells you what you may need to do, if necessary.

6. If you don't want to install the program, click the Back button to return to the previous screen. You can always return to the previous screen by clicking the Back button. This feature enables you to browse the different categories and products and decide what you want to install.

7. To install a program, click the appropriate Install button. The CD-ROM interface drops to the background while the CD-ROM installs the program that you chose.

8. To install other items, repeat steps 5–7.

9. When you've finished installing programs, click the Quit button to close the interface. You can eject the CD-ROM now. Carefully place it back in the plastic jacket of the book for safekeeping.

Note: If you don't install the tutorial files with the CD-ROM interface (if you just copy the files directly from the CD-ROM) and you're using a Windows operating system other than Windows XP, you'll have to change the read-only status of the copied tutorial files. (If you use the interface, the files won't be read-only.) Otherwise, you won't be able to write over the files as you work through the tutorials. To do so, select all the files in a folder that you've copied to your computer. Right-click one of the files and choose Properties. In the Properties dialog box, uncheck Read-only.

Also, I suggest that you instruct Windows to display the filename extensions of the copied tutorial files (if it isn't already set up to show them) so that you can see the file formats (`.psd`, `.tif`, `.jpg`, and so on). Find your Folder Options dialog box. (It's located in a slightly different place in different versions of Windows; in Windows XP, it's in the Appearance and Themes Control Panel; in Windows 2000 and Me, in the My Computer→Tools folder; in Windows 98, in the My Computer→ View folder.) Click the View tab. Uncheck Hide File Extensions for Known File Types, which is checked by default.

Using the CD-ROM with the Macintosh OS

To install the items from the CD-ROM to your hard drive, follow these steps:

1. Insert the CD-ROM into your CD-ROM drive.

2. Double-click the icon for the CD-ROM after it appears on the desktop.

3. Double-click the License Agreement icon. This is the license that you are agreeing to by using the CD-ROM. You can close this window after you've looked over the agreement.

4. Most programs come with installers; for those, simply open the program's folder on the CD-ROM and double-click the Install or Installer icon. ***Note:*** To install some programs, just drag the program's folder from the CD-ROM window and drop it on your hard drive icon.

What's on the CD-ROM

The following sections provide a summary of the software and other materials that you'll find on the CD-ROM.

Tutorial Files

All the tutorial files that you'll use when working through the tutorials in this book are on the CD-ROM in the folder named "Tutorial Files." Within the Tutorial Files folder are subfolders containing the tutorial files for each session. In each session subfolder, you'll find all the files referenced in that session, including a file with the word _end in the filename. The _end file is an example of how the collage that you'll work on in that session should look at the end of the session.

Use the process described in the preceding sections to copy the files to your hard drive. Windows users can access the Tutorial Files from the Start menu. Macintosh users can access the Tutorial Files from the Finder.

Applications

The following applications are on the CD-ROM:

Adobe Acrobat Reader

Freeware version for Windows and Macintosh. This program enables you to view and print PDF files. Go to www.adobe.com for more information and product updates.

Adobe Photoshop (including ImageReady)

Try-out version for Windows 98, 2000, Me, NT and Macintosh OS 9.1, OS 9.2, and OS X. Photoshop is the program that you'll use throughout this book to edit images and put together the film festival project; ImageReady is similar to Photoshop but is designed for making Web graphics. Go to www.adobe.com for more information and product updates. Macintosh users, be sure to review "Project Overview" in Part I for detailed instructions on how to install Photoshop on various configurations of Macintosh OS 9 and X.

Shareware programs are fully functional, trial versions of copyrighted programs. If you like particular programs, register with their authors for a nominal fee and receive licenses, enhanced versions, and technical support. *Freeware programs* are copyrighted games, applications, and utilities that are free for personal use. Unlike shareware, these programs don't require a fee or provide technical support. *GNU software* is governed by its own license, which is included inside the folder of the GNU product. See the GNU license for more details.

Trial, demo, or evaluation versions are usually limited either by time or functionality (such as being unable to save projects). Some trial versions are very sensitive to system date changes. If you alter your computer's date, the programs will "time out" and will no longer be functional.

Troubleshooting

If you have difficulty installing or using any of the materials on the companion CD-ROM, try the following solutions:

» **Turn off any antivirus software that you may have running.** Installers sometimes mimic virus activity and can make your computer incorrectly believe that it is being infected by a virus. (Be sure to turn the antivirus software back on later.)

» **Close all running programs.** The more programs you're running, the less memory is available to other programs. Installers also typically update files and programs; if you keep other programs running, the installation may not work properly.

» **Reference the ReadMe file:** Please refer to the ReadMe file located at the root of the CD-ROM for the latest product information at the time of publication.

If you still have trouble with the CD-ROM, please call the Wiley Publishing Customer Care phone number: (800)762-2974. Outside the United States, call 1(317)572-3994. You can also contact Wiley Publishing Customer Service by e-mail at techsupdum@wiley.com. Wiley Publishing will provide technical support only for installation and other general quality control items; for technical support on the applications themselves, consult the program's vendor or author.

Wiley Publishing, Inc. End User License Agreement

READ THIS. You should carefully read these terms and conditions before opening the software packet(s) included with this book "Book". This is a license agreement "Agreement" between you and Wiley Publishing, Inc. "WPI". By opening the accompanying software packet(s), you acknowledge that you have read and accept the following terms and conditions. If you do not agree and do not want to be bound by such terms and conditions, promptly return the Book and the unopened software packet(s) to the place you obtained them for a full refund.

1. **License Grant.** WPI grants to you (either an individual or entity) a nonexclusive license to use one copy of the enclosed software program(s) (collectively, the "Software") solely for your own personal or business purposes on a single computer (whether a standard computer or a workstation component of a multi-user network). The Software is in use on a computer when it is loaded into temporary memory (RAM) or installed into permanent memory (hard disk, CD-ROM, or other storage device). WPI reserves all rights not expressly granted herein.

2. **Ownership.** WPI is the owner of all right, title, and interest, including copyright, in and to the compilation of the Software recorded on the disk(s) or CD-ROM "Software Media". Copyright to the individual programs recorded on the Software Media is owned by the author or other authorized copyright owner of each program. Ownership of the Software and all proprietary rights relating thereto remain with WPI and its licensers.

3. **Restrictions On Use and Transfer.**

   (a) You may only (i) make one copy of the Software for backup or archival purposes, or (ii) transfer the Software to a single hard disk, provided that you keep the original for backup or archival purposes. You may not (i) rent or lease the Software, (ii) copy or reproduce the Software through a LAN or other network system or through any computer subscriber system or bulletin-board system, or (iii) modify, adapt, or create derivative works based on the Software.

   (b) You may not reverse engineer, decompile, or disassemble the Software. You may transfer the Software and user documentation on a permanent basis, provided that the transferee agrees to accept the terms and conditions of this Agreement and you retain no copies. If the Software is an update or has been updated, any transfer must include the most recent update and all prior versions.

4. **Restrictions on Use of Individual Programs.** You must follow the individual requirements and restrictions detailed for each individual program in Appendix A of this Book. These limitations are also contained in the individual license agreements recorded on the Software Media. These limitations may include a requirement that after using the program for a specified period of time, the user must pay a registration fee or discontinue use. By opening the Software packet(s), you will be agreeing to abide by the licenses and restrictions for these individual programs that are detailed in Appendix A and on the Software Media. None of the material on this Software Media or listed in this Book may ever be redistributed, in original or modified form, for commercial purposes.

5. **Limited Warranty.**

   (a) WPI warrants that the Software and Software Media are free from defects in materials and workmanship under normal use for a period of sixty (60) days from the date of purchase of this Book. If WPI receives notification within the warranty period of defects in materials or workmanship, WPI will replace the defective Software Media.

   (b) WPI AND THE AUTHOR OF THE BOOK DISCLAIM ALL OTHER WARRANTIES, EXPRESS OR IMPLIED, INCLUDING WITHOUT LIMITATION IMPLIED WARRANTIES OF MERCHANTABILITY AND FITNESS FOR A PARTICULAR PURPOSE, WITH RESPECT TO THE SOFTWARE, THE PROGRAMS, THE SOURCE CODE CONTAINED THEREIN, AND/OR THE TECHNIQUES DESCRIBED IN THIS BOOK. WPI DOES NOT WARRANT THAT THE FUNCTIONS CONTAINED IN THE SOFTWARE WILL MEET YOUR REQUIREMENTS OR THAT THE OPERATION OF THE SOFTWARE WILL BE ERROR FREE.

   (c) This limited warranty gives you specific legal rights, and you may have other rights that vary from jurisdiction to jurisdiction.

6. **Remedies.**

   (a) WPI's entire liability and your exclusive remedy for defects in materials and workmanship shall be limited to replacement of the Software Media, which may be returned to WPI with a copy of your receipt at the following address: Software Media Fulfillment Department, Attn.: *Photoshop 7 Complete Course*, Wiley Publishing, Inc., 10475 Crosspoint Blvd., Indianapolis, IN 46256, or call 1-800-762-2974. Please allow four to six weeks for delivery. This Limited Warranty is void if failure of the Software Media has resulted from accident, abuse, or misapplication. Any replacement Software Media will be warranted for the remainder of the original warranty period or thirty (30) days, whichever is longer.

   (b) In no event shall WPI or the author be liable for any damages whatsoever (including without limitation damages for loss of business profits, business interruption, loss of business information, or any other pecuniary loss) arising from the use of or inability to use the Book or the Software, even if WPI has been advised of the possibility of such damages.

   (c) Because some jurisdictions do not allow the exclusion or limitation of liability for consequential or incidental damages, the above limitation or exclusion may not apply to you.

7. **U.S. Government Restricted Rights.** Use, duplication, or disclosure of the Software for or on behalf of the United States of America, its agencies and/or instrumentalities "U.S. Government" is subject to restrictions as stated in paragraph (c)(1)(ii) of the Rights in Technical Data and Computer Software clause of DFARS 252.227-7013, or subparagraphs (c) (1) and (2) of the Commercial Computer Software - Restricted Rights clause at FAR 52.227-19, and in similar clauses in the NASA FAR supplement, as applicable.

8. **General.** This Agreement constitutes the entire understanding of the parties and revokes and supersedes all prior agreements, oral or written, between them and may not be modified or amended except in a writing signed by both parties hereto that specifically refers to this Agreement. This Agreement shall take precedence over any other documents that may be in conflict herewith. If any one or more provisions contained in this Agreement are held by any court or tribunal to be invalid, illegal, or otherwise unenforceable, each and every other provision shall remain in full force and effect.

Index

Tool Presets, 23, 48–50

toolbox, 22, 39, 42, 47, 103

tools

    access methods, 38–41

    focus, 20

    painting, 20

    pixel-based, 20

    preference settings, 48–50

    restoring to default settings, 50

    rollover icons, 22, 39

    vector-based, 20

    vector-based drawing, 156–187

ToolTips, 6, 39

tpl (Tool Presets) file extension, 50

tracking, defined, 324

transformations, 15, 208–210, 238

transparency

    creating, 449

    layer opacity, 234–235

    layers, 224

    locking/unlocking, 119

    preference settings, 43

Transparency Dither, 24

transparent GIFs, creating, 24

transparent pixels, GIF versus JPEG, 448

Trash, deleting images, 65

troubleshooting, 475

tutorial files, 474

tutorials, session stages, 33–34

tweening, animation method, 439

type, 7, 20

type layers, 316, 341, 347–349

Type tool, 24, 48–50, 226, 316–318, 418

U

U.S. Prepress Defaults, 101–102

undoing mistakes, 68–71

units of measurement, 43, 54–55, 89

Unsharp Mask filter, 286, 369–370

user slice, 422

V

vector graphics, 158

vector masks, 261–266

vector objects, 118, 158, 261

vector-based drawing, 155–185

vector-based tools, 20

vector-based type, 20, 316

vertical rulers, 274

Vertical Type tool, 320

vignette, image feathering, 212

virtual memory, scratch disks, 44

visibility, layers, 229–230

W–Y

Web browsers, types, 31

Web graphics, 20, 421

Web hosting, color, 406

Web pages, 24, 416–420, 425, 443–450

Web palette, disadvantages, 446

Web Photo Gallery, 24, 454

Web sites

    Adobe, 26

    Internet Explorer, 31

    made by Photoshop, 454–455

    Netscape Navigator, 31

    posting to Web, 455

Web-ready images, outputting, 451–453

White Arrow (Direct Selection) tool, 164

Windows 2000, 20, 26

Windows 98, 20, 26

Windows Me, 20, 26

Windows NT, 20, 26

Windows OS, 26, 31–32, 38, 100, 472–473

Windows XP, 20, 22

Work Path, Paths palette, 150

workspaces, 23, 45–47, 87–88

Z

Zip image compression, 464

Zoom tool, 77–79

zooms, 76–79, 81

We actually like
the new kid on the block.

© Index Stock Imagery, Inc. / Peter Cross

All Photoshop 7 Complete Course readers receive a

10% discount

on their first purchase at...

Index Stock Imagery offers a wide selection of over 650,000 rights-protected and royalty-free photographs and illustrations that you can use on all your Photoshop projects.

Visit us at www.indexstock.com to enjoy the savings, or mention this ad when you call us at (800) 690-6979 or (212) 929-4644 and also receive a free catalog.

About Seybold Seminars and Publications

Seybold Seminars and Publications is your complete guide
to the publishing industry. For more than 30 years it
has been the most trusted source for technology events,
news, and insider intelligence.

SEYBOLD
CONSULTING / PUBLICATIONS ℠

SEYBOLD
SEMINARS

Produced by

PUBLICATIONS

Today, Seybold Publications and Consulting continues to guide publishing professionals around the world in their purchasing decisions and business strategies through newsletters, online resources, consulting, and custom corporate services.

○ **The Seybold Report: Analyzing Publishing Technologies**

The Seybold Report analyzes the cross-media tools, technologies, and trends shaping professional publishing today. Each in-depth newsletter delves into the topics changing the marketplace. *The Seybold Report* covers critical analyses of the business issues and market conditions that determine the success of new products, technologies, and companies. Read about the latest developments in mission-critical topic areas, including content and asset management, color management and proofing, industry standards, and cross-media workflows. A subscription to *The Seybold Report* (24 issues per year) includes our weekly email news service, *The Bulletin,* and full access to the seyboldreports.com archives.

○ **The Bulletin: Seybold News & Views on Electronic Publishing**

The Bulletin: Seybold News & Views on Electronic Publishing is Seybold Publications' weekly email news service covering all aspects of electronic publishing. Every week *The Bulletin* brings you all the important news in a concise, easy-to-read format.

For more information on **NEWSLETTER SUBSCRIPTIONS,**
please visit **seyboldreports.com**.

CUSTOM SERVICES

In addition to newsletters and online information resources, Seybold
Publications and Consulting offers a variety of custom corporate services
designed to meet your organization's specific needs.

○ **Strategic Technology Advisory Research Service (STARS)**
The STARS program includes a group license to *The Seybold Report* and
The Bulletin, phone access to our analysts, access to online archives at
seyboldreports.com, an on-site visit by one of our analysts, and much more.

○ **Personalized Seminars**
Our team of skilled consultants and subject experts work with you to create a
custom presentation that gets your employees up to speed on topics spanning
the full spectrum of prepress and publishing technologies covered in our publications. Full-day and half-day seminars are available.

○ **Site Licenses**
Our electronic licensing program keeps everyone in your organization, sales
force, or marketing department up to date at a fraction of the cost of buying
individual subscriptions. One hard copy of *The Seybold Report* is included with
each electronic license.

For more information on **CUSTOM CORPORATE SERVICES,**
please visit **seyboldreports.com**.

SEYBOLD SEMINARS

EVENTS

Seybold Seminars facilitates exchange and discussion within the high-tech publishing community several times a year. A hard-hitting lineup of conferences, an opportunity to meet leading media technology vendors, and special events bring innovators and leaders together to share ideas and experiences.

Conferences

Our diverse educational programs are designed to tackle the full range of the latest developments in publishing technology. Topics include:

- Print publishing
- Web publishing
- Design
- Creative tools and standards
- Best practices

- Multimedia
- Content management
- Technology standards
- Security
- Digital rights management

In addition to the conferences, you'll have the opportunity to meet representatives from companies that bring you the newest products and technologies in the publishing marketplace. Test tools, evaluate products, and take free classes from the experts.

For more information on **SEYBOLD SEMINARS EVENTS**, please visit **seyboldseminars.com**.